# THE CATHOLIC BOOK OF DAYS

JOHN DEEDY

THE THOMAS MORE PRESS
CHICAGO, ILLINOIS

**ACKNOWLEDGEMENTS**

Excerpt from *Murder in the Cathedral* by T.S. Eliot, copyright 1935 by Harcourt Brace Jovanovich, Inc., renewed 1963 by T.S. Eliot, reprinted by permission of the publisher.

Reproductions from the *Book of Kells*, courtesy of Bord Failte Eireann, Dublin.

Reproductions from Benedictine Book of Hours, France, 1435; from 16th century Book of Hours, Paris, France; also, leafs from Schedel's *Liber Cronicarum*, Nuremberg, 1493, and from Jacobus de Voragine's *Legenda Aurea*, Nuremberg, 1488, as well as specimens of other incunabula: From files of a private collection; used with permission of owner.

Reproductions of 1897-88 and 1919 union records of Edward Deedy used with permission of Mrs. Louise Buckley and Elizabeth and Mae Deedy.

January 12 (Harris & Ewing, Wash.,D.C.); January 25 (Pix); February 12 (Library of Congress); February 12 (Library of Congress); February 17 (drawing by P. Evans, National Portrait Gallery, London); March 25 (Joe McTyre); April 10 (Mark Gerson); April 20 (National Portrait Gallery, London); May 7 (*Fifty Years of Soviet Art*); May 10 (Bettmann Archive); May 14 (Zell); July 14 (Photo: Religious News Service); July 26 (Lithograph from *Oxford Characters* by William Rothenstein); July 30 (Israel Gov't Tourist Office); September 12 (Ollie Atkins); October 9 (Drawing of John Henry Newman by George Richmond); October 13 (The British Society for the Turin Shroud); October 28 ("Unfinished Portrait" by Madame Elizabeth Shoumatoff); November 6 (Georgetown University); November 24 (Louise Dahl-Wolfe); November 26 (Phillipe Halsman); December 3 (Religous News Service); December 7 (National Portrait Gallery, London); December 10 (Religious News Service)



ISBN 0-88347-249-X

For
Beverly and Connie Buckley
and
Father Paul Bailey
friends, aiders and abettors.

# FOREWORD

**THE IDEA ISN'T EXACTLY NOVEL.** "Books of days" are an old form. They've been compiled for years — part anecdote in content, part biography, part history, part oddities of character and of institutional and human nature....part everything, as a matter of fact. So it is with this book of days. And like its predecessors, it's pegged to calendar days — an event of the day per page of the book, roughly — and it's eclectic.

On the other hand, this book differs from others of its type, at least those that I've seen.

For one thing, the entries are not always neatly packaged for a particular, given date. Some topics were just too large for one day's entry, so I have taken the liberty of letting them run on for two, three, four days. The reader will discover these topics, as the book moves along.

For another, this "book of days" is Catholic-oriented, drawing liberally at the same time on the Judaic roots of Christianity and the common patrimony of the Old Testament.

A Catholic "book of days" is evocative in the way of Catholicism's old "book of hours." Everyone's acquainted with those "books of hours." They were the monastic manuals of prayer and devotion that guided the devout through the twenty-four-hour period with prescribed readings at stated intervals — and still do in many religious orders. This Catholic "book of days" is comparable mostly in the play of words of the title. The "book of days" uses the calendar rather than the clock, and it's scope goes beyond the inspirational and devotional, though there are elements of each in the book too. Have many Catholic books of days been done? Very likely, though I'm not familiar with them.

Finally, there's a seriousness, or so I'd like to think, that sets this book apart from others of the genre, certainly the secular ones. That comes from the subject itself; religion, church and believing tend in overall context to be serious business. And so here.

But mixed in with the serious, which here will be more informational than instructional and elevating, are dashes of the frivolous and the lighthearted. Thus a cautionary note: It might jar some to come occasionally upon a whimsical entry cheek-by-jowl with some sober marking of a date of Catholic history or comment on, say, the deposit of faith. It shouldn't upset; life itself is a dichotomy, or can be. Besides, what's to exclude frivolity or fun from the profession and the living of the faith? Chesterton believed Catholics had more fun than anyone. And why not? The deepest points of life, philosophy *and* religion, are not antithetical to humor, or the possession thereof, and humor in turn is *not* inimical to one's devotional state. As Belloc rejoiced in rhyme:

Where e'er the Catholic sun doth shine,
There's always music and laughter and good red wine.
At least I've always found it so,
*Benedicamus Domino.*

Which reminds, this was a fun book to do — though almost every topic broached left me disappointed that there was not more space for its handling; there was always so much more that could have been added. By the same token, so many additional topics might have been handled. There's a lot of history in Catholicism and a ton of lore in the Judaeo-Christian Bible. But then to have indulged the temptation to expand and run on would have been to produce a different kind of book, and an impossibly long one. Whatever, those who might wish to explore further those subjects broached here might check the bibliography at the rear of the book. They'll know where I've been, and where there's a whole lot more information.

So, yes, it's been fun doing the book.

It's also been something of a sentimental journey — to the old practices of the faith into which I was born, the old prayers, the old traditions, the old influences. On a more personal level, it was particularly moving in dealing with the great social encyclicals of the popes to be able to invoke pictorially, by way of union-membership documents, the shade of my paternal grandfather, a favorite forebear. My grandfather came out of a thatched cottage with earthen floor in Firies, County Kerry. He was a highly intelligent man, and devout in the manner of the old Irish, and when Leo XIII blessed labor unionism, he by the circumstance of emigration would be among the very first to draw, as it were, on the blessing. That was a proud thing, for him and now his descendants.

As for the help and the research that made this book possible — well, what would one do without the feed-in of friends and the book stacks of Cape Ann's libraries? For them, in that Catholic blessing from the language we don't use anymore: each and all, *Benedicamus Domino*--Let us bless the Lord--indeed.

Enjoy!

John Deedy
Rockport, Massachusetts

Annus XXV - Vol. XXV 7 Aprilis 1933 Num. 7

ACTA APOSTOLICAE SEDIS

COMMENTARIUM OFFICIALE

INTER SANCTAM SEDEM ET BADENSEM REMPUBLICAM

SOLLEMNIS CONVENTIO

| CONCORDATO | KONKORDAT |
|---|---|
| FRA LA SANTA SEDE E LA REPUBBLICA DEL BADEN | ZWISCHEN DEM HEILIGEN STUHLE UND DEM FREISTAATE BADEN |
| Sua Santità il Sommo Pontefice | Seine Heiligkeit Papst Pius XI. |

# A NEW YEAR, AN AWKWARD FEAST

**CURIOUS. THE YEAR BEGINS** with a day lost to church and state. The modern state doesn't know what to do with January 1, and lets it be as secular holiday — so a day in the United States for viewing bowl games and recovering from a night lost to revelry. Forget it. Tomorrow we'll get on with the world.

The ancient church? Well, it has its problems too with January 1. It's a holy day, of course, in Catholicism — but a holy day in search of an identity, despite being observed since the sixth century. The holy-day feast has traveled under a number of names, even in our own lifetimes. Currently it's known as the feast of the Solemnity of Mary, Mother of God, being designated to supplant the former feast of the Maternity of Mary, which was observed on October 11. It's a true holy day, as it were, carrying for Catholics the obligation of Mass. In recent years there was sentiment on the part of canonists for removing the obligatory character of the day, but Pope John Paul II nixed the notion in approving the new Code of Canon Law in 1983. The holy-day feast stayed on the liturgical calendar.

So church, like state, is stuck with January 1. What to do with or on it? Well, not quite nothing all of the time. Take January 1 of 1909. On that day, almost two millenia into its existence, the church launched the publication known as *Acta Apostolicae Sedis*. Which seemed appropriate all around. If January 1 was a date for the legalists, it seemed meet and just that on January 1 the church should inaugurate its legalist journal.

*Acta Apostolicae Sedis* is precisely that. It's the church's legal record, its official journal for promulgating the laws of the church and other documents of a weighty kind, such as encyclicals, decretal letters, writings and addresses of the pope, decrees and decisions of the Vatican congregations, tribunals and commissions, the diary of the Curia, episcopal appointments worldwide, and the necrology of bishops and cardinals.

The journal was established in accord with the September 29, 1908, constitution *Promulgandi* of Pius X. It appears at least once a month and forms an annual volume of some 1,000 pages. Usually it's language is Latin, not yet "lost" in Rome, though documents sometimes appear in other languages.

The clergy knows it well, but the *Acta* (as the cumbersome title is commonly telescoped to) is nowhere near so familiar to laics of the world as, say, *L'Osservatore Romano*, the Vatican daily. The two are not to be confused. *L'Osservatore* is the authoritative voice of the Vatican; the *Acta* — it's word's thunder.

# JANUARY 2

Detail from guide for pilgrims visiting the seven churches of Rome, 1575

## WHEN TRAVEL WAS GOOD FOR THE SOUL...

**THE HOLY DAYS** and holidays over, Catholics once upon a time would sit down on this day and plan their travel adventure for the year -- no, not their vacation; rather, their pilgrimage. For long before people traveled for mere change from life's routines, Christians traveled on pilgrimages to holy places. The church encouraged this, not for phsyiological and psychological therapy (though change can be good for a Christian as anyone else), but because it held pilgrimages to be a devotional exercise, a spiritual refreshener, a purifying act for the soul. The church accordingly attached indulgences and other inducements to pilgrimages. As an example, persons under canonical penalties could have these eased or lifted entirely by making pilgrimages.

Pilprimages in fact were once so much a part of the Christian tradition that time-schedules often provided for them in civil and ecclesiastical law. Today the worker receives a two- or three-week vacation. In times of yore the worker, if lucky and of rank, would receive pilgrimage time. Certainly the clerics qualified for pilgrimage time. The canons of Hereford, for instance, allowed clergmen three weeks each year for visiting a shrine within the English kingdom. Seven weeks were available for visiting the tomb of St. Denis in Paris, eight weeks for a pilgrimage to St. Edmund in Pontigny, and 16 weeks for going to Rome or the shrine of St. James at Compostela in Spain. No clergyman was expected to make more than one foreign pilgrimage in his lifetime, but those three-week pilgrimages within the kingdom were usually for the asking.

In this context, it is interesting to note that when Europe reopened to American travelers after World War II, much of the early travel, certainly for Catholics, was in the form of pilgrimages to religious shrines. Whole boat loads of the devout would travel. Church-sponsored pilgrimages are still arranged, but emphases today seem more on the recreational than the devotional.

# JANUARY 3

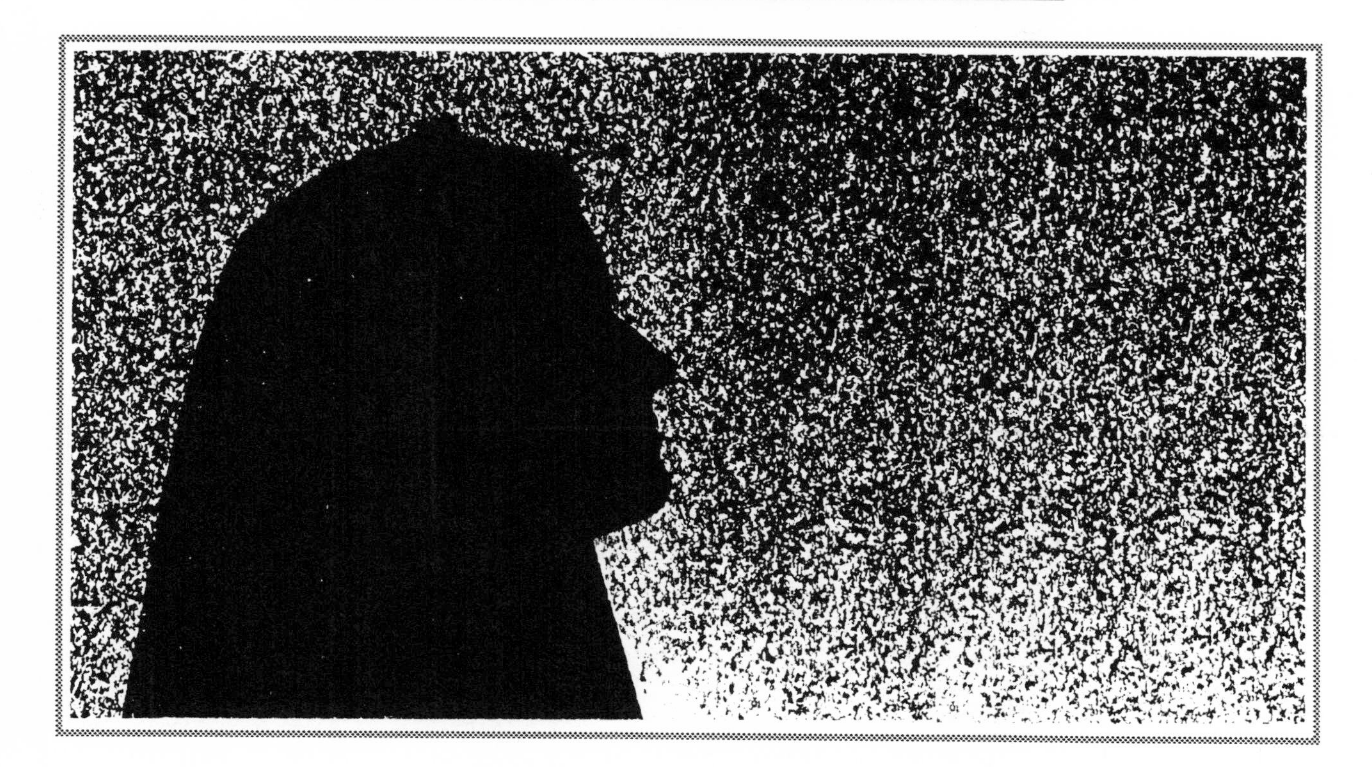

## MARIAN APPARITIONS AND CATHOLIC PIETY

**A DISTINCTIVE FEATURE** of Catholic piety is belief in apparitions of Mary to groups of Catholics, usually with warnings of direly consequential events if certain of her instructions were not followed. One of the first of these Marian appearances is recorded in the Vosges Mountains in northeast France in 1493, and to be sure there were the apparitions at Guadalupe in Mexico in 1531. But mostly Marian apparitions were nineteenth and twentieth century phenomena — as at the motherhouse of the Sisters of Charity on the rue de Bac in Paris in 1830 (to commission of Catherine Laboure the striking of the Miraculous Medal); at La Salette and Lourdes in 1846 and 1858, respectively; at Knock, in Ireland, in 1879; at Fatima, in Portugal, in 1917.

A more recent series of Marian apparitions is credited to Beauraing, near Namur, in Belgium beginning November 29, 1932, and concluding on this day in 1933. A total of thirty-three apparitions were recorded to five children in the garden of their convent school. A chapel was erected on the site, and for a time Beauraing was an exceedingly popular pilgrimage center. The apparitions there were extended reserved approval in 1943, then final approval in 1949. The latter opened the gates more fully for devotional expressions on the part of the faithful. But, whereas apparition sites such as Lourdes and Fatima, and Knock to a lesser extent, were to retain a grip on the Catholic imagination worldwide, that of Beauraing has not. Most Catholics would be hard put to tell you why the place is remembered, or footnoted, in Catholic history.

Marian apparitions are debunked by the skeptical, and indeed the church itself is cautious in their regard, as demonstrated by a seeming reluctance to credit alleged Marian happenings. Official hesitancies over the alleged 1980s apparitions at Medjugorie, Yugoslavia, provide an example. But the Catholic mind remains receptive. Marian apparitions seem part of the Catholic psyche.

# AMERICA'S FIRST HOME-GROWN SAINT

**TODAY IS THE FEAST DAY** of the first United States-born saint, Elizabeth Ann Seton. A native New Yorker born in 1774, Elizabeth Seton was an Anglican by birth. She was devoutly married as a Protestant, and was a mother five times. Her career as a married laywoman was no less important, as the late John Cardinal Wright once said, than her life as a Catholic religious, a sister.

As a young mother, Elizabeth Ann Seton was deeply involved in charitable works, helping to found in 1797 the Society for the Relief of Poor Widows with Small Children. She was widowed at twenty-nine with small children to care for, yet she continued her life of good works as a social planner and founder of a refuge for lepers. It was in 1805 that she entered the Catholic Church, where she would leave her mark as founder of the Sisters of Charity of St. Joseph and also of the American parochial school system. The system had its beginnings in a school for poor children she opened near Emmitsburg, Maryland.

Elizabeth Ann Seton's role in the founding of the religious order was unique, for several of her children were still in her care. She was elected superior of the order in 1812, and her daughters Anna and Rebecca eventually followed her into religious life as members of the community. The fervor of the community won wide admiration, and Elizabeth herself achieved additional fame as a writer and translator. When Elizabeth was elected mother superior for the third time in 1819, she protested that it was an election of the dead. She was right in a way; she died two years later of a pulmonary ailment.

In 1880 Baltimore's Cardinal Gibbons initiated steps toward Elizabeth Ann Seton's canonization, and in 1911 her cause was placed in the hands of a postulator. She was canonized in 1975. St. Elizabeth's guiding principle is as apt today as ever: "Have confidence. Never let the comparison of time and eternity slip an instant from your mind. I find this cures all sorrows."

## PHILADELPHIA'S SAINTED FOURTH BISHOP

**TODAY BELONGS TO** St. John Nepomucene Neumann, an early Bishop of Philadelphia, known for his pioneering of the parochial school system and as the first American male to achieve sainthood. A native of Bohemia, Neumann emigrated to the U.S. and was ordained in New York in 1836. He spent his first years in the priesthood as a missionary among Germans in the Niagara Falls area. In 1840 he joined the Redemptorist order, and in 1842 became the first member of that order to be professed in this country. He served in Pittsburgh and Baltimore before being named Philadelphia's fourth bishop in 1852.

It was in Philadelphia that Neumann founded the first Catholic diocesan school system. He was famous for one thing more: he was the first bishop to prescribe the Forty Hours devotion on a diocesan-wide basis. From Philadelphia the devotion spread nationwide among dioceses before going into eclipse in the postconciliar years, as Catholic devotional preferences changed radically. He was only forty-eight when he died suddenly on a Philadelphia street.

Bishop Neumann was beatified in 1963. The ceremony was scheduled for June 23 with Pope John XXIII presiding, but had to be rescheduled because of John's death on June 3. Paul VI was elected June 21 as the new pope, and Neumann's beatification finally took place three months later. Canonization ceremonies went more smoothly, taking place June 19, 1977, Paul VI again doing the honors.

Paul VI's homily at the beatification ceremonies contained one of the great papal tributes to the American hierarchy. Pope Paul singled out Bishop Neumann as "one of that wonderful chain of bishops who prepared the leaders of the Catholic hierarchy in the United States, and imbued them with those virtues of dedication, zeal, practical efficiency and absolute faithfulness which still distinguish the venerable and exemplary American episcopate.

St. John Nepomucene Neumann's feast is observed January 5.

# JANUARY 6

## A HOLY DAY, BUT A MOVABLE ONE

**TODAY, FEAST OF THE EPIPHANY,** is one of the church's official holy days of obligation. The fact escapes many American Catholics, because here the observance is transferred to Sunday, which means the feast can be observed anytime between January 2 and 8. Not so everywhere. In Italy, for instance, this is not only a holy day, but the day on which La Befana, an old lady similar to Santa Claus, brings children their Christmastide gifts. A few years ago, the Italian Parliament, seeking to reduce the number of national holidays, persuaded the church to move the observance of Epiphany to Sunday, as in the United States. There was a huge uproar and such lack of cooperation by the people that government and church had to abandon the experiment.

Epiphany means manifestation, and that's the key to the feast. The Epiphany commemorates the manifestations of the divinity of Christ — in the adoration of the baby Jesus by the Magi, and in his baptism in the Jordan by John the Baptist.

In the Western church the Magi element long enjoyed the greater emphasis, but with the tighter incorporation of the Magi story into that of Christmas, the baptism element began to come more to the fore. There's a logic to this. The feast is of Eastern origins, and the manifestation or declaration of Christ's divinity in his baptism is an emphasis that has been present in the Eastern church since the feast's adoption between 380 and 430.

Incidentally, the Epiphany is not the only one of the church's official holy days of obligation to be moved into a separate category of observance by the American church. Corpus Christi, a feast designated for the Thursday following Trinity Sunday, is observed in this country on a Sunday, while the feasts of St. Joseph (March 19) and Sts. Peter and Paul (June 29) are marked on their appointed days but with no Mass obligation entailed.

# JANUARY 7

He has done with roofs and men,
Open, Time, and let him pass.

—LOUISE IMOGEN GUINEY
*The Ballad of Kenelm*

## LAUREATE OF THE LOST

**LOUISE IMOGEN GUINEY'S BOOKS** may not be read these days, but in her lifetime she was one of the very few American Catholic writers with a genuine literary fame. She lived from 1861-1920; in fact, she was born on this date in Boston, daughter of an Irish-born father who had a gallant career as a general in the Civil War. In time, though, like Henry James and Edith Wharton, she would become an expatriate. From 1901 she lived permanently in Oxford, turning out poems, essays, short stories, biographies, and studies of the recusant poets of England. Known as the laureate of the lost, she is credited with reviving interest in such authors as Henry Vaughan and William Hazlitt.

Louise Imogen Guiney was steeped in a romantic past, so much so that Sir Edmund Gosse would say that she was "only at ease in a chivalrous and antique dreamland." This was no libel. Guiney connected her father with the cavaliers of Stuart times, and felt herself a cavalier's daughter. Van Wyck Brooks commented in *New England: Indian Summer* (New York, 1940) that she "lived a dream of the 17th century, with other Bostonians of her time, who often shared her interest in the Oxford Movement." Life in England stimulated her dream.

Dr. Oliver Wendell Holmes was charmed by Guiney's poems and called her his "little golden guinea." Brooks was harsher. Her poems had a "fragile beauty," he conceded, but added that they "constantly verged on the false-archaic." Overall Brooks found her work "intensely bookish," though he allowed that "the prose of her later essays was precise and distinguished." Guiney's first poems were published in *The Pilot*. Later she became a regular in *Scribner's* and *Atlantic Monthly*, but she never abandoned the Catholic press, writing often for *Catholic World*, *Ave Maria* and *America*. Louise Imogene Guiney died in Chipping Campden, England. In this country Holy Cross College in Worcester, MA, and Albertus Magnus College in New Haven have large collections of her works and papers.

# JANUARY 8

## "BLESSED BE HIS GLORIOUS NAME"

**THE CHURCH PRAYS FOR PEACE** the year 'round, but especially in January. In fact, with the permission of the local bishop, the Mass for the World Day of Peace may be substituted for the usual holy day Mass on January 1; or that Mass for world peace may be celebrated on any other day of the month. The readings for the peace Mass are optional, though a popular gospel choice is Matthew 5:38-48, in which Jesus speaks of loving one's enemies and praying for one's persecutors. The recommended psalm for the Mass excerpts from Psalm 72. Perhaps composed as one of good wishes for one of David's successors, Catholics consider the psalm messianic in its meaning, the king being a figure of Christ the King. The doxologies are according to the King James version:

"Give the king thy judgments, O God, and thy righteousness unto the king's son. He shall judge thy people with righteousness, and the poor with judgment.

"The mountains shall bring peace to the people, and the little hills, by righteousness. He shall judge the poor of the people, he shall save the children of the needy.

"In his days shall the righteous flourish; and abundance of peace so long as the moon endureth. He shall have dominion also from sea to sea, and from the river unto the ends of the earth.

"For he shall deliver the needy when he crieth; the poor also, and him that hath no helper. He shall spare the poor and needy, and shall save the souls of the needy.

"His name shall endure forever; his name will be continued as long as the sun; and in him will all the tribes of the earth be blessed; all nations shall call him blessed. Blessed be the Lord God...And blessed be his glorious name."

For each doxology the response, appropriately, is: "Justice shall flourish in his time, and fullness of peace forever."

# THE POPE WHO WISHED HE WASN'T

**ADRIAN, CARDINAL OF UTRECHT** and Emperor Charles V's viceroy in Spain, was elected on this day in 1522 to the papacy. It was a huge surprise. Adrian hadn't attended the consistory; he in fact was in Spain at the time, and likely expected, along with many others, that the mantle would fall on Cardinal Wolsey, who dearly wanted the post and who carried the weighty support of King Henry VIII, then still in the fold. Adrian didn't want the job, and obviously many people didn't want him either, for there was a plundering of the Vatican by cardinals before he arrived in Rome to serve as Adrian VI.

Adrian's reign was something of a disaster. He was a total outsider. He didn't speak Italian. Reform-minded, he sought to institute changes, and moved to reduce the splendor of the papal court and cut back on cardinals' privileges and incomes. As much as reform was needed, it cost Adrian support in seeking to cope with urgent problems of ecclesiastical and temporal kinds.

The great failure, however, was Adrian's own. He completely misjudged Luther and his revolt. Adrian thought Luther simply an obstinate and heretical monk, whose acting out could be handled by the usual applications of force and penalty. It was a characteristic way of thinking for one who had been the Inquisitor of Aragon and Navarre in 1517 and of Castile and Leon in 1518, and it was fatal for historical Catholicism. The first pope to face the full impact of Luther's challenge thus misjudged it completely. Adrian wasn't alone in that by any means, then or later. Still, it was not a time for misjudgment.

Adrian's reign was short, lasting but twenty months. He died September 14, 1523, and his epitaph summed up the disillusionment and disappointment that were his: "Here lies Adrian VI, who thought nothing in life more unfortunate than that he became pope."....

There would not be another non-Italian pope until John Paul II's election in 1978, no less than 455 years later.

Woodcut by Albrecht Dürer

# MIGRANTS, REFUGEES AND MARY

**THIS IS THE TIME OF YEAR** when the church asks people to remember the world's migrants and refugees, and reflect on the root causes forcing people to leave homeland and loved ones in search of a better life elsewhere. In 1989 the church built attention to these people around the theme "Migrants and the Blessed Mother." If that theme struck some as a far reach for a liturgical connection, Pope John Paul II provided the response:

"By the way she lived her human vicissitudes, the Blessed Virgin is, indeed, a point of reference for migrants and refugees. Her earthly life was marked by a continual pilgrimage from one place to another; going in haste to her cousin Elizabeth; traveling to Bethlehem for the census, where she gave birth to her son in a cave, since no other place was available; journeying to Jerusalem for the presentation of Jesus in the temple; following Jesus attentively and discretely in his apostolic activities; and being present, coparticipating in suffering, on Mount Calvary.

"Besides all this, Mary knew, by personal experience, the pains of exile in a foreign land. She was forced to do so, by the impending threat to Jesus' life. The Angel of the Lord appeared to Joseph, in a dream, and said, 'Get up, take the child and his mother with you, and escape into Egypt...because Herod intends to search for the child and do away with him' (Matthew 2:13)."

"It was a sudden flight, done in the heart of night, in dramatic circumstances," and Pope John Paul drew a parallel to the tribulations and anguish that migrants and refugees experience: the trauma of detachment from persons and things, the leaving behind of precious hopes, travel to unknown places, search for shelter, the uncertainty of finding work, the air of suspicion, discrimination and rejection often encountered. May these people receive "Christian welcome" at journey's end, prayed the pope. Amen to that.

Cavanaugh, Rev. John J. (C.S.C.), educator; *b.* Owosso, Mich., Jan.23 '99; *s.* Michael Francis and Mary Ann (Keegan) C.; M.A. Univ. of Notre Dame '27, student C.U.A. '27-31, Ph.L. Gregorian U., Rome, '32. Sec. to pres., U. of Notre Dame, '17-19; in adv. dept. Studebaker Corp., S. Bend. '23-25; joined Cong. of the Holy Cross, '26; ordained, '31; prefect of religion, U. of Notre Dame, '33-38; asst. provincial, C.S.C., and v.p. Notre Dame U., '40-46, pres., '46-52; dir. Notre Dame U. Fdn., '52- . *Home:* Notre Dame, Ind.

The American Catholic Who's Who, 1962-63

# AMERICAN CATHOLICS AND THE INTELLECTUAL LIFE

**AT THIS TIME IN 1958** the American Catholic press was in high dungeon, as it reacted to a speech in the closing days of the old year by the former president of Notre Dame, Father John J. Cavanaugh. At a communion breakfast, Cavanaugh asked, "Where are the Catholic Salks, Oppenheimers, Einsteins?" There was "humiliating evidence," he charged, of a lack of Catholic representation in scholarship. For every 100,000 Catholics, only 7 were listed in *Who's Who*; of 303 eminent scientists, only 3 were Catholic; of the 96 U.S. senators, only 10 were Catholics; of the 50 top business leaders, only 2 were Catholic and one of them was a convert.

Foul!, cried the Catholic press, or at least much of it. Cavanaugh's speech was interpreted as a slur on Catholic schools, from the elementary to the university level, which implied in sum that Catholic education was second-rate. (Indeed, Cavanaugh had alluded in his talk to schools "without first-rate teaching personnel.") So what, wrote one writer, if the 2.5 million Catholic alumni and alumnae weren't achieving success in the secular sense; for the most part they were "God-fearing individuals who had been trained in the best Catholic tradition, embracing human life in all its forms" according to the example of Christ himself. One Catholic editorial writer viewed the Cavanaugh talk as a slur on the priesthood itself. What more learned body as a whole could be found, the editorialist wanted to know, than the American priesthood?

The irony of the Cavanaugh speech is that it wasn't exactly ploughing new ground. Monsignor John Tracy Ellis three years before wrote that American Catholics were shamefully remiss in upholding the intellectual traditions of the church. Ellis' forum was different, however. He was writing in *Thought*, the scholarly Fordham quarterly. The muted reaction lent weight to his theory.

John Tracy Ellis

# MORE ON THE "GREAT DEBATE" OF THE 1950s

**MONSIGNOR JOHN TRACY ELLIS'** essay in *Thought* on American Catholics and the intellectual tradition may not have had the wild, instant impact of Father John Cavanaugh's communion breakfast talk, but it fueled the topic that was to be one of the liveliest of the 1950s in Catholic circles. In 1955 Ellis' paper provoked lively discussion at the meeting of the Catholic Commission for Intellectual and Cultural Affairs. In 1956 it appeared in book form under imprint of the Heritage Foundation, Inc., of Chicago. The book's preface was by John J. Wright, then Bishop of Worcester and later a cardinal of the Roman Curia, who moved discussion to larger context, as follows:

"What we have called the 'great debate' raging here in the United States at the moment is doubtless no more than a phase within our own land of an argument that has been going on in Europe for decades. Traditionally, the European intellectual has been acknowledged by his contemporaries, even those who might disagree with him, to have a 'vocation' beyond the limits of his own profession of writing or science or teaching. It is a vocation quite apart from that of the functionary or representative of Church or of State, and it has obvious and grave perils as well as elements of prestige. These perils are as real as ignominy, exile or prison, even death, the frequent destinies of the traditonal intellectuals in Europe. And yet, the intellectual has usually enjoyed a veneration in Europe which scarcely has a parallel in the common American attitude toward those who take on the valiant role of questioner, critic, or intellectual trail blazer."....Wright did not level the charge of anti-intellectualism, not yet. But what a problem it would be for the church, he stated, if "any who might be taken as her representatives in any sense of the world of the campus, the press, or the forum reveal contempt for that 'wild living intellect of man' of which Cardinal Newman spoke..."

# JANUARY 13

## GREAT DEBATE—A SOCIOLOGIST'S VIEW

**THE DEBATE ABOUT CATHOLICS** and the intellectual life was a decidedly intramural affair, and got especially heated with the publication in 1958 of Thomas F. O'Dea's *American Catholic Dilemma*. O'Dea, Harvard-educated and then associate professor at Fordham, rounded on the issue as sociologist. He fingered five factors in the American Catholic environment which he considered detrimental to mature intellectual development. The five:

*Formalism*, or a strong attachment to the external forms and observations of religion, as distinct from a strong intellectual appreciation of faith itself.

*Authoritarianism*, or a readiness to accept positions and statements less on their intrinsic merits than on the authority of those enunciating them, as by pope, priest or nun (this in contradistinction to Thomas Aquinas, who regarded the argument from authority as the least persuasive of all).

*Clericalism*, or what lately is called "creeping infallibilism"; namely, the tendency of the clergy to assimilate errorlessness to their own person and into virtually every statement of their own, and a concomitant disposition on the part of the laity to accept this clerical word as dogma, whatever its context.

*Moralism*, or the impulse to focus on the morality, or rightness or wrongness of a particular reality, rather than truthness or falseness.

*Defensiveness*, the "my church right or wrong" syndrome, which shuts ears to legitimate criticism, retreats from threatening controversy, and indulges in protectiveness, even if it means rewriting history.

Most, if not each of these charges has been rendered obsolete by changes that have taken place since Vatican II. Certainly the charges are not valid to the degree they were when O'Dea wrote his book.ities to protect O'Dea's book from A single word from the pope, or from father, or from sister would no more close an issue today than it would alter a weather pattern. Catholic intellectual life profits from the fact.

# JANUARY 14

*Almighty God, bestow upon us the meaning of words, the light of understanding, the nobility of diction and the faith of the true nature. And grant that what we believe we may also speak.*

— St Hilary of Poitiers

## THE SAINT WHO GAVE HIS NAME TO A UNIVERSITY TERM

**IN THE UNITED STATES,** the academic year is divided on the university level into two semesters, one beginning in September and the other in the New Year. Under the English and Anglo-Irish system, the academic year divides not into two semesters, but rather three terms: Michelmas, Hilary and Trinity. Hilary is the so-called winter term, and traditionally begins around this time. It takes its name from the saint whose feast appeared in both the Anglican and the old Catholic calendars for this date, St. Hilary of Poitiers.

Hilary was one of the great defenders against Arianism, the fourth century heresy that denied the divinity of Christ. A fourth century adult convert from paganism, Hilary was a vigorous theological controversialist, and when Emperor Constantine II tried to impose Arianism on the Western church, he fought back. Hilary was not without standing; he had been Bishop of Potiers since 350.

Arianism was the brainchild of the priest Arius of Alexandria, and represented in essence an attempt to settle the early church question of how Jesus related to God. Arius rejected the idea of a Trinity of Father, Son and Holy Spirit. He described the Son as a second or inferior God, posed midway between the First Cause and creatures, who of course once had not existed.

Hilary's objections to Arianism were so strenuous that he was exiled as a nuisance in 356 to Phrygia in Asia Minor. There he ceased to be quiet. In fact, so effective a defender of causes was he that Constantine decided he would be less of a problem back in Gaul. Hilary thus returned to his diocese in 360 — bringing with him a theology greatly enriched by experiences in the East. One result was Hilary's profound theological treatise *On the Trinity.*

As they don their academic gowns for the new term, chances are that few English and Irish students could say where the term's name originates. But Hilary was a big and important man in his day — a saint, and also a scholar.

# JANUARY 15

## The Act of Faith

*O my God, I firmly believe that thou art one God in three divine persons, the Father, the Son, and the Holy Ghost. I believe that the divine son became man, and died for our sins, and that he will come to judge the living and the dead. I believe these and all the truths which the holy Catholic Church teaches, because thou hast revealed them, who can neither deceive nor be deceived.*

## The Act of Hope

*O my God, relying on thy infinite goodness and promises, I hope to obtain pardon of my sins, the help of thy grace and life everlasting, through the merits of Jesus Christ, my lord and redeemer.*

## The Act of Charity

*O my God, I love thee above all things, with my whole heart and my whole soul, because thou art all good and worthy of all love. I love my neighbor as myself for love of thee. I forgive all who have injured me and ask pardon of all whom I have injured.*

## YESTERDAY'S PRAYERS

**ONE LARGE PHENOMENON** of the post-Vatican Council II era is the number of prayers that have been consigned by neglect to the devotional dust pile. Many of these prayers will be recalled in the course of this project, beginning here with three prayers that once upon a time every parochial school child could recite — indeed, was required to know if he or she expected to pass religion class. How many people even of that period remember the acts of Faith, Hope and Charity? Ah, those Acts of prayerful Catholic piety.

# THE EVOLUTION OF THE EUCHARISTIC FAST

**IN THE FIRST THREE CENTURIES** of the Christian era, there was no such thing as a eucharistic fast. Communion, in fact, was commonly received in conjunction with a communal meal, the *agape*. In the fourth century, things began to change and fasting before communion became so widespread that St. Augustine wrote the custom must have been due to divine inspiration. At first local councils regulated fast requirements. In 1418 the Council of Constance took steps to formalize the code, and in time Catholics receiving communion were expected to fast from the previous midnight from all food and liquids, water included. Indeed, so conscientiously were the requirements observed that people worried whether water accidentally ingested while brushing teeth or food particles lodged between teeth then swallowed broke one's fast. (They didn't.)

The iron eucharistic fast rules of yesterday began to ease on this day in 1953, when Pope Pius XII issued the apostolic constitution *Christus dominus* stating that, though fasting from midnight was still required, water did not break the eucharistic fast, no matter when taken. *Christus dominus* provided further that under certain circumstances other liquids, alcohol excepted, could be taken up to one hour before Mass and communion — as by those engaged in energy-sapping work or those traveling a long distance to Mass.

Other relaxations were to follow. With the motu proprio *Sacram communionem* of 1957 Pius XII abolished the midnight rule and reduced the fast requirements to three hours for solids and one hour for liquids, alcohol again excepted. The change was attributed to Pius' recognition of the social and economic demands of modern society.

The next change, the one by which Catholics live today, came with the close of the third session of Vatican Council II, November 21, 1964, when Pope Paul VI reduced the eucharistic fast requirement to one hour.

# JANUARY 17

## THE UNITY DEVOTION THAT CAME AND WENT

**TOMORROW IS THE FEAST** of the Chair of St. Peter, a liturgical expression of belief in the authority of the episcopacy and hierarchy of the church that has been on the Roman calendar since 336. In more recent times, beginning in 1908 to be precise, the feast marked the opening of what was known as the Chair of Unity Octave, an eight-day devotional period ending with the feast on the Conversion of St. Paul, January 25, during which Catholics prayed for the reunion of Christendom around the Chair of Peter. Catholics still pray for unity during this period, but the lines are no longer so narrowly etched.

The Chair of Unity Octave is of English origins, and grew out of a correspondence between Father Paul Wattson and the Rev. Spencer Jones over the claims of the Holy See as the one true church. Jones wrote a book on the subject (*England and the Holy See*), in which he called on Anglicans to accept every doctrine and practice of the church of Rome. Father Paul was persuaded enough to begin a "Church Unity Octave" in his Episcopal community, and he soon became its first fruit. In 1909 he led his community corporately into the Catholic Church. Pope Pius X blessed his Institute of the Society of the Atonement and endorsed his octave of prayer for unity. In 1927, the Vatican's Congregation of Rites gave the devotion the name Chair of Unity Octave to particularize it from "ecumenical" (meaning Protestant) movements for unity.

Into the 1960s, the Chair of Unity Octave was one of great popularity in Catholicism, the eight days being marked by special prayers at Masses, and with devotional services featuring litanies and Benediction. Then all that pretty much came to an end. Devotional exercises generally waned in the post-Vatican II era, and the Chair of Unity Octave found itself under a further handicap; a narrowly focused ecumenism was not good form. Unity services are still held at this time of year, but with emphases shifted, the old devotion is done.

# JANUARY 18

For a reunion it is above all necessary to know and to love one another. To know one another, because if the efforts of reunion have failed so many times, this is in large measure due to mutual ignorance. If there are prejudices on both sides, these prejudices must fall. Incredible are the errors and equivocations which persist and are handed down among the separated brethren against the Catholic Church; on the other hand, Catholics also have sometimes failed in justly evaluating the truth or, on account of insufficient knowledge, in showing a fraternal spirit. Do we know all that is valuable, good, and Christian in the fragments of ancient Catholic truth? Detached fragments of a gold-bearing rock also contain the precious ore. The ancient Churches of the East have retained so true a holiness that they deserve not only our respect but also our sympathy.

—Speech of Pius XI, January 11, 1927

## UNITY — BACK AND FORTH FROM SQUARE ONE

**AS FATHER PAUL'S** Chair of Unity Octave observance underscored, there was wide interest in the early decades of the century with Christian unity, and for a time the Catholic Church itself seemed interested beyond the narrow focus of its own octave of this unity occurring "around the Chair of Peter." For instance, between 1921 and 1928 Rome joined, however uneasily, in "conversations" with Anglican leaders at Malines, Belgium. They came to naught however, for in 1928, the same year Anglicans published their first report of the "conversations," Pius XI issued *Mortalium animos*, the first papal encyclical on ecumenism. It effectively arrested progress for years.

"The Apostolic See can by no means take part in these [religious unity] assemblies, nor is it in any way lawful for Catholics to give to such enterprises their encouragement or support," the pope wrote. "If they do so, they would be giving countenance to a false Christianity alien to the one Church of Christ." The only way in which religious unity could be fostered, he continued, was "by furthering the return to the one true Church of Christ of those who are separated from it, and this authentic unity "can be born of but one single authority, one sole rule of faith, and one identical Christian belief." The "infallibility of the Roman Pontiff" was to be accorded the same belief and faith as "the incarnation of Our Lord."....The logic behind the 1927 change of name for the church's own unity devotion (c.f. Jan. 17) could not have been more forcefully underscored.

Pius XI's attitude carried forward, Pius XII declining in 1948 to authorize the presence of Catholic observers at the first assembly of the World Council of Churches. But the world would change. In 1984 John Paul II visited World Council of Churches' headquarters in Geneva, calling the visit a pilgrimage in the spirit of *Unitatis redintegratio*, Vatican II's Decree on Ecumenism.

Pius VI greeting Joseph II of Austria in Rome in 1783

# THE VETOING OF PAPAL CANDIDATES

**ONE OF THE PARADOXES** of Catholic history is that a church so jealous of its prerogatives would countenance to an arrangement whereby its most important tradition, the election of popes, would be subject to direct outside influence. Yet such was the case for many centuries. From the sixteenth into the twentieth century several governments, notably those of Spain, France, Austria and Germany, were able to exercise influence over papal elections by what was called *jus exclusivae*, or "right of exclusion." That is, at the time of papal conclaves they could indicate those members of the College of Cardinals who were *personae minus gratae* and therefore whose election as pope would be unacceptable. The conclaves of 1644 and 1655, which produced Innocent X and Alexander VII, respectively, saw Cardinal Giulio Sacchetti excluded *jus exclusivae*, and throughout the eighteenth and nineteenth centuries numerous prominent candidates were eliminated as prospects by similar veto. The Holy See never formally ratified the arrangement, but obviously it tacitly accepted it.

The last papal election subjected to the *jus exclusivae* imposition was that of 1903, which rose up Cardinal Giuseppe Sarto as Pius X. A strong candidate for pope was Cardinal Mariano Rampolla del Tindaro, but he was vetoed by Franz Joseph, emperor of Austria and king of Hungary, the veto being carried into the conclave by Cardinal Kolzielsko Puzina. Rampolla, it is recorded, rose "pale, stately and resplendent with dignity" and protested this "serious attack on the liberty of the church and the dignity of the Sacred College," but his candidacy was finished. Rampolla's support ebbed, and Sarto was elected August 4, 1903.

This day in 1904 would thus be the last for *jus exclusivae*. Moving quickly, the new pope drew up the bull *Commissum nobis* suppressing the right of papal veto or exclusion, and excommunicating any cardinal who was party to any future attempt to exercise one. The bull was dated tomorrow, January 20, 1904.

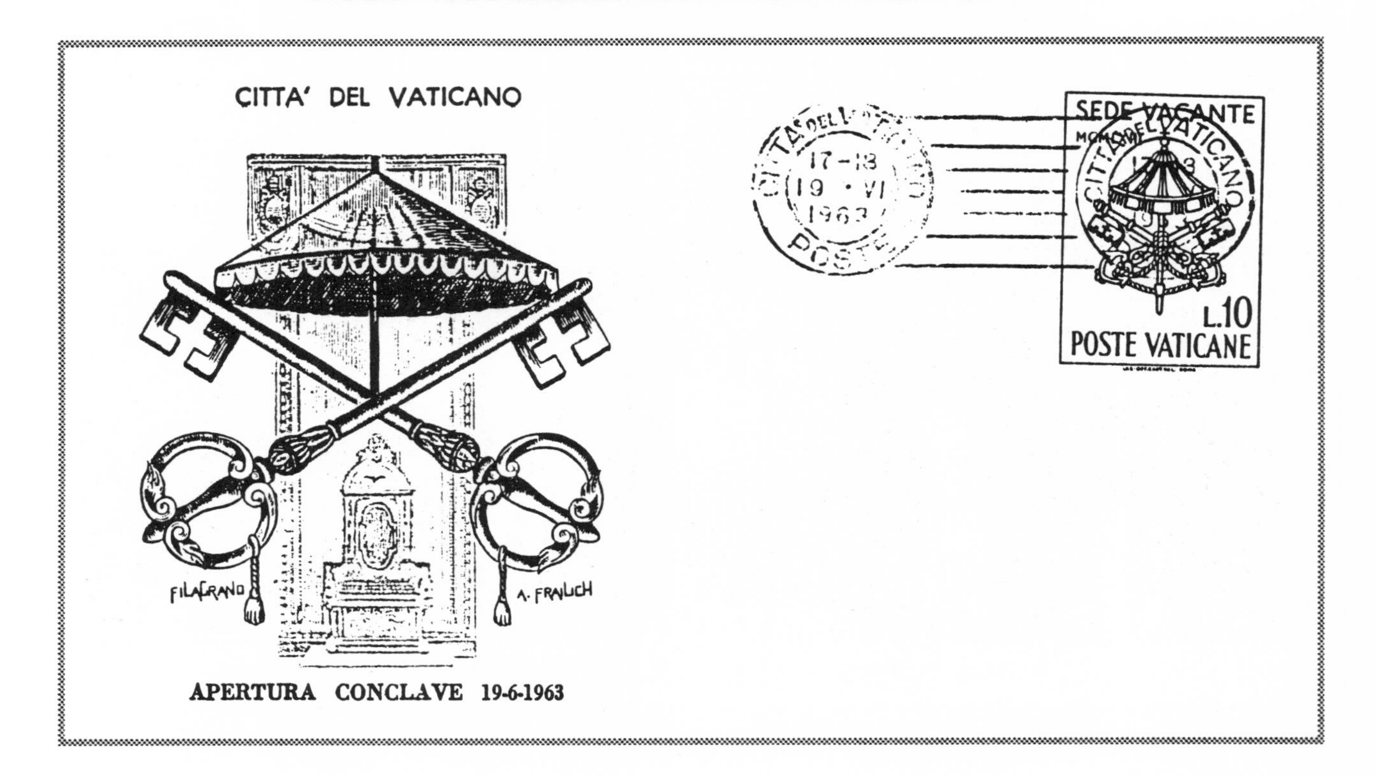


# THE VATICAN AS CITY-STATE

**AS A STATE,** that of Vatican is miniscule — 108.7 acres of land entirely surrounded by the city of Rome, and home to only about 1,000 citizens. Ah, but one of them is the pope, and that makes all the difference. As religious leader of some 841,000,000 Catholics worldwide, 18 percent of the world's population, the pope is a person governments must conjure with, like him and his church or not. More than 110 nations of the world have diplomatic relations with the Vatican, including a few that are Marxist.

On this day in 1984, President Ronald Reagan re-established formal diplomatic ties between the United States and the Vatican after a hiatus of 117 years. To be sure, beginning with President Franklin D. Roosevelt a series of presidents named personal representatives to the Vatican, but all were without portfolio. Persuaded of the importance of the Vatican as a window on the world, President Reagan appointed an ambassador to the Holy See. Not everyone liked the idea, for religious and constitutional reasons. The White House told critics the step was taken to improve communications at a time when papacy and pope had become increasingly involved in international affairs.

The Reagan move restored an old tradition. From 1779 to 1848, American consuls were posted to the Papal States. In 1848 President James Polk upgraded U.S. representation to that of a mission, and resident ministers then were assigned until 1867, when the mission was closed after Congress cut off funds. The action was based on reports that the papal government had ordered the American Protestant church in Rome to move outside the walls of the city. The reports proved false, but the decision of Congress stood.

In 1951 President Harry Truman attempted to name a U.S. ambassador to the Vatican, but there was a huge outcry from Protestants and "constitutionalists."

The political and religious climate was better for President Reagan.

St. Agnes' Eve—Ah, bitter chill it was!
The owl, for all his feathers, was a-cold.
The hare limped trembling through the fro-
 zen grass,
And silent was the flock in wooly fold

—from "The Eve of St. Agnes" by John Keats

## ST. AGNES' DOUBLE MARTYRDOM

**THIS IS** the feast of St. Agnes, a saint whom the church reveres as a double martyr — one of modesty and one of witness. She lived in the fourth-century, and as a youngster declared herself a Christian during one of Rome's most terrible persecutions, probably that of Diocletian. By some accounts, she was consigned by her persecutors to a brothel, where a young man is said to have turned a lacivious look on her, only to be struck blind for the deed. She was then ordered to martyrdom by fire, and while tied to the stake is reported to have been less concerned with the flames than using her long hair to veil "her chaste body which had been exposed to the gaze of the heathen multitude." When fire didn't work, the flames being miraculously extinguished, it is said that Agnes was killed by the officer in charge — either by stabbing or beheading.

Agnes' story, however embellished, had a profound effect on people of the early church. St. Ambrose and St. Augustine wrote glowingly of her, and Pope Damasus (366-384), accenting her youth, spoke of her as one leaping bravely to martyrdom from the lap of her mother or nurse. Ambrose placed Agnes' age at twelve, Augustine's at thirteen. Whatever, her fame was great and Agnes soon became one of the best known and most honored of Roman martyrs. Her remains were placed in a sepulchre on the Via Nomentana, and around her tomb grew the catacomb that bears her name. A basilica was raised over her place of martyrdom in the Piazza Navona, and traditionally on her feast day two lambs are blessed, and from their wool are made the palliums sent by the pope to new archbishops.

St. Agnes' fame was no local phenomenon. As the patron of young girls, her feast was widely observed, including in rural England, where unmarried women indulged in exotic forms of country magic on St. Agnes' Eve with a view to discovering who would one day be their husband. The practice was immortalized in John Keats' 1819 poem "The Eve of St. Agnes."

Leo XIII

# THE DAY "AMERICANISM" WAS CONDEMNED

**IT'S THE ESOTERIC HISTORIAN** who can associate this date with Catholic history, few others. But on January 22, 1899, Pope Leo XIII issued the encyclical *Testem benevolentiae*, the document condemning the alleged heresy labeled "Americanism." The heresy was a libel on American Catholics. From the beginning the "heresy" was more European than American. What's the background?

Marveling at the rapid growth of the Catholic Church in the United States, certain circles of European Catholics, in France particularly, seized upon a popularized and imprecisely translated biography of Father Isaac Hecker (cf. Dec. 22), who came to Catholicism partly through New England transcendentalism, to press for secular and ecumenical accommodations that theoretically would be as beneficial for the church in Europe as they had been for the church in America. Liberal European Catholics seemed especially impressed by the health and vigor a church could enjoy where it was independent from state patronage.

Isaac Hecker, to return to him, was founder of course of the Missionary Society of St. Paul the Apostle, better known as the Paulists. He acquired a wide reputation for winning converts, in part by emphasizing those things which Catholics and Protestants held in common, rather than those which separated them. That approach, highlighted in the translation, is the cornerstone of the modern ecumenical movement, but in 1899 it smacked of compromise, of dilution of doctrine, of a waiving of prerogatives. The very idea was anathema in Rome. Problem was, in issuing his condemnations, Leo was addressing the wrong audience.

Though the "Americanism" name given the incident would stick, the reality was that the issues that troubled Leo did not exist in the American church. The church was not in radical ferment; it was loyalist. Leo XIII subsequently realized this, and three years later issued a congratulatory message to American Catholics for their loyalty and "liberality."

# JANUARY 23

## THE PRACTICE OF COUNTING QUARANTINES

**MANY OLD CATHOLIC PRACTICES** have gone by the boards in the post-Vatican II era, but probably none more so that the storing up of indulgences — accumulated "good" time as an offset against one's time-sentence to purgatory in the afterlife. For instance, one January day in 1917, Pope Benedict XV granted three hundred days' indulgence against time in purgatory for recitation of the Marian ejaculation, "My Mother, my trust." One could also get three hundred days for whispering "Holy Mary, deliver us from the pains of hell" or "Mary, Virgin Mother of God, pray to Jesus for me"; and for more involved devotional practices such as litanies, novenas and stations of the cross there were indulgences involving years, quarantines and lifetimes. A plenary indulgence, for instance, wiped out all temporal punishment due to sin.

Under such an arrangement, some Catholics inevitably would be conscientious hoarders of indulgences. The record may have been set, however, way back in the thirteenth century. In one twelve-month period, the pious Elector of Saxony, Frederick the Wise, made up no less than 127,799 years' worth of indulgences — a grand sum, but hardly an overload at a time when even a forgiven sin was believed to require the equivalent of seven years in purgatory before the soul qualified for admission to heaven. That was a lot of heat for one sin.

Emphases are quite different now than they were in Frederick the Wise's time, or for that matter in Benedict XV's. The church no longer doles out what might be called "matching grants" for the performance of acts of piety. Said another way, though the church still believes in the efficacy of pious practices, and though it still lists some seventy grants in its official handbook of indulgences, its stress is not on the selfish beefing-up of one's personal treasury of indulgences, but instead on the spirit of joyful and efficacious participation in the communion of saints and the prayer life of the church.

Charles Maurras

# THE PHENOMENON OF ACTION FRANCAISE

**THIS WAS THE WEEKEND** in 1927 that the church lowered the boom on Action Francaise, the French movement which initially championed traditional Catholicism over the extremes of twentieth-century liberalism, but which evolved into a reactionary political force seeking the return of the monarchy and with it the resurrection of glorious yesterdays. The leader of Action Francaise was Charles Maurras, a brilliant journalist and theoretician — and elitist. He scorned liberalism and the petit-bourgeois, and he propelled his newspaper, *L'Action Francaise*, into enormous prominence. Maurras built a particularly strong following among Catholics for his attacks on the liberal regimes of the Third Republic, at whose hands the church had suffered much. At one time eleven of France's seventeen cardinals and bishops publicly sided with Maurras. But Maurras' politics brought him in conflict with the Vatican, notably over post-World War I policies toward Germany. The Vatican was anxious for reconciliations; Maurras chauvinistically crusaded for the prerogatives of the victor. When a survey of Belgian youth confirmed the influence of Maurras' writings among the Catholic youth of Europe, Rome acted. Maurras was too dangerous a thinker.

Thus it was that on January 24, 1927, the archbishop of Paris published a pastoral prohibiting Catholics from reading *L'Action Francaise* and declaring Maurras' writings to be on the Index. Rome followed with an edict forbidding French clergy — bishop or simple priest — to baptize, marry, confess or bury persons subscribing to or reading *L'Action Francaise*. One consequence was that the French Academician, Jacques Bainville, a member of Action Francaise, was refused a Catholic burial. Similarly, the cardinal who placed the tiara on Pius XI's head, Louis Billot, was stripped of the red hat for opposing condemnation of Action Francaise. Much resentment was seeded, but by 1935 Action Francaise was history and the Vatican was decorating French leaders.

# JANUARY 25

John XIII in garden at Castel Gondolfo

## VATICAN COUNCIL II'S FIGURATIVE BIRTH DAY

**JOHN XXIII WAS A POPE** hardly three months. On this day in 1959, the feast celebrated as the Conversion of St. Paul, he went to the Basilica of St. Paul Outside the Walls to conclude the then-popular ecumenical devotion known as of the Chair of Unity Octave. Before seventeen area cardinals assembled in the chapter-room of the abbey, Pope John dropped his bombshell. It was cushioned in the Vatican Press Office's communique, which said: "The Holy Father, inspired by the age-old traditions of the church, announced three events of the greatest importance: a diocesan Synod for Rome, an ecumenical Council for the Universal Church, and the *aggiornamento* of the Code of Canon Law..."

The "sandwich-ing" of the news of the council between two events of markedly lesser importance clued to a larger truth. The Vatican bureaucracy was displeased, or at least nonplussed. The world now knows that to a man the cardinals sat mute at the news. They uttered "not a single word of response," Xavier Rynne reported in the *New Yorker*. For its part, *Osservatore Romano*, the official Vatican daily, made no mention of the council the day of announcement. John XXIII was deeply disappointed, particularly with the cardinals. The Jesuit Giovanni Caprile quoted him saying, "Humanly speaking, we would have expected that the cardinals, after listening to our address, might have crowded round to express their approval, and good wishes." No way. Actually, the cardinals' reaction was not unexpected. Pope John himself was reported to be genuinely apprehensive about how they would react. But — again according to Rynne — he put "the kindest and most charitable light on their unanimous failure to show any immediate reaction."

Many Catholics are still second-guessing John XXIII's decision to call a council. But this much seems certain: As turbulent as the scene became after the council, it is as nothing to what it would have been without one.

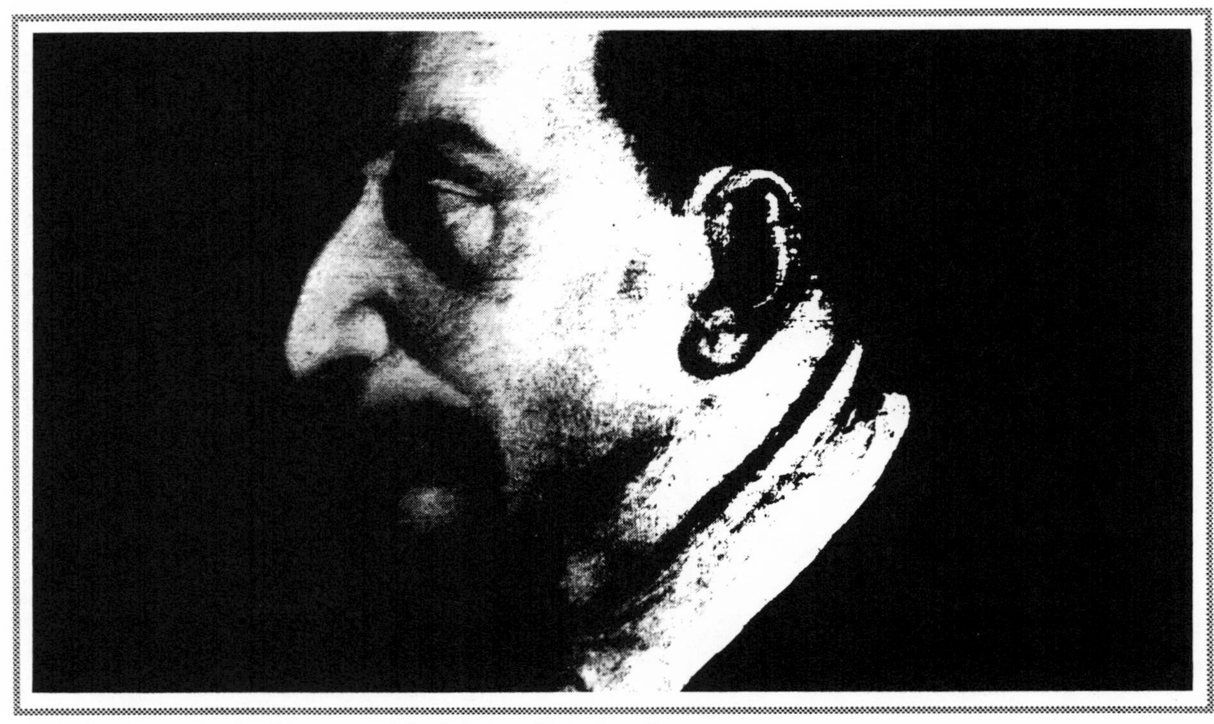

Charles Borromeo (detail from portrait by Guiseppe Maria Crespi)

# THE COUNTER-REFORMATION?

**AS A COUNCIL OF RECONCILIATION,** Trent was a signal failure. But as a council of doctrine and discipline, it was a signal success, and this was the day in 1564 that Pope Pius IV approved its decrees without alteration and, in effect, launched the Counter-Reformation. Or is that the wrong term? Some Catholic historians, Henri Daniel-Rops for one, have rejected the term — not so much for its reactionary tone, but because they have found it misleading. As Daniel-Rops wrote, the term Counter-Reformation "cannot rightly be applied, logically or chronologically, to that sudden awakening as of a startled giant." The more accurate term, he argued, was renascence — or better, the title of his own two-volume work on the subject, *The Catholic Reformation.*

But Counter-Reformation remains the common term for that period of Catholic revival that stretched from the pontificate of Pius IV to the close of the Thirty Years' War in 1648 during which the church of Rome put its house in order after the debacle of the Reformation. Three remarkable popes exerted influence as reformers — Pius V (1566-1572), Gregory XIII (1572-1585) and Sixtus V (1585-1590) — and enormous spiritual zeal characterized the period. New religious orders multiplied, and old ones reformed in fortuitous ways. The Franciscan reform, for instance, spun off the Capuchins, who were instrumental in securing Italy, France and sizable parts of Germany for Roman Catholicism. The Jesuit order, approved in 1540, came to prominence as a bulwark of the faith in the Netherlands, Bavaria and Poland. Leaders were raised up whose names would become legends of history — among them, Francis de Sales, Charles Borromeo, Peter Canisius, Philip Neri, Teresa of Avila and John of the Cross.

One further development contributed significantly to the revival of the church's fortunes: the age of exploration. The opening of the New World broadened visions as well as horizons, and the church was in the vanguard.

Excerpt from *Dictatus Papae*, twenty-seven propositions drawn up by Pope Gregory VII asserting his claim to power over both Church and State. Proposition XII states that the pope can depose emperors.

# GOING TO CANOSSA

**THIS WAS THE DAY IN 1077** that Pope Gregory VII ended the three-day ordeal of King Henry IV of Germany. Gregory had excommunicated Henry the year before in a dispute that had pitted the rights of monarchial powers against those of the papacy, notably in the conferring of bishoprics. Gregory had held the rights of the papacy to be literally limitless in all matters, and in excommunicating Henry he both neutralized and isolated him. Since at the time Christians were forbidden to associate with excommunicates, Henry's excommunication meant that oaths of allegiance of his subjects were suspended, and in doubt were concordats between Henry and other Christian leaders.

Hearing that Gregory was staying at Canossa, a castle of Matilda of Tuscany in the foothills of the Apennines, Henry hurried to Canossa to make his peace with the pope and do penance in hopes of the excommunication being lifted. Henry arrived before the castle gate on January 25, and in the dress of a pentitent cried out for the pope's forgiveness. For three days and nights the pope left Henry kneeling in the snow, foodless and shelterless it is said, before finally, "moved by the royal compunctions and the importunities of his royal entourage, among them Matilda," he received him and lifted his penalty. Details of the event have undoubtedly been colored over the centuries. Nonetheless, it was an incident that was to inspire one of the most famous catch-word phrases of history: "to go to Canossa" — meaning, to do penance and surrender to the claims of the church.

As for the incident itself, it is usually described as a victory for the spiritual power of the papacy. In point of fact, it proved an act of political subversion, for it lent sparks to a civil war that raised up a rival German king. Henry outlasted that king, only to die in 1106 while trying to put down a rebellion led by a namesake son. It wasn't always fun to be a king.

# ANGELIC DOCTOR, ENORMOUS MAN

**CALL HIM DOCTOR COMMUNIS,** Doctor Angelicus, the Great Synthesizer, but know him as St. Thomas Aquinas, the church's thirteenth-century Dominican genius who harmonized faith and reason, theology and philosophy, particularly that of Aristotle, and who systematized the body of Catholic doctrinal belief into a package that stayed tightly knotted for centuries.

To theologians trained until then largely in the Platonic tradition, Thomas Aquinas was deeply suspect for preoccupation with Aristotle and Aristotelian knowledge, bursting forth with new translations from Arabic and the original Greek. Today Thomas Aquinas' name is almost synonymous with conservatism, but he was revolutionary for his times. Distinguishing between revelation and reason, theology and philosophy, the sacred and the profane, he produced numerous treatises, the masterwork of which is the *Summa Theologica*, a standard seminary text yet for its synthesis of Latin and Greek patristic traditions.

Thomas Aquinas lived from 1225-1274, and was a man of great girth. He is said to have had a hole cut into his desk to fit his stomach. Indeed, his size was a matter of sport to his brother monks, and one day one of them excitedly exclaimed, looking out the window, "Come quick, look at the cow flying!" Aquinas is said to have been up from his desk and across the room like a young sprinter — to see nothing, of course. The monks howled with laughter, but Thomas Aquinas had his historic rejoinder: "I thought it more likely that a cow would fly than a monk would lie."

Thomas Aquinas was educated at Monte Cassino and the University of Naples, but it was as a professor and writer at the University of Paris that he gained his fame. After his return to Naples, Thomas Aquinas was summoned to take part in the Second Council of Lyons. He never got there, dying in route at Fossanova. The weight didn't help; he was not yet fifty years old. Today is his feast day.

# JANUARY 29

## LISTENING TO PRELATES AND BARBERS

**ONE OF THE GREAT** American worries at the time of the Civil War was that European nations might align with the Confederacy. Concern became especially acute after Great Britain, France and Spain signed the 1861 Treaty of London for the protection of their respective interests in Mexico. It was well known that all three signators were friendly to the Confederacy.

New York's Archbishop John Hughes and President Lincoln's Secretary of State, William H. Seward, were in close correspondence on the issue, and in October 1861, Seward asked Hughes to travel abroad and lobby the Union's cause. On this day in 1863, Archbishop Hughes wrote back to Seward from Paris: "Permit me to state my course, as a loyal citizen, since I came to France. I had no encouragement from our officials. But, independent of their patronage, I have had...the entree to the best Society in Paris — as an American Bishop. At dinners & soirees it has come up invariably that the company, either before, or during, or after dinner referred to me for an explanation of the Civil War that is now existing between two sections of our once United States. I did explain as well as I could, perfectly satisfied that whatever I said would reach the ears of one or other of the Ministers within 24 hours after its utterance. Besides, during my interview with the Emperor, I felt no hesitation in stating what none of his Ministers would venture to say. I might almost add that on the same occasion I had the effrontery even to give advice. It is generally thought that certain men are above being influenced. This is a mistake. If there ever was a man of such a type it would be General Jackson. And yet whilst General Jackson would disregard, under certain circumstances, the opinion of his whole Cabinet, General Jackson might take up and reflect upon a phrase uttered by the barber who shaved him. At all events, I think we might have fared worse in France than we have done.

# JANUARY 30

Pope Clement VIII

## THE POPE CAUGHT IN THE MIDDLE

**JANUARY IS A QUIET MONTH** as the election of popes goes. In fact, one has to go back to this date in 1592 to find the last man elected to the papacy in January. He was Ippolyto Aldobrandini, who took the name Clement VIII. Clement was an interesting man, but receives mixed grades from history. He emancipated the papacy from Spanish influence, and brought thirty years of religious war within France to an end by legitimating the birth and claims of Henry IV. Efforts, however, to steer England back to the fold and to draw slavs of the East into an alliance against the Turks were unsuccessful. Large areas of Germany and Poland were won back from Protestantism during his reign, but at the same time he was the pope who was reigning when Giordano Bruno went to the stake (q.v. Feb. 8). Clement was a close friend of Philip Neri, and in the eyes of some was so imbued with his spirit that it was as if the future saint were himself occupying the chair of Peter. The Forty Hours devotion is credited to Clement, as is the revised text known as the Clementine Vulgate.

A fascinating footnote to the story is Clement's role in the famous theological dispute between the Jesuits and the Dominicians over the nature of grace in the competing contexts of free will and predestination. The dispute, highly technical and nuanced, claimed Rome's attention, and Clement decided to settle the matter personally. He presided over sixty-eight sessions before retiring exhausted when neither side would budge. Clement is pictured as being persuaded by the Dominican logic, but as not wanting to offend the Jesuits. Thus he refused to decide on the debate. He named the chief Jesuit spokesman, Robert Bellarmine, to be Archbishop of Capua, a consolation prize. Soon after he had second thoughts that maybe the Jesuits were right after all. Too late.

The dispute ended with his successor, Pope Paul V. In 1611, Paul prohibted all further discussion of the question *de auxilis.*

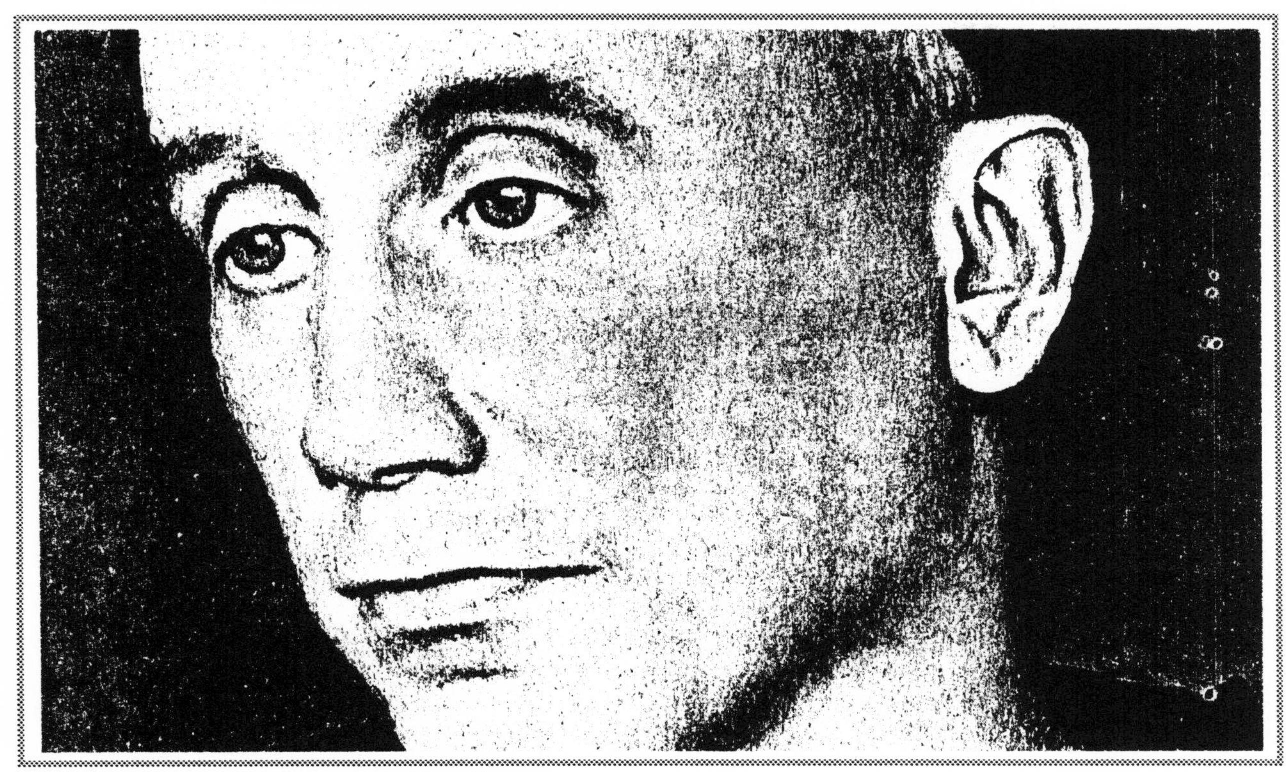

Thomas Merton (detail from sketch by Victor Hammer)

# A MAN OF PEACE IN AN UNPEACEFUL WORLD

**ON THIS DAY IN 1915** in Padres, France, a son was born to an English landscape artist and an American Quaker mother, who in the twenty years between 1948 and 1968 would have an enormous social and spiritual influence in the United States. He was Thomas Merton, poet, author, monk — a paradox of his times, a man who spoke to the twentieth century from the seventeenth-century world of a Trappist monastery. Merton studied in France and England; left Cambridge under something of a shadow; flirted with Communism while a student at Columbia University in New York — and converted to Catholicism in 1938, a decision which stabilized his life and turned it toward religion. He joined the Trappists in 1941, and in 1948, after three books of poetry, published his first book of prose, an autobiographical account of family life and the forces that led him to religion. The book was a smash bestseller that made Merton famous overnight: *The Seven Storey Mountain.*

New books followed at the rate of one and two a year, many of them reflections on the condition of the secular world in the context of peace, poverty, civil and social justice, and all permeated with his commitments to pacificism and nonviolence. Merton was haunted by the specter of the nuclear arms race, and on the immediate level by the war in Vietnam, and he grew increasingly pessimistic that humankind could ever achieve a permanent peace.

Paradoxically this man of the cloister was to die far from the monastery at Gethsemani, Kentucky, where he had lived as a Trappist. He died December 10, 1968, in Bangkok, Thailand, where he had gone a few months before to delve into Eastern mysticism. The circumstances were bizarre; an electrical fan toppled over and electrocuted him as he rested atop a bed. His remains were returned home aboard a plane carrying the bodies of young men killed in Vietnam. Thomas Merton, Father Louis, OCSO, was laid to rest at Gethsemani.

# FEBRUARY 1

## THE SAINT WHO PRAYED FOR MARTYRDOM

**BEFORE THE SHUFFLING** of the liturgical calendar in recent years, February 1 long belonged to St. Ignatius of Antioch. His feast is now marked on October 17 according to general Roman-Rite calendars — which incidentally is when Antioch always observed it. The Greek church honors him on December 10. But, as mentioned, this was his feast day, so let's cite him here.

Who was he? St. Ignatius of Antioch bridged the first and second centuries, and was one of the early church's great theologians. Of Syrian origin and a convert from paganism, Ignatius served as bishop at Antioch when it was a great center of trade and learning. He was a man in the tradition of St. Paul. He traveled widely, as did Paul, and wrote stirring letters to local Christian communities whose contents were strongly Pauline in Christology and moral counsel, notably those on marriage and celibacy; e.g., "if any man can remain continent to the honor of the flesh of the Lord, let him do so without boasting." Ignatius' major departure was in focusing more on the Hellenic than Judaic experience.

But perhaps Ignatius' most fascinating letter was that in which, under threat of martyrdom, he spurned thoughts of a pardon and expressed his wish to consummate his union with Christ by dying while sharing his passion: "Suffer me to be eaten by the beasts through whom I can attain to God. I am God's wheat and I am ground by the teeth of wild beasts that I may be found pure bread of Christ...I long for the beasts that are prepared for me...Let there come on me fire and cross and struggles with wild beasts...mangling of limbs, crushing of my whole body...May I but attain to Jesus Christ. I am learning in my bones to give up all desires...and there is in me no fire or love for material things; but only water living and saying to me from within, 'Come to the Father.'"

Ignatius of Antioch's wish was granted. He was martyred during the reign of Trajan (98-117), being torn apart by wild beasts in a Roman arena.

# FEBRUARY 2

## ANOTHER FEAST WITH CHANGED EMPHASES

**LIKE THAT OF JANUARY 1,** this is another church feast of altered emphasis. The feast goes today under the title of the Presentation of the Lord, and it commemorates the presentation of the young Jesus in the Temple, according to the prescriptions of Mosaic Law. That's quite new. For centuries, the feast was known as the Purification of the Blessed Virgin Mary.

Purification from what? From childbirth. Mosaic Law held that a woman who had given birth to a male child was unclean for forty days, and further she was to remain three and thirty days "in the blood of her purification." If the offspring was a female, the time was double. When the time period was over, the woman presented herself in the Temple with "a lamb for a holocaust and a young turtle dove for sin." If she could not afford a lamb, two turtle doves would do, or two pigeons. The Temple priest prayed with her, and the woman was considered clean again. The mother brought her child along for the ritual, and this constituted the child's solemn introduction into the house of God. When Mary was purified, accordingly, the baby Jesus was with her.

Thus it was that in the Eastern church, the feast was traditionally observed as one of Our Lord. But in the Western church the feast's emphases were squarely on Mary — until 1970, that is, and the revision of the liturgical calendar. The practice in the western Church of "churching" women after childbirth, a practice only lately abandoned, derived directly from the focus on Mary's "churching" or purification. To be sure, new mothers were never bound under pain of sin to be churched. Even so, at one time it was common for women to absent themselves from church after a childbirth, as if unpure, until they had been churched. The practice of churching women waned in the 1940's, and was just about gone entirely by the 1950's. Providentially so. The women's liberation movement of the 1960's would have annihilated it.

# THE CANTICLE OF SIMEON

**ONE OF THE GREAT CANTICLES** of the New Testament — the first of the three so-called "Evangelical Canticles" — is associated with yesterday's feast. It is the Canticle of Simeon, better known as the *Nunc Dimittis* from its opening words in the Latin Vulgate. A canticle quite simply is a sacred song that draws its text from the Bible, and some are so moving as to pass into the common prayers of the faithful. Such it is with the *Nunc Dimittis*. The *Nunc Dimittis* ranks in solemnity with the Canticle of Mary, the *Magnificat* (q.v. May 31), and the Canticle of Zachary, the Benedictus (q.v. February 4).

The setting is known to most everyone. Mary has gone to the Temple for her ritualistic purification, and she has along with her her son, her first born, whom she will present at the same time to the Lord as an offering. At the temple is a just and pious old man named Simeon, who has been awaiting the "consolation of Israel," the Holy Spirit having told him that he would not die until he had seen the "Anointed of the Lord." Inspired by the Spirit, Simeon was present in the Temple when Mary and Joseph arrived with Jesus for the customary ritual of the law. Simeon took the child Jesus in his arms and blessed the Lord in the immortal words of the *Nunc Dimittis* (Luke 2:29-32):

> Now thou canst dismiss thy servant, O Lord, according to thy word in peace. Because my eyes have seen thy salvation, which thou hast prepared for all peoples to see: A light to the revelation of the Gentiles and the glory of thy people Israel.

The Canticle of Simeon receives great prominence in yesterday's liturgy for the feast of the Lord's presentation. It is also incorporated into the church's daily prayer life as a part of compline, where it is preceded by the responsorial phrase familiar to most Catholics: *In manus tuus, Domine, commendo spiritum meum*...."Into your hands O Lord, I commend my spirit."

### The Benedictus

*Blessed be the name of the Lord, the God of Israel, for he has visited and redeemed his people. And he has raised up a horn of salvation for us in the house of David his servant, as he promised through the mouth of his holy ones, the prophets from of old; salvation from our enemies, and from the hands of all who hate us, to show mercy to our forefathers and to be mindful of his holy covenant, of the oath that he swore to Abraham our father, that he would grant us, that, delivered from the hand of our enemies, we should serve him without fear, in holiness and justice before him all our days. And thou, child, shall be called the prophet of the Most High, for thou shalt go before the face of the Lord to prepare his ways, to give to his people knowledge of salvation through forgiveness of their sins, because of the tender mercy of our God, wherewith the dayspring from on high has visited us, to give light to them that sit in the darkness and in the shadow of death, to guide our feet into the way of peace.*

## THE CANTICLE OF ZACHARY

**SEQUENTIALLY,** the Canticle of Zachary is the second of the church's great evangelical canticles. Also called the *Benedictus*, again from its opening Latin word, the canticle is the hymn of praise sung by Zachary, the father of John the Baptist, in gratitude for the son who would be the precursor of Jesus and his baptizer. Some background: Zachary was the husband of Elizabeth, who in turn was a cousin of Mary. Zachary was an old man and his wife was advanced in years and seemingly hopelessly barren, when the angel Gabriel appeared to him and told him that he would be the father of a son. Zachary was incredulous and because he doubted, he lost his power of speech — struck speechless, as they say. He would not regain it until the day of his ritualistic circumcision, and he wrote that his son's name would be John. Immediately Zachary broke out in the hymn of praise, the *Benedictus*. Again the canticle is found in Luke, 1:68-79:

# FEBRUARY 5

## THE SAINT WHO LOST BREASTS AND LIFE

**ST. AGATHA** has been on the church's liturgical calendar for centuries, but she's another about whom not a whole lot is known. A woman of striking beauty, she was born in Sicily (perhaps Catania, perhaps Palermo) of noble parentage, and was martyred at Catania around the year 250, apparently because she refused to move in with Quintian, the governor of Sicily, as his concubine. Incensed by her refusal, the spurned governor ordered Agatha ripped by iron hooks, and had her breasts cut off. In her agony, Agatha is piously said to have been consoled by a vision of St. Peter, then to have been cured by Peter himself of her afflictions. But the tortures were renewed, and in a last gesture of cruelty her tormentors threw her on burning coals—whereupon Catania was reportedly rocked by an earthquake.

That's about all that's known. But it was enough to have built for Agatha a huge devotional following. She was accorded a feast of her own, and a Mass with the Introit prayer: "Let us all rejoice in the Lord, celebrating a festival in honor of blessed Agatha, virgin and martyr, at whose passion the angels rejoice and give praise to the Son of God." In the sixth century the poet Venantus Fortunatus celebrated Agatha as virgin and martyr, and a hymn in her honor is ascribed to Pope Damasus. For years in some places, specially baked bread was blessed at Masses on her feast day and known as Agatha's bread. Her feast was traditionally kept on February 5, and it survives in the streamlined church calendar of the post-Vatican II church.

Agatha's story has ever inspired the creative, and there's a famous painting of her by Bernardino Luini in Rome's Galleria Borghese. Because of the breast mutilation, medieval art tended to feature her carrying her breasts around on a salver, or tray. She's invoked against breast diseases, and in the region of Mount Etna against eruptions of the volcano. She's also the patroness of nurses.

# FEBRUARY 6

## THE BIBLE AND EVERYDAY SPEECH

In many homes the Bbile may indeed be the dustiest book on the shelf. Yet many everyday figures of speech come directly from that dusty book and slip from the tongue with little conscious sense of their origin. Examples:

*Feet of clay.*
— Daniel 2:33

*Apple of one's eye.*
— Deuteronomy 32:10

*Salt of the earth.*
— Matthew *5:13*

*There were giants in the earth in those days.*
— Genesis 6:4

*A land flowing with milk and honey.*
— Exodus 3:8 and 33:3

*Set one's house in order.*
— 2 Kings 20:1

*Sweeter also than honey and the honeycomb.*
— Psalm 19:10

*My cup runneth over.*
— Psalm 23:5

*At wit's end.*
— Psalm 107:27

*Pride goeth before the fall.*
— Psalms *16:18*

*A merry heart doth good like a medicine.*
— Shakespeare? Proverbs 17:22

*Vanity of vanities; all is vanity.*
— Ecclesiastes l:2 and 12:8

*To eat, drink, and be merry.*
— Surely Shakespeare! No; Ecclesiastes 8:15

*The race is not to the swift.*
— Ecclesiastes 9:11

*Can the...leopard change his spots?*
— Jeremiah 13:23

*Old men shall dream dreams and young men shall see visions.*
— Joel 2:28

*Neither cast pearls before swine.*
— Now Shakespeare? No; Matthew 7:6

*He passed by on the other side.*
— Luke 10:31

*Eat, drink, and be merry.*
— No, not Ecclesiastes again; see Luke 12:19

*The wind blows where it will.*
— John 3:8

*It is more blessed to give than to receive.*
— Acts 20:35

*Labor of love.*
— 1 Thessalonians 1:3

*God forbid!*
— Romans 3:31.......Interested in more? See February 18.

Cardinal Petro Gasparri

# THE SETTLING OF THE "ROMAN QUESTION"

**TEMPORAL POWER RETURNED** to the Vatican on this day in 1929. For fifty-nine years popes had been so-called "prisoners of the Vatican" (cf. Sept. 20). Not one pope had stepped outside the Vatican over all those years in protest over Italy's annexation of the Papal States in 1870. The protest had become anachronistic, and everyone with sense wanted to settle the dispute, including Benito Mussolini, Italy's Fascist leader and prime minister.

The possibility of negotiations was broached in 1927, and proceeded with such speed that the pope, Pius XI, thought he was being rushed into an agreement. He preferred a slower pace and, not prevailing there, proposed completing the negotiations but leaving the actual signing to his successor — to which his Secretary of State, Cardinal Pietro Gasparri, is said to have protested, "No, no, Your Holiness! Now or never!" The pope acceded, and on February 7, 1929, Gasparri called together heads of the diplomatic community and officially announced that the "Roman Question," as the issue had come to be called, had been resolved.

The terms of the agreement were ratified four days later as the Lateran Concordat, and by any historical reassessment they were as much as the Vatican realistically could hope for. The Italian state renounced all claim to Vatican territory in Rome, and the Vatican became a city-state of 108.7 acres — not a large area, but sufficiently large to insure temporal independence, while protecting political and spiritual integrity for its head, the pope. In addition, the Vatican received 1,750 million lire ($100 million) and specified rights in Italy itself in the realm of education and over mores controlled by law. Roman Catholicism was declared the state religion, and the church assumed sweeping controls over Italian life that would last until the signing of a new concordat in 1984. Pius XI was to reign for ten more years, convinced, in his words, that he had "given Italy back to God, and God back to Italy."

# A KNIGHT-ERRANT OF THE RENAISSANCE

**THE CHURCH** doesn't talk much about Giordano Bruno, and if the reason is embarrassment, it's understandable. The Roman Inquisition handed him over to the secular arm on this day in 1600, and nine days later Bruno was burned at the stake in the Campo dei Fiori in central Rome. In 1889 a heroic-sized statue to Giordano Bruno was erected on the spot to his memory by admirers, but there's been no ecclesiastical rehabilitation, as with Galileo.

Giordano Bruno was forever a large problem, and to others than just Catholic officials. Though he steadfastly denied ever belonging to a reformed faith, the Calvinist Council excommunicated him. So did the Lutherans. The Venetian Inquisition probed him, but he slipped away with an imaginative use of the principle of the "two-fold truth," Bruno holding that errors imputed to him were held by him "as a philosopher, and not as an honest Christian." Even so he "abjured" all errors and doubts alleged to him apropos Catholic doctrine and practice. The Roman Inquisition intervened, slapped him in jail for six years, retried him for heresy, and finally allowed his execution. A sad day.

Bruno was born in Campania in 1548. He joined the Dominicans at fifteen and in 1572 was ordained a priest. A fiery type, he cast off the order's discipline and wandered from country to country tilting at sacred theories and hallowed traditions. He found pedantry in Geneva, and he dismissed Oxford professors as people who knew more about beer than Greek. At a time when masters and bachelors not following Aristotle faithfully were liable to fines of five shillings, Bruno held him in "perfect hatred." Yet he respected Aristotelians like Albert the Great and Thomas Aquinas. As a philosopher of the Renaissance, Giordano Bruno brimmed with new thought. He was absorbed by Copernicus, and saw whole other worlds revealed through astronomy. He viewed God and nature as one. The orthodox deemed him an incoherent pantheist. For this he died.

Pope Gregory IX (Detail from fresco by Raphael)

# THE POPE AT WHOM THE FINGER IS POINTED

**THE CHURCH** got into the business of dispatching heretics in a serious way with Pope Gregory IX in the thirteenth century. In the ninth century, Pope Nicholas I declared the use of torture to be unconscionably un-Christian, but with heretics seeming to be coming out of the woodwork, Gregory winked at torture and in February 1231 approved the death penalty for heresy — heretics then being looked upon as traitors. He did this by enacting a law for Rome providing that heretics condemned by an ecclesiastical court be delivered to the secular power for "due punishment." This translated to life imprisonment for the penitent and death by fire for the obstinate — Giordano Bruno's fate.

Gregory in effect systematized the Inquisition, placing it at the same time in the hands of the Dominicans with rules that would remain in force until the reign of Sixtus V, 1585-1590. You're talking thus of a couple centuries plus.

The paradox is that Gregory IX, along with numerous other popes of the Inquisition, was a remarkable man, and with luck might have been judged kindly by history. He was famed for his learning and eloquence, led a blameless moral life, and had great strength of character. An admirer of Francis of Assisi, he would often don the Franciscan garb and walk about barefooted with Francis and his friends. He canonized Francis of Assisi — and St. Anthony of Padua, St. Dominic and St. Elizabeth of Thuringia as well. He championed the rise of the medieval university, promoted Aristotelianism as the basis of scholastic philosophy, and was especially solicitous for the welfare of his alma mater, the University of Paris. Yet history judges him an ogre. Not without reason.

The severity of the Inquisition eased to be sure, but inquisitorial notions would be around a long time. In fact, it was not until 1908 that the Curia's Congregation of the Holy Office of the Inquisition became known simply as the Holy Office....today's very same Congregation for the Doctrine of the Faith.

# THE COMING AND GOING OF NOVENAS

**THE WORD "NOVENA"** derives from the Latin word for nine, *novem*, and historically designates a period of prayer spread over nine days or weeks. The practice is thought to have its origins in the nine-day interval between the Ascension and the coming of the Holy Ghost on Pentecost, and over the centuries it took many forms. In the Middle Ages, for instance, the rich and powerful would provide in their wills for a novena of Masses to be said on the nine days after their death. Later, major feasts of the church, notably that of Christmas, were ushered in with novenas of preparation. The novenas that today's generations of Catholics came to know — novenas of petition or, more accurately, indulgenced novenas — were largely a ninteenth century innovation.

To be sure, in the seventeenth century Alexander VII indulgenced a novena in honor of St. Francis Xavier, but it wasn't until the eighteenth century that the first indulgenced novena was approved for the city of Rome — Clement XI acting on this day in 1713 in favor of a novena in preparation for the feast of St. Joseph. But the approval was for one church only, that of St. Ignatius. And so it was to be for years. When novenas were approved, it was on a local basis only.

The universalization of novenas began early in the ninteenth century, in an effort to enrich the whole church with indulgences, not just pockets of it. Soon there were no fewer than thirty-two indulgenced novenas, honoring such heavenly hosts as the Guardian Angel and the Archangels Michael, Gabriel and Raphael. St. Joseph had two, one memorializing his "seven sorrows," the other his "seven joys." But going into the twentieth century, Mary was clearly the leader with no less than eleven. Perhaps the most popular was the novena of the Most Holy Rosary. In time, the novena passed from vogue, and maybe with cause. Some had become exotic — like that to St. Hubert for cures against madness due to the bite of a mad dog or wolf. Still novenas had their day, and they're missed by many.

# FEBRUARY 11

St.. Bernadette

## "I AM THE IMMACULATE CONCEPTION"

**THIS IS THE ANNIVERSARY** of the first of the apparitions at Lourdes in 1858. The story is a familiar one. Bernadette Soubirous, fourteen, set off with her sister and a friend to gather firewood from the common land by the banks of the river Gave. Bernadette fell behind the others, and as she was removing her shoes and stockings before crossing the mill stream near the grotto of Massabielle, she was visited by a woman no bigger than herself, dressed in a white robe, with a blue sash knotted at her waist. The woman was the Blessed Virgin, and she revealed herself under the title of the Immaculate Conception. Eighteen times the Virgin was to appear to Bernadette. They prayed the rosary together, and Bernadette conveyed the Virgin's wish that a chapel be built on the site of the vision. The Virgin also told Bernadette to drink from a fountain in the grotto. There was no grotto, but when Bernadette scratched at the spot designated in the apparition, a spring began to flow, whose waters proved subsequently to have a wondrous healing power.

Millions flock annually to Lourdes from all over the world, and since 1933 Bernadette herself has been officially hailed by the church as a saint. But she had a hard time in her lifetime. She was besieged by skeptics — bullied, cajoled and endlessly cross-examined. She entered the convent of the Sisters of Nevers in 1866, and her lot was another trial, for she had a mistress of novices and a mother superior who found it impossible to believe that Mary would appear to a peasant girl rather than someone more exalted like one or the other of them. In Bernadette's words she was "ground like a grain of corn."

Lourdes and its continuing miracles have obscured the life of this remarkable saint. Parents seldom name daughters after her anymore, as they did in the 1930s, 1940s. But Bernadette's story lives, as does her shrine, which is yet a singular place of pilgrimage; in fact, one of the most popular.

# FEBRUARY 12

Guglielmo Marconi

## THE VATICAN TAKES TO THE ETHER

**ONE OF THE MAGIC NAMES** in the early part of the century was that of Guglielmo Marconi, the native of Bologna who invented the radio and who shared the Nobel Prize for physics in 1909 with Ferdinand Braun. On this day in 1931 Marconi inaugurated Vatican Radio. The project was initiated after the signing of the Lateran pacts of 1929 re-establishing the Vatican's territorial independence. The Vatican now being a sovereign state, Pius XI wanted for it what was then in the new field of wireless telegraphy the ultimate in electronic sophistication: a radio station. Who better to start one than the inventor of the wireless himself? Pius made Marconi an offer which Marconi as a Catholic and an Italian to boot could hardly refuse; he assigned him the radio project, much as earlier popes assigned artistic projects to Raphael, Michelangelo and other artists. In fairness to Marconi, he seemed happier about being asked and about serving than some others extended "papal command" assignments. Marconi introduced Pius XI for the station's first papal message, and he supervised the station's operations until his death in 1937.

Vatican Radio has grown enormously since the February day in 1931 that the pope defined its mission to carry "the voice of the Supreme Pastor...across the waves of ether, to the utmost ends of the earth, for the glory of Christ and for the spiritual help of souls." Vatican Radio's signal, or sign-call, is the same — the bells of St. Peter's — but most everything else of a physical kind is different, including location. In 1957 a new transmission center was opened twenty miles north of Rome on an extra-territorial site whose area is almost ten times larger than Vatican City itself. Today Vatican Radio is one of the most far-reaching in the world. It is on the air twenty-four hours a day, and broadcasts regularly in thirty-four languages. It reports fully on the pope, and also airs daily a Latin Mass, the rosary, news and commentary of religious interest, and music.

# FEBRUARY 13

## SALVATION BY PARENTICIDE?

**LOOK IT UP YOURSELF.** You'll find there are thirty-nine St. Julians in the Roman Martyrology, and a slew of others of later centuries. But the principal Julian is probably Julian the Hospitaller, and once upon a time this was a feast day of his. You don't hear much about Julian the Hospitaller, although in 1877 one of the stories in French novelist Gustave Flaubert's *Trois contes* was titled *Saint Julien—l'Hospitalier*, none other. The American novelist Truman Capote recalled the story in the "Nocturnal Turning" episode of his 1980 book *Music for Chameleons*. According to Capote's precis, Julian loved to hunt about his parents' estate, and got so caught up in slaying that somehow or another he killed his mother and father. Rendered a pariah, Julian wandered the world in penitence, barefoot and in rags. One day he was approached near a river (the River Styx? asks Capote) by a particularly hideous leprous old man. The leper was God, and he tested Julian to see if he had achieved true penitence. The leper asked Julian if he could share his blanket, which Julian did; he asked Julian to embrace him, which Julian did; he asked Julian to kiss his diseased, rotting lips, which Julian did — whereupon the leper was radiantly transformed as God, and Julian, having seen the light, went on to heaven and sainthood.

You get a different version in Catholic books of hagiography, or those that touch the story. One has Julian killing his parents after finding them in his wife's bed, she having gone off to morning Mass and he, returning from somewhere or another, not knowing that there in bed before his very eyes were his parents, jumped to conclusions, and wham! Two corpses. Appalled by his deed, Julian atoned by building a hospital by a river for the poor and devoting the rest of his life to their care. Hence, Julian the Hospitaller.

Nowadays Julian the Hospitaller gets short shrift. But he was once the patron of boatsmen, travellers and innkeepers....Wonder why not marksmen too?

# FEBRUARY 14

## VALENTINE: SAINT OR SWEETHEART?

**THIS IS ST. VALENTINE'S DAY**, but how it came to be known and observed as such, with the exchange of valentines and all, is anyone's guess.

To be sure there was a feast of Saint Valentine on the old church calendar, and it was observed on February 14. Coincidentally, ancient legend had it that birds began to pair on this date. Hence it seemed appropriate that young women and men should also formally choose one another, or at least send each other greetings on the day. Because of the church calendar, the custom came under the patronage of St. Valentine, and the greetings themselves became known as "valentines."

The custom reached across much of Christendom. In medieval France and England, for instance, young people would gather on St. Valentine's eve, and names would be drawn from a receptacle. The person whose name was pulled was the "valentine" or sweetheart of the drawer for the ensuing year.

As for St. Valentine, who he was is again anyone's guess. There may have been no Valentine. Then, too, there may have been two — a priest who was beheaded in Rome during the persecutions of Claudius the Goth around 269; and a bishop, also said to have been beheaded, but at Terni, near Rome.

The church settled the confusion on this day in 1969, when Pope Paul VI issued his apostolic letter *Mysterii paschalis celebrationem*, revising the calendar of saints. St. Valentine received no valentine. His feast was suppressed, and he passed into obscurity along with Canute, Alexius, Christopher, Eustace, Philomena and others.

But interesting enough St. Valentine's Day survives, though nowadays it's more likely to be called just Valentine's Day. "Valentines" are dropped on school desks, and they fly through the mails between grandparents and grandchildren. It's a lovely custom, be there a St. Valentine or not.

# FEBRUARY 15

## The Divine Praises

*Blessed be God.*

*Blessed be his holy name.*

*Blessed be Jesus Christ, true God and true man.*

*Blessed be the name of Jesus.*

*Blessed be his most sacred heart.*

*Blessed be Jesus Christ in the most holy sacrament of the altar.*

*Blessed be the great mother of God, Mary most holy.*

*Blessed be her holy and Immaculate Conception.*

*Blessed be the name of Mary, virgin and mother.*

*Blessed be St. Joseph her most chaste spouse.*

*Blessed be God in his angels and in his saints.*

## YESTERDAY'S PRAYERS

**A VERY POPULAR** afternoon or evening devotion in the pre-Vatican II church was Benediction of the Blessed Sacrament, a fifteenth-century ceremony that grew out of Catholic fascination with the sacred host. At one time the devout would rush from church to church to witness the elevation of the host at the consecration of the Mass, and the dying were brought the host simply to gaze upon. These practices were eventually discouraged, but in the meanwhile legitimate devotions came along to satisfy the urge to worship God in the sacred host, notably Benediction of the Blessed Sacrament, a ceremony first recorded at Hildesheim, Germany. The ceremony was to take various forms country to country, but the point was constant: to enshrine the host in a monstrance, expose it for viewing, sing hymns (*O Salutaris Hostia* and *Tantum Ergo Sacramentum*), then bless the faithful with the host, silently making over them the sign of the cross with the monstrance. In the United States, the ceremony then concluded with a recitation of the Divine Praises (above) — known more formally as the Act of Reparation for Profane Language.

# BUT IS THE DRINK INDULGENCED?

**AS MENTIONED YESTERDAY**, fascination with the divine presence in the eucharistic elements was enormous in centuries gone by, and nowhere did it hit a higher fever pitch than at Fécamp, a seaport community of northern France. The town actually grew up around a convent founded in 658 to guard the relic of the True Blood, which, legend has it, was found in the trunk of a fig tree that had drifted to the area from Palestine. In the tenth century, a priest saying Mass in a small chapel three miles from Fécamp's Benedictine abbey church found neither bread nor wine before him at the moment of consecration but the actual flesh and blood of Christ. Naturally this caused a great stir when reported back at the abbey, but the miracle was "confirmed," and chalice, paten and species were enshrined beneath the chapel's main altar.

Greater fame of another kind awaited Fécamp, however. For it was at Fécamp's Benedictine abbey that the monk Don Bernardo Vincelli concocted a beverage with fresh lemon peel, cardamoms, hyssop tops, angelica, peppermint, thyme, cinnamon, nutmegs, cloves and arnica flowers — the exact combination of the ingredients is a carefully guarded secret — that was to prove a salubrious blessing to humankind. Indeed a medieval archbishop of Rouen hailed Vincelli as a man as important to the race for his inspiration as any saint.

What Vincelli had produced was the liqueur the world knows as Benedictine. It was first made about 1510, and Vincelli and his colleagues in their piety dedicated the product "to the greater glory of God." The monastery was destroyed in the eighteenth century during the French Revolution, but the monks preserved their secret formula and fifty years later production was resumed by a man named A. Legrand in a distillery on the site of the old abbey. The label of each bottle carries the faint outline of a cross and the bold letters D.O.M., for *Deo optimo maximo*, "for the most good and great God."

# REMEMBERING MONSIGNOR RONALD KNOX

**THERE WERE** two famous Knox brothers, sons of the Anglican Right Reverend E. A. Knox, D.D. — Edmund George Valpy Knox and Ronald Arbuthnot Knox. Edmund was the celebrated humorist, the versifier and parodist "Evoe" of Punch, who eventually succeeded to the editor's chair. Ronald, whom Catholics remember better, was the celebrated convert, churchman (monsignor), and author. He was born on this date in 1888 in Kibworth, Leicestershire, England.

Ronald Arbuthnot Knox had all the proper credentials: Eton, Oxford, Trinity fellow, and as of 1912 Anglican orders. He served as chaplain at Oxford until 1917, and then he converted to Roman Catholicism. Two years later he was ordained a priest, and proceeded to become one of the most influential Catholic apologists in England. He wrote numerous books, from spiritual treatises to erudite detective novels, and was known forever for his witty satire.

In 1925 Ronald Knox returned to Oxford as Catholic chaplain, and regularly took part in Oxford Union debates. He is said to have been perhaps the Union's most popular speaker ever. He was also a private tutor of note, including to Harold Macmillan. The arrangement was of limited duration, being ended by the Macmillan family for fear of Knox's Catholicizing influence. The fear may not have been misplaced, for in 1957, when Mr. Macmillan as prime minister attended Knox's funeral, he was heard to remark wistfully, "I am too old to change now."

Knox left Oxford in 1939 to devote himself to a new translation of the Scriptures from the Vulgate. The task was undertaken on the request of Cardinal Arthur Hinsley, who wanted a wholly modern translation characterized by clarity and beauty of language. The Knox Bible, which went through many printings, never achieved the success hoped for it. But it did point up one urgency in translating the Scriptures, subsequently met in the post-Vatican II period: to go beyond the Vulgate to the original languages themselves.

# FEBRUARY 18

## MORE ECHOES FROM THE BIBLE

(Continuing with the entry for February 6)

*Garments of gladness.*
—Judith 10:3

*Be quick to hear, slow to speak, slow to anger.*
—James 1:19

*Fight the good fight.*
—1 Timothy 6:12

*Touch not, taste not, handle not.*
—Ben Franklin? Try Colossians 2:21

*It is hard for thee to kick against the pricks.*
—Acts 9:5, King James Version.

*The poor you will always have with you.*
—John 12:8

*He was a good man.*
—Luke 23:50

*Is there no balm in Gilead, no physician there?*
—Jeremiah 8:22

*A bruised reed....a smoldering wick.*
—Isaiah 42:3

*The ancient and honorable...*
—Hibernians? Nope, Isaiah 9:15

*The borrower is servant to the lender.*
—Ah, Shakespeare at last. Wrong again. Proverbs 22:7

*The beauty of old men is the grey head.*
—Proverbs 20:29

*The hearing ear and the seeing eye.*
—Proverbs 20:12

*They go from strength to strength.*
—Psalm 84:7

*A broken and contrite heart.*
—Psalm 51:17

*God save the king.*
—1 Samuel 10:24

*To rise as one man.*
—Judges 20:8

*When we sat by the fleshpots.*
—Exodus 16:3

*My brother's keeper.*
—Stanislaus Joyce? Yes. But first, Genesis 4:9

*A stranger in a strange land.*
—Exodus 2:22

*The sun stood still, and the moon stayed.*
—Hemingway? Could be, but it's Joshua 10:13

*The naked truth.*
—John 8:32? Caught ya! Shakespeare, at last: *Love's Labour's Lost*, Act 5, Scene 2, line 715

## FIDDLING WHILE ROME BURNED

**IT IS INEVITABLE** in the long history of the papacy and rule by pronouncement that some statements would be less cosmic than others. On this day in 1749 Benedict XIV, the same who four years earlier issued *Vix prevenit*, declaring interest rates on money loaned a "crime," released *Annus qui hunc*, an encyclical addressed to the bishops of the Papal States on, guess what? — clean churches and sacred music. This is Benedict, warming to his subjects:

"...We do not intend with these words to insist on sumptuous or magnificent accouterments for holy buildings, nor on rich or expensive furnishings; we are aware these are not everywhere possible; what we wish is decency and cleanliness. These can coexist with poverty, and can be adapted to....The second point upon which we would rouse your zeal and your solicitude is that you take care that the canonical hours be sung or recited as is customary or is the rule in each church, with the care and the respect due by those who are obligated to them....

"Great care must be exercised lest the chant be hurried or sung faster than it should; that the pauses be made in the appropriate place; and that one part of the choir does not begin the following verse of a psalm before the other has finished the preceding verse. It is this chant which excites the souls of the faithful to devotion and to piety; and it is this chant which, if it is executed according to the rules and with the decorum which is required inside the churches of God, which the faithful prefer....

"The third thing of which we wish to warn you is that 'musical' chant which modern usage has commonly introduced into churches, and is accompanied by organs and other instruments, should be executed in such a way that it does not convey a profane, worldly or theatrical impression. The use of organs and of other instruments is not yet admitted throughout the Christian world."

# THE DEAD SEA SCROLLS

**IT WAS ABOUT THIS TIME**, February or March, in 1947 that a young Bedouin man of the Ta'amirch tribe, one Muhammad adh-Dhib, searching for a lost goat, entered a cave on the west coast of the Dead Sea, south of Jericho, and discovered a set of jars, twenty-five to thirty inches high and ten inches wide, containing strange leather scrolls wrapped in linen. Were they any good? Did they mean anything? The scrolls were shown to a Muslim elder in Jerusalem, who was not particularly impressed, then offered to a dealer in antiquities for twenty pounds. The dealer turned them down as a poor risk. His was a poorer business sense. The scrolls were the first of the documents known as the Dead Sea Scrolls.

Five of Muhammad adh-Dhib's scrolls were subsequently bought by the archbishop of the Syrian Orthodox monastery at Jerusalem, Mar (Lord) Athanasius Samuel, and three by an official at the Hebrew University at Jerusalem, Eliezer Sukenik. It did not take Sukenik long to recognize the great age and importance of the scrolls. It was urgent, he felt, that the documents be kept together. That proved a problem, however, for Mar Athanasius fled the Middle East and the blood and turmoil that acompanied creation of the Jewish state of Israel in 1947, taking the scrolls with him. He turned up in New York, where, anxious to capitalize on the scrolls, he offered them for sale in *The Wall Street Journal*. By remarkable coincidence, Sukenik's son, Yigael Yadin, was in New York at the time and saw the advertisement, and through a wealthy friend, D. Samuel Gottesman, Yadin managed to purchase the scrolls. The price was $250,000 — steep, but a colossal bargain for something in fact priceless. The scrolls were returned to Israel, joined to the Sukenik scrolls, and today constitute what Israeli scholar Herbert A. Kenny calls the core of the collection at Hebrew University's Shrine of the Book — the "book" in this case being not the Torah or the Bible, but the Book of Isaiah. Read on. »»»

# BRIDGE BETWEEN THE TWO TESTAMENTS

**THE DEAD SEA SCROLLS** found by Muhammad adh-Dhib proved to be but the beginning of the most remarkable manuscript discovery of modern times. By 1970, more than six-hundred manuscripts, including ten complete documents and thousands of fragments, were found in eleven caves of the Desert of Juda west of the Dead Sea. With one exception, the scrolls are in Hebrew. A quarter are biblical texts, the remainder being commentaries, hymns, psalms and theological writings of the Qumram community, a branch of the Essenes, an ascetic, celibate brotherhood of Jews that first appeared two centuries before Christ.

The great importance of the Dead Sea scrolls lies in the descriptions and insights they provide into Jewish history and Hebrew literature during the crucial transition period between the Old and the New Testaments. The scrolls by their antiquity also help confirm the time-fixing of certain books of the Old Testament. The Book of Isaiah scroll mentioned yesterday, for instance, moved known Hebrew manuscripts of the tract back centuries. Hitherto the oldest known Hebrew manuscripts of the book dated from the tenth century C.E.

How did this wealth of scrolls ever come to be in such a remote place as the caves of a desert? No one knows for sure, though it is obvious pains were taken to conceal and preserve a vast library — perhaps for security against vandalism and plunder; perhaps to insure that after Hellenizing influences of the period had run their course there was a reliable record of true Judaism to refer back to. Who knows? The tragedy is that the library likely was considerably larger than that found. There is a third-century account, for instance, of a translation of the Psalms being found in a jar near Jericho, and in the year 800 the Nestorian patriarch Timothy I wrote of a "little house of books" being found near Jericho by a sheperd. There are other accounts of a similar sort. What seems certain is that someone got to the scrolls before the Bedouin goatherd Muhammad adh-Dhib -- and, alas, it's all lost.

# FEBRUARY 22

## LATIN'S LAST GREAT ECCLESIASTICAL GASP

**LOOK BACK TO THIS DAY** in 1962 to realize that the immutable, unchangeable church is really mutable after all. For that was the day Pope John XXIII issued the apostolic constitution *Veterum sapientia* celebrating the Latin language for its "immutable" qualities, reconfirming its place as the official language of the church, and imposing (or reimposing) it as the teaching medium of philosophy and theology in seminaries. Well, we all know what happened. The Latin tradition was undone in less than two years' time by the very first decree of Vatican II, the Constitution on the Sacred Liturgy, which provided for the worldwide replacement of Latin with the vernacular in the Mass and for other liturgical functions. For us in the United States, that meant Mass in English. We've hardly heard a word of Latin since.

To be sure *Veterum sapientia* ("The Wisdom of the Ancients") was, in the words of John XXIII's biographer Peter Hebblethwaite, "the most ineffectual document" ever published by John. But that's not the point. The point is that church is not frozen in time. It does change, and the displacement of Latin is a dramatic example of that fact. It has changed in other notable ways as well within the lifetimes of most living Catholics. For instance, we no longer have to fast from midnight to receive communion. We can eat meat on Friday in good conscience, if not also in good health: fish is better for us.

Most of the modern changes occurred during the papacy of Paul VI, and he handled the issue of change by saying "the church is consistent with itself." Which may be another way of saying that if the church does not change, it does evolve. But theologians have said that all along. Cardinal Newman used to speak of the "development of doctrine." A more contemporary theologian, Jesuit Father Avery Dulles, uses the word "reconceptualization." Either way, if the church doesn't change, it takes on mighty different hues at times.

## THE MORNING OFFERING

**TIME WAS** when morning prayers were said rigorously and inevitably included the prayer known as the "Morning Offering." Several variations of the prayer were in vogue. The one many Catholics learned from Sister in parochial school went as follows:

"O Jesus, through the Immaculate Heart of Mary, I offer all my prayers, works and suffering of this day, for all the intentions of thy Sacred Heart, in union with the holy sacrifice of the Mass throughout the world, in reparation for my sins and for the intentions of all my associates, and in particular for the general intention recommended for this month."

One seldom knew or heard what the "general intention" was, but specificity was of no particular importance, as an all-knowing God could be counted upon to handle the ambiguity and make the proper consignment. Presumably the "general intention" was that of the popes. But there was also a "mission intention," which originated, it seemed likely, with the Propagation of the Faith. The church, incidentally, has not given up on these general and mission intentions, and many feast day calendars include them month by month, revised year to year.

Some typical "general intentions": Reverence and respect for life by all; reconciliation in the church and among all humanity; unity of the church in the faith and in the life of Christians; acceptance of Mary as our model for prayer; the sanctification of weekends and leisure time (an August intention); fulfillment of lay persons of their specific mission in the church and world.

Some typical "mission intentions": Esteem and support for Pontifical Missionary Works by all Catholics; prayerful solidarity of all contemplative communities with the missions; the Catholic Church in Sri Lanka; those suffering from leprosy; awareness by lay persons of their responsibility to the missions; the full communion of Chinese Catholics with the church.

Dorothy Day

# DOROTHY DAY, COMFORTER OF THE AFFLICTED

**THE THOUGHT WAS ALIEN** to everything that motivated her, but even in her lifetime Dorothy Day was looked upon as something of a saint. Thus it was that seven years before her death — on this date in 1973, to be exact — Colman McCarthy could write in the New Republic that she had "the wild extreme notion that Christianity is a workable system, the bizarre idea that religion has more to do with what you work at than what you believe."

Dorothy Day worked at helping the poor. For forty-five years she energized the Catholic Worker movement, supervising its soup kitchens, distributing food and clothing, providing free shelter, and espousing a voluntary poverty — all in the name of Christian charity. She wandered the country visiting Catholic Worker houses and defending causes and people, such as migrant workers. She called once on "residents" at a women's prison in West Virginia. "Why are you here?" an inmate asked. "We have come to wash your feet," Dorothy answered.

When people referred to her as a saint, she protested, for she felt saints were easily dismissed as persons to be admired rather than imitated. But her unofficial canonization did have a rationale. Dorothy Day belonged to a social and spiritual elite.

But not in the beginning. She was born in 1897 and as a young woman lived the Bohemian life. Her friends included Mike Gold, Max Eastman and Eugene O'Neill; she was a women's suffragist, World War I pacifist, and flirter with communism. She likely underwent an abortion. Her one child, a daughter, Tamar, was born of a common-law relationship. But her life was to change. In 1927 Dorothy Day became a Catholic, and in 1933 she met the impassioned social theorist Peter Maurin, and came under his influence. The Catholic Worker was born of that association, and the rest is history. Dorothy Day died in 1980, and indeed saint she may one day officially be. Her cause is being promoted.

# THE LAST OF THE MEDIEVAL POPES

**POPE BONIFACE VIII** reigned from 1294 to 1303, and historians account him the last of the medieval popes. Certainly he was a man with a full sense of power, spiritual and temporal. Unfortunately for him, the times were changing. The authority that the papacy enjoyed in the feudal order was slipping away, and rather than adjust or accommodate, Benedict resisted, notably with the issuance of two extraordinarily autocratic bulls.

The first of these came on this day in 1296, *Clericis laicos*, in response to the levying of taxes in France on the clergy. Boniface forbade clergy to pay any tax not authorized by the pope, and those who imposed such taxes were declared excommunicated. Benedict speedily retreated from that position when a considerable sum of money belonging to the Holy See and currently in France was in danger of being impounded. Still, he was not about to abandon ancient papal prerogatives. Thus in 1302 followed *Unam sanctam*, one of the strongest official statements ever of papal authority, and the same bull, incidentally, which enunciated that there was but one true church, the Catholic Church, outside of which there was no salvation (q.v. July 28).

Boniface was a proud and arrogant man, and was embroiled constantly in disputes with rulers in France, Denmark, Scotland, England and Germany, to say nothing about elements within the church and the Italian peninsula. Though the tides had turned against him, even on his deathbed he was counting as mere straws all earthly rulers. Compounding difficulties, his nepotism was open and notorious. Not surprisingly, history has not been kind. But then neither were the shapers of his times. Fra Jacopone da Todi, the Franciscan author of *Stabat Mater*, satirized Benedict in lyric and song, and Dante branded him in the *Inferno* as the "Prince of the new Pharisees," adding in the *Purgatorio* that "in his Vicar Christ was made a captive" and was "mocked a second time."

# THE ORIGINS OF LENT AND THE LENTEN FAST

**BY NOW CATHOLICS** should be settled into their current Lent, the forty-day period of fast and penitential practices that begins on Ash Wednesday and extends to Holy Saturday, the day before Easter. Funny thing about Lent, though. As deeply rooted as it is in the Christian tradition, there is no apostolic history connected to the observance. In fact, the word itself means nothing more than spring or the spring season, and over time it was the confusion of the Teutonic word for the season with the Latin word for the pre-Easter fast, *quadragesima*, that resulted in our ecclesiastical Lent with capital "L."

In fact, it was several centuries into the Christian era before Lent was even fixed at forty days. Initially, it seems, the period of preparation for Easter was not forty days but the forty hours between the afternoon of Good Friday and Easter Sunday morning. It wasn't until the seventh century, well after the Easter-date contoversy was settled, that the Lenten period was fixed in its present form and the requirements of fast and abstinence generally agreed upon.

As for the nature of the Lenten fast, it has varied of course in time and place — as well as in rigorousness of demand. Today's fast pales beside that of just a quarter-century ago, and yesterday's pales alongside that of the early Middle Ages — when, for instance, fast requirements, tough to begin with, were intensified for Holy Week.

Then as now the principal item to be fasted from was meat, although in the Middle Ages eggs, cheese and milk were also forbidden — by ecclesiastical canon and by civil law too. In England, the law was enforced until the reign of William III, 1689-1702. How seriously were the laws taken? Well, we know that in the seige of Orleans in 1429, defenders of the city were reduced to starvation because of lack of Lenten food; they went hungry, although there were on hand ample stores of meat and other supplies. Read on. »»»

# FISH AS SYMBOL AND COUNTERSYMBOL

**FROM THE EARLIEST LENTS,** fish dominated the Catholic diet, and thus it was that Catholics came to be known, derogatorily, as fish-eaters. In fact, fish became so much a "Catholic" symbol that some Protestants — Puritans for instance — ostentatiously avoided fish to dramatize their theological separateness. The writer John Taylor took note of this proclivity in *Jack a Lent* in 1620, remarking, "I have often noted that if any superfluous feasting or gormandizing, paunch-cramming assembly do meet, it is so ordered that it must be either in Lent, upon a Friday, or a fasting: for the meat does not relish well except it be sauced with disobedience and contempt of authority."

There's some political background to Taylor's remark. With the Reformation, Lenten fasting quickly began to become a thing of the past, and in order to protect the fishing industry against economic ruin, fasting laws were hurriedly re-entered into the books. Fines were imposed on butchers who slaughtered animals during Lent (twenty pounds per offense during Elizabeth I's reign), and it was said that not even royalty, queen or king, had the license to excuse herself/himself and eat flesh meat on fish days. But statutes and proclamations served small purpose. English Protestants continued to turn against fish. The English fishing industry went into ruin, and that circumstance, it is said, is what turned many English mariners into pirates.

The concern for the fishing industry sounds exotic, but that episode of history had a small parallel centuries later when the Catholic Church in 1966 dropped its Friday abstinence requirement, and the "fish-on-Friday" tradition went by the boards (q.v. Dec. 2). One of the loudest complaints against the change came from Boston's Cardinal Richard J. Cushing, who worried that it would put fishermen from Gloucester, a major Massachusetts fishing port with a heavy Catholic population, out of business.

# ISAIAH AND TRUE FASTING

**ON THE OTHER HAND,** perhaps Catholic emphasis in fasting should be less on the stomach and more of the nature prescribed in Isaiah 58:1-9:

> Cry out, full-blooded and unsparingly, lift up your voice like a trumpet blast, and tell my people their wickedness, and the house of Jacob their sins.
>
> Yet they seek me daily, and delight to know my ways, as a nation that has done what is just and not abandoned the ordinance of their God.
>
> Why have we fasted, they say, and you do not see it? Why do we afflict ourselves, and you take no notice of it? Behold, on your fast day you find pleasure, and exact all your labors.
>
> Behold, your fast ends in strife and quarreling, and striking with the fist of wickedness. Would that today you might fast as to make your voice heard on high.
>
> Is it such a fast that I have chosen? A day for a man to afflict his soul? Is it to bow down his head like a bulrush, and to spread sackcloth and ashes under him? Will you call this a fast, and an acceptable day to the Lord?
>
> This rather is the fasting that I wish: to release those bound unjustly, to undo the heavy burdens, and to let the oppressed go free, and that you break every yoke.
>
> To share your bread with the hungry, to shelter the oppressed and the homeless, to clothe the naked when you see them, and not turn your back on your own.
>
> Then shall your light break forth as the morning, and your health shall spring forth speedily; and your righteousness shall go before you, and the glory of the Lord shall be your reward.
>
> Then you shall call and the Lord will answer. You will cry, and he will say, "Here I am!"

# FEBRUARY 29

## DESERT EXPERIENCES

As yesterdays's reading from Isaiah makes plain, Lent is a time when the church reminds people of their obligations in justice and charity to others. It does this by first reminding, however, that ashes we are and into ashes we shall return — the Ash Wednesday ritual. Nothing could be a more humbling reminder than that of one's mortality, and vulnerability.

But then, a few days later, on the very first Sunday of Lent, the church provides a Gospel reading that seems precisely gauged to give heart to any who might be changed by Lent's emphases into being Job's comforters. The Gospel is from Luke 4:1-13. It is the church's reminder that we all have our desert experiences, as did Christ himself; that we can overcome, as did Christ — but also that we're likely to be tempted again, as of course would be Christ. The reading:

> And Jesus being full of the Holy Ghost returned from Jordan, and was led by the Spirit into the wilderness,
>
> Being forty days tempted by the devil. And in those days he did eat nothing: and when they were ended, he afterward hungered.
>
> And the devil said unto him, If thou be the Son of God, command this stone that it be made bread.
>
> And Jesus answered him, saying, It is written that man shall not live by bread alone, but by every word of God.
>
> And the devil, taking him up into a high mountain, showed unto him all the kingdoms of the world in a moment of time.
>
> And the devil said unto him, All this power will I give thee, and the glory of them: for that is delivered unto me; and to whomever I will I give it.
>
> If thou therefore will worship me, all shall be thine.
>
> And Jesus answered and said unto him: Get thee behind me, Satan; for it is written, Thou shalt worship the Lord thy God, and him only shalt thou serve.
>
> And he brought him to Jerusalem, and set him on a pinnacle of the temple, and said unto him, If thou be the Son of God, cast thyself down from hence:
>
> For it is written, He shall give his angels charge over thee, to keep thee:
>
> And in their hands they shall bear thee up, lest at any time thou dash thy foot against a stone.
>
> And Jesus answering said unto him, It is said, thou shalt not tempt the Lord thy God.
>
> And when the devil had ended all the temptation, he departed from him for a season.

# MARCH 1

## A LEEK A DAY KEEPS THE DOCTOR AWAY

**THE IRISH PLANT PEAS** on St. Patrick's Day. The Welsh wear leeks in their hats on St. David's Day. That's today, and the custom traces back to the 6th century, when on St. David's advice his cohorts stuck leeks in their hats to distinguish themselves from the enemy in battle against the Saxons.

David is revered as the patron of Wales, though in truth little is known about him. Legend has it that his mother was a nun, Nonna, who was violated by the Prince of Keretica (Cardiganshire), one Sandde ab Ceredig ab Cunedda, and that his birth was foretold 30 years beforehand to St. Patrick. David is said to have founded or restored 12 monasteries, mostly in Southern Wales, before he and his monks settled in the Vale of Ross, where they lived a life of extreme austerity in the face of severe temptations due to "the obscene antics of the maid-servants of the wife of Boia, a local chieftain."

Some of the monks, their heads perhaps turned by maid-servants, seem not to have been completely loyal to David, as they plotted to poison him. David, however, was saved by Scuthyn, who crossed from Ireland by night on the back of a sea monster. Scuthyn blessed the poisoned bread — the unholy instrument of poison — and ate it himself, without harm. Iron stomach. Scuthyn too is a saint today, as obviously he should be.

As for David, he lived to the great age of 147, probably because he ate a lot of leeks. Leeks are good for you. They're a hardy vegetable, and tasty. The Israelites loved them. The Bible records (1 Numbers 11:4-5) that while the Israelites were in the desert the strangers among them complained: "Would that we had meat for food. We remember the fish we used to eat without cost in Egypt, and the cucumbers, the melons, *the leeks*, the onions, and the garlic." Now all they had before them was manna, and manna tasted like "coriander weed." Bah! Seedy, chewy. Have you had your leek today?

# MARCH 2

## HEAVENLY MUSIC AND HUNTERS' HART

**MANY SAINTS** of pre-Reformation England are lost to memory, their stories collecting dust in old books of hagiography. St. Chad is one of them. He lived in the 7th century and came from a family of priests, four brothers taking holy orders and two going on to the episcopate — Chad and older brother Cedd. Chad was no martyr; he was a devout man with a reputation for sanctity, whose claim to fame was winning the East Saxons, the people of London, to the faith. Still, there's a story in his death; no saint dies without one.

Chad's story begins with a monk working in the garden of Chad's retreat in Lichfield and hearing sweet music wafting from heaven towards Chad's oratory, filling the oratory for about half an hour, then drifting off again towards heaven. Opening his window, Chad spied the monk and told him to gather the others, for Chad had an announcement to make. The monks convened, Chad spoke of peace and loving one another, then revealed that "that gracious guest who was wont to visit our brethren has vouchsafed to come to me also today and to call me out of this world. Return therefore to the church and speak to the brethren that they in their prayers recommend my passage to the Lord."

Chad then lapsed into what is described as a "languishing distemper." It persisted for seven days, whereupon, "after receiving the body and blood of Our Lord, he departed this life, escorted by the soul of his brother Cedd and by a joyful company of angels." That was in 664. A cult sprung up and soon some 31 churches and several nearby holy wells (q.v. March 8) were dedicated to him.

In Christian art, Chad is depicted with a hart. How come? One day while praying near a stream, Chad's solemn mood was disturbed by a hart and two sons of King Wulfhere hot in pursuit. Chad so effectively lectured the youths on kindness to animals as to convert them to Christianity. Angry over their conversion, the king murdered the sons, but later, seized with remorse, he confessed to Chad and became one of the English church's great patrons.

# MOTHER, NOW BLESSED KATHARINE DREXEL

**PHILADELPHIA'S KATHARINE DREXEL** lived a long life; she was 96-years-old when she died on this date in 1955. A daughter of privilege, educated by governesses, widely traveled, heiress to a huge fortune, she elected as a young adult on a life of religion. In 1889 she joined the Sisters of Mercy, but anxious to do missionary work among blacks and Indians, she left and two years later founded — of necessity, since no existing order fit the vision — her own order, Sisters of the Blessed Sacrament for Indians and Colored People.

As a nun, Mother Drexel lived through calamitous racial upheavals, but never as mere on-looker. Pope John Paul II summarized her life succinctly: "In her day, American Indians and blacks in the United States suffered great injustices as a result of racial prejudice. Seeing clearly the evil of this situation, she set out with determination to combat it and overcome it." Indeed! By the time of her death, her order staffed 66 schools in 23 states, including a college, predominantly black Xavier College in New Orleans. Many of the order's schools were in Indian communities in the Southwest.

Like other religious orders, Mother Drexel's has been forced to retrench in recent years. But the work goes on, including in Harlem, where the Sisters conduct two schools. The order is still to be found in 12 states.

As for Mother Drexel, she's now Blessed. Pope John Paul beatified her on November 20, 1988 — the same occasion on which he saluted her for her apostolate on behalf of American blacks and Indians. The beatification was unusual, for it followed only 33 years after Mother Drexel's death. The elapsed time between death and beatification was accordingly one of the shortest in modern church history. By contrast, three European missionaries to Africa were beatified the same day as she had died 272 years before.

St. Francis Xavier (detail from a work by Rubens)

# REMEMBER THE NOVENA OF GRACE?

**IN THE DAYS WHEN** novenas were a popular facet of Catholic devotional life, one of the most popular began on this date and ran to March 12. Many's the parochial school graduate who can remember being led in ranks, two abreast, from the classroom to the nearby parish church for the services of hymns and prayer, and Benediction of the Blessed Sacrament, and on the last day veneration of a first-class relic of the saint. Who was this saint? Francis Xavier, and the services in his honor were known as the Novena of Grace.

Saint Francis Xavier was the 16th-century Spaniard, who was one of the first recruits to the Jesuit order, and who went off to the Far East to accomplish missionary feats that became legendary. Areas in which he labored are Christian to this day, notably Goa, in India. One of his great missionary goals was Japan, but he got only as far as the island of Sancian, off the coast of China, where he died in 1552, only 46-years-old.

Curious, though the novena of petition to him was held in the month of March, his feast day was, still is, observed on December 3. In Catholic consciousness, however, March is more closely associated with Francis Xavier because on March 12, 1622, he was canonized in a twin ceremony by Pope Gregory XV. Sainted along with him was Ignatius Loyola, founder of the Jesuits.

As for novenas, it is not only Saint Francis Xavier's that has fallen into eclipse. Gone are all the others, at least in the forms and certainly in the degree of popularity that they were once known. None seems to have been spared the shift in Catholic devotional practices, not even the Novena of the Miraculous Medal, another big favorite at one time. It is not easy to explain the shift that has taken place, except that Catholics appear suddenly to have concluded that they do not need intercessors before God, when there is God himself. Or is God a she?

# GALILEO, THE SUN AND THE EARTH

**FEW HAVE EXPERIENCED** triumph and humiliation in measure to Galileo Galilei, the Italian astronomer and experimental philosopher, who lived from 1564 to 1642. In 1611 he was the toast of Rome as he exhibited in the gardens of the Quirinal Palace the telescopic wonders of the heavens to the elite of the pontifical court. By 1615 he would be in disrepute, hauled before the Inquisition and told to renounce his teachings. More trouble followed.

On this day in 1616 the Congregation of the Index, which, while not mentioning Galileo by name, took direct aim at him by declaring heretical theories and works that were his stock in trade. At debate basically was the heliocentric system versus the geocentric; did the earth revolve around the sun, as Galileo contended, or the sun around an immovable earth, as had been taught since Ptolemy and the ancients? It was no small argument, as nothing less was involved than the letter of Scripture. If Galileo were right, large passages of Scripture were quite literally not true. Since it was deemed this could not possibly be, it followed that Galileo was anti-Scriptural and heretical.

Galileo's fortunes ebbed and flowed. In 1633 he was examined under menace of torture on charges that he had written in contravention of the decree of 1616. Galileo denied allegations, then accommodated. On June 22, 1633, he recanted in the Church of Santa Maria sopra Minerva, but still was condemned, as one "vehemently suspected of heresy," to incarceration at the pleasure of the tribunal, and directed to recite the seven penitential psalms once a week for three years. Galileo was never made a prisoner in the traditional sense, but the humiliation was total for the man whose telescopic revelations, and whose discoveries of the thermometer and astronomical clock, made him a person of the ages. The church has rehabilitated Galileo's memory in recent years. But of course. In an age of obscurantism, he was right from the start.

# ROGER BROOKE TANEY AND DRED SCOTT

**THIS DOES NOT RANK** as a particularly glorious day of American Catholic history, at least not so far as 1857 is concerned. For on March 6, 1857, Roger Brooke Taney, the first and indeed only Catholic Supreme Court Chief Justice in the nation's hisory, handed down the infamous Dred Scott decision. Scott, a black slave, had been taken by his owner from Missouri to Illinois in 1834, and on his return to Missouri sued for his liberty on grounds that his stay in free territory had ended his slavery. Taney rejected this argument, ruling in essence that Dred Scott was a slave, and as such was not a citizen and not qualified to sue in Federal court. Taney ruled further that Congress had no power to exclude slavery from the territories opening in the West, and finally that blacks could not become citizens. Wow!

The nation was only four years away from civil war over slavery, so of course the impact of Taney's decision was enormous. The South welcomed the ruling, but its reasoning, like the South's own self-interest, ran counter to dominant social and political trends. History would prove that unmistakably. More immediately, Taney's decision dangerously undermined the prestige of the High Court. It fed the then-common stereotype of the fondness of the Catholic mind for oppression, and it left his reputation in shambles for all time.

The irony is that in his private life Taney, a Southerner, did not believe in slavery. He manumitted the slaves he inherited on his father's death, and he pensioned his freedmen when they grew too old to earn their living. In a similar vein, his pastor recorded that in going to confession Taney insisted on taking his place in line, even though most of those ahead of him were slaves. That glosses nothing, to be sure. Apologists contend that in the Dred Scott case Taney was doing no more than interpreting the law as presently on the books — which glosses nothing either. In plainest language, Taney erred.

# MARCH 7

*Blessed are the poor in spirit,*
*for theirs is the kingdom of heaven.*

*Blessed are the meek,*
*for they shall inherit the land.*

*Blessed are they that mourn,*
*for they shall be comforted.*

*Blessed are they that hunger and thirst after justice,*
*for they shall have their fill.*

*Blessed are the merciful,*
*for they shall obtain mercy.*

*Blessed are the clean of heart,*
*for they shall see God.*

*Blessed are the peacemakers,*
*for they shall be called the children of God.*

## THE BEATITUDES

**LENT IS ALSO A TIME** for prayerful meditation, and what thereby could be a more appropriate than the Sermon on the Mount and, most especially, the section of the sermon containing the Beatitudes? The Beatitudes are more hortatory than admonishing, and thus singularly suitable for meditative purposes — even apart from Lent, for that matter. They speak of the happiness that is possible on earth and in heaven for those who live by their precepts; they embody the substance of God's law and the rule of evangelical perfection — along with promises of specific rewards for particular good works performed.

The Bible does not tell us where the sermon was delivered, except for its being on a hillside near the See of Galilee. It was probably near Capharnaum, and likely at an early stage in Jesus' public life. Matthew devotes three chapters to the Sermon, the Beatitudes appearing in chapter 5:3-10. Luke also records the Beatitudes in somewhat different form, 6:20-22. Luke registers four Beatitudes, Matthew eight.

It is Matthew's version that is the more familiar to most Christians, and so it is rendered here.

# THE LURE OF BRITAIN'S HOLY WELLS

**IN THE MIDDLE AGES,** the divine presence was felt as intimately in nature as in the eucharist, and in nothing more so than the element of water. The discovery of a clear spring in some idyllic setting, or of a spring notable for its unusal origin, taste or flow, excited associations with God and the saints favored of him. This was especially true in Britain, where there were more holy waters — "holy wells," they were called — per shire than perhaps anywhere else in Christendom. The holy well was thought to possess curative powers of a unique sort. Sufferers of the "falling disease" patronized St. Tegla's Well; children with rickets or eye problems were hauled to St. John's Well in Scotland; the waters of Trinity Gask Well enabled one to face the plague without fear. But the most popular holy well of the scores on record was St. Winifred's Well at Holywell in Wales. Small wonder, given its origin.

Winifred was a 7th-century noble maiden pursued by an unwelcome Prince Cradocus. Angry at being spurned, Cradocus lopped off Winifred's head, whereupon his body was immediately swallowed by the earth. Winifred's head, meanwhile, rolled off for itself down a hill, where it was picked up by St. Beuno and reunited to Winifred's body — so skillfully, apparently, that but a faint white scar circled Winifred's neck. Winifred went on to live a life of sanctity for 15 years more. But here's the kicker apropos holy wells: When Beuno picked up the head, a spring gushed forth from the spot washing the pebbles of Winifred's blood and giving the ground moss a marvelous fragrance.

So extravagant was belief in holy wells that the Saxon king Edgar in 963 forbade "worshipping of fountains," and the canons of Anselm in 1102 ruled that no one was to attribute holiness to a well or fountain without the bishop's authority. The decrees stopped nothing. For centuries kings and commoners flocked to Britain's holy wells with petitions and penances due before the practice waned near completely. That wasn't until the nineteenth century, however.

# MARCH 9

## THE WOMAN WHO CONSORTED WITH AN ANGEL

**ONE DOESN'T HEAR** much of St. Frances of Rome, but the calendar says this is her feast. What do the books of hagiography say about Frances?

They say Frances of Rome lived from 1384 to 1440, and was the very model of the model Roman housewife. In an age when women married much younger than now, she wed at fourteen and began raising a family. Devoted wife and mother, she also plunged into works of piety and charity outside the home. With her sister-in-law Vannozza, she made regular visits to the poor and distressed, cared for the most difficult of hospital cases, and worked heroically through a scary Roman plague. She was, in a few words, a woman of the home and of the world.

Frances of Rome lost two children in that plague, and she herself was sick for a time almost beyond hope. But she recovered, and, committed as ever to charity and good works, she organized the religious group known as the Oblates of Tor de' Specchi, which later became affiliated with the Benedictines. After the death of her husband, Frances entered the community and eventually became its superior, though reluctantly so, it seems.

Her last years, we are told, were marked by great austerities and by supernatural gifts, which complemented earlier powers of healing.

But probably the most wondrous detail of her life is this: During her last twenty three years she was guided by an archangel visible only to herself. She had it made. Others should be so lucky. Not everyone has an angel at beck and call.

Frances' privileged status was commemorated in the prayer of the old Latin Mass in her honor: "O God, who, among other gifts of thy grace, didst honor blessed Frances, thine handmaid, with the familiar companionship of an angel, grant, we beseech thee, that by the help of her intercession we may deserve to attain the company of angels. Through Christ, Our Lord, amen."

Frances of Rome was canonized in 1680.

# ROME AND REPRODUCTIVE ETHICS

**NO FIELD OF SCIENTIFIC MEDICINE** has exploded with such suddeness as that of reproductive technologies. This day in 1987 Rome let it be known that it wanted nothing of it, or at least very little, for that day it released its official doctrinal position on the subject, a forty-page document entitled "Instruction on Respect for Human Life in Its Origin and on the Dignity of Procreation." The document may have been awkwardly titled, but there was no mistaking where the Vatican stood on seemingly every conceivable detail of reproductive biomedicine.

The Vatican was against surrogate motherhood and experimentations on human embryos. It was against virtually all forms of artificial insemination, approving only medical interference in human reproduction when it assisted married couples who have engaged in the "normal" sex act; this put Rome on record even against in vitro or test-tube fertilization, a procedure already incorporated into the medical practices of many Catholic hospitals around the world. The Vatican also took a position against genetic counseling, embryo and sperm banks, donor insemination — and, further, called on all governments to enact laws on the subject. That call extended Rome's hand into the legal field in seeking limits on medical interference in human reproduction.

The condemnation of reproductive technologies followed decades of rising concern, nowhere more so than at the Vatican, over the ethical implications of new medical/scientific technologies for assisting reproduction. There was some sharp dissent to Rome's instruction, including among some Catholics, who would have preferred more flexibility in several areas, as in aiding couples who are infertile. On the other hand, the *New York Times* editorially welcomed the instruction, declaring that it offered a considered set of views warranting attention, as secular society argues out its positions in biomedical ethics.

# GOOD FRIDAY AND THE "TRE ORE"

**IT WAS IN 325** that the Western church established the formula for calculating the date on which Easter should be celebrated annually. It would be observed on the first Sunday following the first full moon of spring — Sunday, because from earliest Christian times it was believed that Christ rose from the dead on the first day of the week. The arrangement meant that Easter could fall as early as March 22 or as late as April 25. But whether Easter comes early or late, right now Christians everywhere are well along in their Lenten season. Ahead lies Holy Week and the awesome events that propel Jesus — and emotionally all Christian believers — from the triumphal entry into Jerusalem, Palm Sunday, to the ignominious death on the cross. It is the most solemn of seasons in the church's calendar.

The most somber day of Holy Week is of course Good Friday. There's no consecration of the Eucharist on that day, no Mass, but there is a communion service, and in most churches other special devotions of a commemorative kind marking Christ's death on the cross.

One of the more popular of the latter — though, again, not conducted everywhere — is the Tre Ore, the three-hour afternoon service featuring as a rule hymns, prayers, sermons and meditations of the seven last words of Christ. The devotion, known commonly as the Service of the Seven Last Words, is not a formally approved liturgy, but rather is held in the spirit of Vatican II's Constitution on the Sacred Liturgy, which encouraged non-liturgical devotions that "harmonize with the liturgical seasons, accord with the sacred liturgy, are in some fashion derived from it, and lead people to it." (15)

Whatever the day, however, whether it be Good Friday or not, the seven last words make for ideal lenten spiritual reflection. Let's review them and their setting here.... Read on.

# MARCH 12

## THE SEVEN LAST WORDS OF CHRIST

1 — Jesus is led to Golgotha to be crucified along with two criminals. He speaks: *Father, forgive them; they know not what they do.* (Luke 23:32-34)

2 — Jesus and the two criminals are nailed to their separate crosses. One criminal blasphemes Jesus, only to be rebuked by the other criminal, who says to him, "We are only paying the price for what we have done, but this man has done nothing wrong." Jesus responds to his defender: *I assure you: This day thou shalt be with me in paradise.* (Luke 23:39-43)

3 — Near the foot of the cross is his mother, Mary, his mother's sister, Mary the wife of Clopas, Mary Magdelene, and the Apostle John. Jesus addresses Mary in the context of John: *Woman, behold thy son*! Then, turning to John, he says, *Behold thy mother*! (John 19:25-27)

4 — The afternoon wears on; the pain is agonizing. Jesus cries out in a loud voice: *Eli, Eli, lama sabachthani*, that is to say, *My God, my God, why hast thou forsaken me*? (Matthew 27:45-46)

5 — The end is near. Jesus, knowing that all has been done in fulfillment of the scripture, says: *I thirst.* (John 19:28)

6 — There is a jug nearby of vinegary wine. A soldier sops a sponge in the wine, puts it upon a sprig of hyssop, and raises it to Jesus' lips. Jesus exclaims: *Now it is finished.* (John 19:29-30)

7 — It is around midday. Darkness has been over the land for three hours with an eclipse of the sun. The veil of the Temple has been rent in two. Jesus utters a loud cry: *Father, into thy hands I commend my spirit.* (Luke 23:44-46)

# A PROMINENT CATHOLIC PUBLISHER

**THIS WAS THE DAY** in 1835 that Mathew Carey came to explain how he happened to write *The Olive Branch*, published some years before with a view to reconciling embittered American Federalists and Republicans split over the politics of Thomas Jefferson and Alexander Hamilton, and with astonishing success. Andrew Jackson read a copy, and the future president effusively wrote to Mathew Carey that the book "by unveiling the eyes of many who have been long hoodwinked by the misrepresentations of folly and falsehood, must have a salutary effect in allaying that factious spirit which threatens so much evil to our happy government." Said Mathew Carey: "The publication of the *Olive Branch* was one of the most important incidents of my life...."

Maybe so. The country was not only at ideological loggerheads internally, but on foreign policy was deeply divided on issues related to the renewal of conflict between France and England. Still, instrumental as *The Olive Branch* undoubtedly was in harmonizing factional feelings, few remember Mathew Carey today for *The Olive Branch*. Check the annuals, and his claim on history is religious, not political. Mathew Carey — native Dubliner, Philadelphia entrepreneur — was the first Catholic publisher of prominence in the U.S., and in 1790 he printed the first Catholic Bible in this country, a Douay Version.

Mathew Carey was a friend of Lafayette; in fact, Lafayette once staked him to $400 to help with Mathew Carey's *Pennsylvania Herald*, a journal of record which achieved wide circulation beginning in 1785 publishing the debates of the House of Assembly. Alas, Mathew Carey never entered the certified canon of American Catholic heroes. Why? Maybe because he became entangled, however anonymously, in a notorious lay-trustee parish fight involving one "rebellious" Father William Hogan and St. Mary's Church in Philadelphia. However, try today to buy a Mathew Carey Bible. If available, it's financially way out of reach.

# DISOWNING THE NOTION OF "DEICIDE"

**THE OLD "CHRISTIAN" LIBEL** against the Jews, that of deicide, was finally laid to rest, expunged, dismissed, rejected by Vatican Council II. Etymologically, deicide means "killer of God" or Christ killer, and it was applied by some to the Jews in connection with the Crucifixion. The application, which resulted from implication or inference rather than from direct, official teaching, was long a point of contention between Christians and Jews, and without doubt a source of considerable Christian anti-Semitism.

Vatican II's formal disowning of the deicide notion was made in *Nostra aetate*, the Declaration on the Relationship of the Church to Non-Christians. After expressing admiration for the Jews, remarking that "Jews still remain most dear to God because of their fathers," the declaration went on record: "True, authorities of the Jews and those who followed their lead pressed for the death of Christ (cf. John 19:6); still, what happened in his passion cannot be blamed upon all Jews then living, without distinction, nor upon the Jews of today. Although the church is the new people of God, the Jews should not be presented as repudiated or cursed by God, as if such views followed from the holy Scriptures. All should take pains, then, lest in catechetical instruction and in the preaching of God's word they teach anything out of harmony with the truth of the gospel and the spirit of Christ.

"The church repudiates all persecutions against any man. Moreover, mindful of her common patrimony with the Jews, and motivated by the gospel's spiritual love and by no political considerations, she deplores the hatred, persecutions, and displays of anti-Semitism directed against the Jews at any time and from any source" (4).

The declaration also said that "in company with the prophets," the church awaits that day, known only to God, "on which all peoples will address the Lord in a single voice and 'serve him with one accord'"(4). Read on.»»»

# POPE JOHN XXIII AND JEWS

**CURIOUSLY ENOUGH,** though *Nostra aetate*, the Declaration on the Relationship of the Church to Non-Christians, rejected the deicide canard, it ended up not using the word itself. The phrase "or guilty of deicide" was included in the sentence stating that "the Jews should not be presented as repudiated or cursed by God," but it was dropped before the document's final ratification. This spurred charges that the deletion came under pressure from Arab governments. It was explained, however, that many Council Fathers asked for the deletion, feeling that the phrase was ambiguous and might even suggest to some that the church no longer regarded Jesus as God.

It is too bad the council document could not have been unmistakably explicit, but nonetheless the point was made, and, though John XXIII was by then dead, it seemed singularly appropriate that it should come in a gathering that had come to be called "Pope John's Council."

For in 1959, three years before the council opened, John went far in setting the stage for *Nostra aetate* when, at Good Friday services in St. Peter's, he halted a priest in mid-flight as he intoned from the old liturgy the prayer *Oremus et pro perfidis Judaeis: ut Deus and Dominus noster auferat velamen de cordibus eorum*...."Let us pray for the perfidious Jews, that Our Lord and God may take away the veil from their hearts." The pope ordered the priest to go repeat the prayer from the start, omitting the word *perfidis*.

It would follow that in the collect or prayer following that *Oremus* the reference *Judaicam perfidiam*, "Jewish perfidity," would also be purged.

There was nothing surprising about Pope John's action. This is the same man who, as a Vatican diplomat in Turkey during the Holocaust years, risked being the conduit for getting immigration certificates issued by the Palestine Jewish Agency to sources in Hungary and Bulgaria, saving no one knows how many lives. To Jews he was one thing; in his own words: "I am your brother."

# MARCH 16

## THE SIGN OF THE CROSS

**IN WESTERN CHRISTIANITY** nothing so clearly identities the Catholic Christian than the sign of the cross. Eastern Christians, Orthodox and Uniate, use the gesture, which traces the cross from forehead to breast and shoulder to shoulder to the words, "In the name of the Father and of the Son and of the Holy Spirit. Amen." But Protestants have largely abandoned the act.

The sign of the cross is one of the earliest ways by which the Christian expressed the faith, though in apostolic times, when persecution was rife, the sign often had to be used surreptitiously by the believer to escape detection. The believer would then track a small sign of the cross on the forehead with the right thumb or a finger, and perhaps continue on to the lips and breast.

As Christianity developed, the sign of the cross took on symbolic meanings and aspects of a liturgical art. The sweeping sign, from forehead to breast to shoulders, appears to have resulted, at least indirectly, from the fifth-century Monophysite controversy over the two natures of Christ. The sign of the cross fortified the concept of a Trinity and the dual nature of Christ, human and divine. But how precisely was the sign of the cross to be self-administered?

Some argued for the cross to be signed with two fingers (thumb and forefinger or thumb and middle finger) to typify the two natures and two wills of Christ. Some preferred a signing with three fingers displayed (first three) and two (ring and little fingers) folded back to the palm — the three fingers denoting the Trinity and the two fingers the two natures or wills of Christ. This last is the form commonly used in the East to this day, with a left cross from shoulder to shoulder. Latin Christians, on the other hand, use a right cross (per the mid-nineteenth-century instruction of Leo IV) and keep the signing hand open. How come the latter? Maybe mere convenience, being for some less awkward. Whatever the reason, the open palm was in use in the West since long before the close of the Middle Ages.

# MARCH 17

## WHEN EVERYONE'S IRISH FOR THE DAY

**THERE'S NO ESCAPING** St. Patrick's Day. In Ireland it's a holy day of obligation, but in the United States it's a day of fun and revelry. The American observance is somewhat incongruous in the light of much that has been happening in Ireland in recent years. It seems a travesty to be wearing the green, when back in "holy Ireland" wearers of the green are plotting and killing in the name of patriotism — on both ideological sides. The day would better be one of prayer and atonement for the brutalities and murders that are a scandal to all who profess interest and love for Ireland.

And who better to pray to than St. Patrick, patron of Ireland? There's a lot of legend connected to Patrick, like the business of driving the snakes out of Ireland. But, unlike some other popular "saints" of Christendom, we know he existed. No spurious character, he.

Patrick arrived in Ireland around 461, and died there around 492. In those thirty-one years he converted the country from paganism, and indeed planted the faith so firmly that soon Irish missionaries were fanning out from Ireland as evangelizers to the then known world. To this day missionaries are one of the country's prime exports.

Where did he come from, this Patrick? Who knows? Pious legend has it that he was the son of a Roman collector of taxes, who lived in Wales, near the river Severn, and that he was kidnapped by pirates at age sixteen. Taken to Ireland, he was sold as a slave and for six years labored as a swineherd in County Antrim. Patrick escaped to Britain, studied for the priesthood in Gaul, and allegedly returned to Ireland in response to voices in a talking letter delivered in a dream by an angel named Victor. The voices cried for him to come back to Erin.... Nonsense? I suppose.

But Patrick did go back to Ireland. The rest of the story we know.

# MARCH 18

**The Anima Christi**

*Soul of Christ, be my sanctification.*

*Body of Christ, be my salvation.*

*Blood of Christ, fill all my veins.*

*Water of Christ's side, wash out my stains.*

*Passion of Christ, my comfort be.*

*O good Jesu, listen to me.*

*In thy wounds I fain would hide,*

*Ne'er to be parted from thy side.*

*Guard me should the foe assail me.*

*Call me when my life shall fail me.*

*Bid me come to thee above,*

*With thy saints to sing thy love*

*World without end. Amen.*

## YESTERDAY'S PRAYERS

**NOT TOO LONG AGO,** when the Mass was essentially the private devotion of the celebrant (the priest mumbling away in Latin, his back to the congregation), many Catholics spent much of their Mass time in private devotions of their own — such as in "prayers of preparation" prior to communion and "prayers of welcome" after, read from a missal or popular paraliturgical prayer-book.

A favorite post-communion prayer from those years was the *Anima Christi*, the recitation of which Pope Pius IX richly indulgenced in 1854 (three hundred days per recitation; seven years if said after communion; plenary, once a month under the usual conditions). Cardinal Newman's translation (above) was rampant.

Ejaculations could be tacked onto this, like "Eucharistic heart of Jesus, have mercy on us," or "Divine Heart of Jesus, convert sinners, save the dying, set free the holy souls in purgatory," but you get the idea.

## THE SPOUSE WHO LIVED IN HUMBLE SILENCE

**THIS IS THE FEAST** of St. Joseph, and in some places — Gloucester, Massachusetts, for instance — it is celebrated by ethnic groups with the gusto that the Irish reserve for St. Patrick. Thus in Gloucester, Italian Catholics erect parlor shrines to St. Joseph, and compete with one another in their elaborateness; prayer services are conducted in the saint's honor; visits are made from home to home, and festivity builds with the visits.

Joseph deserves the attention; he got precious little of it in his lifetime. Though he figured prominently in several biblical episodes, he nonetheless moves through the Gospels as a docile, somewhat amorphous figure — a carpenter by trade, a dutiful husband and father, but forever in the background. If he was still alive at the time of the wedding feast at Cana, he wasn't brought along. There's no mention of him being at the Crucifixion. In fact, the last we hear of Joseph is in the Temple episode, when Jesus, then twelve, was found preaching to the elders. Luke tell us (2:41-52) that Jesus then went back to Nazareth and was subject to him. Likely Joseph was dead before his son's Crucifixion, but how come the Gospels never recorded the death?

The church itself long scanted Joseph. He did not even have an annual feast day of his own until 1481, when one was finally declared by Pope Sixtus IV. Since then, however, the church has raced to make up. Pius IX declared Joseph Protector of the Universal Church in 1870, and Leo XIII singled him out as a model father for families. Benedict XV put workers under his protection; Pius XI cited him as the exemplar of social justice; and Pius XII established a second feast in his honor, that of St. Joseph the Worker. Pius XII had an ulterior motive, as he pointedly set the feast on May 1 as a counterbalance to communist observance of May Day. The May 1 feast never particularly caught on.

# THE ADVENTURE THAT WAS THE CRUSADES

**ONE OF THE MOST** astonishing adventure stories in human history is that of the crusades, the ill-fated effort on the part of Catholic Christians to deliver the Holy Land from Islam. The adventure extended over several centuries and engaged popes, emperors, kings, princes, mercenaries, unnumbered thousands of the devout, and a horde of chancers, who, anxious to escape an unprivileged life at home, leaped at the opportunity to join in a "holy war," which lent them status, prestige and the prospect of striking it rich in the East. The church fostered such illusions by granting temporal privileges, such as exemption from civil jurisdiction and inviolability of persons and lands, and lavishing indulgences on those who swore the solemn oath and sewed on their cloaks the cross made of cloth that was the crusaders' badge. The Council of Clermont, for instance, in 1095 enacted the so-called Crusader Indulgence, excusing from "all penance" those who "set out for the liberation of the church of God in Jerusalem." There were conditions, to be sure; the crusader was to be motivated "from devotion alone" and not out of "purposes of gaining honors and wealth." Notwithstanding, the crusades attracted a rough lot, many of whom were not above plunder, rape and murder.

The First Crusade was not launched until near the close of the eleventh century, but as early as the ninth century it was considered an act of piety to fight for the defense of Christianity and the church. In 878 Pope John VIII promised absolution from their sins to those who died defending Christians against Moslems, who were then invading Italy, and in 1063 Pope Alexander II conveyed the same guarantee to Christians fighting Moslems in Spain. After the defeat of Byzantine troops at Manzikert in 1071 by forces of the Mahommedan revival Gregory VII contemplated a crusade to the East and actually assembled a considerable army. It never marched, but others would. Read on. »»»

# THE FATEFUL FIRST CRUSADE

**IT WAS THE FRENCH POPE,** Urban II, who gave shape to Gregory VII's plans and launched the first crusade. The date was 1096, with the crusade comprising two parts — the crusade of the people and the crusade of the princes. One proved as disastrous as the other.

The crusade of the people consisted of five divisions of poor pilgrims, *pauperes*, mobilized by a band of wandering preachers, of which Peter the Hermit was the most famous. The crusaders, poorly armed and badly led, moved off in four wings, headed for Constantinople, but were effectively dispersed and massacred by the Hungarians and Turks — with few tears shed for the wing that proceeded via the Rhine valley and was decimated by the Hungarians. Some 10,000 Jews perished because of the "crusading zeal" of that wing.

The crusade of the princes was better organized, and assembled somewhere between 300,000 and 600,000 crusaders at the gates of Constantinople. The crusade moved towards Jerusalem hugging the shore as much as possible so it could be kept supplied with provisions and munitions of war by Italian ships. It swept down the coast of the Levant, took Jerusalem in 1099, and established the first of the Crusader States in the region, the Kingdom of Jerusalem. In time there would be five more Crusader States founded in the East by Western crusaders: the County of Edessa, County of Tripoli, Principality of Antioch, Kingdom of Cyprus and Latin Empire of Constantinople. These Crusader States rooted papal presence in the region, but ultimately caused as many problems as those thought solved, for every attack on a Crusader State was deemed an attack on the pope and papal territory, exciting retributions and further crusades.

When Jerusalem fell, the Burgundian, Lombard, German and Poitevin crusaders headed back home. They never got there, being annihilated by the Turks in 1101 while crossing Asia Minor. Read on.»»»

# THE SAD LEGACY OF THE CRUSADES

**SEVEN MORE CRUSADES** to the East would follow between 1096 and 1270, most of them under more favorable auspices than the first, as emperor and king would replace princes as leaders. King Louis VII of France and King Conrad III of Germany, for instance, led the Second Crusade, and Emperor Frederick I Barbarossa took the cross for the Third Crusade. (When Emperor Frederick II took the cross of the Sixth Crusade, then procrastinated, Pope Gregory IX excommunicated him.) The crusades would have their triumphs, wholly temporary, and their catastrophies; the loss in human life was appalling — on both sides.

The crusades are a blot on history, but as late as 1967 there were still apologists for them. For example, the entry on the crusades in the *New Catholic Encyclopedia* concludes thus: "The crusades were not an act of intolerance: they aimed neither at the forced conversion of non-Christian (sic) nor at the massacre of 'infidels.' These expeditions had, indeed, military, financial, and economic aspects, but above all else they can be characterized as a penitential act and as a voluntary effort in the service of God. The notion of bearing arms in God's service, though it may seem paradoxical, was perfectly attuned to the mentality of the Middle Ages and, in the last analysis, assured the success (sic) of the crusades. The concept of devoting considerable effort to a task in the service of God guarantees lasting favor to the crusade idea as applied in our day to the works of peace."

Absolute rubbish. Despite their spiritual motivation, the crusaders were self-righteous. They were a disgrace. Further, whatever gains they achieved in terms of Christian access to the holy places of the Middle East were offset by new antagonisms and an alienation between East and West that persists to this day. In fact, nothing in history is more striking than the recession of Christianity in the East following the crusades. It can hardly be accounted mere coincidence. One last word tomorrow.

# THE CHILDREN'S CRUSADE

**IN 1212, THE CRUSADE IDEA** reached a height of naivete with the organization of what history knows as the Children's Crusade. The crusade is not counted among the eight to the East, and for good reason; it never got beyond the seaports of France and Italy.

The crusade developed on two fronts. In France, a young shepherd named Stephen from Cloyes-sur-le-Loir, near Vendome, had a vision in which he claimed Jesus appeared to him disguised as a pilgrim with an inspiration for the liberating of the Holy Land from the Moslems. The Holy Land would be conquered by the love of young innocents instead of by force. Stephen began preaching a crusade and attracted followers by the thousands. Meanwhile, a second group was marshalling in Germany's Rhineland behind a ten-year-old named Nicholas.

The boy preachers prophesied that Jerusalem would be liberated from Islam by miracle. How would they ever get there? The sea would divide for them, and they would cross dry-shod, like the Israelites of old crossing the Red Sea ahead of the pursuing armies of Pharoah. So convinced, the French youths — 30,000-strong— made their way to Marseilles. The German youths — 20,000-strong — crossed the Alps into Italy, where they began to split up, some heading for Genoa, some for Brindisi on the Adriatic in southeast Italy. The seas there refused, however, to part, and the young "crusaders" found themselves beset by hunger and exhaustion, and prey to disreputable merchants, who shipped them off to slave markets. The French youths were sold to the slave markets of Africa; the Germans to those of the East. It is said that "a few" of the German band made their way to Rome, where Innocent III "took pity" and released them from their crusade vows so that they could go back home.

One would have thought that the debacle would kill the whole idea of crusades. Not at all. The Children's Crusade ended in disaster, but it helped spark the Fifth Crusade that stepped off in 1217. Footnote tomorrow.

# THE MODIFYING OF THE CRUSADE IDEA

**THOUGH THE LAST** of the crusades to the East ended in the thirteenth century, it was hard for Rome to let go of the idea of "holy wars" fought in behalf of the faith — the very concept, incidentally, for which certain Eastern militant faith factions are today berated. Indeed, the crusade idea haunted Western Christianity into the seventeenth and eighteenth centuries, and wars closer to home took on the character of crusades as popes sought to bulwark the church against the assaults of "infidels," which translated now mainly as Turks.

In 1517, for instance, Pope Leo X proposed to lead personally a crusade backed by Emperor Charles V and France's King Francis I, which would lay seige to Constantinople with three hundred ships. Charles and Francis became at odds with one another, however, and the plans were aborted. In any instance, the leaders of the Reformation opposed Leo's proposal, Martin Luther declaring it sinful to war against the Turks, because God had made them his instrument in punishing the sins of Christians.

Similarly, the expedition of Don Juan of Austria that culminated with the defeat of the Ottoman fleet in the Straits of Lepanto in 1571 was in the nature of a crusade. The pope, Pius V, who was so thrilled by the victory, believing that it saved Christendom, that he commemorated it by instituting the feast of the Most Holy Rosary, long marked on the first Sunday in October. Similarly again, the sixteenth and seventeenth century expeditions in the form of Holy Leagues against the Turks in Hungary continued the idea of the crusades of the Middle Ages, popes furnishing subsidies and indulgences and directives for public prayers. And as late as 1715, Clement XI was blessing an expedition of Venetians into Greece.

These "holy wars" were essentially papal enterprises from start to finish. The waning of the Ottoman empire and the Turkish threat to Western Europe at last pacified the popes. But it was bloody business before it all ended.

Flannery O'Connor

# A CATHOLIC WRITER STEEPED IN TRAGICOMEDY

**FLANNERY O'CONNOR LIVED** only thirty-nine years, and left a relatively small opus — two novels, two collections of short stories, some incidental writings and lectures that were collected into books after her death. But her mark as writer and Catholic was as few other Americans of this century. Was she a Catholic writer? Was she rather an odd writer of Southern Gothic? Flannery O'Connor said simply that she considered herself "a Catholic peculiarly possessed of the modern consciousness." That consciousness was once thought Southern, almost uniquely regional. But it is proving to be universal.

Flannery O'Connor was born in Savannah on this day in 1925, and lived most of her years in Milledgeville. She attempted to live in New York, and for a year and a half rented a room above a gararge on Sally and Robert Fitzgerald's farm in Connecticut. But her health was frail, and forced her back to Georgia. In 1950 she contracted disseminated lupus, which she had to cope with until her death in 1964. She seemingly acquired lupus genetically; her father died of it in 1941.

In her study *Flannery O'Connor: A Study of the Short Fiction* (Twayne, 1988), Suzanne Morrow Paulson presents her subject as a modern moralist whose vision of humankind transcends the Catholic and Southern Gothic labels some critics would impose upon her. Paulson's conclusion: Flannery O'Connor's "mix of the comic and the tragic elements of human life...will preserve her art in the centuries to come — especially as her insights into modern life and 'the mystery of personality' are better understood."

That's fair enough. Flannery O'Connor was a graphic writer, but also one of great subtlety. Her emphases were on the flaws of human judgment, but her epiphanies, says Paulson, were in terms of the sacred glimpse physical reality afforded those who seek spiritual dimensions. Fate cut her short in expanding her propositions, but the legacy is awesome nonetheless.

# PAUL VI'S CALL FOR A NEW HUMANISM

**BY PAPAL STANDARDS,** Paul VI wasn't a particularly busy encyclical writer. Over fifteen years he wrote only seven of them, in contrast to Leo XIII's eighty-eight, Pius X's sixteen, Pius XI's thirty and Pius XII's forty-one. Even John XXIII wrote more, turning out eight encyclicals in his short five-year reign.

As fate would have it, much of Paul VI's reputation is pegged to his last encyclical, the one which restated the church's traditional position against artificial birth control, *Humanae vitae*. His other encyclicals are not fixed in the public mind, although one should be — *Populorum progressio* ("On the development of people"), a 20,000-word document issued on this day in 1967. *Populorum progressio* struck a note that was to be picked up on time and again by John Paul II: the imbalance of privilege between nations of the first and third worlds, and the responsibility of first-world nations to help rather than exploit those nations less well off. "It is a question...of building a world," Paul VI wrote, "where every man, no matter what his race, religion or nationality, can live a fully human life, freed from servitude imposed by other men or by natural forces over which he has not sufficient control; a world where freedom is not an empty word and where the poor man Lazarus can sit down at the same table with the rich man." Rich nations, the pope charged, were obliged to help those "struggling to free themselves from the yoke of hunger, misery, disease and ignorance, who seek a larger share in the fruits of civilization and a more active realization of their human personality."

The media hailed Pope Paul for his compassion and foresight. *Populorum progressio* was termed "the church's definitive answer to Marxism" (John Courtney Murray), and the National Council of Churches recommended it for immediate study. Even Planned Parenthood welcomed the remarks on demography. But the honeymoon would be short. In sixteen months there would be *Humanae vitae*.

# MARCH 27

## THE STATIONS OF THE CROSS

**THE WAY OR STATIONS OF THE CROSS**, the devotional exercise which traces Christ's passion and death from the palace of Pilate to Calvary and burial, must be accounted yet another casualty of post-Vatican II Catholicism. The Stations were once one of the most popular of Lenten devotions, but they were not exclusive to the season. They were said year-round too. Many's the knee that bent before the fourteen stations before Mass, during Mass and on visits to church, back when churches were routinely open all day long. The Stations of the Cross are still said, but not anywhere near the numbers saying the Our Father and Hail Mary and meditating station to station as of old.

Actually, as a devotional exercise, the Way of the Cross is of relatively recent vintage. The erection and devotional use of the stations did not become general before the end of the seventeenth century, though in the fifthteenth and sixteenth centuries reproductions of the holy stations were being erected as shrines to keep fresh the memory of the scenes of Christ's passion and death, and as devotional aids to the large numbers of Christians who would never have the means or physical strength to make a Holy Land pilgrimage themselves.

Tradition says that it was the Virgin Mary who inspired the devotion of the Way of the Cross by making daily visits to the scenes of Christ's painful walk to death, pausing for prayer at spots along the way hallowed by special incidents. If so, her example was a long time exerting itself, for it was not until the fifteenth century that Mary's *via crucis* was adopted for the faithful into a devotional way of the cross, at least as known in the modern sense.

It was the Franciscans who were the primary promoters of the devotion, largely due to the coincidence of their being entrusted in 1342 with the guardianship of the holy places. The latitudes are greater today, but in 1731 Clement XII decreed that only Franciscans could erect Stations of the Cross. They were the instruments; the fruits followed, for a time. Read on.»»»

# ARRIVING AT FOURTEEN STATIONS

**THE STATIONS OF THE CROSS** did not arrive in a tidy, neat package. For centuries the stations varied widely in number and designation; in a few places there was even another name for the devotion.

At Neuremberg, for instance, the stations numbered seven and the devotion was known as the Seven Falls, after the representations by artist Adam Krafft, which depicted Christ either prostrate or sinking under the weight of the cross. In other places the stations varied from as few as nine to as many as thirty-seven. The Diocese of Vienna set the number at eleven, only five of which correspond to today's stations.

No one knows for sure how the church finally arrived at fourteen stations, though it seems likely the number was decided by devotional writers of the Middle Ages rather than actual devotional practice along the Holy Land's *via crucis* itself. It was Clement XII who, in entrusting the devotion to the Franciscans, fixed the number at fourteen. Again, that was in 1731. The fourteen are as follows:

(1) Jesus is condemned to death; (2) Jesus takes up his cross; (3) Jesus falls the first time; (4) Jesus meets his afflicted mother; (5) Simon of Cyrene helps Jesus carry the cross; (6) Veronica wipes the face of Jesus; (7) Jesus falls the second time; (8) Jesus comforts the women of Jerusalem; (9) Jesus falls the third time; (10) Jesus is stripped of his garments; (11) Jesus is nailed to the cross; (12) Jesus dies on the cross; (13) Jesus is taken down from the cross; (14) Jesus is laid in the tomb.

There is some modern opinion that the Way or Stations of the Cross is liturgically and psychologically incomplete because it ends without reference to the Resurrection. Some thus propose a fifteenth station for meditation upon the Resurrection; others argue that this is unnecessary, as the place of Jesus' entombment was also the place of his Resurrection, and therefore meditation on the one can be extended to the other. Discussion on the point seems largely academic, however, with the devotion gone into such an eclipse.

## THE FOUNDING OF THE KNIGHTS OF COLUMBUS

**IT WAS CHARTERED** by the Connecticut General Assembly on this day in 1882 as the first fraternal benefit society of Catholic men in the United States, and within twenty-five years the group could be found in every state of the Union, in most of the provinces of Canada, in Mexico and in the Philippines. What's its name? The Knights of Columbus.

The organization was the brainchild of Father Michael J. Givney, and had its origins in New Haven, where it is still headquartered. In the rush-tide of fraternalism, the local Knights of Columbus hall was a busy and popular place. Indeed, the "K. of C." was the vehicle for many an immigrant's rite of passage from Old World mores to those of the New.

Changing social tastes and home TV took a toll, if not at first on membership figures, then certainly on the fraternalism of the clubroom. But the Knights of Columbus' fate was a common one for fraternal orders. Fortunately, the Knights of Columbus had more to fall back on than many counterpart groups, as an insurance company (with more than $8.34 billion in force in 1984) and as an organization concerned about religious and patriotic values. Dedicated to the ideals of religious freedom and the principles of the Catholic faith, the Knights of Columbus evolved into something of a Catholic anti-defamation society. At the same time, as an organization of growing means, it became a bankroller of notable church-related projects, such as the microfilming in the 1950s of the Vatican Library — 9,500,000 manuscript pages for starters, for housing at St. Louis University in Missouri — and the 1975 underwriting of "up-link" costs for telecasting papal ceremonies throughout the world via satellite.

The Knights of Columbus is not every Catholic's cup of tea. But, as Christopher Kauffman has written, it is a group no one can dismiss lightly, thanks to its "unique blend of Catholic idealism and American practicality."

Karl Rahner

# THE THEOLOGIAN WHO INFLUENCED VATICAN II

**ONE OF THE TWENTIETH CENTURY'S** leading theologians died at age eighty on this day in 1984, the Austrian Jesuit Father Karl Rahner. Like the American Jesuit Father John Courtney Murray, Father Rahner was unwelcome by entrenched conservative elements at Vatican Council II, but he got there anyway. However, whereas Murray's influence was over a single document, religious liberty, Rahner's was pervasive. The entire work and spirit of the council are now recognized as derivative of his thinking and approach to theology.

Karl Rahner is typed as a transcendental theologian, one whose objective it was not to pass beyond the corpus of inherited thought and theory, but to take what exists and develop what is implicit and presupposed in what is already known. Viewed from this perspective, as William A. Herr noted in *Catholic Thinkers in the Clear* (Thomas More, 1985), "the real purpose of the Gospel message is not to bring us news about some exterior reality, but to help us understand more fully who and what we are." Thus, with respect to salvation, the question which is foremost in most Christian minds:

"Salvation is not a kind of posthumous spiritual reward for good behavior, granted to some and withheld from others; it is simply a continuation of what has taken place during one's life, a sharing in God to the extent that each person has developed a capacity for it through the practice of faith, hope and love. Heaven and hell are, in a sense, the same thing — remaining whatever you have made of yourself, forever."

That's a theology to clash with much of what is to be found in the Baltimore Catechism, and maybe it will never fly, as they say. But more and more people are beginning to think as did Karl Rahner, and to compare him in the process to Thomas Aquinas.

Preposterous!!!!

Perhaps. But then history is still being written. Wait a century or two.

# SYMBOLS, SYMBOLS, EVERYWHERE.

**DO ANY OF US** ever stop to note how much of our lives is defined by symbols — the wedding ring, the decoration worn in our lapel, the old school tie rummaged out for special occasions? As individuals we are forever being described by abstract items and concepts. And not just us. The larger society is also defined to remarkable extent by symbols — the flag, the eagle, the dollar sign — and, of course, so is the church. Symbols are sown and consciously cultivated, always have been, for the meanings they invest in other meaningful things — marriage, military service, college affiliation, patriotism, and so on.

The church, though hardly claiming any monopoly on the idea, has indulged in the use of symbols from the start to convey to the faithful the inner meanings of things and as expressions of religious ideals. Some church symbols are as familiar as that of the ring which in secular life connects to marriage; some are obscure; all are interesting.

Let's review some of the church's more fascinating symbols — emphasizing the word *some,* for there are hundreds, indeed thousands of them. Remember, nearly every saint in heaven has been assigned a symbol. Let's take some of the church's more common symbols and see how many are familiar:

***Fish and loaves of bread.*** Easy; they're the symbol of the Eucharist.

***Ship.*** Again easy. It's the church, Peter's bark, the symbol of hope in immortality, the ship sailing along towards the life of the blessed.

***Anchor.*** Less easy. It too is a symbol of hope — the anchor of the soul, sure and steadfast.

***Scallop shell.*** The symbol of the crusader, the scallop shell being a souvenir of the journey East, where it served as a drinking vessel.

***Keys.*** Simple; the symbol of power and of the office of the pope.

***Sheep.*** In the Old Testament, the sheep served as a symbol of dependence or helplessness; in the New Testament, as a symbol of Christ's humility — also, as a significance of Christ's ministry, as dramatized in the parable of the shepherd and the sheep.

***Crowing cock.*** This is the resurrection symbol. The cock announces the dawn and proclaims the life of the world to come.

***Cross.*** The symbol of salvation — the symbol on which the theology of the New Testament converges.

The sacraments are full of symbols, of course — the white robe of baptism, for instance, symbolizing innocence and purity. So are the fruits of the biblical trees; the pomergranate symbolizes fertility because it has so many pips. The lion symbolizes strength; a road or path indicates action, purpose and direction. One could go on to the symbols of the saints: Luke, a book, palette and brush, for he was reputed to be a painter as well as a writer; Patrick, a harp, serpent, shamrock, baptismal font — everyone knows why; Peter, keys, boat and cock; etc., etc., etc.

One final point of symbolism. Did you know that in the early centuries, churches were built facing East. Why? Because that's where Christ lived and died, and that's where the sun rises emblematic of him who was the Sun of Justice?

# FOOLING AROUND FROM TIME IMMEMORIAL

**IF YOU'RE WISHED** "Happy New Year" today, don't be too quick to dismiss the greeting as an April Fools' Day joke. April 1 was the day of revelry that in Roman times climaxed the old New Year's — the eight days of festivity after the vernal equinox, March 25. In the Christian era, April 1 marked the eighth day or end of the octave of the Annunciation, the Archangel Gabriel's announcing unto Mary on March 25 that nine months hence she would deliver a baby and call him Jesus. Once again April 1 was a day of special celebration — the counterpart of sorts of today's January 1, New Year's Day, which happens also to be the eighth day of Christmas, holy day and holiday.

As holiday, this New Year's of ours is of relatively new date. For centuries on end New Year's was observed on March 25, and was not moved to January 1 until the adoption of the Gregorian calendar in the sixteenth century.

The French were the first to accept the reformed calendar, Charles IX decreeing in 1564 that henceforth the new year would begin, not on March 25, but rather January 1, the close of the octave of Christmas. Many did not like the idea, because April 1, the close of the octave of the Annunciation, was France's traditional day for gift-giving and New Year's visits to friends and relatives. They refused to change, and insisted on observing April 1 according to old ways. Quickly they became objects of sport for wits, who sent them mock gifts, paid them comic court, and subjected them to pranks, like sending them on fools' errands, a favorite trick. Thus was born April Fools' Day.

At least that's one theory for the origin of April Fools' Day. There are others — like the theory that, the Crucifixion having occurred on or about April 1, the day is a burlesque commemoration of Christ's being sent from Annas to Caiaphas, from Caiaphas to Pilate, from Pilate to Herod, from Herod back to Pilate. But the French theory holds more water. Or is that water mirage?

# THE EASTER CONTROVERSY

**EASTER, THE CORNERSTONE** of the Christian faith, the feast which Pope Leo I called *festum festorum*, the "feast of feasts" — so great a feast in fact that Leo said Christmas was celebrated only as a preparation for Easter. In the early church every Sunday of the year was regarded by many as a commemoration of Easter, the Resurrection of Christ, which they earnestly believed took place on a Sunday. At the same time, however, Easter is a movable feast; that is, one whose date may vary from year to year.

Not being a fixed date that one can situate on a given calendar day, as with Christmas, readers may find Easter's placement in this daybook coinciding with a weekday. The dislocation should not startle; in the early church, Easter, as a movable feast, was once widely observed on a weekday. This practice clashed with that of those who associated Easter with Sunday, and thus was seeded the contention known as the Easter Controversy.

The controversy has three phases. The first involved Christians of Jewish descent (who held that the paschal fast ended on the fourteenth day of the moon, on which the Jewish people were commanded to sacrifice the lamb, with the Easter festival immediately following, whatever the day of the week) and Christians of Gentile descent (who, unfettered by Jewish traditions, identified the first day of the week with the Resurrection and accordingly wanted adjustments relative to moon phases so that Easter coincided with a Sunday).

Generally speaking, Christians of the West opted for the Sunday observance, but in the East the tendency was to follow Jewish rule and mark Easter on the fourteenth day of Nisan, which again meant that Easter might occur any day of the week. Because of fixation with the number 14, those of the latter school were known as *Quartodecimani*. Polycrates, metropolitan of proconsular Asia, visited Pope Victor I in Rome in 197 to discuss the issue. Victor responded by excommunicating Polycrates and all who continued the Eastern usage. Read on.»»»

# EASTER SUNDAY....BUT WHICH SUNDAY?

**COOLER LOGIC** stayed Victor from enforcing his excommunications of the Asiatics, notably that of Irenaeus and the bishops of Gaul. The interest of Gaul's bishops was not surprising, as they had long since despaired of the all paschal computations, and preferred the simple solution of a fixed date for Easter; namely, March 27, with March 25 being observed as Good Friday. That preference did not prevail either. Instead, most Christian communities gradually moved to Sunday observance of Easter.

With that the Easter Controversy entered a new phase — namely, if Sunday it be, which Sunday would be observed as Easter? The question was thrashed out at the Council of Nicaea in 325, and was settled by the Council Fathers with unecumenical bluntness. They severed the issue completely from Jewish tradition ("...it appear[s] an unworthy thing that in the celebration of this most holy feast we should follow the practice of the Jews, who have impiously defiled their hands with enormous sin..."), then settled on a four-part rule: (1) Easter must be celebrated thoughout the world by all on the same Sunday; (2) that Sunday must follow the fourteenth day of the paschal moon; (3) the moon to be accounted the paschal moon was the one following fourteen days after the spring equinox; (4) the determination of the precise date for Easter was to be made, probably by the church of Alexandria as best skilled in astronomical calculations, then conveyed to Christendom at large. Harmony would then be achieved — or so they thought.

It wasn't. There were lunar variations in different longitudes. Also, different parts of the world were following different lunar cycles — some the Jewish cycle of 84 years, some the Roman cycle of 532 years. Chaos. In 387, for instance, Augustine recorded that Easter was observed on March 21 in Gaul, April 18 in Italy, and April 25 in Egypt. In 455 Leo I noted that there was an eight-day difference between the Roman and Alexandrine Easters. Read on.»»»

# FROM SEVERAL EASTER DATES TO TWO

**THE EASTER CONTROVERSY** was so tangled that some despaired of ever finding a solution. There was even scattered sentiment for returning to the custom of the church's earliest days, when it was believed the Resurrection was sufficiently commemorated by the weekly Sunday. Of course that would not do as Easter came to be recognized as the central fact of the Christian faith and a feast of supreme importance. So the hunt for a solution continued.

Eventually a lunar cycle of nineteen years was agreed upon, and that coordinated the Easter Sunday date, although not everywhere. Roman missionaries arriving in England and Ireland at the turn of the seventh century found the churches there following old Asian custom and observing Easter in the seventeenth day of the Jewish month of Nisan, irrespective of the day of the week on which the seventeenth occurred. In defending their position, the English and Irish churches appealed to the authority of St. John and St. Philip. The Romans insisted, however, on a Sunday observance of Easter, and the issue was settled in the Romans' favor at the Synod of Whitby in 664. Still, it would be several years before Ireland would fall into line, and accept the Sunday rule. The issue was then settled, in the West at least, but not forever.

In 1582 came the displacement of the Julian calendar by the more accurate Gregorian calendar (q.v. Oct. 14), and once again Easter was being observed on different dates in much of the church. Eastern churches alienated from Rome declined to correct their calendars according to Gregorian formula. Similarly, many countries were slow in adopting the new calendar — England and Ireland, for instance, not doing so until 1752 — with the result that in the West itself churches were observing Easter on a Sunday different from Rome's. Date differences due to national policy ended as countries one by one accepted the Gregorian calendar. But with Eastern churches retaining the Julian calendar, the Easter Controversy was never tidied up into a neat, coordinated solution.

# PURGING THE BIBLE OF SEXISM

**THIS WAS THE DAY** in 1987 that the American Catholic bishops introduced their updated text of the New Testament purified of much of its sexist language. The male-oriented old version, with its constant use of words like man, men, sonship, him, brothers, brotherhood, had become of late a major irritant, particularly with feminists. Many resented being addressed as "men" or "sons," bundled into the generic term "mankind," or, more insufferably, being called nothing at all. The revised, so-called "inclusive" text, six years in the devising, does not go as far as the 1983 collection of Bible readings issued by the National Council of Churches for experimental use in Protestant churches, but it does clean up all of the chauvinist language of the old text. For instance, the verse from Matthew 4:4, "Not on bread alone is man to live," has been revised to read, "One does not live by bread alone." Similarly, Matthew 16:23, "You are not judging by God's standards, but by man's," becomes "You are thinking not as God does, but as human beings do."

Other changes have been made as well to reflect other sensitivities of the times. The new text, for example, treats homosexuals less judgmentally. Thus it clarifies the references to homosexuals in 1 Corinthians 6:9-10, where Paul speaks of those who will be excluded from the kingdom of God. The old text reads, "no adulterers, no sodomites, no thieves"; the new, "nor adulterers nor boy prostitutes nor practicing homosexuals." This is a change not merely of semantics; it reflects a whole new set of Catholic attitudes by distinguishing between sexually practicing homosexuals and those who have what is called a homosexual orientation. The former are reprobated, not the latter.

Do changes such as these really make a difference? It is impossible to argue that they do not. Sexist language obstructs any message, including that of the Bible. The entire community of belivers benefits from its elimination.

# BIBLICAL INERRANCY VS. MISCHIEVOUS PRINTERS

**YESTERDAY'S READING** demonstrates that, though the Bible is the word of God, and though the Bible is inerrant, each of these attributes has to be understood in a special context. The Bible is not literally true in each and every word. Science and history have demonstrated that. For instance, the earth is not stationary, despite Ecclesiastes, Chapter 1; and Darius the Mede did not succeed Belshazzar, as he does twice in Daniel. The explanations for inaccuracies such as these is that God "in his condescension deigned to entrust his revelation to the frail vessel of human language." Also, passages with inaccuracies like those cited echo common opinions of the day without making them objects of teaching — in other words, they're *not* the very word of God.

It is well to beware belief in the Bible's absolute literalness of fact for the additional reason that Bibles have not escaped bloopers. Mark the 1560 "Breeches" Bible published in Geneva. It took its name from the passage in Genesis 3:7, and the publishers' belief that it was more seemly that Adam and Eve sew their fig leaves into breeches than mere loincloths or frontal aprons.

Then in Hereford, England, there's the "Cider" Bible, so named because the 1400 copyist amended Luke's admonition on the drinking of wine to include cider, "He shall drink ne wine ne cider" — understandable mayhaps given the region's reputation for strong cider.

Two London printers, Robert Barker and Martin Lucas, received stiff 300-pound fines in 1632 for their "Adulterer's" Bible, so called because they dropped the negative from the Sixth Commandment, thus allowing it to read: "Thou shalt commit adultery." Similarly, a seventeenth-century English printer was fined 3,000 pounds for substituting an *a* for a *no* in Psalm 14, making it read, "The fool has said in his heart there is a god." The prize, though, goes to the "Bathroom" Bible published in the U.S. in 1971, wherein in 1 Samuel 24:3 Saul goes into a cave, not to cover his feet, but "to go to the bathroom."

# APRIL 7

## EASTER'S DATE AND HIRSUTE PRIESTS

**TODAY'S FEAST RETURNS US** to the Easter Controversy (q.v. April 2-4), when it was in its early stages. The feast is that of Anicetus, second-century pope and saint. No household name his, but he left a double mark on history.

First, Anicetus was the pope who met in 159 with Polycarp, the disciple of John the Evangelist, on the Easter issue. It was an ecclesiastical summit meeting in the truest sense. Polycarp, also a future saint, was bishop of Smyrna when he came to Rome seeking to resolve differences between the Eastern and Western churches on the termination of the paschal fast and the observance of Easter. Was Easter to be celebrated on the fourteenth day of the Jewish month of Nisan, no matter what the day of the week, as proposed by Polycarp, or was the feast to be observed always on Sunday, as held by Anicetus? Forty years later prelates would be threatening one another with excommunication over this issue, but not Anicetus and Polycarp. They met in an atmosphere of civility. They did not bring uniformity of date to the Easter observance (as we know, no one ever would), but they ruptured no church links. As the historian Eusebius recorded, "Polycarp could not persuade the pope, nor the pope, Polycarp. The controversy was not ended but the bonds of charity were not broken."

Anicetus, more accommodating than the pope who would be reigning a quarter-century later, Victor I, permitted Polycarp to celebrate Easter on the day traditional for the church at Smyrna. Rome went its way, and East and West lived in peaceful coexistence on the issue until the Council of Nicaea in 325 settled on the Sunday following the first full moon after the vernal equinox. Nicaea didn't solve matters for all nor for all time, of course, but it helped.

As for that second mark that Anicetus left on history: It has to do with our well-barbered clergy....or maybe so. Anicetus forbade priests to wear their hair long. By and large to this day priests are better barbered than the rest of Catholic Christian males in the pews. Or is that one's imagination?

# THE AMERICAN CHURCH MOVES WEST

**LIKE THE COUNTRY,** the church began in the East and moved gradually West. It all began on this day in 1808, when Pope Pius VII split up the original diocese of Baltimore, mother see in the United States, and erected four new dioceses. All were in the East, except for one, designated for west of the Allegheny Mountains. This was the diocese of Bardstown, Kentucky, since renamed the diocese of Louisville. Appointed its first bishop was a French-born Sulpician priest, Benedict Joseph Flaget. He didn't want the job, and was so poor he didn't even have money to cover traveling expenses to Kentucky.

The papers for Flaget's elevation to the episcopacy reached him in September, 1808, but it was more than two years — November, 1810 — before he accepted consecration as a bishop from Bishop John Carroll. It was another six months before he left Baltimore for his see in what then was quite literally a wilderness. He traveled over the Alleghenies to Pittsburgh, and there boarded a river boat chartered specially for the purpose, and floated down the Ohio to Louisville. He arrived in Louisville June 4, 1811, and five days later entered Bardstown. There was as yet no church there.

Bishop Flaget had his work cut out for him. His diocese embraced all of Kentucky and Tennessee, but he was also assigned spiritual jurisdiction over the whole United States northwest, states and territories, until dioceses could be prudently and strategically established. This area added the present states of Michigan, Ohio, Indiana, Illinois, Missouri, Wisconsin, Iowa and half of Arkansas to his responsibility. The reluctant bishop accepted the challenge.

In 1832 Bishop Flaget, now sixty-nine, resigned his bishopric, but then found himself reappointed when his successor stepped down after a short tenure. He served another seventeen years. He supervised transfer of the diocesan seat to Louisville, and consecrated numerous bishops for a burgeoning Midwest church.

# APRIL 9

## OF EASTER EGGS AND EASTER JOKES....

**RETURNING FOR ONE** last time to Easter....there are a number of colorful customs connected to the season, like coloring eggs and things like that. Did you ever wonder about their origin? Let's look at some of them.

***Easter eggs.*** The coloring of them goes back to when the use of eggs was forbidden in accordance with the Lenten fast. People colored them at Easter as an expression of the Easter joy. The Lord was risen; eggs were back on the table — and they arrived there brightly colored, the symbol of the new life of the church and the germinating life of spring.

***The Easter rabbit.*** The rabbit theoretically lays the Easter egg; thus the egg hunt of Easter Sunday morning. The rabbit was a pagan symbol, but it fit nicely into Christian mythology as the emblem of fertility and new life.

***The Easter fire.*** Here's another pagan custom carried into Christian tradition. For pagans this was the new fire that signified the victory of spring over winter. The church incorporated the tradition into the Easter liturgy as the symbol of the new life of the Resurrection.

***Easter water.*** This is the holy water, once upon a time blessed only twice a year, on the vigils of Easter and Pentecost, and in the old liturgy distributed to the faithful before the holy oils were poured in it. Catholic Christians of old attached great healing power to the Easter water.

***The Easter blessing.*** It was extended to homes (in memory of the passing of the angel in Egypt and the signing of the doorposts with the blood of the paschal lamb), and among some ethnic groups is still sought for the foods of the Easter table, so that what was for forty days banned by the church might now be blessed in the Lord.

***Easter laughter (Risus Paschalis).*** The somberness of Lent behind, priests inserted jokes and funny stories into the sermons of Easter, and drew their moral, as the congregation laughed. Clement X barred the custom as unseemly.

Evelyn Waugh

# THE MAN WHO LOVED TO TAUNT

**YOU'VE READ HIS BOOKS;** you've seen *Brideshead Revisited* on television; you know the person we're talking about: Evelyn Waugh passed on this day in 1966 into the world he spared. "Bad cess for that world," as the Irish would say, "he spared nothing here." Indeed he didn't. Evelyn Waugh was a prize curmudgeon. He was also a literary genius, however — and he wore his Catholicism (to which he was converted in 1930) on his sleeve.

When the American literary critic Edmund Wilson objected to *Brideshead's* emphases, Waugh shot back in *Life* magazine, then at the height of its influence: "He was outraged (quite legitimately by his standards) at finding God introduced into my story. I believe that you can only leave God out by making your characters pure abstractions....[Modern novelists] try to represent the whole human mind and soul, yet omit its determining character — that of being God's creature with a defined purpose. So in my future books there will be two things to make them unpopular: a preoccupation with style and the attempt to represent man more fully, which, to me, means one thing, man in his relation to God." He kidded not, though of all his books *Brideshead* was to remain Evelyn Waugh's masterpiece.

Conservative to the point of reaction, Waugh's politics were Jacobite (seventeenth century) and his Catholicism Tridentine (sixteenth century). He was such an anachronism, in fact, that Pope Pius XII, no neo-modernist he, is reported once to have protested charges by Waugh against the church with the words, "But Mr. Waugh, I too am a Catholic!"

Much of Waugh had to be pose. He lived in the twentieth century (1903-1966); he served heroically in World War II on several fronts as a commando with rank of major. He was no plastic citizen or soldier. He was no great admirer of the United States, either. But he served his country well....and his church.

# APRIL 11

Bust of Pope John XXIII by Manzu

## POPE JOHN XXIII'S FINAL GIFT TO THE WORLD

**ONE OF THE TACTFUL** innovations of the pontificate of John XXIII was his addressing of encyclicals not exclusively to Catholics or some sub-group within Catholicism, but to persons of good will throughout the whole world. It began with *Mater et magistra* in 1961, and it continued with *Pacem in terris*, which was issued on this day in 1963. *Pacem in terris* — "Peace on earth" — was John's great human-rights encyclical, the encyclical in which he addressed the dignity of the individual and order between peoples, from the family to the community of nations. There was not a base left untouched. John XXIII denounced racism, defended the right of the individual to worship according to conscience, urged an end to the arms race and a ban on nuclear weapons, and finally supported the concept of a world body "endowed with a breadth of powers, structure and means" to solve problems of worldwide dimensions, the last being interpreted as a ringing endorsement of the United Nations.

The encyclical was extraordinary in scope and had an unparalleled impact on world opinion for the refinements of understanding it brought to issues once approached so one-dimensionally by Rome. For instance, there was John's distinction between communism as an atheistic creed and communism as a social, political and economic reality which was part of the historical order and had to be cooperated and contended with as such. It was the church's first serious concession to "co-existence" in an ideologically pluralistic world.

*Pacem in terris* did not appeal to hard-liners of the Curia and capitalist world, who argued that in trying to speak to everyone John diluted the Christian case and muddled issues he sought to clarify, including human rights and the dignity of the individual. But many more received the encyclical as a blessed breath of fresh air. John died less than two months after issuing the encyclical. *Pacem in terris* was thus something of a last will and testament.

# APRIL 12

## CATCH PHRASE OF THE MODERN CHURCH

**WITH *PACEM IN TERRIS*** Pope John XXIII bequeathed one thing more to the modern church, the term that was to become its catch phrase: "signs of the times." John first used the term in his bull of December 25, 1961, *Humanae salutis*, convoking Vatican Council II in the upcoming year. But other terms in that document caught the public's fancy for their sheer novelty and their optimism, like John's description of the church as "always living and always young" and always feeling "the rhythm of the times."

In *Pacem in terris* John returned three times with the "signs of the times" phrase, using it as a divisional sub-head and proceeding in each instance to note particular developments which were of significance for God and faith in relation to three "signs of the times": the progression of the working classes, the expanding role of women in public life, and the waning of colonialism.

John's successor, Paul VI, picked up the phrase and used it in his 1964 encyclical *Ecclesiam suam*, citing the dialogue between the church and the world among the "signs of the times." And of course the Fathers of Vatican II used the phrase time and again in interventions seeking to relate the ancient church to the modern world. Finally, in *Gaudium et spes*, the pastoral Constitution on the Church in the Modern World, the Fathers gave the phrase a specific theological context, relating it to events characteristic of eras of history which, if properly read, can reveal the presence or absence of God. This the Fathers said in paragraph 4 of *Gaudium et spes*: "...The church has always had the duty of scrutinizing the signs of the times and of interpreting them in the light of the Gospel. Thus, in language intelligible to each generation, she can respond to the perennial questions which men ask about this present life and the life to come, and about the relationship of the one to the other."

Today the phrase falls from lips with the ease of a Hail Mary.

# THE LIMITING OF THE CATCH PHRASE

**FOR ALL THE LATTER-DAY USAGE** of the phrase "signs of the times," it is anything but new. John XXIII gets credit for starting the phrase on the road to popularity, but where did he get it? Where else but out of Matthew's Gospel? It's been sitting there all along in Chapter 16:1-4:

> The Pharisees also with the Sadducees came, and tempting desired him that he would show them a sign from heaven.
>
> He answered and said unto them, When it is evening, ye say, It will be fair weather: for the sky is red.
>
> And in the morning, It will be foul weather today: for the sky is red and lowering. O ye hypocrites, ye can discern the face of the sky, but ye cannot discern the signs of the times.
>
> A wicked and adulterous generation seeketh after a sign; and there shall no sign be given unto it, but the sign of the prophet Jonas. And he left them and departed.

The strict biblical exegete sees Matthew's passage as both christological and eschatological. His "signs of the times" belong, in a word, to the person and activity of Jesus as indications of the coming of the kingdom. In council debate, therefore, some bishops objected to the broadening of the concept and the contemporizing of the phrase for modern contexts and events. In so doing they reflected doubts entertained by many observers at the council from the World Council of Churches. One worry was how to account for ambiguities in human history: when was God speaking and when someone else? Thus, several times "signs of the times" was in and out of *Gaudium et spes*. The phrase made its way into the final text, but only by compromise. It would appear, but without any biblical citation — indicating that the term was to be understood only in the limited sense in which it had been used by John XXIII and Paul VI.

# APRIL 14

## The Tantum Ergo

*Tantum ergo sacramentum*
Down in adoration falling

*Veneremur cernui;*
Lo! the sacred host we hail!

*Et antiquum documentum*
Lo! o'er ancient forms departing

*Novo cedat ritui;*
Newer rites of grace prevail;

*Praestet fides supplementum*
Faith for all defects supplying

*Sensuum defectui.*
Where the feeble senses fail.

*Genitori, Genitoque*
To the everlasting Father,

*Laus et jubilatio!*
And the Son who reigns on high

*Salus, honor, virtus quoque*
With the Holy Ghost prodeeding

*Sit et Benedictio;*
Forth from each eternally,

*Procedenti ab utroque*
Be salvation, honor, blessing

*Compar sit laudatio. Amen*
Might, and endless majesty. Amen.

# YESTERDAY'S PRAYERS

**IN THE FIELD OF SPIRITUAL** composition, Thomas Aquinas was a triple threat. When he wasn't busy with the *Summa*, he was apt to be writing prayers and hymns. One of the most beautiful of the last was *Pange Lingua* ("Sing with tongue"), a Latin hymn composed in honor of the Blessed Sacrament for vespers of the Office of Corpus Christi, the feast created in 1264 by Pope Urban IV for the Thursday after Trinity Sunday — a holy day in some countries, but observed in the United States on the Sunday following Trinity Sunday. *Pange Lingua* was sung in a solemn procession of the Blessed Sacrament associated with the feast. It was also sung in the old liturgy of Holy Thursday, as the Blessed Sacrament was being placed in the special repository set up for the day. Most Catholics of a given age know the tune of *Pange Lingua*; they *all* know its last two stanzas — hymn and prayer at the one time. The stanzas comprise the *Tantum Ergo*, sung during Benediction when it was a devotion most popular:

# APRIL 15

## THE HOLY MAN OF MOLOKAI

**WHEN THE TERRITORY** of Hawaii became the fiftieth United State in 1959, it qualified to place statues of two of its illustrious dead in the capitol building in Washington, D.C. Selected were the warrior-chieftian King Kamehameha, who united the Hawaiian Islands in the late eighteenth-century, and a peasant Belgium priest, who arrived in Hawaii in 1864 and whose missionary work among lepers of Molokai made him celebrated worldwide before his death on this day in 1889. His name was Joseph de Veuster, better known as Father Damien.

Medical science knows oceans about leprosy and its treatment today. However, in Damien's day — in fact, back to biblical times — no disease was more dreaded. Leprosy was malodorous and frightfully disfiguring, and held so highly contagious that those contracting it were banished outright from the community. In the Hawaiian Islands, the place of banishment was Kalaupapa on the island of Molokai. Kalaupapa had no priest, and when it was decided in 1873 to assign one there, there was one volunteer: Father Damien. Damien, a member of the Congregation of the Sacred Hearts of Jesus and Mary (Picpus Fathers), had served eight years on the island of Hawaii itself. When he went to Kalaupapa, it would be forever; he would never return alive from the leper colony.

Damien's story is legend. He managed the care of the colony's eight hundred or more lepers for sixteen years, not only as priest, but as physician, counselor, handyman, sheriff, gravedigger, undertaker. He built chapels and founded orphanages; he formed religious groups to counter the licentiousness and lawlessness so often found in a people in social abandonment. His is an inspiring story, and of course the most famous detail, one worthy of Hollywood for its drama, was Damien's moving disclosure on a hot Sunday in 1885 that he too was a leper. In the sermon at early Mass, Damien doffed the chasuble against the heat, and began not with the words "My brethren," as was his custom, but "We lepers."

# FR. DAMIEN AND ROBERT LOUIS STEVENSON

**IN THE MID-NINETEENTH CENTURY**, leprosy was Hawaii's "national blight." The disease had made an "unobtrusive appearance" in the islands in the 1840s, and three decades later was rampant. Leprosy laws were enacted and rigorously enforced. But until Father Damien joined the banished of Molokai, the lepers suffered almost total spiritual neglect. His was a hero's decision, and so recognized. Damien's name became known everywhere.

Living heroes are seldom spared the barbs of the malicious. Most certainly Damien wasn't. In his lifetime and in years immediately after his death in 1889, allegations circulated about his "morals." The principal accuser was one Rev. Charles McEwen Hyde, a Congregational minister of New England background living in Honolulu. Writing to a colleague in Australia shortly after Damien's death, Hyde described Damien as "a coarse, dirty man, headstrong and bigoted," adding that "he was not a pure man in his relations with women, and the leprosy of which he died should be attributed to his vices and carelessness." There it was. At a time when leprosy was associated with syphilis as a fourth stage in the progression of the sexual complaint, it followed judgmentally that Damien's problem was rooted in his own lustfulness.

Hyde's letter made its way into the *Roman Presbyterian*, where it was fallen upon by Robert Louis Stevenson, the celebrated Scottish man of letters. Stevenson, a Protestant, did not know Damien personally, but he exploded at the devaluing of the man's suffering and penned a 6,000-word open letter to the world's press terming Hyde "a man quite beyond and below the reticences of civility" but confessing he rejoiced "to feel the button off the foil and to plunge home." Stevenson's was one of the strongest public rebukes of history, and he expected to be sued. But Hyde merely remarked, "Stevenson is simply a Bohemian crank, a negligible person, whose opinion is of no value to anyone."

Investigations exonerated Damien, and his cause was introduced in Rome.

# APRIL 17

## BIDING TIME AND BECOMING POPE

**THIS DAY IN 1585** Rome was at mid-point in the interregnum between the death of the pope who gave the world today's calendar, Gregory XIII (q.v. Oct. 14), and the pope who loved obelisks, erecting four in Rome, including the one in St. Peter's Square, which he pilfered from Nero's Circus, Sixtus V.

There's a wonderful story told of Sixtus and his election. The times seemed to call for a caretaker pope so that practical minds could bring order to the chaos and near bankruptcy in which the papacy had been left by Gregory. Sixtus, no one's fool, despite most humble origins as a swineherd, feigned infirmities of age and entered the conclave on crutches and appearing a little simple. Of course, as someone who appeared weak and manipulable, he was elected. Thereupon the new pope rose up, smoothed his wrinkled robes, cast aside his crutches, and as the cardinals sang the traditional *Te Deum*, he joined in with a vigor of voice that confounded the conclave's electors. Sixtus then announced that he was seven years younger than supposed, and launched into a five-years' pontificate remarkable for its vigor.

Marvelous story, except it is now generally discounted. The origin of the tale seems to lie in the long years of inactivity that the future Sixtus, then Cardinal Montaldo (he dropped his family name and affected the name of his native village), was forced to endure while Gregory XIII reigned. Montaldo, a Franciscan, and the future Gregory had clashed bitterly while attached as cardinals to the Holy See's Spanish legation; they had been sent by Pius V to Spain to investigate charges of heresy against the archbishop of Toledo. The antagonism between the two was to endure a lifetime. Thus while Gregory was pope, the man who would be his successor quietly occupied himself caring for his villa, editing the works St. Ambrose, and discreetly making no enemies. The tactic was to pay off. Read on.»»»

# SIXTUS V — GENIUS, TYRANT...AND SAINT

**POPE SIXTUS V WAS** iron-fisted. Not surprisingly; as a young priest he was counselor to the Inquisition in Venice, but was recalled on request for displaying excesses of enthusiasm. A first task, accordingly, was to eliminate bandits from the papal state, and Sixtus pursued it with uncommon Franciscan zeal. Some 7,000 "perpetrators" were executed, and Sixtus confided to the French ambassador that he would like to have done away with 20,000 more. There was much that was un-Franciscan in Sixtus' severity. When friends of one gentleman-criminal pleaded that, if die the man must, let it be swiftly by decapitation, Sixtus replied, "No, he shall be hanged, but I will ennoble his execution by attending it myself." When mercy was asked on another occasion for a criminal age sixteen under the death penalty, Sixtus replied, "I will give him ten of my own years to make him subject to the law." Pretty cruel stuff for a person who would be canonized Pope St. Sixtus V in 1712.

On the other hand, there was a genius about Sixtus, and his trademark is on so much of Rome that one visits today. He built the Lateran Palace, completed the Quirinal, restored the Church of Santa Sabina on the Aventine, supervised the erection of the dome over St. Peter's, reconstructed the Vatican Library, situated the obelisks in front of Santa Maria Maggiore and Santa Maria del Popolo, planned the papal apartments in which popes live yet, restored the aqueduct of Severus ("Acqua Felice"), opened magnificent new avenues — all the while building up the Vatican treasury with new taxes and sale of offices.

Nor were internal church matters neglected. Sixtus limited the College of Cardinals to seventy, and he brought efficient government to the church with the establishment of fifteen permanent congregations of the Curia. Religious orders were encouraged....but Sixtus kept a wary eye on the Jesuits. He especially objected to the formal name of their order, Society of Jesus, and was in the process of ordering a change when he died in 1590. His successor let them be.

## THE MARTYR DISPATCHED BY DINNER BONES

**CALL HIM ELPHEGE OR** call him Alphege, he was once one of England's most revered saints, and this was his feast day. A former bishop of Winchester and archbishop of Canterbury, Elphege (the more common spelling) lived from 954 to 1012, a time when the Danes were marauding up and down the countryside. On St. Brice's Day in 1002 — November 12, if you've forgotten Brice's date — there was a massacre of Danes billeted with Anglo-Saxon families, so great as to be compared by historians to the Sicilian Vespers and St. Bartholomew's Day atrocities. Well, the Danes struck back, and in 1011 appeared in assault formations before Canterbury. For twenty days Canterbury held, then its defenses were betrayed by a man named Aelmaer. Elphege was taken captive and was carried about England in chains as the Danes demanded a ransom of 3,000 pieces of silver, else the archbishop's life would be exacted. Their deadline came and went, however, without the ransom being paid. The Danes were not amused.

On this day in 1012, the Danes were celebrating in Greenwich, and "half-mad with south-country wine" they demanded that Elphege be hauled before them, apparently for some drunken sport. "Money, bishop, money," the Danes chanted. "Money, money! Your ransom, bishop, your ransom." Elphege rose and to a quieted hall declared, "Silver and gold have I none; what is mine I freely offer, the knowledge of the one true God."

Infuriated, Danes were on their feet, swinging the bones of the oxen on which they had just dined and had flung about the floor. Elphege, not robust to begin with (he was so wan and transparent of hue that, it was said, the moon could shine through his hand), sunk under the blows, mortally injured. A Dane named Thurm delivered the *coup de grace*, raising his battle axe and with one swift blow cleaving Elphege's skull. Elphege, accordingly, is represented in art with an axe buried in his skull. His remains are in Canterbury.

## THE MAID WHO CROSSED THE KING

**WHEN HENRY VIII WAS PURSUING** his divorce from Queen Catherine, no one protested more strongly "in the name and by the authority of God" than the Holy Maid of Kent. She was one Elizabeth Barton, but history hardly remembers her thus. In her times, as now, she was simply the Holy Maid, the domestic servant at Aldington, Kent, who claimed visionary powers and told of "wondrous things done in other places whilst she was neither herself present nor yet heard to report thereof." Cures were attributed to her, including a self-cure worked in the presence of a large crowd. The cure, she said, came through the intercession of the Virgin Mary. The Maid's following grew, and believers were convinced she was "of marvellous holiness in rebuke of sin and vice." Or was the Maid of Kent fraud and imposter?

Henry VIII's loyalist archbishop of Canterbury, Thomas Cranmer, set out to prove so, less in the interests of religion, it might be said, than of Henry's divorce; the Holy Maid of Kent had proved a most formidable adversary to the King's wants. A commission comprising three Benedictines, two Franciscans, a diocesan official and parish priests was named to investigate her. One of them — the Benedictine Edward Bocking — acting out of what has been termed "a mistaken zeal for the preservation of the ancient Faith," persuaded the Maid to declare herself an inspired emissary for the overthrow of Protestantism and the blocking of Henry's divorce. It was the kiss of death, for both of them.

Of course Henry got his divorce, and in 1533 he married Anne Boleyn. As for the Holy Maid of Kent, Cranmer had her consigned to the Tower of London, along with Bocking and others close to her cause. In January, 1534, a bill of attainer was framed against them, and on this day in 1534 they went, seven in all, to the gallows at Tyburn, the hanging site not far from modern London's Marble Arch. The Holy Maid of Kent was no older than twenty-six.

## A POPE LOCKS HORNS WITH GOD

**FOR POPE PAUL VI** this was an extraordinarily tense night in 1978. His dear friend Aldo Moro, leader of the Italian Christian Democrats, was being held prisoner by the terrorist group the Red Brigades. The day before the Moro family forwarded a letter from Aldo Moro to the pope appealing to him for his help. Paul VI could hardly ignore so direct a request. Thus this night in 1978 he drafted a letter "to the men of the Red Brigades" (a concession to their self-importance) asking for Moro's release, "simply, unconditonally." He said the letter was written "on his knees." He was begging. A telephone number was provided for making contact; it was to Caritas International, a Catholic international relief agency based at the Piazza San Calisto.

What happened was shocking. Aldo Moro was found in the trunk of an automobile shortly thereafter outside Christian Democrat headquarters in central Rome. He was dead. The world was appalled at this act of terrorism.

On May 13 a memorial service for Aldo Moro was conducted by the pope at St. John Lateran Basilica, the cathedral church of the bishop of Rome. Paul VI, to everyone's astonishment, upbraided God for allowing this awful deed to happen. As the London *Tablet* remarked, Paul VI was like Job reproaching the Lord for the condition of the world; his "was not a voice of anger so much as distress and pain that Italy should have reached the point at which young people should think that political violence of this kind could win anyone over."

Ah, but as they say, God writes straight with crooked lines.

The slaying of Aldo Moro united Italy's political parties, and spelled the end of the Red Brigades — at least for the time being. Later, some members of the Red Brigades actually repented and confessed. So was Pope Paul VI's prayer heard or not? The question can be answered either way. On the other hand, when was the last time you heard a pope publicly reproaching God?

## THERE WAS MORE THAN ONE QUASIMODO

**IF THIS WERE** the old church...if Easter were past and today a Sunday, then it just might be Low Sunday, the first Sunday after Easter, so named because of the contrast between it and the solemnity that preceded. Before Vatican II, in most parishes there were no high Masses on Low Sunday. So what's Low Sunday got in common with French literature, and more specifically Victor Hugo's *The Hunchback of Notre Dame*? Nothing, except the principal character of Hugo's 1931 novel shares the name given liturgically to this Sunday: Quasimodo. Yes, there's Quasimodo Sunday and there's Quasimodo the disfigured man (remember Charles Laughton in the old black-and-white movie?) who was abandoned on the steps of Notre Dame Cathedral on Quasimodo Sunday in 1476, lived in the belfry, and went deaf from the din of the bells.

No need to review Victor Hugo's story, but maybe there's reason to recall Quasimodo of the liturgy, if only for auld lang syne.

The name comes from the first two words of the Introit for the Latin Mass of the day: *Quasi modo* (two words here) *geniti infantes, alleluja: rationabiles, sine dolo lac concupiscite, alleluja, alleluja, alleluja. [Ps. 80: 2] Exsultate Deo adjutori nostro: jubilate Deo Jacob*— "As newborn babes, alleluia, desire the rational milk without gile, alleluia, alleluia, alleluia [Ps. 80:2]. Rejoice to God our helper: sing aloud to the God of Jacob."

Strictly speaking, the name for the Sunday in the old liturgy was *Dominica albis depositis*, for it was on this Sunday that the neophytes, the new Christians who were baptized on Easter eve, laid aside their white baptismal albs and appeared in congregations as full-fledged members. The custom was also alluded to in the Eastertide vespers hymn, *Ad reginas Agni dapes*, written in imitation of St. Ambrose's vespers hymn, "Now that daylight dies away/By all thy grace and love/Thee, Maker of the world, we pray/to watch our bed above." All that apropos a life of worship that is lost. Regretably?

# BIRTH OF THE AMERICAN CATHOLIC PRESS

**WHAT IS CREDITED** as being the first Catholic newspaper in the United States made its appearance on this day in 1789, *Courrier de Boston.* It only lasted until October 15, less than six months, and left no great mark, but *Courrier de Boston* helped launch an apostolate that would grow to more than 500 publications with a combined circulation of some 25 million readers.

Nothing contributed more immediately to the development of a Catholic press in the U.S. than the fact that Catholics were strangers in a strange land, and often unwelcome strangers at that. A primary purpose of a church press, therefore, was to conserve the faith of Catholics and represent rights of Catholics in an atmosphere where religious, social and political bias could be very strong. Looking back, though, one is struck by a curious absence of solidarity among early Catholic publications, either in faith or patriotism. As often as not these publications were first Irish, or German, or Slovak, among other possibilities, then Catholic almost in afterthought. The diocesan newspaper, for instance, which today lays claim as the oldest in the U.S., The *Pilot* of Boston, was known in 1834-1835 as The *Irish and Catholic Sentinel*, and though the name changed, concern for things Irish dominated for generations.

Matters were to change, of course. The Catholic press never was the editorial monolith it is sometimes accused by critics of being, but it did outgrow nationality preoccupations and develop common institutional loyalties that if anything have grown stronger with the years, occasional editorial disagreements notwithstanding. Some would say that the American Catholic press never reached its full potential and that even now its influence is not commensurate with the numbers of its readers, or, better, the number of Americans who identify as Catholic. Still, the Catholic press does a job, and the American church would be at a loss without it.

# APRIL 24

Peter Finely Dunne

## PETER FINLEY DUNNE AND "MR. M. DOOLEY"

**THE LIGHTS WENT OUT** for that great American wit, Peter Finley Dunne, on this day in 1924. Today his may not be a household name everywhere in the land; still Peter Finley Dunne occupies a place in the pantheon of humor not far from Mark Twain and Will Rogers. His is a name largely associated with Chicago, but the fact is that Dunne died in New York and was buried from St. Patrick's Cathedral. Dunne had moved to New York in 1900 as an editor and writer, but his fame remained rooted back in Chicago, where as a journalist and columnist he produced comic but acidly pointed pieces on the political and social foibles of the times. He did this in dialogues in thick Irish brogue between one "Mr. Martin Dooley," an imaginary saloonkeeper, and "Hinnissey," his sidekick and sounding board. Snippets from the dialogues are heard regularly to this day, though in the vernacular, most notably Mr. Dooley's comment on decisions of the Supreme Court: "No matter whether th' constitution follows th' flag or not, th' Supreme Coort follows th' illiction results."

Dunne began writing his Mr. Dooley sketches around 1893 in the old Chicago *Post*, and came to national attention for his unceremonious observations on the Spanish-American War and whether, for instance, "Mack" (President McKinley) should "hist a flag over th' Ph'lippeens" or "lave [the matter] to George" (Admiral George Dewey), who "wom thim with th' shells." Henry Steele Commager, the historian, would say of these columns that they "pricked every political bubble and exposed every political fraud" of the transition years of the turn of the century — but their dialect sure makes them hard to read today.

In later years Dunne dropped the Irish dialect in writing the columns "In the Interpreter's House" and "From the Bleachers," but these pieces never achieved the popularity of the Mr. Dooley columns. Those columns are not lost, incidentally. Peter Finley Dunne's writings were collected into eight volumes.

# THE ISSUE OF LIMBO REMAINS IN LIMBO

**THE WORD SLIPS FROM** tongues when people are anxious to indicate a state of uncertainly or nonresolution: It's in *Limbo*; he's in *Limbo*; she's in *Limbo*. What is Limbo? Catholics know. It's that "in between" place where people go who do not deserve hell and its eternal punishments for their life lived on earth, and on the other hand don't merit heaven either because they're unbaptized and thus still burdened by original sin. Thus they end up in Limbo, ablative case singular of the Latin word *limbus,* meaning border or edge.

In Catholic parlance, the word is used most commonly in the context of infants who die without the sacrament of baptism. They go to Limbo, where they suffer the "pain of loss," but no "pain of sense." Theirs is a natural happiness, in other words. They enjoy everything except the beatific vision.

It's all very neat — except the word Limbo appears nowhere in the Scriptures and was never used by the Fathers of the church. Limbo, in sum, is a latter-day theological improvisation to preserve intact the teaching of the church concerning the absolute necessity of baptism for admission to heaven. There *had* to be a Limbo, for obviously innocent children who died in the birthing process or soon afterwards could not charitably be consigned to a hell's fire of eternal damnation — though St. Augustine was prepared to do so. It was Thomas Aquinas who "freed" those in Limbo from the "pain of sense," and that wasn't until the 1200s. Jansenists of the eighteenth century sought to return unbaptized infants to hell's fire, but Pius VI, the last pope to address the problem, defended not Limbo *per se* but the common teaching from slander.

In recent years, a more generous theology proposes substitutes for baptism to provide for infant salvation, like baptism of desire supplied by the parents or by the church in its role as the extension of Christ in the world. But, as the *New Catholic Encyclopedia* says, "The question of Limbo still belongs among the unsettled questions of theology."

# PURGATORY, A MATTER OF TRADITION

**SO WHAT ELSE** in our common code of belief might also have a Limbo aspect connected to it? How about Purgatory — that place or condition in the next world where the souls of the baptized who die in the state of grace, but not yet free from all imperfection, make expiation for unforgiven venial sins or for serious sins on which temporal punishment is yet due? Like Limbo, Purgatory is not explicitly mentioned in the Scriptures, though to be sure in both the Old and New Testaments there's more deductive evidence for a Purgatory than there is for a Limbo.

In the Old Testament only one passage is cited in support of a doctrine of Purgatory, but it's a strong one: 2 Maccabees 12:39-45. This is the passage in which Judas Maccabeus takes up a collection of 2,000 silver drachmas to be sent to Jerusalem for an expiatory offering for his soldiers slain in battle, "inasmuch as he had the resurrection of the dead in view." It would have been "useless and foolish to pray for them in death," Scripture adds, "if [Judas Maccabeus] were not expecting the fallen to rise again." His was "a holy and pious thought," an act of atonement, "that they might be freed from this sin."

Evidence for a place called Purgatory is more frequent in the New Testament, but once again the fact of a Purgatory is indirect. The word is not specifically stated. For instance, the word isn't mentioned in Matthew 12:32, considered one of the stronger textual references: "Whoever says anything against the Son of Man will be forgiven, but whoever says anything against the Holy Spirit will not be forgiven, *either in this world or the world to come*." Nor is it mentioned in Paul's prayer for Onesiphorus in 2 Timothy 1:18, as he petitions: "When [Onesiphorus] stands before the Lord on the great day, may the Lord grant him mercy!"....Again the conclusion of the *New Catholic Encyclopedia*: "In the final analysis, the Catholic doctrine on purgatory is based on tradition, not Sacred Scripture." Read on.»»»

# SO JUST WHAT IS PURGATORY?

**A NUMBER OF PRESUPPOSITIONS** contributed to the church's concept of a Purgatory, notably the teaching that there was a difference between grave (mortal) sin and minor (venial) sin. The former could be serious enough to involve the loss of soul and merit eternal damnation, but hardly the latter. There had to be a place after death where the souls of the just would be cleansed, purified, *purged* of any remains of sin so they could enter heaven. Hence, *Purgatory*. Several councils defended the principle of a purgatory, including Lyons I (1245), Lyons II (1274), Florence (1438-1445) and Trent (1545-1563). Interesting enough, Trent, which was so dogmatic across the range of Catholic belief, treaded softly when it came to Purgatory, out of concern no doubt about the horror stories so common at the time about the miseries and agonies of the place. Trent directed that priests omit from sermons difficult and subtle questions that savor of idle curiosity and superstition, that are scandalous and repulsive, and that would repel rather than edify the faithful. Applied to the subject at hand, it seemed a concession that even though the church was convinced that Purgatory existed, it didn't know what it was or the nature of the punishment meted out there.

Was the principal punishment of Purgatory deprivation of the beatific vision, and was there also some kind of positive physical punishment, like fire? And if there was real fire, what was there to purify or purge when the body was back on earth in the cold, cold ground, or ashes in an urn? Could real fire have an effect on one's soul, which was pure spirit? Theologians of the West had an answer; the soul in Purgatory, though separated from the body, remained in some way related to the material world, and thus liable to its elements. Eastern theologians reject the idea of suffering by fire; they speak of an intermediate state where the good experience foretastes of heaven and the less good some of the torments of hell. Purgatory, in sum, is a puzzle.

# APRIL 28

## HELL FIRE CLUBS OF OLD

**ON THIS DAY** in 1721 authorities in the British Isles sought to bring under control that "fraternity of free-living gentlemen" that profaned religion under the banner Hell Fire Clubs.

Hell Fire Club members were alleged to engage in "profane orgies" debunking religion, usually in odors of sulphurous smoke raised up to give their meetings an atmosphere of "infernal regions." Members adopted grisly nicknames like Old Dragon and King of Tartarus, and dubbed women associates with titles such as Lady Envy and Lady Gomorrah, and together they raised glasses to toasts so blasphemous that some were said to fall over dead after draining their drink. It was uncertain, it is written, whether those righteous deaths resulted from "supernatural intervention," from "the moral strain required for the act," or from "the sudden revulsion of spirits under the pain of remorse," but in any case dead the person was. One Hell Fire Club death was reported to have resulted from an accidental lancing during a mock reenactment of the Crucifixion.

The infamy of Hell Fire Club members was great and presumably followed them to their graves. People paying their last respects to deceased "H. F." members professed to detect in the waking room an unmistakable smell of brimstone, and they noted that horses displayed a decided reluctance to draw the hearses of the "H.F.-ers" to their burial places.

Hence, the order in council of April 28, 1721, denouncing Hell Fire Clubs and seeking their curb. A bill was soon introduced in the House of Peers, but guess what? It was killed, not because the exalted lords of Parliament wisely discounted tales about the clubs, but apparently because, sensitized by earlier persecutorial actions, they did not want to appear to be intolerant in matters religious.

Incidentally, the clubs were centered in London, but there was a notorious branch in Dublin. Something on it and its foiling tomorrow.

# A COUNTRY PRIEST BECOMES A BISHOP

**DUBLIN'S HELL FIRE CLUB WAS,** as said, especially notorious. But a country priest visiting the city announced boldly that he wouldn't be afraid to visit and dine there; in fact, he'd consider it his duty to do so, if asked.

Well, asked he was, and no doubt he enjoyed the specialty of the house — a concoction called *scaltheen.* This was a brew of whiskey and butter, savored in Ireland "before the days of Father Mathew," the famous preacher of temperance known more for his efforts than his results. The problem with *scaltheen* was that it was dastardly tricky to make. If burned too much, the drink was harsh rather than soft and creamy. But the "barkeeps" at Dublin Hell Fire Club had the process mastered, and members drank *scaltheen* with "pious bravado" by roaring fires.

In any case, here's our priest-friend in the Dublin Hell Fire Club. He said grace, despite "a torrent of execrations," but on seeing the club's cat fed first, the priest demurred. The carver explained that it was the custom to respect age, and he believed the cat to be the oldest creature present in the room. The priest said he belived so also, but objected that the cat was really not a cat at all but "an imp of darkness." The remark caused a furor, and instant death was pronounced on the seemingly hapless priest.

What to do? As a last request, the priest was allowed five minutes of prayer — to the annoyance of the wily old cat, which snarled and hissed in indignation. The cat knew, for that country priest was no oaf. Instead of a prayer for himself, the priest pronounced an exorcism, which caused the cat to be turned back into the demon it was, and to rocket away, blasting the roof off the Hell Fire clubhouse. That was the end of the "H.F.-ers" in Dublin. The club was dissolved on the priest's exhortations.

As for our hero clergyman, word circulated of his brave and sagacious deed. Such a deed could not go unrewarded, and wasn't. The country curate was given a bishopric.... The end.

# THE JEKYLL AND HYDE POPE?

**THE NINETEENTH-CENTURY** historian Leopold von Ranke wrote of Pope Pius V that he presented "a strange union of singleness of purpose, austerity and profound religious feeling with sour bigotry, relentless hatred and bloody persecution." It's a harsh judgment for one whom the church reveres as a saint — whose feast day is today, as a matter of fact. Unfortunately the shoe fits.

Pius V reigned from 1566 to 1572, but even after four centuries he touches modern lives in remarkably direct ways. His tomb in the Basilica of St. Mary Major is one of Rome's showpieces; the supplication "Help of Christians" in the Litany of Our Lady is his inspiration; so is the October 7 Marian feast, though he originally named it Our Lady of Victory, to commemorate the victory over the Turks at Lepanto on that day in 1571. Gregory XIII changed the name to the feast of the Most Holy Rosary....which made sense in a way. Pius V was reciting the rosary with fellow Dominicans when word reached Rome of the victory at Lepanto. Pius burst into tears of happiness at the news, for he correctly realized that the westward tide of Moslem Turks had been stemmed.

So much that the man did was historic. He introduced a new catechism and improved breviary and missal; instituted major reforms of the clergy; obliged bishops to live in their own dioceses; set new standards of piety and of charity for religious, publicly embracing lepers and visiting hospitals to sit at the bedside of the sick; banned animal baiting and bullfights (modified by later popes); and proved an implacable foe of nepotism. True, under great pressure he created a nephew a cardinal, but he allowed him no influence.

Nepotism was no newly acquired concern of Pius V. He fell afoul of his predecessor, Pius IV, when as a cardinal himself he offered what has been described as "insurmountable opposition" to Pius IV's attempt to make a cardinal of his thirteen-year-old nephew, Ferdinand de Medici. Pius V carefully scrutinized episcopal elections throughout his reign, and on one occasion blocked the canons of Halberstadt in northern Germany from electing as bishop a six-year-old relative of the Duke of Brunswick.

Unfortunately, Pius V never escaped his past. He was born Antony Ghislieri but took the name Michael when he entered the religious life at the age of fourteen. He rose in the clergy as an inquisitor of unbounded zeal, finally in 1557 being named Inquisitor General for all of Christendom. The term "Fra Michele dell' Inquisizione" became synonymous with terror. He was unsparing, and his election as pope constituted an enthronement of sorts of the Inquisition itself. As pope, Ghislieri established the Congregation of the Index to rout out heretical literature; he banished the prostitutes of Rome to a special section of the city, and in March 1569 expelled Jews from the Papal States, though for what is said to be "commercial reasons" they were allowed to remain "under humiliating conditions in Rome and Ancona." He excommunicated heads of state freely, including England's Elizabeth I, and lest anyone not understand where he was coming from he issued the bull *In coena Domini* reaffirming the supremacy of the Holy See over all civil power. When he died in 1572, the Sultan ordered three days of celebration and rejoicing. Pius V was beatified by Clement X in 1572 and canonized by Clement XI in 1712.

# MAY 1

## MARY'S MONTH AND AN OLD MARIAN PRAYER

**THIS IS THE MONTH** the church dedicates to Mary. Interestingly enough, those origins are Jesuitical and go back only to the latter part of the eighteenth century, when May Marian devotions were promoted at the Roman College of the Society of Jesus to counteract what was termed "infidelity and immorality among the students." From Rome, May devotions spread to other Jesuit colleges and thence throughout the Latin church. Suddenly this was a month for May altars and May processions, and special devotions to Mary. The rosary was a favorite prayer for May. So, too, was St. Bernard of Clairvaux's prayer, "Mary, Star of the Sea." Tastes change, thankfully, but this is the way St. Bernard's prayer went:

"O thou who findest thyself tossed by the tempests in the midst of the shoals of this world, turn not thine eyes from the Star of the Sea, if thou wouldst avoid shipwreck. If the winds of temptation blow, if tribulations rise up like rocks before thee, a look at the star, a sign to Mary, will be thy aid. If waves of pride, ambition, calumny, jealousy threaten to swallow thy soul, look toward the star, pray to Mary. If anger, avarice, or love of pleasure shiver thy frail vessel, seek the eyes of Mary. If horror of thy sins, trouble of conscience, dread of the judgments of God, commence to plunge thee into the gulf of sadness and abyss of despair, attach thy heart to Mary. In thy perils, thy anguish, thy doubts, think of Mary, call on Mary. Let the name of Mary be on thy lips and in thy heart; and in taking refuge with her in petition lose not sight of the example of her virtues. Following her thou canst not wander. While thou prayest to her, thou canst not be without hope. As long as thou thinkest of her, thou wilt be on the right path. Thou canst not fail while she sustains thee; thou hast nothing to fear while she protects thee. If she favor thy voyage thou shalt reach the port of safety without weariness."

# THE ORIGIN OF THE HAIL MARY

**BY FAR** the most familiar Marian prayer of all is the Hail Mary. It is prayed in a single burst of devotion, but it is really of three pieces:

*Hail Mary, full of grace, the Lord is with thee. Blessed art thou amongst women* — being the words of the Angel Gabriel in saluting Mary (Luke 1:28);

*And blessed is the fruit of thy womb [Jesus]* — being Elizabeth's divinely inspired greeting to her cousin Mary (Luke 1:42);

*Holy Mary, Mother of God, pray for us sinners now and at the hour of our death. Amen* — being an appendage of petition added by the church some time in the Middle Ages as the cult of Mary grew in intensity among Catholics.

As a prayer with set formula, there is actually no trace of the Hail Mary until about 1050, and even then the prayer took a variety of forms country to country. In fact, there is no record of the Hail Mary in present common formula until 1495, when with the omission of a single Latin word (the possessive *nostrae*) it appeared at the head of a work by the Dominican monk Girolamo Savonarola, and he, ironically, would be hanged as a heretic in 1498.

Incidentally, the seventh-century Spanish saint, Ildephonsus of Toledo, is said to have entered his church one night and there in the apse found Mary seated in his episcopal throne, surrounded by a choir of virgins singing her praises. Ildephonsus reputedly fell to his knees and approached Mary with a series of genuflections, repeating as he went, "Hail Mary, full of grace, the Lord is with thee. Blessed art thou amongst women, and blessed is the fruit of thy womb." Mary was so pleased, they say, that she rewarded Ildephonsus with the gift of a magnificently woven chasuble. The Ildephonsus story is outrageous rubbish, of course. But how did anything like that get started in the first place? Maybe in someone's pious zeal to situate the Hail Mary of final form as early as possible in church history, thus adding to its devotional character.

# MAY 3

## SAINT HELENA AND THE TRUE CROSS

**BEFORE THE REVISION** of the calendar to eliminate dubious or redundant feasts, today was marked as the feast of the Finding of the True Cross in 326 by the Empress Saint Helena, mother of Constantine. The feast marking the event had seemed from the beginning to be superfluous, for it had always been overshadowed by the older seventh-century feast of the Triumph of the True Cross, which retains its place in the calendar for September 14. Nonetheless, the Finding of the True Cross was ever an intriguing feast.

As mentioned, it was Helena who found it—along with the Holy Sepulchre, Golgotha, and such other incidentals as Christ's manger and the home at Bethany where Martha, Mary and their brother Lazarus lived. Her memoirs and the popular fascination with her discoveries helped establish the Christian tradition of pilgrimages to the Holy Land.

The True Cross has always ranked as the holiest of Christian relics, though there are those who believe that the relics are so numerous as to make its weight implausible. Some said there was enough wood there to build a ship.

On the other hand, there are those who argue that if all the relics of the True Cross were brought together, they would amount to but one-sixth of a cubic foot. One authority calculated that, presuming the cross were made of pine wood, it would have a volume of 178 million cubic millimeters, whereas the known portions of the True Cross amount to only 4 million cubic millimeters.

So take your choice. Are the relics real or are they false? One can believe either way about them. They're not articles of faith. One Holy Land relic of Helena's that surely is false is the INRI plaque ordered by Pilate for the top of the cross. It is preserved in Rome's Santa Croce Church, but, like the Shroud of Turin, is so esoteric that it can only be ascribed the product of a forger's art.

# WHEN POPES DIVIDED THE WORLD

**WITH THE DISCOVERY** of the New World by Christopher Columbus in 1492, the race was on between the two great exploring nations, Spain and Portugal, to broaden their spheres of influence. The church had a stake in the competition between these two countries, for there were souls out there beyond the Ocean Sea and therefore evangelization to be done. Popes were still then in a position to carve up the world, and as Catholic nations Spain and Portugal both applied to the pope for a confirmation of their rights.

In 1455 Pope Nicholas V had granted to Portugal the exclusive right of exploration and conquest on the road to the Indies, which translated to use of the route by the coast of Africa to the south and east via the Cape of Good Hope. Columbus' voyage of 1492, however, revealed other sea lanes of opportunity, so papal pronouncement was necessary to head off points of dispute. Thus it was that on this day in 1493 Pope Alexander VI drew a line north to south 100 leagues west of the Azores and Cape Verde Islands. Spain could claim all to the west; Portugal to the east. The terms were spelled out in the bull *Inter caetera divinae*, and Alexander brooked no nonsense. Anyone of whatever dignity, "imperial or royal," or of whatever "rank, status, order or condition," who intruded on these separate licenses for "trade or any other reason," incurred the penalty of excommunication *latae sententiae*; that is to say, automatically.

Portugal, it developed, protested the division. Obviously; it was getting little more than it already had. So the line was redrawn at a conference at Tordesillas in 1494, and moved 360 leagues west. The pope approved, and thus it was that Brazil came under Portuguese influence, while the rest of America and the West Indies was to be for Spanish trade and settlement. And that's the way it was — until folks like John Cabot and Henry Hudson got into the act.

# YESTERDAY'S PRAYERS

**ANOTHER DEVOTIONAL ARTIFACT** of the post-Vatican II era is the Litany of the Blessed Virgin Mary, once especially popular in the month of May. Sisters led parochial school children in its recital; priests added it to the prayers at the foot of the altar after Mass; families recited it in the home.

After opening salutations to God and the Trinity, accompanied by the pleas "Have mercy on us," the litany proceeded with forty-eight salutations to Mary under the following titles, each followed with the response, "Pray for us":

Holy Mary....Holy Mother of God; Holy virgin of virgins; Mother of Christ; Mother of divine grace; Mother most pure; Mother most chaste; Mother inviolate; Mother undefiled; Mother most amiable; Mother most admirable; Mother of good counsel; Mother of our creator; Mother of our savior; Virgin most prudent; Virgin most venerable; Virgin most renowned; Virgin most powerful; Virgin most merciful; Virgin most faithful; Mirror of justice; Seat of wisdom; Cause of our joy; Spiritual vessel; Vessel of honor; Singular vessel of devotion; Mystical rose; Tower of David; Tower of ivory; House of gold; Ark of the Covenant; Gate of heaven; Morning star; Health of the sick; Refuge of sinners; Comforter of the afflicted; Help of Christians; Queen of angels; Queen of patriarchs; Queen of prophets; Queen of apostles; Queen of martyrs; Queen of confessors; Queen of virgins; Queen of all saints; Queen conceived without original sin; Queen of the most holy rosary; Queen of peace.

The litany then invoked the "Lamb of God" and Mary the Mother of God before concluding with a prayer for health of soul and body, so that by "the glorious intercession of blessed Mary, ever a virgin, when freed from the sorrows of this present life, [we may] enter into that joy which hath no end."

Back when prayers were carefully indulgenced, the Litany of the Blessed Virgin Mary merited seven years; a plenary, if recited daily for a month.

# DID MARY DIE OR DID SHE NOT?

**SPEAKING OF MARY,** and this being Mary's month and all, a question: Did the Blessed Virgin *actually* die? That's no trivia question; for long it has been one of sober Marian theology. Throughout most of Christian history there have been those — "mortalists," so called — who have held that Mary in fact did die and that her assumption into heaven (which is not the issue here) occurred some time thereafter. On the other side, there were those — the "immortalists" — who contended that Mary never died, and that before what would have been actual temporal death something unusual happened....like Jesus himself descending and whisking Mary to heaven, body and soul together.

Theologians long wrestled with this question, but without resolution. Then, on November 1, 1950, Pius XII issued the apostolic constitution, *Munificentissimus Deus*, defining the dogma of Mary's assumption into heaven (q.v. Aug. 15). Presumably the answer would be here and the issue settled for all time.

It wasn't. When it came to the point of addressing the question of Mary's death, Pius became undogmatic. He used the phrase *expleto terrestris vitae cursu* — which supported neither the "moralists" nor the "immortalists" — and thus he left open whether Mary experienced death per se. Rather, Pius said that "Mary, having completed the course of her earthly life, was assumed body and soul into heavenly glory." Was she dead or alive? The pope didn't say.

Today most theologians are "moralists," holding that Mary died a physical death. But in the past opinion has been all over the lot. Epiphanius, a pre-Council of Ephesus (431) saint, speculated that Mary could have been immortal — but then again could have suffered martyrdom or experienced a natural death. Sts. Augustine, Ambrose and Jerome leaned to the popular belief that Mary died rather than being exempted from physical death, and so did Bonaventure in his day. But the door is yet still open....perhaps against some new revelation.

# MAY 7

## THE MAN WHOSE CHORALE WE TRIVIALIZE

**NEEDN'T ASK!** That body you hear turning in its grave each time you sing the recessional at Mass, "Joyful, Joyful, We Adore Thee," is Ludwig van Beethoven's. He has reason to be upset. The recessional's tempo is wrong; the singing is frightful. The music belongs to Beethoven's Symphony No. 9 in D Minor; it's the concluding chorale. Otto Klemperer and the Philharmonia Orchestra and Chorus had a right to handle it. The Boston Symphony does. But do parish choirs and people in the pews? We should be more respectful.

That co-opted "recessional" happens to be one of the most magnificent pieces of music ever created. It was performed for the first time on this day in 1824, at Vienna's Karntnertor Theater. The chorale is titled *An die freude,* "Ode to Joy." The ode was Schiller's of course, and it sang of a glorious brotherhood of creations, united under a common Father — "vast heaven, wide earth, and the joy that we shall feel in knowing that we have a place in the scheme of eternity," as the critic William Mann phrased it. Nothing so lofty about the recessional's lyrics; they were writen by Henry van Dyke, 1852-1933.

Paradoxically, the Ninth Symphony immortalized a man who never heard a note of it. By 1824 Beethoven (1770-1827) was stone deaf; had been since 1814. As for opening night, contralto Karolina Unger left behind this moving memory: "The master...heard nothing of it at all, and was not even sensible of the applause of the audience at the end of this great work but continued standing with his back to the audience and beating time till Fraulein Unger turned him, or induced him to turn and face the people who were still clapping their hands and giving way to the greatest demonstration of pleasure. He turned about, and the sudden conviction thereby forced on everybody that he had not done so before because he could not hear what was going on acted like an electric shock on all present, and a volanic explosion of sympathy and admiration followed."

"Joan of Arc before Orleans" (17th century engraving by Mariette)

# THE WOMAN WHO SAVED FRANCE

**JOAN OF ARC** grew up in the chaotic years of wars between France and England and the Burgundian alliance. Of course she proved to be France's savior, and this day in 1429 was a particularly significant one in her brilliant career. It was the day Joan raised the siege of Orleans and opened the road to Rheims for the crowning of the dauphin as King Charles VII.

Joan's story is familiar enough. She was the peasant girl of Arc who heard "voices" belonging to Sts. Michael, Margaret and Catherine urging her to seek out the dauphin and tell him she had been sent by God to lead his armies against the English occupation and save France from its national degradation. It was a preposterous suggestion, in retrospect, but Joan pulled it off. At seventeen she donned the armor of battle and led her soldiers to spectacular (some say miraculous) victories that loosened England's hold on France.

Her lot was an unhappy one, alas. On May 24, 1430, Joan was taken prisoner by the Burgundians during a skirmish at Compiegne. Sold to the English, she was brought to trial, and after a scandalously unfair proceeding was condemned as a relapsed heretic and sorceress. Joan was burned at the stake on May 30, 1431, at a spot within the shadow of Rouen Cathedral's Butter Tower hallowed to this day. Her ashes were cast into the Seine. Twenty-four years later Joan of Arc would be formally exonerated. Canonization would follow in 1920.

Today, as saint and warrior, Joan of Arc belongs largely to the age of nationalism, when wars could be fought spared worries of cosmic consequences. Still, she has a strong modern relevance, especially for women, as one who functioned in the world of men, daring even to wear her hair short and dress like a man. Strange as it might seem now, those were major points of prejudice against her, for the practices stirred sick notions about sexual orientation. Who said times haven't improved?

# GETTING TO KNOW THE HOLY SPIRIT BETTER

**IT IS SAID,** half-facetiously, half-seriously, that Catholics are close to being closet Unitarians — that they profess the Trinity in the Nicene Creed, that they bless themselves with the sign of the Trinity, but that they have limited real understanding of the Trinity. They know God the Father, of course, and God the Son, but God the Holy Spirit is a stranger. Charismatics appreciate this Third Person, but to the person in the pew the Holy Spirit may as well be....well, a ghost. Which, come to think of it, the Third Person was until the polishing of the vernacular, when "Holy Ghost" became "Holy Spirit."

This is no latter-day problem, which is no doubt why Leo XIII troubled to write an encyclical on the subject, *Divinum illud munus*. The document was issued on this day in 1897, and stands as a major papal explication of Catholic belief in the Trinity. Here's what Leo had to say therein of the Holy Spirit:

"...The Holy Spirit is the ultimate cause of all things, since, as the will and all other things finally rest in their end, so He, who is the divine goodness and the mutual love of the Father and the Son, completes and perfects, by His strong yet gentle power, the secret work of man's eternal salvation. 'In Him are all things,' *in Him* referring to the Holy Spirit.

"...[T]he Gospels thus speak of the Blessed Virgin: She was found with child of the Holy Spirit and that which is conceived in her is of the Holy Spirit. And this is rightly attributed to Him who is the Love of the Father and the Son, since this *great mystery of piety* proceeds from the infinite love of God towards man, as St. John tells us: 'God so loved the world as to give His only begotten Son.' Moreover, human nature was thereby elevated to a personal union with the Word; and this dignity is given, not on account of any merits, but entirely and absolutely through grace, and therefore, as it were, through the special gifts of the Holy Spirit."

# MAY 10

Matthew Ricci, S.J. (left) and mandarin convert.

## RICCI'S ILL-FATED OPENING TO THE EAST

**WHEN THE CHURCH'S** lost opportunities are pondered, among the largest invariably looms Father Matteo Ricci's mission to China. Ricci was the Italian Jesuit who entered China in 1582 and had astonishing impact as a scientist and, as priest, as one who adopted Chinese manners, customs and dress, and accepted as part of Catholic liturgical practice certain Chinese traditions and language. For instance, Ricci was tolerant about the honoring of ancestors and of Confucious, and had no problem in accepting such terms as *T'ien* for heaven and *Shang-ti* (Sovereign Lord) for God. Rome did have a problem, though, and in 1704 and 1715 Pope Clement XI rejected Ricci's opening to the East. Ricci was long dead by then, of course, having died at Peking (Beijing) May 10, 1610. But the implications of his life are with the church yet. Less Western precommitments and more tolerant Roman attitudes at the time toward the cultures of others could have changed religious history in the Far East.

Father Ricci was vindicated in 1939, when Rome at last allowed certain indigenous Chinese codes within the Catholic prescript by recognizing, for instance, the regard in which Confucius is held and by accepting the reverence which the Chinese have for their ancestors. But by then it was much too late to reshape evangelical history. China was long lost to Roman Catholicism.

Interestingly enough, Ricci's latter day rehabilitation in Rome has been accompanied by rehabilitation in China itself. Ricci's grave was seriously damaged by Red Guards during the Cultural Revolution of the 1960s. However, China's current communist government, perhaps more mindful of Ricci's service as astronomer to the Chinese imperial court at the end of the sixteenth century, saw to its restoration in 1984. A bigger surprise was the announcement in 1987 of Chinese plans for a Ricci monument at Zhaoqing (Shiu Hing, near Canton), where Ricci had his first mission, gained his first convert, and lived for six years.

# THE FLOWER THAT HONORS MARY

**IF YOU'RE SETTING OUT** a flower garden, it's safe by now to plant your marigolds. You'll be guaranteed a wonderful showy flower until frost hits in the fall. You'll also have a flower that serves practical as well as aesthetic purposes, for the marigold deters certain animals, like the rabbit, and fends off nematodes, microscopic plant pests that strike tender plants and shoots — which is why the marigold is commonly used as a border plant. The pot marigold was even used at one time as a medicinal poultice, being applied to wounds.

Why all the talk in a book like this about the marigold? Because the marigold is another everyday word in the vocabulary with a hidden or lost religious association. The word evokes Mary, the mother of Jesus. Marigold is nothing more than a simple compounding of the words "Mary's gold," just as Maryland, the state, results from a fusing of the words "Mary's land."

In the 1950s, Illinois' Senator Everett Dirksen pressed in Congress to have the marigold declared the national flower of the United States. There was no religious inspiration behind the attempt; Dirksen was not a Marianist, let alone a Catholic. He just liked the flower. His effort went nowhere, but it was a strange cause to undertake in the first place. The marigold isn't native to the United States, as one might expect a national flower to be.

The marigold species known in the United States are several, and have been grown in gardens of the land for some four hundred years. They originate, however, in the tropics of Mexico and Central America. Similarly, in Europe. The marigold flowers profusely there, but it was brought to the area by crusaders returning from the Middle East. They found the flower there, and were so captivated by its beauty and golden color that they named it for the Virgin; hence, Mary's gold. The flower would be bred into a number of colors, including red and orange, but it is still yellow that predominates and dazzles — Mary's gold.

# MAY 12

## THE POET WHO CHASTIZED THE EXALTED

**DANTE ALIGHIERI** lived in parlous times. Italy was bloodied by jealousies and passions between families and states, and Dante — a Florentine, the greatest of that land's poets — was in the thick of much of it, as warrior, politician and poet. Thrice he was condemned to be burned alive if he came into the power of the republic, and much of his life was lived in exile or on the run. It suited him. Dante's biggest scorn was for those "sorry souls who lived without infamy and without renown, displeasing to God and God's enemies."

Dante was born toward mid-May in 1265 in Florence (the exact day we don't know) and died in Ravenna in 1321. The quarrels and wars of the Italian peninsula distressed him, and with his pen he heaped scorn and vindictive on those he regarded as fosterers of problems that contributed to the fracturing of the peninsula. Dante spared not emperor, pope, king, poet, prince or warrior, consigning all he viewed jaundicely to the depths of the hell or a seven-storied purgatory he concocted in an epic he called his *Commedia.* He put Mohammed there too, condemning him to one of the lower circles of hell, split in two, for promoting schisms — an inclusion infuriating to present-day Moslem fundamentalists, who recently threatened to blow up Dante's tomb at Ravenna.

The epithet *divina*, incidentally, was not given to the work by Dante himself; in fact, the word did not appear on a title page until 1555. But *Divina Commedia*, "The Divine Comedy," it is today. The poem is written as a memorial to the Beatrice he loved as a child (he married someone else); he includes Beatrice in the feminist triumvirate in heaven (Mary and St. Lucy being the others) who commission Virgil to escort Dante to the netherworld.

There is an astonishing legacy of writings from Dante, but the *Commedia* is of course the classic. Curiously, in the sixteenth century Dante's reputation went into eclipse, and in the seventeenth and early eighteenth centuries his work was almost totally neglected. That's been repaired. Dante's fame is immortal.

# THE DAY THE POPE WAS SHOT

**IT WAS A BLESSEDLY BEAUTIFUL** 1981 spring day, and Pope John Paul II moved in an open car through St. Peter's Square, blessing the faithful lining the way. Suddenly shots rang out, and John Paul slumped into the arms of attendants with bullet wounds of the abdomen, right forearm and left hand. The car sped to Gemelli Hospital, two miles from the Vatican, where the pope underwent two and a half hours of surgery, including a colostomy made necessary by damage to the intestinal area. The pope recovered, of course, and even the colostomy was closed in time. But it had been a close call. John Paul attributed his survival to the Virgin Mary, none other. Certainly the date was auspicious; May 13 marked the first of her six appearances at Fatima in 1917.

The man who shot the pope was Mehmet Ali Agca, twenty-three, a convicted murderer who had escaped in 1979 from a maximum-security Turkish prison, where he was under sentence of death. The case against Agca enveloped alleged co-conspirators, and dragged on for five years in the courts. By trial's end, Agca was serving a life sentence, but charges against three Bulgarians and three Turks for complicity in the deed ultimately were dropped "for lack of proof," an Italian legal nicety which stopped short of full acquittal and implied that evidence existed to support both the guilt and the innocence of the defendants. Did a wide, even international conspiracy exist to kill the pope? Agca was the state's key witness in its effort to prove so, but his credibility eroded, and with it the state's case, as he experienced what came to be called religious deleriums. Several times Agca proclaimed himself Jesus Christ reincarnated.

Papal security has been beefed up since the 1981 shooting, but it should have come sooner. There had been a forewarning. In 1970 Paul VI narrowly escaped assassination when a man disguised as a priest rushed at him with a knife in Manila, and actually got within a few feet before being subdued.

# MAY 14

Michelangelo

## THE "DOME-ING" OF ST. PETER'S

**IN THE 1500s,** the Vatican was transforming itself under the aegis of several popes into an architectural wonder. This day in 1590 was Sixtus V's great moment of satisfaction, for that wonder of wonders, Michelangelo's dome of St. Peter's, stood completed for the admiration of people, believers and non-believers, for centuries to come. The basilica would not be entirely completed and ready for dedication by Urban VIII until November 18, 1626, but the project that Nicholas V began dreaming of in 1450 and that Julius II stirred to life with his election in 1503 was at last in its final stages.

Everyone had to be relieved, for the project seemed endless. Popes, architects and designers tumbled one upon another, and the project bogged down several times over controversy whether the design should be square-ish in the form of a Greek cross or, have the extended nave of a Latin cross. A Greek cross with a dome was favored by Michelangelo. He got his dome, strengthening the central piers of an earlier Bramante design so the basilica could carry its weight. However, Paul V revised other plans so that the basilica would form a Latin cross after all, with Baroque facade.

Michelangelo became chief architect of the project in 1548, on the death of Giuliano de Sangallo, and remained in charge until his death in 1564. He rejected most of Sangallo's ideas in favor of Bramante's coupled to his own genius. The result is a basilica of heroic proportions (it's length is 693.8 feet, longer than two football fields) and spectacular line, the particular showpiece of course being the dome. From basilica floor to the top of the cross at the dome's tip is a remarkable 434.7 feet.

Michelangelo did not live to see the dome completed, but his successor, Giacomo della Porter, was so faithful to his blueprints that it was as if Michelangelo were still clerk of the works.

# MAY 15

GEORGETOWN UNIVERSITY

## THE COUNTRY'S FIRST CATHOLIC COLLEGE

**ONE OF THE PROUDEST** institutional accomplishments of the church in the United States is its system of Catholic higher education — some 245 colleges and universities with an enrollment of more than a half million students. If this system has a birthday, it is today. For it was on May 15 in 1789 that under the initiative of Father (soon Bishop) John Carroll, a meeting of priests issued the prospectus outlining plans for an academy at "George Town, Patowmack River, Maryland," and asking public subscriptions of support.

"The object of the proposed institution," the prospectus declared, "is to unite the means of communicating Science with an effectual provision for guarding and preserving the Morals of Youth.... It will therefore receive Pupils as soon as they have learned the first Elements of Letters, and will conduct them through the several Branches of Classical Learning to that Stage of Education from which they may proceed with Advantage to the Study of higher Sciences in the University of this or those of the neighboring States. Thus it will be calculated for every Class of Citizens; — as Reading, Writing, Arithmetic, the earlier Branches of the Mathematics, and the Grammars of our native Tongue, will be attended to no less than the learned Languages."

Nor was the institution to be narrowly denominational. "Agreeably to the liberal Principal of our Constitution," said the prospectus, the institution was to be "open to Students of every religious profession."

Funding lagged, and it took three years to get the project off the ground. The doors of the institution finally opened in September, 1791, with William Gaston, a future associate justice of North Carolina's supreme court, as the first pupil. The name of this "furtive little academy," as the noted Catholic historian Monsignor John Tracy Ellis once called it, is spelled differently from the 1789 prospectus, but everyone knows it: Georgetown University.

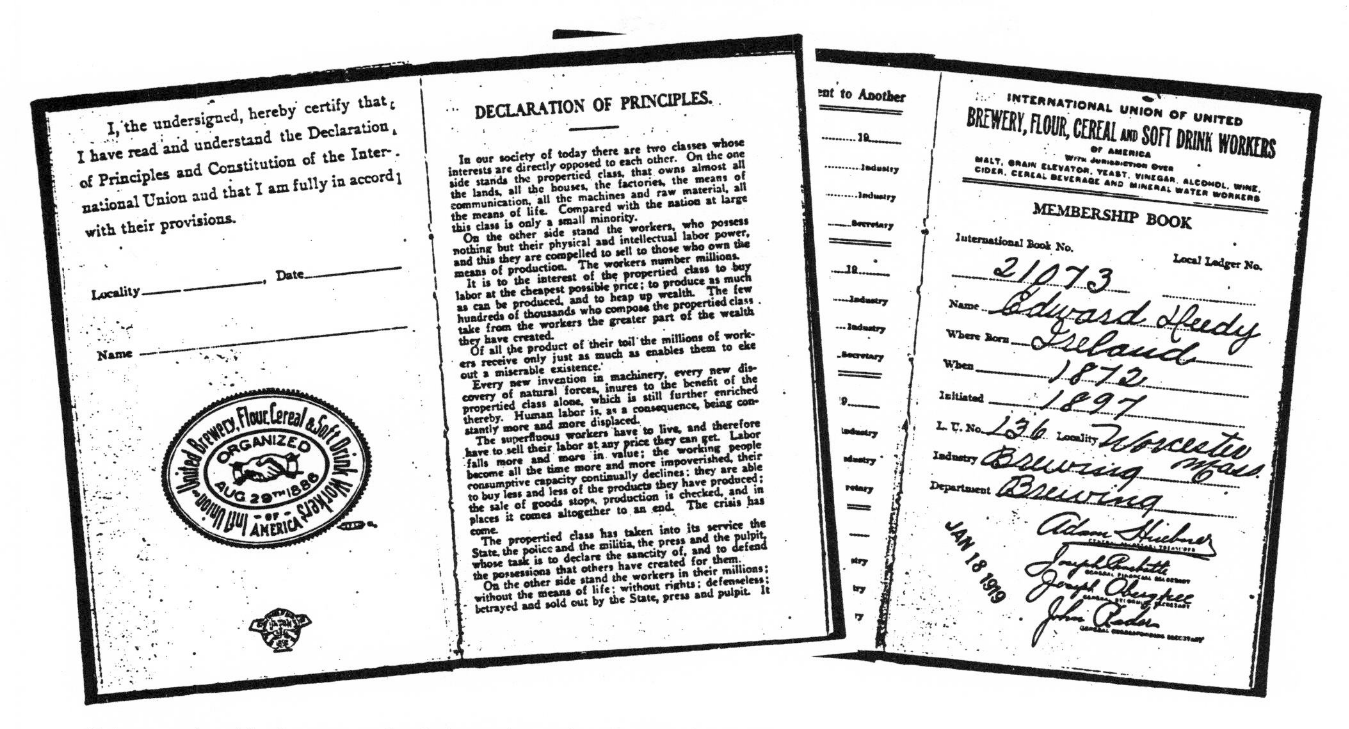

I, the undersigned, hereby certify that I have read and understand the Declaration of Principles and Constitution of the International Union and that I am fully in accord with their provisions.

Locality__________, Date__________

Name__________

United Brewery, Flour, Cereal & Soft Drink Workers
Int'l Union of America
Organized Aug 29th 1886

DECLARATION OF PRINCIPLES.

In our society of today there are two classes whose interests are directly opposed to each other. On the one side stands the propertied class, that owns almost all the lands, all the houses, the factories, the means of communication, all the machines and raw material, all the means of life. Compared with the nation at large this class is only a small minority.

On the other side stand the workers, who possess nothing but their physical and intellectual labor power, and this they are compelled to sell to those who own the means of production. The workers number millions.

It is to the interest of the propertied class to buy labor at the cheapest possible price; to produce as much as can be produced, and to heap up wealth. The few hundreds of thousands who compose the propertied class take from the workers the greater part of the wealth they have created.

Of all the product of their toil the millions of workers receive only just as much as enables them to eke out a miserable existence.

Every new invention in machinery, every new discovery of natural forces, inures to the benefit of the propertied class alone, which is still further enriched thereby. Human labor is, as a consequence, being constantly more and more displaced.

The superfluous workers have to live, and therefore have to sell their labor at any price they can get. Labor falls more and more in value; the working people become all the time more and more impoverished, their consumptive capacity continually declines: they are able to buy less and less of the products they have produced; the sale of goods stops, production is checked, and in places it comes altogether to an end. The crisis has come.

The propertied class has taken into its service the State, the police and the militia, the press and the pulpit, whose task is to declare the sanctity of, and to defend the possessions that others have created for them.

On the other side stand the workers in their millions; without the means of life; without rights; defenseless; betrayed and sold out by the State, press and pulpit. It

ent to Another
19
Industry
Industry
Secretary
19
Industry
Industry
Secretary

INTERNATIONAL UNION OF UNITED
BREWERY, FLOUR, CEREAL AND SOFT DRINK WORKERS
OF AMERICA
WITH JURISDICTION OVER
MALT, GRAIN ELEVATOR, YEAST, VINEGAR, ALCOHOL, WINE, CIDER, CEREAL BEVERAGE AND MINERAL WATER WORKERS

MEMBERSHIP BOOK

International Book No. 21073
Local Ledger No.
Name Edward Heedy
Where Born Ireland
When 1872
Initiated 1897
L. U. No. 136 Locality Worcester Mass.
Industry Brewing
Department Brewing

JAN 18 1919

Union membership documents that belonged to author's paternal grandfather.

# LEO XIII'S CONTRIBUTION TO ECONOMIC ORDER

**POPE LEO XIII** had to be satisfied this day in 1891. Leo was an inveterate writer of encyclicals; he wrote eighty-eight in all. But the encyclical issued the day before was especially pertinent historically, and Leo must have known so. He had brought the church to grips at last with major concerns of the proletariat of Europe and America by acknowledging the legitimacy of their grievances over poor wages and working conditions, and joining the church's voice in a call for justice and equality in the work place. Above all, Leo wrote, the working person had a right to organize labor unions. The encyclical was *Rerum novarum* ("Of new things"), cornerstone of Catholic social teaching.

It is hard to appreciate now the impact of Leo's comments. Today most of his recommendations are part and parcel of standard labor-management relations, but in the context of the times what Leo said smacked of the revolutionary. For lines were hardening at the end of the nineteenth century. Society was rapidly dividing in Europe and America between the haves and the have-nots, and class warfare was more than some wild possibility, as history was to prove. To the extent that it was heeded, *Rerum novarum* helped ease much social pressure.

Leo wrote unequivocally in defense of the worker, "whom the present age has handed over, each alone and defenseless, to the inhumanity of employers and the unbridled greed of competitors." His key recommendation: "Let it be taken for granted that workman and employer should, as a rule, make free agreements, and in particular should agree freely as to wages; nevertheless, there is a dictate of natural justice more imperious and ancient than any bargain between man and man, that remuneration should be sufficient to maintain the wage-earner in reasonable and frugal comfort. If through necessity or fear of a worse evil the workman accept harder conditions because an employer or contractor will afford no better, he is made the victim of force and injustice."

Pius XI

# PIUS XI ON BEHALF OF THE PROLETARIAT

**IN 1931, ON THE FORTIETH** anniversary of *Rerum novarum*, Pope Pius XI commemorated Leo's great encyclical on the reconstruction of the social order with a labor encyclical of his own no less historic, *Quadragesimo anno* ("In the fortieth year"). Pius attacked big business, stock-market speculation, socialism, communism, and the Fascist corporate state, which he said "risks serving political aims rather than contributing to the initiation of a better social order." The thrust of the encyclical was outlined a few days earlier in a radio address, an English translation of which was read to the world by a young American priest then resident in Rome, Francis J. Spellman. Pius XI speaking:

"In the past there has been, beyond question, an excessive and unjust disproportion of the commodities of life between capital and labor, for on the one hand immense riches are accumulated in the hands of a few, while on the other the proletariat, who form a multitude beyond all counting, have nothing of their own save their hands and the sweat of their brow.

"It is therefore absolutely necessary to reconstruct the whole economic system by bringing it back to the requirements of social justice so as to insure a more equitable distribution of the united proceeds of capital and labor.

"The differences in social conditions in the human family, which were wisely decreed by the Creator, must not and cannot ever be abolished, but on the other hand the condition of the proletariat worker cannot forever be the normal condition of the bulk of mankind. It is essential that the proletariat be enabled gradually to obtain some of the advantages enjoyed by proprietors.

"In the present order this can be accomplished only by a fair and just wage. Wages, therefore, must be such as really to satisfy the legitimate requirements of an honest workingman, not only for his person, but also for his family, and to make it possible for him to improve his condition...."

# CONCERN FOR WOMEN IN THE WORK FORCE

**IN 1981, FOR THE NINETIETH** anniversary of *Rerum novarum* and the fiftieth of *Quadragesimo anno*, Pope John Paul II readied a companion encyclical to update the church's social concerns. The result was *Laborem exercens* ("On human work"). Issuance was planned for May 15, the actual anniversary date of its historic predecessors, but the assassination attempt on John Paul (q.v. May 13) forced a delay. *Laborem exercens* thus did not appear until September. It was the third encyclical of John Paul's reign and thus far it is his most memorable.

Echoing Leo XIII and Pius XI, John Paul II termed labor unions "an indispensable element" of modern industrialized society and a vehicle "for the struggle for social justice," but then he took the church's social thought beyond earlier encyclicals by including women workers in the thought equation. Women who work, he said, must be provided "suitable working conditions," and "should be able to fulfill their tasks in accordance with their own nature without being discriminated against and without being excluded from jobs for which they are capable." He added that respect was due "for their family aspirations and for their specific role in contributing, together with men, to the good of society."

But John Paul II was not sounding a rallying cry for women to join the work force. A "family wage" was needed, he argued, a sufficient single salary paid the head of the family so that the other spouse, presumably the wife, does not have to take up gainful employment outside the home. In similar context, the pope urged "measures such as family allowances or grants" so that mothers can be able to devote themselves exclusively to their families.

The encyclical also broke new ground in addressing issues of health care, handicapped workers, unemployment benefits, foreign work pools and modern technology, which he said should be the worker's ally, not boss and enslaver.

John Paul II in 1988 moved social/labor discussions to a new and in some ways loftier international plain with an even more controversial social encyclical, entitled *Sollicitudo rei socialis*, "The Social Concerns of the Church." The encyclical charged that rivalry between the world's superpowers was subjecting the Third World nations to imperialistic "structures of sin" that deny them freedom and economic development, and it held accountable for this both "liberal capitalism and Marxist collectivism," though not specifying any nations by name. It was hardly any secret, however, about whom he was talking. The encyclical attributed to nations of those two ideological blocs "an unacceptably exaggerated concern for security, which deadens the impulse toward united cooperation for all the common good," and it appealed for a turn away from the competition between East and West to solidarity and interdependence, said to be necessary for the elimination of social inequities between rich and poor nations. Among correctives recommended were a reworking of the international trade system, revision of international debt structures, new forms of technology transfer, and "review and possible correction" of the operating methods of international organizations.

With *Sollicitudo rei socialis*, the church widened the lens on a watch Leo XIII began in 1891. Now it was international survival.

# MAY 19

## YESTERDAY'S PRAYERS

**THE THIRTEENTH CENTURY** produced a wealth of hymns and prayers, few more popular in their time than *Stabat Mater*, a poetic chant of such vivid spiritual and lyrical character as to stir the talents of composers of the stature of Palestrina, Pergolesi, Hadyn, Ramondi and Rossini. *Stabat Mater* has been ascribed to Sts. Gregory the Great, Bernard of Clairvaux and Bonaventure, among others, but chances are that the Franciscan Jacopone da Todi (1220-1306) is the true author.

It was commonly chanted during the Stations of the Cross devotion, and it provided the sequence in the old Latin Mass for the feast of the Seven Dolors (Sorrows) of the Blessed Virgin. *Stabat Mater* divided conveniently into three parts, and thus provided the office hymns at vespers, matins and lauds on the feast. The vespers section with the title words opens:

*Stabat Mater dolorosa*
Next the cross in tears unceasing

*Juxta crucem lacrymosa*
Worn by sorrow aye increasing

*Dum pendebat Filius.*
Stood the Mother 'neath her Son.

*Stabat Mater* continues with a lengthy, prayerful recapitulation in triplets of the emotions that had to be Mary's at Calvary. The poetry is charged in power, and becomes even more gripping in effective combination with solemn music. The German poet Johann Tieck, for instance, said that on hearing Giovanni Pergolesi's *Stabat* he "had to turn away to hide my tears," especially when the music combined with the words:

*Vidit suum dulcem natum*
She beheld her dear Begotten

*Moriendo desolatum*
Stretched in death by all forgotten

*Dum emisit spiritum*
As on hoisted rood He hang.

# HAWTHORNE'S OBLIQUE GIFT TO THE CHURCH

**NATHANIEL HAWTHORNE** harbored many jaundices. He hated Salem. He didn't particularly like Lincoln either, and at a low ebb for Union forces during the Civil War wrote an abrasive article for the *Atlantic Monthly* which characterized an "Uncle Abe" of coarse physiognomy and sly instincts pursuing a goal better abandoned. The Lincoln allusions were tactfully edited out of the article, though preserved and made public after Hawthorne's death. As it was, the article caused stir enough, arguing as it did that the only reason for fighting the Civil War was so that the North could determine "where our diseased members shall be lop't off." Hawthorne considered the United States too vast and multicultural. Indeed, he would have been perfectly content for his native New England to go it alone as a separate nation.

Something else Hawthorne was also jaundiced about — Catholicism. He spent two years in Italy after his service as U.S. consul at Liverpool, and much of what he saw didn't like. He managed a magnanimity when his daughter Una leaned towards Anglicanism, but it was probably as well he wasn't alive when his youngest daughter Rose converted to Catholicism. To Hawthorne, Catholicism was that "old, corrupted faith" peopled by "torpid recluses" closed off in monasteries and convents. Rose Hawthorne was thirteen when her father died. By a twist of fate, she would become one of those "recluses" her father scorned.

Rose Hawthorne was born in this day in 1851 — "a child of spring," her brother Julian would one day write, "and spring never vanished from her nature." She too was a writer, though a far more modest one than her father. Still her work appeared in the leading magazines of the day — *Harper's Bazaar*, *St. Nicholas* and *Scribners*, among others — and she did write a book or two, including one on the Georgetown Visitation Convent in collaboration with her husband, George Parsons Lathrop. Her marriage was disastrous, but paradoxically it led her to a noble life's mission. Read on.»»»

# ROSE HAWTHORNE LATHROP

**GEORGE PARSONS LATHROP** was one of the promising young talents of the day — an assistant editor of the *Atlantic Monthly*, supervisor of an edition of his father-in-law's collected works, and Hawthorne's first biographer. His was the inside track, but Lathrop proved an uninspired, pedestrian writer. He also developed into a lush, and after a series of separations and reconciliations, Rose Hawthorne Lathrop, who had converted to Catholicism in 1891 at age forty, turned to the church for counseling. From one priest-counselor she learned of a young seamstress who was being sent to Blackwell's Island to die of cancer, Blackwell's being the old name for Welfare Island in the East River. Touched by the woman's plight, Rose Hawthorne Lathrop resolved to devote her life to indigent people dying from inoperable cancer. She trained for three months at New York Cancer Hospital, then began her own apostolate on the Lower East Side.

Rose Hawthorne Lathrop worked in the slums — on Scammel Street, Water Street, Cherry Street — and this woman of genteel background was at first terrified of the people among whom she placed herself. But she reassured herself, telling herself, "Well, my dear, you have set out to love everybody and to make everybody love each other. Of course, you can do very little, and you are as stupid as you can be. But the moment we set ourselves free from selfishness and sloth, everybody is refreshed. It works wonders — just as though God had brushed you aside and said, 'I am here.'"

Rose Hawthorne Lathrop's apostolate was to spawn St. Rose's Free Home in lower Manhattan; then a religious order, the Dominican Congregation of St. Rose of Lima, incorporated as the Servants of Relief for Incurable Cancer; then a large center in Westchester County, north of White Plains, known at Rosary Hill — where cancer victims were to be considered "guests," not "patients." As a religious of the order she helped found, Rose became Mother Alphonsa. She died in 1926 at age seventy-seven. Her work continues to this day.

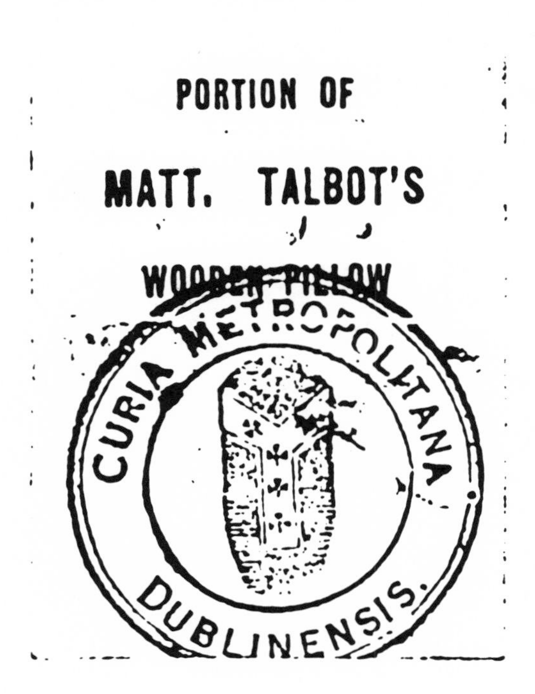


## DUBLIN'S INSPIRATION FOR ALCOHOLICS

**A REFLEX OF THE CHURCH** is to raise up exemplars for any and all problem situations of a human kind. One such exemplar belongs to this day — Matt Talbot, the so-called "saint in overalls," who is held up in some quarters as a model for recovering alcoholics. Matt Talbot died this day in Dublin in 1925, after turning a life of drunkenness into one of great holiness.

Matt Talbot was born in Dublin in 1856, and worked on its docks. But first he was a messenger for wine merchants, and the easy access to alcohol proved more than he could handle. By twenty-five he was in the gutter, a hopeless alcoholic, shunned by all. With neither a farthing for drink nor a friend to stand a round, Talbot sobered and returned to the sacraments. He took the pledge, but doubting his ability to keep it, pledged for only three months. Successful for that time, he took the pledge for a year, then a lifetime. He never relapsed. Meanwhile, he developed a reputation for sanctity, though no one knew immediately the degree of that holiness. It was a common sight to see Matt Talbot kneeling mornings on the church steps, waiting for the first Mass to begin, or to see him returning to church to attend a second Sunday Mass. In fact, when he died, it was on the street as he was hurrying to a second Mass of a Trinity Sunday. Stripped at the morgue, chains were found imbedded in his flesh; Talbot had bound his body in chains as a follower of Louis-Marie de Montfort, the eighteenth-century French saint of poverty and humiliations.

The secrets of Matt Talbot's life came speedily to light. He slept but three and a half hours a night, rising at 2 a.m. to pray before attending Mass at 6 a.m. He slept on two rough planks and his pillow was of wood. He fasted; his noon meal was a slice of dry bread and a cup of cold tea, and he took no meat nine months of the year. Hailed for holiness, Matt Talbot's cause was opened in 1931. In 1947 the apostolic process began, and continues now.

# BELGIAN JESUIT AMONG AMERICAN INDIANS

**THE CHURCH'S MISSION** to the native American has never been a particularly vibrant one, but certain names have stood out, none greater than that of the Jesuit Pierre-Jean De Smet. De Smet roamed the West when it was truly the wilds, and by the time of his death in St. Louis, he had been a friend of President Lincoln and a confidant of generals and highest government commissioners. De Smet's fame was in his standing among Indians. From Council Bluffs, Iowa, to Astoria, Oregon, he was their trusted friend and counsellor.

Pierre-Jean De Smet came to this country from Belgium, and joined the Jesuits at Whitemarsh, Maryland. Poor health forced his return to Belgium, but four years later he was back in the United States and again with the Jesuits. In 1838 he went on his first assignment among the Indians, founding a mission at Council Bluffs among the Potawatomi. Subsequently he worked among the Sioux and the Blackfeet Indians, and established numerous mission stations in the Rocky Mountains region. He wrote extensively of his adventures, and his writings won large audiences in this country and Europe, making him one of the best known priests of his day. He pleaded Indian causes in Europe and Washington, and at Washington's request he was present as a pacificator at the 1851 conference in Horse Creek Valley near Fort Laramie aimed at easing tensions over the white influx into California and Oregon. In 1858 he went along as chaplain on General William Harney's expedition against the Mormons, the so-called Mormon War, and he helped Harney on various other campaigns. He refused, however, to lend his support in 1862 to an expedition against the Sioux at the start of the Civil War, after learning it was to be punitive in nature. In 1868 he acted as counsellor to Sitting Bull in peace negotiations with Washington. It is said no one else would have been acceptable to the Sioux chieftain. Decorated and lionized, Father De Smet died on this day in 1867.

# MAY 24

## WINNING FRIENDS AND INFLUENCING PEOPLE

**THIS WAS THE DAY** in 1844 that Samuel F.B. Morse tapped out his famous message in dits and dahs, "What hath God wrought?" It was the birth of the Morse alphabet, the Morse Code and the modern electrical telegraph (though judging from court suits others had been onto the idea earlier). But, wait, Morse was more than a dabbler in electronics. He was also an artist, and a good one — and the epitome of the nineteenth-century bigot. He was convinced that "all America west of the Alleghenies will eventually be a Catholic country," and that prospect he did not like. What got the idea into his head?

Robert Leckie offers a theory in his 1970 book *American and Catholic*. According to Leckie, Morse was in Rome in 1830, a Holy Year, not out of religious ideals but as an artist to study Catholic art. One day, Leckie writes, Morse stood watching a papal procession, when, quoting Morse, "in an instant, without the slightest notice, my hat was struck off to the distance of several yards by a soldier, or rather by a poltroon in a soldier's uniform, and this courteous manoeuver was performed with the gun and bayonet, accompanied with curses and taunts and the expression of a demon on his countenance." Why? Samuel F.B. Morse had neglected to uncover his head as the pope passed.

Small offenses can have curious consequences, and this was one of them. The incident made Morse, in Leckie's words, "a bitter enemy of Catholicism." Morse's Roman visit confirmed suspicions of a plot, which Morse codified in 1834 in a series of twelve letters entitled *A Foreign Conspiracy Against the Liberties of the United States*. So well received were they that Morse produced another series elaborating Rome's evil designs, exclaiming: "Up! Up! I beseech you. Awake! To your posts! Let the tocsin sound from Maine to Louisiana. Fly to protect the vulnerable places of your Constitution and Laws. Place your guards; you will need them, and quickly too. — And first, shut your gates."

# THE OTHER "POPE" JOHN XXIII

**IT IS NOT COMMONLY KNOWN,** but there were actually two John XXIIIs. The one of our mid-century everyone remembers. The earlier one the church would just as soon forget. He was the antipope of the Pisa party who claimed the papacy for five years. He was consecrated and crowned pope on this day in 1410, having been ordained priest the day before. It meant that there were now three "popes" simultaneously running the church, or parts thereof — Gregory XII, in Rome; Benedict XIII, the Avignon claimant; and of course John XXIII.

This John was no prize. History's judgment is that he was "utterly worldly minded, ambitious, crafty, unscrupulous, and immoral, a good soldier but no churchman." His formal name was Baldassare Cossa, and he entered the service of the church after a career as a soldier. A Neapolitan, he rose to the rank of cardinal and, deserting Gregory XII in 1408, he helped organize the Council of Pisa, which elected the antipope Alexander V. When Alexander died eleven months later, Cossa succeeded, taking the name John XXIII.

When the possibility loomed of yet another pope being elected, which would have raised the number of claimants to four, the Emperor Sigismund forced the calling of the Council of Constance (1414-1418) to bring order to the church. Sensing the precariousness of his position, John XXIII fled Constance with the intention of revoking the council's convocation and starting a countermovement of his own. However, he was caught, arrested, tried on charges of simony, corruption and maladministration, and deposed as pope. That was May 29, 1415.

All was not lost, however. After two and a half years of custody, Cossa was released, and the new pope, Martin V, named him Cardinal-Bishop of Tusculum. He died a few months later and was buried in the baptistery of the cathedral at Florence. With him the name John disappeared from papal registers until it was rehabilitated by the Good Pope John in 1958, over 500 years later.

# HOW ABOUT A TWO-HOUR MASS?

**THIS IS THE FEAST OF ST. PHILIP NERI,** 1515-1595, a Florentine who lived most of his life in Rome, and with such sanctity as to become known as the Apostle of Rome. Rome was a loose and dissolute city in Philip Neri's time, but he did not withdraw from it nor condemn it. He scarcely even criticized it, choosing instead to combat sin and mischief by promoting the counter-attractions of holiness, purity, truth and gaiety — above all gaiety. More on that tomorrow, but today St. Philip Neri....

As a priest, he advocated frequent confession and communion, but there was nothing of the zealot in him, at least in his dealings with others. Once, when an earnest penitent asked Philip Neri for permission to wear a hair shirt, Philip Neri responded, "Certainly, provided you wear it *outside* your clothes." For him the sacrament of confession (reconciliation, now) was as good for the psyche as it was for the soul.

Yet, though zealot he may not have been with others, he was with himself. In later years, he would say Mass in a private chapel, according to the custom of the time. The only one in attendance would be the server, and just before the communion of the Mass, the server would withdraw in order to leave Philip Neri alone in devotion with the Lord, consecrated in the sacred species. For two hours or more, Philip Neri would remain in meditation before the server was recalled and the Mass brought to a close.

At one point in his life, Philip Neri thought of joining Francis Xavier (q.v. March 4), the Jesuit, in his mission to the Indies. But a priest-counselor advised otherwise, telling him, "Your Indies are in Rome." So Philip Neri stayed put. Sixty of his eighty years would therefore be lived in Rome. By coincidence, when he was canonized in 1622, who should be raised to the honors of the altar at the same ceremony? Francis Xavier.

# THE ORIGINS OF ORATORIO

**BELIEVING THE IDLE BRAIN** to be the devil's workshop, Philip Neri opened his room to the boys and young men of Rome as a place to congregate for talk and song and laughter — prayer too, and an occasional discourse on the Gospels. The room came to be known as "the home of Christian mirth," and when it proved too small to hold the crowds being attracted, the scene shifted to a larger space, which Philip and his friends called "the Oratory." Thus came to be born the name for the musical composition known as the oratorio, and thus came to be born also the name of the order called Congregation of the Oratory.

An oratorio, quite simply, is the name associated with a form of religious music with chorus, solo voices and instruments, performed independent of or at least separate from the liturgy. The form began in connection with activities promoted by Philip Neri as part of his apostolate to the young adults of Rome, and was soon a feature of the run-down church in central Rome that Gregory XIII gave to Philip Neri as a headquarters for his work.

That church was to attract not only music lovers, but also other priests — admirers of Philip Neri. They became known as priests of the Oratory, and were to form a separate clerical order, the Congregation of the Oratory. Neri's rule for membership stipulated that members were to live as secular priests without any further vows than those of ordination; they were to be bound together by mutual love and common purpose; and they were to be concerned mainly with prayer, preaching and the sacraments. The first individual house of the order, the Roman Oratory, was established in 1575 in the church conveyed to Philip by Gregory. It remains the most famous of all oratories, although a close second may be one founded years later — Birmingham, 1848 —by the man who has been the Oratory's most illustrious enrollee, Cardinal John Henry Newman (q.v. Oct. 9, 10).

# MAY 28

## THE FLOWERS THAT BLOOM IN THE SPRING....

**APRIL SHOWERS HAVE BROUGHT** the flowers that bloom in the spring, tra la. What kind of flowers did Jesus walk among in the Holy Land? Those who know the area think it must have been a veritable paradise, for the Holy Land in spring is a sea of flowers, notably yellow flowers of the chrysanthemum family. It is curious, though. Whereas the Bible has considerable to say about fruits and vegetables of the area (q.v. Sept. 15-17), it has remarkably little to say about its flowers. Hundreds of species of flora, plant life, are found in the Holy Land, and nearly one hundred are specifically mentioned in the Bible. But only a relatively few of them are flowers. Matthew (6:28) and Luke (12:27) tell in their Gospels of the familiar "lilies of the field," and the rose of Sharon and the saffron, a type of crocus, are cited in the Song of Solomon (2:1 and 4:14, respectively). But it is more common to speak generally of flowers, as when the flowers of spring are rhapsodied as again in the Song of Solomon: "For, lo, the winter is past, the rain is over and gone; the flowers appear on earth; the time of the singing of birds is come, and the voice of the turtle is heard in our land" (2:11-12).

So what flowers are mentioned? Well, there's the oleander, rose, narcissus, mallow and colchicum. But more common are the references to the blossoming flowers of vines, plants and shrubs, and of fruit and nut trees, such as the almond, olive, pomegranate, lotus, henna, flax and fig — which clues to the likelihood that it was the blossom of dietary and utilitarian value rather than one of mere show, however beautiful, that was appreciated more and thus worthy of special note.

Flowers are mere literary props in the Scripture texts. They are the reminders of the God who put them there, and symbols of larger realities, like the transitory nature of human life. It's something to remember now as tulips break ground and lilacs send forth their wonderful fragrance.

# MAY 29

## A MAN WHO DIED BEFORE HIS TIME

**ON THIS DAY IN 1913** the person who would become the first Catholic president of the United States, John Fitzgerald Kennedy, was born in Brookline, Massachusetts. Going on three decades since his assassination in Dallas on that fateful day of November 22, 1963, the name "Jack" Kennedy is invoked with a reverence accorded no other slain American national hero, except perhaps Abraham Lincoln. The reasons are perhaps less those of accomplishment, or of character, than they are of youth and of vision. John Fitzgerald Kennedy, elected president at age forty-three and president from 1960-1963, symbolized the nation's break with the past; he opened the country to new frontiers — though in truth he did not live long enough to dot the i's and cross the t's on the core programs of his initiation, civil rights and a denuclearized world.

John Kennedy was the son of a wealthy financier who was also ambassador to Great Britain from 1937-1940. He was the grandson of a Boston mayor, John F. "Honey Fitz" Fitzgerald; Harvard educated; World War II combat veteran; congressman, senator, Pulitzer Prize winner (*Profiles in Courage*, 1956); husband of one of the most glamorous women of the age (Jacqueline Bouvier); and father of a son and daughter. He was, in sum, a character out of mythology.

"Jack" Kennedy was only forty-six when he died. He was shot by a curious drifter named Lee Harvey Oswald, who while in police custody was shot in turn by an equally curious local character named Jack Ruby. The bizarre sequence of events feeds theories to this day that a broad political conspiracy was at work to eliminate John Kennedy and snuff the light that for one brief shining moment was Camelot. A presidential commission dismissed the conspiracy theory, but there are still those who believe yet that "outsiders" were behind things, specifically communists.... But then there were those who long believed that Lincoln's assassination was a Catholic conspiracy. The big C again.

# MAY 30

## THE SECULAR EQUIVALENT OF ALL SOULS DAY

**THIS IS MEMORIAL DAY,** the nation's secular equivalent of sorts to the church's All Souls Day. It is the day when cemeteries are visited, graves are marked with flowers and flags, knees are bent and heads lowered in prayers.

It has a curious history, this day. Its origins are in a Southern custom of women going to cemeteries in early spring and strewing the graves of loved ones with the first flowers of the season. The day took on military overtones in 1868, when General John A. Logan, commander in chief of the Grand Army of the Republic, issued an order designating May 30 as the day for commemorating the dead of the Civil War. Though not so intended, the day took on a decidedly Northern focus, and was long primarily observed in Northern states. Because the day's principal activity was the decoration of soldiers' graves, May 30 became known as Decoration Day. It was much later — after Civil War feelings had waned, and the emphases of the day themselves had changed — that May 30 became known as Memorial Day and took on a distinctly national character.

Since the shifting of most national holidays to Monday in the interests of longer weekends, Memorial Day may or may not now be observed on May 30. But there is the holiday, and veterans' organizations bestir themselves, planting small flags at the graves of the dead of all wars, not just the Civil, and conducting memorial services in cemeteries, often after parades that become thinner and harder to sustain by the year.

For time has blurred the initial purposes of the day. The war dead are remembered yet, but more and more Memorial Day has become one for remembering all the dead, not just those who were military. Accordingly, cemeteries are crowded today with people visiting the graves of the near and dear who have gone ahead — parents, children, friends. It's a felicitous change.

# THE MAGNIFICENT MAGNIFICAT

**THIS IS THE FEAST** of the Visitation of the Blessed Virgin Mary to her older cousin Elizabeth, after the annunciation to Mary that she was to be the mother of God. The event, detailed by Luke (1:39-56), is a familiar one.

When Elizabeth, pregnant also, heard Mary's salutation, the baby lept in her womb and, filled with the Holy Spirit, the words rushed from Elizabeth's lips, "Blessed art thou amongst women, and blessed is the fruit of thy womb." They are the very words of the Hail Mary, of course.

Mary's response is the Canticle of Mary, known as the Magnificat:

"My soul doth magnify the Lord, and my spirit rejoices in God, my Savior; because he has regarded the lowliness of his hand-maid; for, behold, henceforth all generations shall call me blessed; because he who is mighty has done great things for me, and holy is his name; and his mercy is from generation to generation on those who fear him. He has shown might with his arm, he has scattered the proud in the conceit of their heart. He has put down the mighty from their thrones, and he has exalted the lowly. He has filled the hungry with good things, and the rich he has sent away empty. He has given help to Israel, his servant, mindful of his mercy — even as he spoke to our fathers — to Abraham and to his posterity forever."

The prayer is one of the most beautiful in the Scriptures, and traditionally is said at vespers or evensong as part of the canonical hours (q.v. Nov. 26). Composers such as Palestrina, Suriano, di Lasso, Gabrieli and Cesar Franck set the prayer — Mary's song, Mary's canticle — to music. More than fifty settings by di Lasso alone could be found in the Royal Library at Munich, and he was said to have actually composed twice as many more.

Apart from its intrinsic beauty, the prayer has a special place in Catholic ecclesiology for the manner in which it bridges the Old Testament and the New.

# JUNE 1

## MONTH OF A MOST MACABRE DEVOTION

**IN 1863, POPE PIUS IX** declared this month dedicated to devotion to the Sacred Heart. The devotion, which hardly exists today, grew out of a Middle Ages fascination with the twin natures of Christ, the human and divine. The devotion took shape over several centuries, and was rooted in the belief in patristic times that the wound of Christ's side and the blood flowing therefrom during the Crucifixion were a source or stream of unending grace. Basically, the devotion celebrated God's redemptive love through the humanity of Jesus, and the heart then as now being the central human organ of life, it became the symbol through which the humanity of Jesus was to be most exactly expressed, the heart commending itself as the battery of life and avenue of salvation.

In the thirteenth and fourteenth centuries, devotion to the Sacred Heart enjoyed enormous popularity. It went into a decline in the seventeenth century, then was rejuvenated when word spread of apparitions to the Visitation nun Sister Margaret Mary Alacoque (q.v. June 2), directing her to foster devotions to the Sacred Heart. And so it came to pass that by the twentieth century, devotion to the Sacred Heart of Jesus was one of the most popular in the Western church. In time, excesses outstripped piety. The devotion came under fire for being sentimental and macabre, and many worshippers were turned off by artistic representations of the Sacred Heart that were to rival those of horror movies in another age. The fleshy heart, girdled by thorns, dripping blood, shooting flames, crowned with cross, was much too graphic for many of subdued piety.

A special feast of the Sacred Heart was duly proclaimed by Pius IX, and renewed by Leo XIII. The devotion, meanwhile, was placed in the hands of the Jesuits, who promoted it under the organizational name of the Apostleship of Prayer. Tens of thousands of Catholic families "enthroned" the Sacred Heart in their houses, but that enthronement custom is virtually unknown today.

# THE SACRED HEART'S "CONFIDANT"

**SISTER MARGARET** Mary Alacoque, the great proponent of devotion to the Sacred Heart, lived from 1647-1690. She was born in the Charolais district of Burgundy, France, and at age fourteen privately vowed to the Blessed Virgin to become "one of her daughters," if cured from a debilitating illness that for four years had left her virtually immobile. In that very instant she is said to have been cured. In 1671 she entered the Visitation order, and during a retreat before her profession experienced a vision from Our Lord, who said, "Behold the wound in my side, wherein thou art to make thine actual abode, now and forever." That presaged four visions in which Christ by her words revealed his Sacred Heart, uttering on one occasion, "My divine heart is so inflamed with love for men, and for thee in particular, that being unable any longer to contain within itself the flames of its burning charity, it must spread them abroad by any means." Christ was to clarify this; during another vision he recommended, among other new devotions, that of the nine First Fridays.

Henri Gheon, the French hagiographer, wrote that Sister Margaret Mary Alacoque bore on her breast "the name of her Saviour which she had cut there with a knife; and in her side was that pain which came to agony on each first Friday of the month." In fact, wrote Gheon, "they had to bleed her, such was the burning pressure of blood with her."

Many of Sister Margaret Mary's co-religious thought her deranged, and she suffered "tribulations at their hands." A Jesuit, Pere Claude la Colombiere, quieted matters when he confirmed Sister Margaret Mary's ecstacies and directed her to commit all her visions to writing, but there were still "stout souls" in the convent who did not buy the package. Sister Margaret Mary was to prevail, however. She was made mistress of novices, and the devotion she espoused was blooming before at age forty-three she herself died "in an ardent transport of love."

# JUNE 3

## THE SACRED HEART AND JUDGMENTAL PIETY

**CATHOLIC FASCINATION WITH** the Sacred Heart of Jesus may belong largely to the past, but it was long enduring. As recently as 1956 an encyclical, Pius XII's *Haurietis aquas*, was devoted to devotion to the Sacred Heart. The last of the truly great papal enthusiasts though was Pius XI. He not only published a Sacred Heart encyclical, *Miserentissimus Redemptor*, 1928, but three years earlier called for the annual consecration of the human race to the Sacred Heart on the feast of Christ the King. The text of that act of consecration conveys the tone and judgmental nature of yesterday's "piety":

"Most sweet Jesus, Redeemer of the human race, look down upon us, humbly prostrate before thy altar. We are thine and thine we wish to be; but to be more surely united with thee, behold each one of us freely consecrates himself (sic) today to thy most Sacred Heart. Many, indeed, have never known thee; many, too, despising thy precepts, have rejected thee. Have mercy on them all, most merciful Jesus, and draw them to thy Sacred Heart. Be thou king, O Lord, not only of the faithful who have never abandoned thee, but also of the prodigal children who have abandoned thee; grant that they may quickly return to their Father's house, lest they die of wretchedness and hunger. Be thou king of all those who are involved in the darkness of idolatry or of Islamism, and refuse not to draw them all into the light and kingdom of God. Turn thine eyes of mercy toward the children of that race, once thy chosen people. Of old they called down upon themselves the blood of the Savior; may it now descend upon them a layer of redemption and of life. Grant, O Lord, to thy church assurance of freedom and immunity from harm; give peace and order to all nations, and to make the earth resound from pole to pole with one cry: Praise to the divine Heart that wrought our salvation; to it be glory and honor forever. Amen."

MARIE PAULINE JARICOT
prima die

# PAULINE JARICOT'S MISSION OF LOVE

**CALL IT SERENDIPITY,** call it divine providence, but one person's devotion to the Sacred Heart helped bring about an organization that serves the church proudly still: the Society for the Propagation of the Faith (not to be confused with the old Vatican congregation of that name; q.v. June 28). The Society for the Propagation of the Faith grew out of the intuition of a young French woman, Pauline Jaricot, who at age seventeen took a vow of perpetual virginity and established a union of prayer among pious servant girls to "repair" the sins of neglect and ingratitude committed against the Sacred Heart of Jesus. Pauline Jaricot's enlistees were known as Reparatrices du Sacre-Coeur de Jesus-Christ, and through them she began collecting funds for the foreign missions, out of which grew her Society for the Propagation of the Faith. The society gained canonical status in 1822, and diocesan units today exist worldwide.

Pauline Jaricot's society was based in Lyons, her birthplace, and became so well known (and affluent) that its French name, *de Propaganda Fide*, would often be translated to that of the Roman congregation. The society's generosity was soon legend and, interesting enough, the country that today is one of its greatest benefactors was early on its greatest beneficiary: the United States. In 1822 the society sent the American church its first donation, $4,582, and over the next ten years it received 42 percent of its entire allocations.

In 1922, the society would be transferred from Lyons to Rome and placed under the governance of the Vatican congregation of same name. Paradoxically, the American church would be instrumental in the transfer. Over the years, bishops of several countries, the U.S. especially, had grown displeased by French monopoly over the distribution of the society's funds, and campaigned for a transfer. Actually, the change was to prove beneficial, for it gave the society wider scope and aspect. Pauline Jaricot no doubt approves it all.

# JUNE 5

## THE CHURCH'S BABYLONIAN CAPTIVITY

**THIS DAY PROVED FATEFUL** for church history for a period of almost seven decades. It was the day in 1305 that Clement V, a Frenchman, was elected pope — a fateful day, for four years later Clement moved the papal court from Rome to Avignon, on the Rhone in southeast France. So began the sixty-eight-year-period known as the Avignon Papacy or, more sinisterly, the Babylonian Captivity.

Theoretically, Avignon was politically independent, but for all practical purposes, the region was squarely within French orbits of influence. Clement was but the first of seven successive French popes who would be virtually totally subservient to King Philip IV of France. Furthermore, banks and commercial houses moved to Avignon, and concomitantly the machinery of church government passed largely into French hands. Nothing illustrated more graphically the magnitude of the new French influence than the recomposition of the College of Cardinals. Of the 134 cardinals created between 1305 and 1377, 113 were French.

For the church it was a dangerous interlude. The autonomy of the Papal States and the temporal authority of the pope in Italy began to meet challenges, and throughout the then known world people began to regard the church less as a universal institution than a national one. Conditions helped spawn election of an antipope, Nicholas V, in 1328, and that complicated matters further.

Urban V, sixth in the line of French popes, began the movement to return the papacy to Rome, but it was his successor, Gregory XI, who got the job done. Two women were influential in the return to Rome — St. Catherine of Siena, who chastized Gregory for neglecting his duties as bishop of Rome; and St. Bridget of Sweden, whose ominous prophecies about Urban's longevity sobered Gregory into hieing himself to Rome, lest he too die prematurely.

The pope returned to Rome January 17, 1377, and they've been there since.

# JUNE 6

## APOCALYPSE AND THE SIGN OF THE BEAST

**FROM TIME IMMEMORIAL,** the use of numbers as signs and symbols of cosmic significance has been common. Ancient civilizations read meaning into numbers, and used numbers as messages or portents. So have interpreters of the Scriptures. By applied analyses of exegetes, the number 1, for instance, is associated with uniqueness, God's; 3 with totality (a person thrice blessed has blessings overflowing); 7 with completeness (the duration of a week); 12 with wholeness and the perfection of order (the twelve tribes of Israel, the twelve Apostles, the twelve gates of the new Jerusalem in the Apocalypse), etc.

This is the sixth day of the sixth month. With one more six one would have the most cryptic and most charged number in all of Scripture — 666, the number that is the sign of the beast in Apocalypse 13:18: "Here is wisdom. Let him that hath understanding count the number of the beast: for it is the number of a man; and his number is six hundred threescore and six."

The number 666 is accepted as the sign of the antichrist, but who is the man alluded to by John, writer of the Apocalypse? Many biblical exegetes, applying numerical values of the Hebrew and Greek alphabets to discover a name whose total numerical value would equal 666, have come up with the name Nero Caesar. Others, less friendly to Roman Catholicism and the papacy be it said, have proposed that the antichrist is the pope. The papal-antichrist theory developed between the eleventh and sixteenth centuries, and was propagated mainly by the Albigenses, Waldenses and Fraticelli, heretical sects all. It was effectively refuted by St. Robert Bellarmine and Cardinal John Newman, but the canard was used effectively in England by John Wyclif and in Bohemia by John Hus. Newman argued that since Christ himself was called Beelzebub, the church must expect similar reproach. Thus, by his logic, the papal-antichrist theory was less insult than further proof of the Catholic Church's true character.

# GUIDELINES FOR RECEIVING COMMUNION

**NO MONTH OF THE YEAR** is more popular as a time for marrying than June. Why shouldn't it be thus? No month is so innocent as June, as Emily Dickinson said; no month has days more perfectly rare, to paraphrase James Russell Lowell. So couples proceed to the altar in numbers that dwarf those for other months.

Whether they come as principals or guests, this means an influx into Catholic churches for marriage ceremonies of many who are not Catholic, as well as many who are Catholic but have been away from the regular practice of their religion. When the marriage ceremony they are attending is connected to the liturgy of the Mass, the question inevitably comes up, at communion-time who is free to receive?

That is a question that of course can arise on other occasions, such as a funeral Mass or an ecumenical service. But what's the answer?

The Committee on the Liturgy of the National Conference of Catholic Bishops in 1986 published a set of guidelines governing such situations, and applying to Catholics and others. Those for Catholics follow here; those for others are reproduced under tomorrow's date.

*For Catholics*:

"Catholics fully participate in the celebration of the Eucharist when they receive Holy Communion in fulfillment of Christ's command to eat His Body and drink His blood. In order to be properly disposed to receive Communion, communicants should not be conscious of grave sin, have fasted for an hour, and seek to live in charity and love with their neighbors. Persons conscious of grave sin must first be reconciled with God and the Church through the sacrament of Penance. A frequent reception of the sacrament of Penance is encouraged for all."

# GUIDELINES FOR NON-CATHOLICS

**CONTINUING YESTERDAY'S ENTRY,** there follow here the communion-reception guidelines of the liturgy committee of the National Conference of Catholic Bishops for people other than Catholics. The guidelines are taken from a liturgical missalette provided in the pews of American Catholic churches, which accounts for the manner of address and the presumption that the guidelines are being read after arrival in the Catholic church building.

*For Other Christians*:

"We welcome to this celebration of the Eucharist those Christians who are not fully united to us. It is a consequence of the sad divisions in Christianity that we cannot extend to them a general invitation to receive Communion. Catholics believe that the Eucharist is an action of the celebrating community signifying a oneness in faith, life, and worship of the community. Reception of the Eucharist by Christians not fully united with us would imply a oneness which does not yet exist, and for which we must all pray."

*For Those Not Receiving Communion*:

"Those not receiving sacramental Communion are encouraged to express in their hearts a prayerful desire for unity with the Lord Jesus and with one another."

*For Non-Christians*:

"We also welcome to this celebration those who do not share our faith in Jesus. While we cannot extend to them an invitation to receive Communion, we do invite them to be united with us in prayer."

# JUNE 9

## THE MEANING OF CHRISTIAN LOVE

**THESE DAYS MARRYING COUPLES** select the readings themselves for their wedding Mass. A particular favorite is the section from St. Paul's first letter to the Corinthians outlining the meaning of Christian love (1 Corinthians 12:31, 13:1-13). In old versions, the word love is commonly rendered as charity, but the new usage fits current contexts better. This unquestionably is one of the Bible's most beautiful passages:

Set your hearts on the greater things.

I will show unto you a more excellent way. Though I speak with the tongues of men and of angels, and have not love, I am become as sounding brass or a tinkling cymbal. And though I have the gift of prophecy, and understand all mysteries, and all knowledge; and though I have all faith, so that I could move mountains, yet do not have love, I am nothing. And though I bestow all my goods to feed the poor, and though I give my body to be burned, and have not love, it profits me nothing.

Love is patient, love is kind; love does not envy, is not pretentious, is not puffed up, is not self-seeking, is not provoked; thinks no evil, rejoices not in iniquity, but rejoices with the truth; bears all things, believes all things, hopes in all things, endures all things.

Love never fails, whereas prophecies will disappear, and tongues will cease, and knowledge will be destroyed. For we know in part and we prophesy in part. But when that which is perfect has come, that which is imperfect shall be done away with. When I was a child, I spoke as a child, I felt as a child, I thought as a child. But when I became a man, I put away the things of a child. For now we see through a glass, darkly; but then face to face. Now I know in part; but then I shall know even as I have been known. So there abide faith, hope and love, these three. And the greatest of these is love.

# JUNE 10

## SOLVING THE MYSTERY OF THE MISSISSIPPI

**PERE JACQUES MARQUETTE,** Jesuit, was an enormous celebrity in his day as missionary and explorer, and re-discoverer with Louis Joliet of the mighty Mississippi. Marquette was born in Laon in northern France on this day in 1637. He entered the Society of Jesus at age seventeen, and in 1666, when most Jesuit missionaries were being sent to the Far East, he drew Canada — perhaps because of his great facility with languages and the notorious difficulty which Indian dialects presented. He became fluent in six of them.

At the time there were extravagant tales of a great waterway that cut across North America, but no one had any idea where it went. The early Spanish explorers spied a wide river that emptied into the Gulf of Mexico and called it the Rio del Spiritu Santo, but was this the same waterway? The French mounted an expedition with Louis Joliet as commander. Marquette was the inevitable clerical presence for the converting of natives.

Marquette and Joliet navigated the northern shore of Lake Michigan, Green Bay and the Fox River, crossed Lake Winnebago, and portaged to the Wisconsin. They then canoed to the headwaters of the waterway that was their goal.

Although uncertain of where it would lead, Marquette doubted that the river emptied into the Gulf of California, thus supplying European adventurers that long hoped for passage to the East, or that it lead to the Chesapeake Bay, another fairly common theory. He believed that the river flowed due south into the Gulf of Mexico, and when he reached a latitude of 33 degrees 40 minutes, he was certain. He was at a point below the present Memphis and realized from known latitudes for the Gulf of Mexico that it was only two or three days away. Assured, the party turned home. But tragedy struck, which would give chief honors to Marquette. Joliet's canoe capsized and he lost all his records; Marquette's survived as the trip's official document. Marquette, however, would not enjoy his fame for long. He contacted dysentery and died in 1675. He was only thirty-eight.

# THE SEVENTEENTH APOSTLE

**ON THE CHURCH'S CALENDAR** this is the feast of St. Barnabas, Apostle. But wait. The Synoptic Gospels of Matthew, Mark and Luke don't list Barnabas among the Twelve. They list Peter, Andrew, James the Greater, John, Philip, Bartholomew, Thomas, Matthew, James the Less, Jude, Simon and Judas Iscariot. No Barnabas there.

Right. But remember there were more than twelve Apostles. Twelve is only the common count. The real number is more like seventeen. There were the twelve summoned by Christ and given authority to expel unclean spirits and cure sickness and disease of all kind, the twelve listed above (Matthew 10:2-4, Mark 3:16-19, Luke 6:13-16). Then there were five more: Paul, Luke, Mark, Matthias and Barnabas.

Paul ranked as an Apostle by special call of Christ.

Luke and Mark were closely associated with the apostolic college, and of course were two of the four evangelists, or writers of the gospel. (Matthew and John were the other two.) They rank as Apostles by virtue of their intimacy with the others.

Matthias was elected an Apostle to replace Judas Iscariot, after Judas' betrayal of Christ. He was chosen by lots over Joseph, also known as Barsabbas.

Finally, there was the Apostle the church honors today, Barnabas.

A Levite of Cypriot origin, Barnabas is the person cited in the Acts of the Apostles (4:36-37), who sold his farm and laid the money at the Apostles' feet to support their mission. He was first named Joseph, but was given the name Barnabas by those he encouraged, his new name meaning, not coincidentally, "son of encouragement." Barnabas labored in the lands at the eastern end of the Mediterranean Sea, and ranks as an Apostle because of his close collaboration with Paul, notably at Antioch and Jerusalem. Tradition has it that he suffered a martyr's death, by stoning, on the Island of Cyprus.

# JUNE 12

## THE RECOMMITMENT TO CLERICAL CELIBACY

**THIS DAY IN 1984,** Pope John Paul II began a four-day visit to Switzerland. Papal tours abroad have become so frequent as to blend into one another, in message and importance. But John Paul's trip to Switzerland is one set apart, for it was on this visit that at an assembly of priests he personally addressed the issue of celibacy head-on. Change in the church's celibacy laws has been one of the continuing agitations of post-Vatican II times. John Paul II let it be known on the fourth day of his visit that priests should expect no change during his papacy. "Celibacy is not simply a juridical addition to the sacrament of orders," he said. "It is a commitment of the person, taken in full maturity, to Christ and the church." It's solid. "Dispensations, even if they are possible, must not be allowed to suppress, diminish, or threaten with oblivion the character of this commitment."

In so speaking, John Paul II echoed, nay complemented Paul VI, who in his 1967 encyclical *Sacerdotalis celibatus*, pointedly admonished those probing the church's celibacy discipline, telling them, "They had better things to do."

The modern church's commitment to clerical celibacy is unqualified (*except* for "raids" on Anglican communions). *Except, too,* it wasn't that way in the beginning. A married, non-celibate clergy was once common in the church. Not only were some of the Apostles married, but Peter is said even to have taken his wife on his missionary journeys. This is not to suggest that clerical celibacy was not an early ideal; it was. It is only to say that clerical celibacy did not become a mandate in Western Catholicism (it's still possible in the East) until the eleventh century, when Leo IX and Gregory VII exerted their reforms. Even then the considerations were not exclusively personal, sexual sanctity. The overriding consideration was simony. Priests and bishops were playing loose with church properties, generously bequeathing them to heirs.

# JUNE 13

## SAINTED RETRIEVER OF LOST OBJECTS

**THIS IS ST. ANTHONY OF PADUA'S** feast day. He helped make the thirteenth what people of faith refer to as the greatest of centuries. He was a native of Portugal, who joined the Canons Regular of St. Augustine at age sixteen. But it was in Italy that he made his reputation, and in Padua most specifically. His fame came as a confessor, convert-maker and preacher. When he was scheduled to preach, shops shuttered-up, courts closed, markets suspended business, and everyone flocked to hear. He preached outdoors, as no mere cathedral could hold the throngs, estimated to have been as large as 30,000. (He must have had one powerful set of lungs to have been heard.) Hagiography says he once held the Christ Child, and the pose has been his representation in popular religious art since the seventeenth century.

But most Catholics of a given age remember St. Anthony as the patron of those seeking lost objects, and devotional books encouraged the practice of invoking him for the recovery of lost items with this prayer:

"O blessed St. Anthony, the grace of God has made you a powerful advocate in all our needs, and the patron for the restoring of things lost or stolen. I turn to you today with childlike love and deep confidence.

"You are the counsellor of the erring, the comforter of the troubled, the healer of the sick, the refuge of the fallen. You have helped countless children of God to find the things they have lost — material things, and, more importantly (sic), the things of the spirit, faith and hope, and love.

"I come to you with confidence. Help me in my present need. I recommend what I have lost to your care, in the hope that God will restore it to me if it is his holy will. Amen."

For those without prayerbooks handy, there was a shorthand version: "Anthony, Anthony, look around. Something's lost and can't be found."

# JUNE 14

G. K. Chesterton and Hilaire Belloc (Painting by James Gunn)

## THE MAN WHO COULD MOVE MOUNTAINS

**WHEN GILBERT KEITH CHESTERTON** was conducting a class in Dante at Milbrook Junior College in California during a visit to America, a student who had lost her place exclaimed: "Where in hell are we?" The class roared. Chesterton warmed to the ejaculation. "I rather like that phrase," he responded, "Good Catholic expression. A Catholic doesn't live in Milbrook or in England, but *sub specie aeternitatis*, and the question always is, where in hell are we, or where in heaven are we, or where in purgatory are we. We live in that spaceless, timeless commonwealth and the question is very important."

The response was a measure of the depth of Chesterton's faith. He was born in 1872, and became a Catholic in 1922. Observers wondered why it had taken so long, so Catholic were his beliefs and writings. Still there were skeptics. "This is going too far," said George Bernard Shaw, who regarded the conversion as something of a stunt. But then Chesterton and Shaw were forever needling one another. Once on meeting in a restaurant the huge, 350-pound Chesterton remarked to the tall, string-like Shaw, "To look at you, people would think there was a famine in England," to which Shaw rejoined, "And to look at you, they would think you were the cause of it." Chesterton once said that if he were ever going to hang himself, he'd use Shaw as a rope. He was a great wit.

Chesterton was also one of the great controversialists of his age, and jousted with everyone in sight, including Wells and Kipling. He formed a team with Hilaire Belloc, and like Belloc was militant in defense of the Catholic Church. As to why he became a Catholic, Chesterton said simply: "To get rid of my sins." As a writer he was extraordinarily prolific, producing essays, biographies, novels, criticism, poetry — even a series of Father Brown detective stories, his priest-detective being modeled on the Father John O'Connor who received him as a Catholic. Chesterton died on this day in 1936.

# THE MISSIONIZING OF OREGON

**THE UNITED STATES** and Great Britain signed the Oregon Treaty on this day in 1846, establishing the 49th parallel as the boundary between the U.S. and British Northwest territories. With the treaty, Idaho, Oregon, Washington and part of Montana became undisputed U.S. territory. Still the agreement represented a substantial compromise by the U.S. The U.S. had claimed to the 40th parallel — up to what was Russian territory then, Alaska now.

One of the immediate results of the treaty was to stimulate migration to the American northwest. Arriving with the first waves of settlers were missionaries of the Oblates of Mary Immaculate. In 1849 one of them, Father Eugene Casimir Chirouse, wrote of life at Holy Cross mission, Simkone:"...At this moment savages from nearly all the neighboring nations are assembled at Holy Cross. I count 60 cabins in my village, around 100 families. There I have *Yellow-Serpent* [chief of the Yakima tribe] with his following as an opponent. He himself presides at all the abominations which are spoken or committed in his infernal den. An old trickster does his best to help him to embarrass me: irritated because my instructions are contrary to his maxims and diabolical acts, he has invented this strange calumny in order that I might be put to death: 'The Blackrobe,' he says, 'catches rattlesnakes, and makes them vomit a black poison with which he poisons the tobacco with the intention of killing everyone.' That is the reason I no longer give tobacco to anyone... [Thus] the men are furious against the old calumniator. I am afraid of only one thing, that is that they will hang him at the first opportunity.

"In spite of all the shafts of the enemy, I have only thanks to render to the Lord and to congratulate myself on the numerous blessings which he has bestowed on my feeble efforts. In the space of a month or two I have been able to baptize over 30 children and seven adults...."

# THE "OUR FATHER" AND HENRY VIII

**THE LORD'S PRAYER,** the "Our Father," is the most universal of prayers. How many of them are there? One, you say. How about two? There's one according to Luke (11:2-4), and another according to Matthew (6:9-13).

First, Luke's: "Father, may thy name be hallowed; may thy kingdom come; our bread for the morrow give us day by day; and forgive us our sins, for we also forgive all who are indebted to us. And lead us not into temptation."

Now, Matthew's: "Our Father in heaven, hallowed be your name, your kingdom come, your will be done on earth as it is in heaven. Give us today our daily bread, and forgive us the wrong we have done, as we forgive those who have wronged us. Subject us not to trial, but deliver us from the evil one."

But, you say, this isn't the Our Father we learned as tots: "Our Father, who art in heaven, hallowed by thy name; thy kingdom come; thy will be done, on earth as it is in heaven. Give us this day out daily bread, and forgive us our trespasses as we forgive those who trespass against us. And lead us not into temptation, but deliver us from evil."

Where does that Our Father come from? No, not the Douay or Rheims Bible. It comes from the version imposed on England during the reign of Henry VIII, when Henry was making his break with Rome and Anglicizing the liturgy. The prayer hitherto had always been said in Latin, even by the uneducated, and was known as the *Pater Noster* from its opening words. Anyway, with Henry VIII the *Pater Noster* became the Our Father, and went into the Book of Common Prayer in 1549 and 1552. The prayer passed into Roman Catholicism with only slight modifications, like "who art" for "which art" and "on earth" for "in earth." Incidentally, the doxology, "For thine is the kingdom, power and glory, etc.," came later to the Book of Common Prayer, then after Vatican II to Catholic liturgy, but separated, it will be noticed, by a short prayer from the Our Father itself.

# JUNE 17

## Twenty-third Psalm

*The Lord is my shepherd; I shall not want.*

*He maketh me to lie down in green pastures: he leadeth me beside the still waters.*

*He restoreth my soul: he leadeth me in the paths of righteousness for his name's sake.*

*Yea, though I walk through the valley of the shadow of death, I will fear no evil; for thou art with me; thy rod and thy staff they comfort me.*

*Thou preparest a table before me in the presence of mine enemies: thou anointest my head with oil; my cup runneth over.*

*Surely goodness and mercy shall follow me all the days of my life; and I will dwell in the house of the Lord for ever.*

## A PSALM OF DAVID

**THE LORD'S PRAYER,** the Our Father, may be the most efficacious of prayers, being the prayer that Christ himself recommended. But for sheer beauty, what is there to compare with the Twenty-third Psalm, a psalm of David? The majesty of the psalm is in its paeans, but the beauty is helped by the rendering, most notably that of the King James Bible (above).

Compare that version with what one hears in liturgical services in Catholic churches:"In verdant (yuk!) pastures he gives me respose"...."Beside restful waters he leads me"...."Even though I walk in the dark valley I fear no evil"...."You spread the table before me in the sight of my foes"...."And I shall dwell in the house of the Lord for years to come." The translation smacks of change for change's sake; it is no improvement at all.

# JUNE 18

## IS A CLERICALISM OF THE LAITY FORMING?

**THIS WAS THE DAY** in 1967 that Pope Paul VI promulgated *Sacrum Diaconatus Ordinem,* the document restoring the office of permanent deacon in the Roman Rite. The action implemented a recommendation of Vatican II, and greatly heightened the visibility of the lay person in the church's new liturgical life. With lay persons acting as eucharistic ministers and lectors at the Mass, and the functions of acolyte being pushed outward to include females, ministerial profiles did indeed seem to be changing, and to such an extent that some began speaking of a new clericalism — that of the laity.

One who obviously shares that concern is England's Archbishop Derek Worlock of Liverpool, and he broached the subject in delivering the 1988 Masie Ward Sheed Memorial Lecture sponsored by England's Catholic Housing Aid Society. Why is it, he asked, that for the first time in his memory there was no Catholic member of the prime minister's cabinet, no Catholic trade union leader, no prominent Catholic helping shape the mores and customs of Britain, so many fewer Catholic councillors in local government? He contrasted this to the many thousands of extraordinary eucharistic ministers and otherwise liturgically involved laity.

However, whereas another might have found consolation in the latter reality, Worlock had a question: "Have our exciting new insights into ecclesiology entrapped otherwise energetic lay men and women within where the altar-rails once were?" Is the laity becoming too "churchy"?

Worlock did not seem to be hankering for a return to the glory days of Catholic action of the 1950s, 1960s — much of which some now think came as response to the perceived communist threat rather than from pure inspirations of Catholic social thought. Worlock's concern was more pointed; namely, that the new liturgical involvements of the laity were coming at the expense of the homeless, the poor, the needy. Is that a worry that applies in the U.S.?

# JUNE 19

## The Adoro Te Devote

*O Godhead hid, devotedly I adore thee.*
*Who truly art within the forms before me;*
*To thee my heart I bow with bended knee*
*As failing quite in contemplating thee.*
*Sight, touch, and taste in thee are each deceived*
*The ear alone most safely is believed:*
*I believe all the son of God has spoken,*
*Than Truth's own word there is no truer token...*

*O thou memorial of Our Lord's own dying!*
*O living bread, to mortals life supplying!*
*Make thou my soul henceforth on thee to live:*
*Ever a taste of heavenly sweetness give.*

*O living Pelican! O Jesu Lord!*
*Unclean I am, but clean I am in thy blood*
*Of which a single drop, for sinners split,*
*Can purge the entire world from all its guilt.*
*Jesu! Whom for the present veil'd I see,*
*What I so thirst for, oh, vouchsafe to me:*
*That I may see thy countenance unfolding,*
*And may be blest thy glory in beholding.*

## YESTERDAY'S PRAYERS

**IN THE MIDDLE AGES,** the Eucharist came to be known as the Blessed Sacrament by way of accenting its supreme position among all the sacraments. Devotion to the Blessed Sacrament excited, in turn, fervent expressions of faith on the part of the pious; hence, this hymn of prayer by Thomas Aquinas, *Adoro Te Devote*, "Devotedly I Adore Thee," the major portion of which is shown above.

# THOSE HEADY, HEADY DAYS OF SUMMER SCHOOLS

This is the last day of spring, the vigil of summer, as it were -- the season in the old days when young Catholic flocked to summer schools of Catholic action to be indoctrinated in...well, Catholic action. Father Daniel Lord, SJ, conducted a huge on out of St. Louis, moving from city to city, Catholic campus to Catholic campus, enrolling tens of thousands in the process, and mobilizing a large percentage thereof, it was hoped, to witness -- except it was called witness then. It was called Catholic Action.

Summer schools there still are, but different from the old days. Today's enrollees are making up credits pr prep-ing for a more sophisticated type of apostolic involvement, like being directors of religious education, not covert operators in the big game of salvation. The Catholic-cation scene has changed. That's not to say that it is dead. Unconstructed? Undoubtedly! Dead. No way!

No way, when one hears of a young Catholic college graduate passing up a promising, capitalistic-type job to work for a Catholic Worker House in Minnesota. Or when one encounters young siblings ladling our soup in a Connecticut house of hospitality.

In defense of he new generation of activists, their Catholic dedications are often misread. Much of the action today may be so unstructured that some people are oblivious to challenges; but very many are involved. By the same token, that lack of organization makes it likely that many beyond personal active involvement are oblivious to much being done in terms of what they remember as "Catholic action."

An old Catholic activist expressed it succinctly a few years ago to an interviewer for a national Catholic magazine. "Look at the area of peace," he said. "We no longer have the Catholic Association for International Peace, but we have Pax Christi, which is more international than the CAP even was. And we have the Catholic Peace Fellowship. The old Catholic action isn't dead; it's just taken on different colorations."

Any other difference? "We have come to a deeper awareness of the complexities of the tasks that confront us. There are no easy theoretical answers anymore. If the structures of society are to be reformed in the light of the Gospels imperatives, then careful scrutiny, rigorous study and long-term dedication are necessary. In the old day we operated with simple theories and easy answers. They weren't sufficient -- which is why so many of the old apostolates went under. Today's better. Maybe the scene's not as flashy nor the numbers so mind-boggling. But the work's more solid."

May we hope so.

# THE GONZAGA SAGA

**LIKE THE VISCONTI,** Sforza and d'Este families, the Gonzagas were people to conjure with in medieval Italy. They entered history around the year 1100, and for centuries they were big players in the affairs of the fractious and fractured peninsula as overseers, printers and patrons of the arts. The Gonzaga palace loomed like a fortress over Mantua, and the family survived one assassination attempt after another before self-destructing primarily from within toward the end of the sixteenth century. But while it lasted, it was grand — as in 1328, when Luigi Gonzaga, his son and grandson all took new brides on the same day (it was Luigi's third), and the three brides entered Mantua in spectacular triumph. One member of the clan would become an archbishop at age eight and a cardinal at fourteen. Inevitably there one day would be a Gonzaga saint. He's none other than Aloysius Gonzaga, 1568-1591, whose feast is marked today.

Aloysius Gonzaga made sainthood via the Jesuits, though religious life was hardly the future his family had in mind for him. Not only did he have to overcome family opposition to the idea of his being a priest; as an imperial prince allied to the royal houses, he also needed the approval of the emperor. This obtained, in 1584 he renounced his heritage in favor of his brother. But it was hard to leave his exalted past entirely behind. The Gonzaga name was such that doctors taking his pulse reportedly would exclaim excitedly about the Gonzaga pulse and the Gonzaga blood coursing beneath their fingers.

As a Jesuit, Aloysius Gonzaga's career would not be a long one. He had a reputation for brilliance and sanctity, and it was said he cured his mother in a vision, after she was stabbed and left for dead in the street by vassals exacting revenge. Two brothers died in that violent outburst.

In Gonzaga's fourth year of theology, plague broke out in Rome. Though himself in frail health, Gonzaga threw himself into the emergency, lugging the ill to hospitals on his back. He soon fell ill himself. There was recovery, then relapse. The pride of the Gonzagas was dead at twenty-three.

# JUNE 22

Thomas More (Detail from painting by Holbein)

## A SAINT FOR ALL SEASONS

**THE WRITER DAN HERR** once commented that St. Thomas More is a person to whom twentieth-century Americans can especially relate. He lived in times of great political flux and of turmoil within the church, when sincere people might disagree on the solutions of grave problems. He lived at a time when faith was exasperatingly elusive, and when hope was difficult to sustain. In the sixteenth century, so in the twentieth. Thomas More sustained, and this Englishman became sainted model for Catholic believers for the ages.

The playwright Robert Bolt called Thomas More a man for all seasons. That he was, and remains. Scholar, tutor to the future king, lawyer, family man, renowned wit, Lord Chancellor of the Realm, figure at royal court — Thomas More had everything....and sacrificed everything on an issue of religious principle. He refused to take the oath, provided in the Act of Succession, repudiating the pope, rejecting King Henry VIII's first marriage to Catherine of Aragon as invalid, and recognizing the offspring of Henry and second wife Anne Boleyn as lawful heir to the throne. His integrity cost him his head.

But first there was the Tower of London, where family implored him to relent in his stubbornness. More countered that he stood on religious principle, and the constitutional principle that silence was not a crime but a right; least of all was silence a capital charge. The crown disagreed. Thomas More went to the scaffold in 1535.

## CARDINAL SPELLMAN GOES TO CANOSSA

**PEOPLE OF A CERTAIN AGE** will remember Eleanor Roosevelt's column "My Day." It revealed what was on the mind of one of the most celebrated women of her day, and was widely read in syndication. On this day in 1949, parochial schools were on Mrs. Roosevelt's mind, and she wrote that though these schools made a contribution to the community, they should not receive tax support, a hot congressional issue at the moment, for such would be a violation of the Constitution's separation clause. In New York, Cardinal Francis Spellman exploded, and fired off a public letter saying he would "not again publicly acknowledge" her and that her "record of anti-Catholicism stands for all to see — a record which you yourself wrote on the pages of history which cannot be recalled — documents of discrimination unworthy of an American mother."

It was an astonishing spectacle — the leading American Catholic prelate excoriating the woman who until just recently had been the First Lady of the land. Of course Mrs. Roosevelt stood her ground, responding with aplomb, "I assure you I have no sense of being 'an unworthy American mother.'"

The issue dragged on, muddying state and national politics to such an extent that in mid-summer President Truman asked New York Democratic boss Edward Flynn to fly to Rome and take the case to Pope Pius XII. Rome listened, and Spellman was directed to make a public act of reconciliation. Spellman is reported to have felt humiliated by the order, but he obeyed, visiting Mrs. Roosevelt at Hyde Park one August day on what was said to be an "unannounced and unplanned" call. It was neither, of course. Mrs. Roosevelt was triumphant but refused to gloat. She told of the visit in her column, remarking graciously, "The Cardinal had dropped in on his way to dedicate a Chapel in Peekskill. We had a pleasant chat and I hope the country proved as much of a tonic for him as it always is for me." Episode closed.

# JUNE 24

## "FILIOQUE" AND THE EAST-WEST SCHISM

**THE SECOND COUNCIL OF LYONS** was in session, and in 1274 this was one of its most momentous days, for it witnessed the arrival of the Greek envoys — the former patriarch of Constantinople, the archbishop of Nicea, and the logothete (chancellor) of the emperor. Their presence was vital, for a major point of the council was reunion with the Greeks. Accordingly, this meant discussion of the festering *filioque* issue in context of the Nicene Creed. In 1274 this was no minor theological debate between East and West, for more was involved than the simple introduction by the West of a controversial formula into a creed the Greeks held sacrosanct. The bottom line involved heresy. *Filioque* — Latin for the term "and the Son" — was promoted by the Western church to express the double procession of the Holy Spirit from the Father *and* from the Son. The Eastern or Greek church rejected the concept as heretical, holding that the Spirit proceeds not *from* the Son, but from the Father *through* the Son. Church history has often pivoted on such fine distinctions.

Interestingly enough, at the council's fourth session on July 6, the Greek envoys accepted the prescribed profession of faith that contained recognition of papal primacy, and actually took part in a Mass during which the creed was sung in Latin and Greek with the *filioque* clause included. The gesture seemed to signal a mending of the sorry theological breach between East and West. After the Greek envoys had thus professed their faith in terms of the *filioque*, permission was extended to retain the traditional text of the creed in the Eastern church, and at last fences appeared to be mended.

But it was only so momentarily. The union did not last. The emperor, Michael of Constantinople, supported the agreement out of mere political motives, and the Greek bishops would have none of it. The schism between East and West that had begun in 1054 was to continue. It does to this day.

# JUNE 25

## THE AMERICAN BISHOPS BITE THE BULLET

**IN SPRINGTIME** the American bishops meet in Collegeville, Minnesota, a long way from Washington, traditionally the site of their annual fall meeting. But then Collegeville is a more pastoral place, and recently they have met there on business preliminary to what is transacted in fall. So they were there on this day in 1988, and they approved a report on nuclear weapons that questioned the morality of deploying a system of space-based defenses against missles. You know the system better as "star wars." The bishops said that "anything beyond a well-defined research and development program clearly within the restraints" of the existing treaty limiting anti-missile systems is, so to speak, anathema; it violates good sense — and existing agreements.

That report, subsequently ratified at the bishops' fall Washington assembly, reaffirmed and updated the pastoral letter on nuclear warfare issued by them in 1983, "The Challenge of Peace: God's Promise and Our Response." The Reagan administration lobbied hard against that letter and its update — for obvious reasons. It cut against long-standing American military policy. The letter stopped short of declaring that nuclear weapons could never be used, offensively or as a means of retaliation, but it asserted that it could never imagine a situation that would justify their use. Strong stuff! The letter called for a halt to the production and deployment of new nuclear weapons and gave only "strictly conditioned" acceptance to existing nuclear deterrents, adding that their maintenance should be linked to serious arms-reduction talks.

Should bishops be talking about questions such as this? Why not? Other hierarchies do — the Irish, West German, French, Dutch, Italian, and so on. In fact, in 1983 none other than John Paul II called on world scientists to refuse involvement in fields of research "inevitably destined" for deadly purposes. Rather, he said, they should "work for justice, love, and peace."

Katherina .CCXLIIII.

Jacobus de Voragine: *Legenda Aurea* (Printed by Anton Koberger; Nuremberg, 1488)

# GUTENBERG'S REMARKABLE INVENTION

**ABOUT THIS TIME** in 1900, several German cities, notably Mainz and Leipzig, were tidying up after observing the 500th anniversary of the birth of Johann Gutenberg. It was an arbitrary anniversary, June 24. No one knows exactly when Gutenberg was born, when he died, or for that matter where he is buried—although tradition favors the Franciscan church at Mainz as his place of burial. But, more important, everyone knows what Johann Gutenberg did. In the mid-fifteenth century he invented the process of printing from movable type, and the world would never again be the same. Learning and knowledge exploded, for now books, hitherto composed by the painfully slow process of hand, could be mass produced and would henceforth be more readily accessible to the populace.

The immediate effect of Gutenberg's invention, however, was to multiply the books of religion rather than those of general learning. His first product was a printed Bible, followed shortly by a Latin *Psalterium*. But soon literary works of ancient Greece and Rome were flowing from the presses, and by 1493 broadsides — sheets printed on one side for posting in public places for perusal by common folk began to appear. These broadsides were the forerunners of the modern newspaper. Germany dominated the printing scene for decades, but the first newspapers were to appear in Italy, and were called *Gazettas* after the coin, *gazeta*, paid for them. Hence the newspaper name common worldwide: "Gazette."

Gutenberg's invention ranks as one of the great events of human history. No longer would learning and culture be the privilege of the aristocratic few and of monks. Secular science, undergoing boon times too, could propagate ideas more immediately. Intellectual cross-fertilization was far more of a given of human society. The irony is that for Gutenberg his invention was no commercial success. He was forced to borrow constantly, and six years after his death in 1468 his estate was still being dunned for funds in arrears.

Page from the Book of Kells

# THE ART AND FASCINATION WITH ILLUMINATION

**BEFORE JOHANN GUTENBERG** and his printing press, bookmaking in the Christian era was for the most part the work of monks, certainly in the West. Monasteries maintained scriptoriums, and there monks sat writing their tracts, usually devotional, or copying the manuscripts of others. They worked in an old tradition, actually. The Dead Sea Scrolls and papyrus rolls of ancient Egypt demonstrate that the instinct to record and pass on history and knowledge belonged to the civilizing process itself — and of course those Hebrew and Egyptian scrolls are but part of the heritage of the word immortalized.

A related specialty that the monks brought to a high art was that of illumination; that is, the embellishment of text with colorful designs and rich, elaborate touches of gold and silver. Astonishingly beautiful documents emanated from monastic scriptoriums, which today are counted as treasures of civilization itself — examples such as the ninth-century Rushworth Gospels at the Bodleian Library at Oxford, and gospel manuscripts of the Abbot Uigbald, who presided at Lindisfarne in the late eighth, early ninth centuries, now found in the collections of the Vatican and the State Public Library in Leningrad.

But the prize of all may be the seventh-century Book of Kells, centerpiece of the "Long Room" of the library of Trinity College, Dublin. The decorations of this illuminated gospel are so intricate that one page's work reportedly demanded a lifetime's work from the illuminator. The claim is probably exaggerated, but certainly the Book of Kells is a most splendid example of Western illuminated manuscripts. Page after page is a fantasy of colored arabesque — animated intials, robed monks, elongated animals....fish, dogs, birds, even snakes, though there weren't supposed to be any in Ireland. The book came out of the monastery at Kells in County Meath, and is one of Ireland's proudest boasts. One page is turned a day for viewing by visitors.

Pius X

# THE AMERICAN CHURCH'S COMING OF AGE

**GIVEN THE SIZE,** stability and affluence of the American Catholic Church, it may be difficult to believe that until eight years into this century it was classified by Rome as a mission church. This day in 1908 would be its last in that category, for the next day, June 29, 1908, Pope Pius X would issue the apostolic constitution *Sapienti consilio* removing the United States (Great Britain, Luxembourg and southern Canada too) from the jurisdiction of the Congregation for the Propagation of the Faith, the Vatican agency that nurtured development of the faith in lands where Catholics were neither strong in numbers nor self-supporting in terms of funds and priests. The American church had officially come of age, and took a place as a peer church alongside those of France, Germany, Italy and other historic centers of Catholic Christianity.

As for the Congregation for the Propagation of the Faith, it is now known as the Congregation for the Evangelization of Peoples, a change of a semantic kind that relieves it of a word that in this century acquired heavy overtones; i.e., propaganda. Originally conceived as a committee of cardinals by Gregory XIII in 1573 for the reconciliation of Eastern Christians, the body was expanded and formally constituted by Gregory XV in 1622 as the Congregation for the Propagation of the Faith. The name was commonly telescoped to Propaganda, a name which conveyed unfortunate connotations come the twentieth-century's time of dictators with their ministries of propaganda. So, new name — but old focus.

Today the Congregation for the Evangelization of Peoples coordinates the church's missionary work throughout the world. In this respect it propagates (oops!) one of the two primary reasons for its coming into being: to bring unity to mission methodology. The other reason long since took care of itself: to wrest from Spain and Portugal the excessive control which they exercised over the missions as explorer nations and by prior rights of patronage.

# PIUS XI'S OUT-MANEUVERING OF MUSSOLINI

**ONE OF THE FASCINATING ADVENTURE** stories of modern Vatican history began on this day in 1931, and intimately involved a man who would be a future archbishop of New York, Francis J. Spellman. Pius XI was pope in 1931, and the dictator Benito Mussolini ruled Italy. The Fascist grip was tightening over Italian youths, and Pius planned in response an encyclical, which would be a defense of Catholic Action in Italy and a criticism of the youth program of the Fascists. But how to avoid the risk of suppression of the encyclical, and how to insure its publication free of Fascist censorship? That was the dilemma.

Pius XI went to great pains. He wrote the encyclical — *Non abbiamo bisogno* ("We have no need") — in his own hand and had it printed in great secrecy in the Vatican printing shop. Pius XI's secretary of state, Cardinal Eugenio Pacelli, knew of the project, but few others. On June 29, 1931, Pius XI signed the encyclical, but it would not be released to the world from Italy. Spellman, then a young monsignor and protege of Pacelli (the future Pius XII of course), was summoned to Pius XI's private library and instructed to make a trip to Paris in the role of diplomatic courier, delivering some official letters to the apostolic nuncio there. In the packet too would be a copy of *Non abbiamo bisogno*, and a letter from the Associated Press bureau chief in Rome to his counterpart in Paris, saying, "You may have absolute confidence in the bearer. He is fully authorized to say whatever he says and to do whatever he does. Please offer him every facility of whatever nature that he wishes."

Thus it came to be that *Non abbiamo bisogno* reached the world free of censorship. The encyclical was not particularly memorable for its message, but the fact that a pope had to take such a step to insure the integrity of a document of his spoke reams to the world about the situation in Italy. As for Spellman, he returned uneventfully to Rome, his future more assured then ever.

# THE SCHISM BORN OF VATICAN II

**ECUMENICAL COUNCILS** are a wonderful vehicle for clarifying doctrine and promoting the faith. Alas, they also spin off the occasional schism.

Vatican Council I produced the sect known as the Old Catholics. Mainly French, Dutch and Germans, Old Catholics broke away in 1870 over the issue of papal infallibility, which was promulgated by the council.

Vatican II — well, it produced a schism yet without name, but originated by the dissident French archisbishop Marcel Lefebvre, once head of the archdiocese of Dakar in what was once French West Africa, and is now Senegal. The Lefebvre schism was formalized on this day in 1988, when, in direct defiance of an order from Pope John Paul II, Lefebvre consecrated four men as bishops at ceremonies in Econe, Switzerland.

Over several years, Archbishop Lefebvre had ordained some 250 priests, also in defiance of papal authority, to the Priestly Society of St. Pius X, a religious order of his founding. But ordaining a priest was one thing; consecrating a bishop was another. Ordination lives and dies with the person ordained. Bishops on the other hand can perpetuate themselves. The Lefebvre action thus constituted in effect establishment of an independent, self-sufficient, renewable hierarchy. Until Lefebvre ordained his bishops, his movement faced likely extinction with his death; it would die with its priests.

What bugged Archbishop Lefebvre? The reforms of Vatican II, notably new ecumenical trends and the vernacularization of the Mass, innovations which he labeled "satanic" and "modernistic." The church had been taken over by "anti-Christs," he charged. As for Pope John Paul II, he was held to be "a disciple of the Father of Lies" and a dupe of "Freemasons and Communists."

Lefebvre aides claim more than a million followers for their movement, most of them French, Swiss and American. Vatican officals estimate the number more conservatively at between 100,000 and 500,000. Large or small, however, the schism is a heartache for those who look for Christians to love one another.

# JULY 1

## CONSCIENCE AND THE CATHOLIC

**THIS IS THE MONTH** of national freedom and independence, and thus an occasion for some related thinking on conscience and the Catholic.

Conscience we know; we all have one. It is, quite simply, that intrinsic faculty by which we arrive at a judgment concerning the rightness or wrongness of a particular act. Historically, the church has honored the primacy of conscience, while holding that the best-formed conscience is one aided by good will, by the right use of emotions, by the external experience of living, and by certain external helps. Among the latter is the magisterium, or teaching authority of the church. But to say this is also to set up a dichotomy.

Conscience is the "voice of reason" or the "voice of God," and in Catholic understanding a person who follows/obeys the dictates of conscience shall never offend God. At the same time, however, Catholic understanding ties conscience to obedience, and further exalts obedience to a virtue when the individual subjects his or her will to that of another for God's sake. Conscience thus is absolute, but it is also subject to obedience.

The dichotomy is glimpsed in successive paragraphs of Vatican II's Constitution on the Church in the Modern World, *Gaudium et spes*, specifically Section 16 dealing with the dignity of the moral conscience:

"In the depths of his conscience, man detects a law which he does not impose upon himself, but which holds him to obedience....

"Conscience is the most secret core and sanctuary of a man. There he is alone with God, whose voice echoes in his depths. In a wonderful manner conscience reveals that law which is fulfilled by love of God and neighbor...."

This dichotomy makes for certain complications, at least one of which many find surprising. Read on.»»»

# THE NON-CONFORMING CONSCIENCE

**THE CHURCH SO RESPECTS** conscience that it holds free from guilt wrongful acts arising from a certain but erroneous conscience. This is not to say that the wrongful act is itself made good by the erroneous conscience, but rather that the individual is not held responsible before God for the wrongful act, because the conscience knows no better. The same council document cited yesterday makes the point succinctly: "Conscience frequently errs from invincible ignorance without losing its dignity" (16).

That conscience can err accounts for the church's emphasis on a properly formed conscience — in the church's parlance, a correct conscience. A correct conscience is one that is in harmony with church teaching. Which is to say, the individual Catholic is responsible for knowing and following the position of the church by conforming his or her conscience to that position.

Once upon a time, the act of "conforming" was almost automatic within Catholicism, but in recent years this has been less so. Large numbers of Catholics take different readings of conscience from that oaf the teaching authority (as on artificial birth control) and have made individual moral decisions at variance with official teaching, thus rounding full circle on the church's own principle of the supremacy of the individual conscience. Thus the phenonenon: whereas obedience to the teaching authority long stabilized the church, the exaltation of conscience has introduced displays of independence which are dramatically new in Catholicism, both in the moral and behavioral realms.

These exertions of independence are deplored by some, but there could be another reading, one far more positive. They might also be seen as signs of the vibrancy of the church, and of the latitudes of belief and the expression of faith now possible within Catholicism. At the very least they have enabled some to "stay" who might otherwise have been forced to take their leave. Not a bad thing.

# THE SAINT WHO REFUSED TO AGE

**POPE JOHN PAUL II** elevated the fourth American to the rank of sainthood on this day in 1988 — Sister Rose Philippine Duchesne of the Society of the Sacred Heart. A fascinating soul, St. Rose. She entered the sisterhood against her father's will, she braved the American frontier, and she founded the first free school west of the Mississippi at St. Charles, Missouri. At seventy-two, an age when most people are resting on their oars, she helped begin a school for Potawatami Indians, in what is now Sugar Creek, Kansas.

A native of France, where she was born in 1769, Sister Rose had difficulty learning the English language, and had virtually no grasp at all of Indian dialect. Instead, she taught through example — prayer, nursing and mending clothes. To the Potawatami she was "Quah-kah-ka-num-ad," the woman who prays.

In canonizing Sister Rose, Pope John Paul II said her life was a reminder that "the call to holiness is universal, and does not know the boundaries of nation, political system, culture or race."

The Claretian newsletter *Generation*, a publication out of Chicago for the spiritual enrichment of older Catholics, cited columnist Lou Jacquet on St. Rose: "The next time I think I am too set in my ways, I will think of this brave woman from pioneer America. Reviewing the life of our newest saint reminds us of how foolish it is to think of oneself as locked forever into any one lifestyle just because we have passed a certain birthday."

*Generation* was then moved to suggest a prayer to the new saint:"Dear Saint Rose, thank you for the examples you gave us: the faith that took you to a new land, the love that inspired you to live among the poorest of God's people, the trust that enabled you to turn over your life to God's will. May your life in turn lead us to follow the way you have shown, so that one day we may join you in singing his eternal praise. Amen."

# SHOULD HOLIDAY BE MADE HOLY DAY?

**OUR NATIONAL DAY OF INDEPENDENCE**, commemorating of course the signing of the Declaration of Independence on July 4, 1776, in Philadelphia by members of the Second Continental Congress. It is a patriotic holiday rather than a religious holy day, but some Catholics would like to see the two elements combined in some more direct way than is presently the case.

Currently a common practice in Catholic churches is to mark the holiday on the Sunday preceeding July 4 (or on July 4 itself, if the holiday falls on a Sunday) with the singing of patriotic songs at Mass instead of the usual religious hymns — songs such as Samuel Francis Smith's *America* ("My country 'tis of thee"), Katharine Lee Bates' *America the Beautiful* ("Oh beautiful, for spacious skies"), or Julia Ward Howe's *Battle Hymn of the Republic* ("Mine eyes have seen the glory of the coming of the Lord"). Paradoxically, the first song is totally derivative in tune of the British national anthem; the second has been coopted by some as the gay national anthem because of the words of stanza one, line four; the third is a mere word variation of a popular Civil War marching song ("John Brown's body lies a-mouldering in the grave").

Some Catholics would like to have a more authentic religious experience on this day, and a few have even proposed that, along with Thanksgiving, the Fourth of July be declared a holy day of obligation in the United States. That's not likely to happen — although so far as church law is concerned there is nothing particularly to militate against it. National hierarchies decide their own holy days of obligation, and it's likely that if one looked hard enough, some religious cover could be found to justify marking the day as a holy day. Actually, July 4 would seem to make more sense as a patronal feast day than December 8.

But then, if this were a holy day, some of us might be late for the parade.

# THE JONES BOY, THE JONES BOY....

**THE JONES'** might live next door, but Inigo Jones is no household name, at least not in this country. In England, however, it's another story. Inigo Jones was the celebrated seventeenth-century architect. About 1612 he was appointed surveyor-general of royal buildings by King James I, and he is credited with designing the queen's home at Greenwich, Lincoln's Inn Chapel, the banqueting hall at Whitehall, Covent Garden piazza, and the reconstruction of St. Paul's Cathedral. It was Inigo Jones who added the Ionic facade to St. Paul's. The touch was in keeping with his background. As one who studied and worked on the Continent, from Denmark to Greece, Inigo Jones was imbued with continental influences. Back in England, his Palladian principles broke completely in England with prevailing design (Jones was often referred to as "the English Palladio"), and architecturally marked the starting point of England's classical period.

Son of a Catholic clothworker of London, he began in life as a designer of sets for court masques (a popular form of aristocratic entertainment at the time) that would shift scenes and do other wondrous things. He also designed dresses for the events. As for the masques, they were written by the likes of Ben Jonson, Daniel, Heywood and D'Avenant. Jones' forte was the technical. Among other things, he could design sets that moved.

Inigo Jones was painted twice by the Flemish master Antoon Van Dyck, but socially and religiously he had his problems. He quarreled with Jonson, and for that Jonson made him the frequent butt of his satire. For instance, he was satirized as "In-and-In-Medley" in Jonson's 1633 comedy *A Tale of a Tub*. Several years later — 1646, to be precise — Inigo Jones was fined for being a favorite of the king and a Catholic.

Inigo Jones, born in 1573, died in poverty in London on this day in 1651.

Thomas More and his family (artist unknown)

# THE WIT AND WISDOM OF THOMAS MORE

**THIS WAS THE DAY** in 1535 that Thomas More's great battle of wits with Henry VIII and legalists of the crown came to an end. More — from 1529-1532 England's lord chancellor; now a saint of the Roman Church — went to the gallows at age fifty-seven for refusing to take the oath provided in the Act of Succession repudiating the pope and recognizing the divorced Henry's marriage to Anne Boleyn and the rights of succession of their offspring.

Ascending the scaffold, More seemed weak and ready to fall. "I pray thee, see me safe up," he said to his guard, "and for my coming down, let me shift for myself."

He was offered wine. "My Master had easell and gall, not wine, given him to drink," he replied.

He could even jest with his executioner.

"Pluck up thy spirits, man," he advised him, "and be not afraid to do thine office. My neck is very short. Take heed therefore thou strike not awry for saving thine honesty."

Then, laying his head on the block, he moved aside his beard, remarking to the executioner to take care in the beheading lest he cut the beard, since it at least was innocent of treason.

His last words are immortal, and the inspiration since for all who have been forced to choose between conscience and convenience, principle and accommodation: "I die the king's good servant, but God's first."

# JULY 7

## THE BIBLE AS SOCIAL DOCUMENT

**THE BIBLE IS PRIMARILY A BOOK** of inspiration, devotion and moral guidance. But the Bible also contains its share of high literary moments, and, for those looking for more, it is an important social document for the data it conveys to the customs and mores of the day — as with respect to weddings.

There was in early biblical times no elaborate wedding ritual as such beyond the giving away of the bride by her father, the unveiling of the bride, and the joining in hands — customs actually pagan in their origins. But the wedding itself was a good time, and families prepared for it with enormous care for detail and effect. For one thing, the wedding was timed to the harvest, when food was most bountiful. The invitations were delivered by special messengers (Matthew 22:1-13), and acceptance was expected; in fact, excuses were regarded as insults. Especially affluent hosts might send textiles along with the invitations, so that the guests would be recognized on arrival, and also well dressed. In any instance, they were expected to come dressed in finery.

As for the bride and groom, their days were busy, busy, busy — the bride receiving ceremonial washings and beauty treatments; the groom enjoying his last days of bachelorhood. Jeremiah speaks several times of "the voice of mirth" of the bridegroom and of the bride connected with preliminary festivities, presumably comparable to today's bridal shower and bachelor's party. The wedding festivities themselves went on for a week or more, and for many participants were major social occasions in otherwise lackluster lives, out of which other new bridal matches might come. The consumption of food and drink was conspicuous, and there was great embarrassment, indeed near panic if a host ran short — which accounts for Mary's concern at the wedding feast of Cana when it was discovered there was no more wine (John 2:3-10); she persuaded Jesus to work his first miracle. Obviously, then as now weddings were fun to attend.

# THE COMING AND GOING OF THE INDEX

**RELATIVELY FEW EVER SAW** a copy of it, and fewer still knew what titles were on it, yet for centuries it stood as the great symbol of Catholic authoritarianism and mind control. The reference is to the Index of Forbidden Books, that list of books condemned because their contents were deemed to be heretical, dangerous to morals, or otherwise objectionable, and which Catholics were forbidden to read, possess or sell under penalty of excommunication.

The church had proscribed books as early as the reign of Pope Gelasius in 494, and the first Roman Index of Forbidden Books *(Index Librorum Prohibitorum)* had appeared in 1559 during the reign of Paul IV. But this was an especially significant date in the Index's history, for it was on this day in 1753 that the Index process was confirmed and codified by Benedict XIV's bull *Sollicita ac provida*. The bull was tampered with by subsequent popes, but by and large it regulated book censorship in the Catholic Church into the twentieth century. The bull detailed the process of examination to be followed on books "denounced" to Rome, the responsibilities of "revisors" involved in the examination, who might read condemned books and under what circumstances, etc. Paradoxically, very few English books were to appear on the Index, but thousands in other languages did, until by mid-twentieth century the list contained several thousand titles either entirely condemned or forbidden until satisfactorily revised. Others were outlawed simply by falling into categories covered by general norms.

Of course it all came to an end. By the twentieth century the Index was a total anachronism, and with popes like Pius XII talking about the importance of freedom of information in the church as in the wider society, the Index was an embarrassment as well. Paul VI finally bit the bullet, and on June 14, 1966, the Congregation for the Doctrine of the Faith declared that the Index and its related penalties of excommunication no longer had the force of church law.

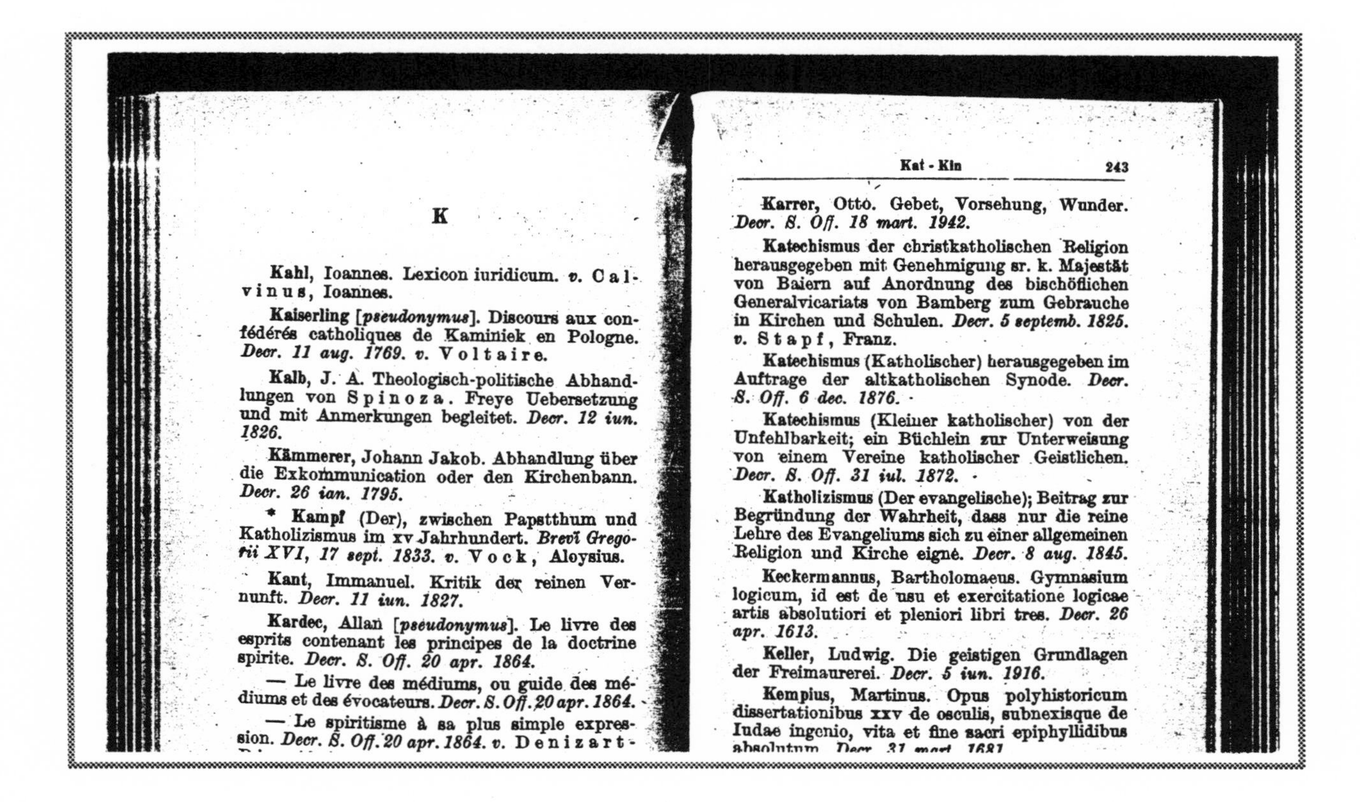

K

**Kahl**, Ioannes. Lexicon iuridicum. *v.* Calvinus, Ioannes.

**Kaiserling** [*pseudonymus*]. Discours aux confédérés catholiques de Kaminiek en Pologne. *Decr. 11 aug. 1769. v.* Voltaire.

**Kalb**, J. A. Theologisch-politische Abhandlungen von Spinoza. Freye Uebersetzung und mit Anmerkungen begleitet. *Decr. 12 iun. 1826.*

**Kämmerer**, Johann Jakob. Abhandlung über die Exkommunication oder den Kirchenbann. *Decr. 26 ian. 1795.*

* **Kampf** (Der), zwischen Papstthum und Katholizismus im xv Jahrhundert. *Brevi Gregorii XVI, 17 sept. 1833. v.* Vock, Aloysius.

**Kant**, Immanuel. Kritik der reinen Vernunft. *Decr. 11 iun. 1827.*

**Kardec**, Allan [*pseudonymus*]. Le livre des esprits contenant les principes de la doctrine spirite. *Decr. S. Off. 20 apr. 1864.*

— Le livre des médiums, ou guide des médiums et des évocateurs. *Decr. S. Off. 20 apr. 1864.*

— Le spiritisme à sa plus simple expression. *Decr. S. Off. 20 apr. 1864. v.* Denizart-

Kat - Kin 243

**Karrer**, Otto. Gebet, Vorsehung, Wunder. *Decr. S. Off. 18 mart. 1942.*

**Katechismus** der christkatholischen Religion herausgegeben mit Genehmigung sr. k. Majestät von Baiern auf Anordnung des bischöflichen Generalvicariats von Bamberg zum Gebrauche in Kirchen und Schulen. *Decr. 5 septemb. 1825. v.* Stapf, Franz.

**Katechismus** (Katholischer) herausgegeben im Auftrage der altkatholischen Synode. *Decr. S. Off. 6 dec. 1876.*

**Katechismus** (Kleiner katholischer) von der Unfehlbarkeit; ein Büchlein zur Unterweisung von einem Vereine katholischer Geistlichen. *Decr. S. Off. 31 iul. 1872.*

**Katholizismus** (Der evangelische); Beitrag zur Begründung der Wahrheit, dass nur die reine Lehre des Evangeliums sich zu einer allgemeinen Religion und Kirche eigne. *Decr. 8 aug. 1845.*

**Keckermannus**, Bartholomaeus. Gymnasium logicum, id est de usu et exercitatione logicae artis absolutiori et pleniori libri tres. *Decr. 26 apr. 1613.*

**Keller**, Ludwig. Die geistigen Grundlagen der Freimaurerei. *Decr. 5 iun. 1916.*

**Kempius**, Martinus. Opus polyhistoricum dissertationibus xxv de osculis, subnexisque de Iudae ingenio, vita et fine sacri epiphyllidibus absolutum. *Decr. 31 mart. 1681.*

# SAMPLINGS FROM THE INDEX

**THE INDEX WAS REVISED** at the turn of the century and some 3,000 titles pruned from the list. Nonetheless, the Index of 1900 still ran to 450 pages, and was soon back to its old size. A 1930 edition needed 563 pages for a listing covering between 7,000 and 8,000 books. (A precise count was impossible as some entries just cited the author's name and after it *opera omnes*, "all works," or *omnes fabulae amatoriae*, "all love stories," which could have meant a few books or many.) An unusual detail about the 1930 edition was its inclusion of *L'Action Francaise* (q.v. Jan. 23), the super-Catholic French newspaper. Ordinarily the Index did not cite the periodical press, ephemeral by its nature, and focused instead on formal book publishing.

Some Index items were extraordinarily esoteric. The first item on the 1930 Index was *Abauzit, Firmin V. Reflexions impartiales sur les evangiles*; the second, *Abbadie, Jacques. Traite de la verite de la religion cretienne, Decr. 5 jul. 1695.* But along with the esoteric were works by some of history's most famous writers and thinkers — people such as Addison, Goldsmith, Victor Hugo, Spinoza, Bergson, Bossuet, Bacon, Kant, Descartes, Heine, Hobbes, Locke, Sir Thomas Browne, Lord Acton, Milton and Balzac. In banning wholesale, the church exposed itself to charges of being terribly insecure and anti-intellectual.

There were also incongruities, like the appearance on the Index of Thomas a Kempis' *Imitation of Christ*. Apologists countered that it was only the Sebastiano Castellione edition that was banned, just as it was only the German edition of Acton's history of Vatican Council I that was "index-ed." Special pleading. The fact was the Index was subject to ignorance — and to *whim*! How else account for the appearance next to Pascal's *Pensees* of *The Priest: A Tale of Modernism in New England* by William L. Sullivan? Just who was this William L. Sullivan elevated by the Index to the ranks of a Defoe and a D'Annunzio?

# FELICITY AND THE SEVEN HOLY BROTHERS

**IN MATTERS RELIGIOUS,** as in the rolling of dice, there's a mystical significance to the number 7. It pops up all the time. There are the seven petitions of the Our Father, the seven gifts of the Holy Spirit, the seven sacraments, the seven heavens, the seven pillars of wisdom, the seven champions of Christendom (the national saints of England, Scotland, Ireland, Wales, France, Spain and Italy) — and, of course, the Seven Holy Brothers, whose feast, once upon a time, was observed on this day.

The Seven Holy Brothers — Felix, Philip, Martial, Vitalis, Alexander, Silanus and Januarius — were reputed to be the sons of St. Felicity. Legend has it that they were martyred for the faith in her presence, all seven going to their deaths "encouraged by her exhortations." Felicity too was martyred, so there's no accusing her of sadistic indifference to the fate of her own.

But is the story true? Most hagiographers regard the story of the Seven Holy Brothers as nothing more than a New Testament adaptation of the seven sons of the Maccabean Mother of the Old, who also suffered ignominious deaths as mother looked on and encouraged them in their religious resolve (2 Maccabees 7:1-42). And maybe they're right, for the brothers are buried in four different catacombs. Wouldn't they be buried together, if they were brothers and martyrs? Well, not necessarily. The brothers went before four different judges, who condemned them to various modes of death, their remains then being consigned to catacombs within the respective judges' districts.

Whatever, Felicity and her sons were honored as early as the fourth century, and in Pope Damasus' time (366-384) were hailed in the poem of praise: *Discrite quid meriti praestet pro rege feriri;/Femina non timuit gladium, cum natis obivit,/Confessa Christum meruit per secula nomen....* "Learn how meritorious it is to die for the king (Christ); /This woman feared not the sword, but perished with her sons, / She confessed Christ and merited eternal reward."

# FOUNDER OF WESTERN MONASTICISM

**THE MONASTIC IDEAL** in Catholic Christianity was seeded in the church's earliest centuries, and in the West by the person the church honors today, St. Benedict. Benedict lived from about 480 to about 546, and founded the famous Abbeys of Monte Cassino and Subiaco — and along with them the rule that was to propel Benedictine life throughout Western Christendom. The great Abbeys of Ampleforth, Downside and Glastonbury in England are Benedictine; so is Melk in Austria; Mont St. Michel, St. Denis and Clairvaux in France; Montserrat and Valladolid in Spain; and in the U.S., St. John's in Collegeville, Minnesota, Mount Angel in St. Benedict, Oregon, and Belmont Alley in Belmont, North Carolina — among many more. Interesting enough, the Order of St. Benedict is not a centralized institute. It is more a federation of congregations of monks, and nuns, following the rule of Benedict. Each abbey is an autonomous body, a family, almost in the literal sense, the abbot being elected for life.

As for Benedict, he was of a distinguished family of Norcia in central Italy, who on first donning the habit became a hermit in a grotto near Subiaco on the face of Monte Calvo, by the artificial lake of Nero's ancient villa. Tensions with a local cleric and the evolution of his own spiritual concepts induced him to move away after three years to Monte Cassino, taking a small band of followers with him. There he destroyed the pagan temples and sacred woods at the summit, and planted the roots of Benedictism.

They say that St. Benedict's character is revealed in every page of his rule — his paternal love and compassion, and his insistence "that in all things Christ shall be glorified." His rule forbade excessive austerities, and sensibly divided life between prayer, labor and learning. Benedict died at Monte Cassino, but are his relics still there, or were they translated to the monastery at Fleury, near Orleans, after Cassino was abandoned around 577 during the Lombard invasion? The answer seems lost to history. Read on.»»»

## THE GLORY AND AGONIES OF MONTE CASSINO

**MONTE CASSINO,** in central Italy on a mountaintop dominating the main artery between Rome and Naples, has always been regarded as St. Benedict's principal foundation. The coherence and discipline of Western monasticism fanned out from there. Benedict never left Monte Cassino after settling there.

An absolutely awesome physical facility was established on the mountain, bolstered by cyclopean walls twenty-six feet high and fourteen feet thick. Buildings of classical magnificence were erected, a vast library was collected, and artists were commissioned from as near as Amalfi and as far away as Constantinople to supervise and decorate. In times before the printing press, Monte Cassino's school of copyists was one of the most important in the West; equally notable was its school of miniature painters. The community grew to more than two hundred members, and the abbot was overlord of sorts over the whole surrounding area.

The big problem for Monte Cassino proved its strategic location. From its heights the countryside could be surveyed for miles around — and controlled. Monte Cassino, therefore, was forever a pawn in the political and military battles that were waged up and down the Italian peninsula. As mentioned, the Lombards pillaged and destroyed it in the sixth century. The monastery was restored and reconsecrated by Pope Zachary in 748, but a little over a century later the Saracens overran the place, killing the abbot and dispersing the monks. In 1239 the monks were again driven from the monastery by the German king and emperor Frederick II. In 1799 it was the turn of the French, who took the abbey and plundered it in their invasion against the kingdom of Naples.

The Italians themselves were ready to move against Monte Cassino in their dissolution of religious houses in 1866, but the monastery was spared, thanks largely to English supporters of a united Italy. Monte Cassino was declared a national monument, and the monks recognized as custodians. But Monte Cassino's problems were not behind it. The worst was still to come. Read on.»»»

# MONTE CASSINO'S LEVELING IN WORLD WAR II

**AS SO OFTEN IN EARLIER WARS,** Monte Cassino during World War II found itself in the battle path of contending armies, in this instance the British Eighth Army under General Sir Bernard L. Montgomery and the Fifth Army, part British, part American, under Lieutenant General Mark W. Clark, advancing north against the German forces led by Field Marshal Albert Kesselring. In January, 1944, the Allies had reached Cassino, sixty miles south of Rome. Three battles were fought for control of the town, with the Allies turned back each time. The blame was fixed on Monte Cassino. Allied leaders believed that the Germans were using the monastery as an observation post, and that as long as they enjoyed that advantage the road to Rome was closed. After great debate, much of it public, the controversial decision was made to bomb Monte Cassino.

On Feb. 14, Allied planes dropped leaflets on the abbey warning the monks and civilian refugees who had taken shelter there to leave. The next day, 229 bombers came over in waves, dropped 453 tons of bombs, and reduced the abbey to rubble. A double irony was involved: the Germans, it was discovered, had not been using Monte Cassino as an observation post; second, the bombing turned the abbey into a fortress, for the Germans moved into the rubble, where they were strategically stronger than ever. For weeks then Monte Cassino was pounded by bombers and artillery before, having been turned from the rear and supplies cut off, it finally fell on May 18. The abbey was by now a virtual dust heap.

The bombing and shelling of Monte Cassino ranked with the major cultural barbarisms committed by the Allies in World War II. Protest was fierce, but Monte Cassino was rebuilt — stone by stone — almost as a gesture of defiance to demonstrate that the power of the spirit is mightier than than any combination of explosives. Most of the funds were provided by the Italian government. Paul VI consecrated the monastery anew October 24, 1964, and from Monte Cassino proclaimed St. Benedict patron saint of Europe.

Statue of Kateri Tekakwitha on the main door of St. Patrick's Cathedral, New York

# THE LILY OF THE MOHAWKS

**TODAY'S FEAST BELONGS** to one of America's own people — Blessed Kateri Tekakwitha, a true American Indian. Kateri Tekakwitha was born about 1656 to a Christian Algonquin, who had been raised among the French at Trois Rivieres in Quebec before being captured by the Iroquis and taken to the Indian village of Ossernenon, now Auresieville in upper New York State. It was there that Kateri was born and there too that she was orphaned about the age of four — her parents and a brother dying during a smallpox epidemic. The epidemic did not spare Kateri entirely. She was left terribly disfigured by the disease and with badly damaged eyesight. An uncle raised her, and in time aunts began to shape marriage prospects for her.

But Kateri, who had come under Catholic influence, shunned marriage. Shunned in return by relatives, and subject to abuses, Kateri Tekakwitha fled to a Christian village two hundred miles distant, near Montreal. There, only eighteen, she persuaded the French missionary Jesuit Jacques de Lamberville to baptize her. On Christmas Day, 1677, she received her first communion, and she lived thereafter a life of austerity and prayer that was inspiration to all with whom she came in contact. Her "mortifications" were accounted "severe," such that she is said to have "attained the most perfect union with God in prayer." She died at Caughnawaga, Canada, April 17, 1680, not yet in her mid-thirties.

Her fame was such that her grave quickly became a place of pilgrimage for Christian Indians, and miracles began to be attributed to her. In 1884 an imposing monument was erected at Kateri Tekakwitha's grave by Father Clarence Walworth, and the nineteenth-century councils of Baltimore and Quebec petitioned her cause to Rome. In 1943 Pius XII declared her venerable, and in 1980 she was beatified by John Paul II. History knows her as the "Lily of the Mohawks" and the "Genevieve of New France." Her memory is enshrined further in the name of an annual conference of Catholic native Americans.

# JULY 15

## IF IT RAINS, FOR FORTY DAYS IT MIGHT REMAIN

**IT WAS MARK TWAIN** who said, everyone talks about the weather but no one does anything about it. Well, that's not exactly right. St. Swithin's been monkeying with the weather since this July day in 1315 (or was it 971?), when tradition has it that he sent a tremendous downpour on those who decided to move his remains from the churchyard at Winchester to a more fitting indoor shrine. Swithin had specifically requested that he be buried in "a vile and unworthy place" where passers-by would trod over his grave and raindrops from the eaves would fall upon it. Obviously, he didn't like being messed with. Hence the storm, and a piece of doggerel associated with it:

> St. Swithin's day if thou dost rain
> For forty days it will remain;
> St. Swithin's day if thou be fair
> For forty days 'twill rain na mair.

It's a bit uncertain what happened as a result of the storm. One legend has it that the would-be translators of Swithin's remains got the message, and let him be. It seems, however, that the remains were indeed moved indoors, where they became a source of grand and wondrous events. There was a glittering shrine to St. Swithin at Winchester for centuries. Henry VIII eyed it, and the shrine was looted in 1538. The gold and jewels proved to be phony.

Swithin lived in the ninth century, and as bishop of Winchester was widely known for his humility. He journeyed about his diocese on foot, and when he gave a banquet, he invited the poor rather than the rich. In his lifetime he is said to have performed a number of "agreeably humble miracles" — like restoring to their shells a basket of eggs dropped by an old woman.

Where's Swithin's grave now? Gone. St. Swithin's relics were scattered at the time of the shrine's looting.

# JULY 16

## OF DOGS, FIRES AND OTHER SAINTLY THINGS

**LIKE YESTERDAY'S** St. Swithin's Day, so much else in life, language and the calendar traces back to Christian saints. Take the St. Bernard dog, for instance. No, the dog did not plod around with nips of brandy dangling from its neck, but it was bred by monks to track down and rescue travelers lost in the blizzards and avalanches of Mons Jovis Pass, 8,098 feet up in the Alps. The dog, a cross between a bulldog and a Pyrenean shepherd dog or Molossian hound, was named after Bernard de Menthon, the eleventh-century saint who founded a hospice on Mons Jovis back when the Alps could only be crossed on foot.

Then there's St. Elmo's fire, the glow that accompanies the slow discharge of electricity from the atmosphere to earth, and which appears as a tip of light on the extremities of objects, like the masts of ships, and sends out crackling and fizzing noises. The fire takes its name from a corruption of St. Erasmus, *Sant' Ermo*, and is regarded by sailors as a sign that their ship has been taken under heavenly protection. To English sailors St. Elmo's fires were known as corposants, which derives from the Italian *corpo santo*, "holy body," a reference to the Eucharist.

Then we have items like St. Patrick's cabbage, St. Martin's goose, St. Ignatius' bean, St. Elizabeth's flowers and St. Peter's cock, the last a thin flat fish (*Zeus faber*) with oval spots, said to be the fingermarks of Peter the Apostle, a fisherman of course. The fish is also known as the John Dory.

But my favorite is St. Boniface's cup. It's a term used as reason or excuse for having an extra drink. The term derives from either Pope St. Boniface I or Pope St. Boniface VI. Neither man cast a long shadow over history, but one or the other of them purportedly established an indulgence for anyone drinking to his health. Hence, that extra cup of cheer, St. Boniface's cup. *Salut*.... Oh, and how about a slice of *Bischofsbrot*, Bishop's Bread; very rich — maybe too rich for the average layperson's taste.

## STUFF TO FORTIFY THE FAITH

**COMING UP IN A COUPLE OF DAYS** — three to be exact — is a feast that once belonged to Uncumber, a saint more mythical than real, but a person nonetheless to whom once belonged a considerable cult, particularly in the fifteenth and sixteenth centuries, when her name was making its way into breviaries and martyrologies, and antiphones and prayers were chanted in her honor.

Uncumber might be called the patroness of misanthropes. Allegedly she was the daughter of a pagan king of Portugal. She cherished her chastity and did not want to marry but finding herself being pushed into a match, Uncumber (also known as Wilgefortis, Liberata, Cumerana, Komina, among other covers) prayed to God for a disfigurement that would keep men at arm's length. He, hearing her pleas, caused a beard to grow on her face so that she might live her life *uncumbered* by men. Get it? *Uncumber, uncumbered.* Neat. It didn't work out totally well for poor Uncumber, however. Her father, or was it a rejected suitor?, was so enraged by her collusion with God that he had her crucified.

Anyway the cult of St. Uncumber grew, and as it did she was appropriated by unhappily married women as their patron. Sir Thomas More, for instance, wrote that "women [later] changed her name [to St. Uncumber] because they recken that for a pecke of oats she will not fail to uncumber them of their husbondys."

Numerous other legends are connected to good St. Uncumber, like that of the fiddler and the golden shoe. Seems Uncumber rewarded a destitute fiddler with a golden shoe for playing before her image or crucified body. The fiddler, however, was thought to have stolen the shoe and so was condemned to death. Granted a final request to play once more before Uncumber, he performed; she kicked off the other shoe, thus establishing the man's innocence.

As for Uncumber and that beard business, hagiographers deny that the legend is a Christian adaptation of the Hermaphroditos story of Greek mythology.

# THE DEFINING OF PAPAL INFALLIBILITY

**THIS WAS THE DAY** in 1870 that the church finally bit the bullet on the infallibility issue. The church from the beginning exercised its authority with the confidence of being infallible, but an explicit declaration of papal infallibility awaited Vatican Council I. Curiously enough, however, when the council was convened, the issue was not formally on the agenda. To be sure there were chapters on primacy and the pontifical magisterium, but papal infallibility was not added until later — and then with a certain hesitancy on the part of the council presidents. Once the issue was on the floor debate was intense, and the infallibility chapter went through several drafts and a number of amendments before a final text was agreed upon. Thus was born the dogmatic constitution *Pastor aeternus* and the decisive passage:

"We teach and define...that the Roman Pontiff, when he speaks *ex cathedra*, that is, when in the exercise of his office as pastor and teacher of all Christians, he defines, by virtue of his supreme apostolic authority, a doctrine of faith or morals to be held by the whole church — is, by reason of the divine assistance promised to him in blessed Peter, possessed of that infallibility with which the Divine Redeemer wished his church to be endowed in defining doctrines of faith and morals; and consequently that such definitions of the Roman Pontiff are irreformable of their own nature, and not by reason of the church's consent."

The last phrase, incidentally, put to rout the rear-guard element — those who held that infallibility was a collective power residing in the church at large and its ecumenical councils, rather than in a single individual.

The vote of adoption was overwhelming — 433 *placets* ("it pleases") and only 2 *non-placets* ("it does not please"). However, sixty-one Council Fathers absented themselves, choosing to leave Rome on the eve of the crucial session.

Pius IX

# THE DECLARATION OF INFALLIBILITY

**CONTINUING** on yesterday's subject, It should be said in fairness to at least some of the sixty-one who were absent when papal infallibility came to a final vote that they had reason to be elsewhere — not all to be sure, as written objections left behind would indicate, but, as said, at least some. Political tensions were at fever pitch in central Europe, and indeed the Franco-Prussian War erupted almost simultaneously with the infallibility vote. The urgency which some bishops felt to be home as soon as possible was not misplaced. A war had come which ultimately would claim 180,000 lives.

As for those written objections, they clued to something. Many genuinely feared a large and troublesome schism. And a schism did develop, spawning the sect known as the Old Catholics. But not involving bishops, the sect never achieved great influence or impact. Bishops who objected to the infallibility declaration quickly made their peace. The two who voted against it in the aula (one of the two was Bishop Edward Fitzgerald of Little Rock) made immediate submissions to Pope Pius IX, who presided at the session. In a few places, notably parts of Germany and Austria, some bishops were slow in signifying acceptance by publishing the decrees of the council in their dioceses. But within a year or two all had done so. Episcopal lines had bent, but, again, there was no breakaway bishop — which is what a schism needs for viability.

The declaration of infallibility quickly proved beneficial for the Vatican. Two months after the adoption of *Pastor aeternus*, the Papal States were swallowed up in the Italian Risorgimento, and the temporal authority which belonged to the papacy for a millenium was for all practical purposes gone forever. The pope was now purely a spiritual leader. But papal primacy and infallibility so strengthened other dimensions of the pope's office that the loss of temporal authority in the long run proved benefit rather than bane.

# "INFALLIBILITY" IN THE FIFTH CENTURY

**AS MENTIONED,** the church always regarded itself as infallible. This, for instance, is the way a fifth-century pope now sainted, Leo the Great, 440-461, conceived of papal authority and its inerrancy:

"...He has delegated the care of his sheep to shepherds, yet he has not abandoned the guardianship of the flock. And with his overruling and eternal protection we have received the support of the Apostles' aid also, which assistance does not cease from its operation; and the strength of the foundation, on which the whole superstructure is reared, is not troubled by the weight of the temple that rests upon it. For the solidity of that faith which was praised in the chief of the Apostles is perpetuated; and as that remains which Peter believed in Christ, so that remains which Christ instituted in Peter....

"The dispensation of truth...abides and the blessed Peter persevering in the strength of the Rock, which he has received, has not abandoned the helm of the church, which he undertook. For he was ordained before the rest in such a way that from his being called the Rock, from his being pronounced foundation, from his being constituted the Doorkeeper of the kingdom of heaven, from his being set as umpire to judge and loose, whose judgments shall retain their validity in heaven, from all these mystical titles we might know the nature of his association with Christ. And still today he fully and effectually performs what is entrusted to him and carries out every part of his duty and charge in Him and with Him through Whom he has been glorified. And so if anything is done rightly and rightly decreed by us, if anything is won from the mercy of God by our supplications, it is of his work and merits whose power lives and whose authority prevails in his see. For throughout the church Peter daily says, "Thou are the Christ, the Son of the living God."

## BAPTISM OF FIRE

**HARKING BACK FOR A MOMENT** to the Franco-Prussian War (q.v. July 19), its outbreak not only sent bishops scurrying, it also effectively terminated Vatican Council I. The council was recessed, never resumed, and thus never formally closed. Another incidental piece of religious history connected with that war: it provided the term "baptism of fire" its particular modern application; namely, a soldier's first experience in battle.

The term "baptism of fire" has obvious roots in Christian history, as one of the substitutes for baptism by water. To provide for those who through no fault of their own never received the sacrament of baptism (and who presumably were barred therefore from entering heaven), the church devised the categories of baptism by blood (*baptismus sanguinis*) and baptism by fire (*baptismus flaminis*). The use of the Latin word *flamen* in the latter context was intended to signify Holy Spirit, *flamen* being the name for the Holy Spirit and the Spirit's symbol, flame — close enough in anyone's lexicon to the word fire. Unbaptized martyrs who died at the stake thus experienced a "baptism of fire."

The term's application to a soldier's life came about when Napoleon III (Louis Napoleon Bonaparte) ordered his son and heir, Prince Louis Napoleon, just fourteen at the time, into battle at Saarbrucken. With irony, the French labeled the experience the prince's *bapteme de feu*, his "baptism of fire."

The prince survived the battle, but after several French defeats crossed to England with his mother, Empress Eugenie. On his father's death in 1873, he became Napoleon IV, official pretender to the French throne. Thinking military prestige would facilitate his return to France, imperialists persuaded him to volunteer on the English expedition of 1879 to Zululand in southern Africa. It was fatal advice. He was killed by Zulus while out on a reconnaissance mission with a few troopers. It was June 1, 1879 — and he was only twenty-three years old.

# JULY 22

## THE SWEET PEA UNLOCKS THE GENETIC CODE

**JOHANN MENDEL WAS BORN** on this day in 1822 at Heinzendorf near Odrau in Austrian Silesia. He added the first name Gregor on becoming an Augustinian monk. Thus, Gregor Johann Mendel. Does the name mean anything to you? It should. Gregor Johann Mendel was an amateur botanist who crossbred varieties of the common green pea, *Pisum sativum*, and opened the doors of science on heredity and life itself. By 1866 he had defined the basic laws of genetics.

In the beginning, however, the emphasis was on plants and animals — tomatoes, horses, hens and of course peas. Mendel discovered that in plants and animals pairs of opposed features behaved in regard to their characteristics, not in haphazard fashion, but in terms of a so-called natural law, so that different pairs of hereditary traits were independently assorted from each other. Mendel's laws led later scientists to the human person and the spiraling molecule that proved to be the life strand of all living cells: deoxyribonucleic acid, or DNA. They found that there were no less than three billion DNA base-pair genes in the human body, and by 1970 they were able to isolate, analyze, splice, clone and otherwise manipulate individual genes.

Science was now in a position, in effect, to play God so far as life was concerned. It could fuse elements of life in a test tube; it could determine the genetic future of life, down to such details as the color of eyes and whether the person should be left-handed or right. That, of course, is only the beginning. Pandora's box is open on an endless group of biomedical possibilities. With them come an equally endless array of ethical and moral questions. Do we have a resposibility to bear only perfect children? Is there a place in society for people with birth defects and propensities, say, to mid-life diseases? Tough questions, but don't blame modern science that we have them. They trace back to an Augustinian monk who wanted a sweeter sweet pea.

# JULY 23

## THE MIRACLES OF THE BIBLE

**HOW MANY MIRACLES** of Christ are recorded in the Bible for his thirty-three years of public life? Answer: thirty-five. That may not be the sum of Christ's miracles; there may have been some that went unrecorded — in fact, no doubt were. But thirty-five we know of, thanks to Matthew, Mark, Luke and John.

Miracles were essential to Christ's mission. The most dramatic of them — the raising of the dead to life (Matthew 9:18-26, Luke 7:11-17, John 11:1-44), the multiplication of the loaves and fishes (Matthew 14:15-21, 15:32-39), and most especially his own Resurrection — are actions placing a divine seal on his life and message. They accent Christ's own divinity. The miracle of the loaves and fishes, for instance, relates to the Eucharist as much as to the divine power to provide for human needs.

Other of Christ's miracles — making the blind see, cripples walk, lepers clean, the deaf hear (Matthew 11:4-5) etc. — are regarded as special manifestations of God's mercy and love for humankind, and also as works confirming some point of teaching. The miracles of healing, for instance, are related symbolically to the power of Christ and subsequently the church to cure the spiritual sickness of sin.

Christ's miracles, in sum, are demonstrations of God's goodness and interest in humankind's welfare and happiness, and of his concern for the eternal salvation of his creatures. They belong to divine prerogative.

Miracles did not end with Christ's mission on earth, any more than they began with that mission. The Old Testament records numerous miracles, like Moses' parting of the sea (Exodus 14:21ff) and Elijah's multiplication of the flour and cooking oil (1 Kings 17:11ff). Miracles happened in biblical times, and so do they continue to occur, since Christ promised the power of miracles to the church as a sign of its divine mission (Mark 16:17-18). Read on.»»»

# THE MEANING OF MIRACLES

**THE CURIOUS THING** is that there is a lowered expectation of miracles in today's church, despite Christ's promise in Mark 16:17-18: "Signs like these will accompany those who have professed their faith. They will use my name to expel demons; they will speak in new tongues; they will be able to handle serpents; if they drink a deadly poison, it shall not harm them; and the sick will recover upon whom they lay their lands." Has a large cynicism taken root?

Not necessarily. Back in the sixteenth century, when the age of faith was in full flower, the Spanish mystic St. John of the Cross was expressing distrust of post-biblical miracles and cautioning that there likely were natural explanations for such phenomena as visions, the experiencing of the stigmata, wondrous signs and seemingly magical interventions of the divine in human affairs. John of the Cross was not denying the power of God to work miracles directly or through instruments of his will, but only suggesting that the wise person should look to self and surroundings, since in the normal course God speaks to individuals through the persons, places, situations and events that form the context of everyday life.

Obviously something of this has coalesced in Catholics of the twentieth century. Even the official church had grown cautious about accepting an astonishing happening as a miracle of God. That does not mean, however, that the church is any less believing in miracles. It means only that it has come to a different appreciation of what a miracle may mean. Miracles do not happen to awe, as some athletic or scientific feat might. As in biblical times, they happen to work effects on people. Said another way, miracles are not demonstrations of divine stuntsmanship, but signs of the larger power that controls the universe. As such, their meaning and import are defined in terms of what people feel and experience. In this context, a faith restored may today be a greater miracle than a sight restored. Who's to say otherwise?

Paul VI (Sculpture by Robert Berks)

# PAUL VI AND CAFETERIA CATHOLICS

**THIS DAY IN 1968** proved one of the most momentous for modern Catholicism. It was the day that Pope Paul VI issued *Humanae vitae*, the enyclical reiterating the church's traditional ban on the use of artifical contraceptives and reaffirming that "every conjugal act must be open to the transmission of life." As we know, the encyclical served as catalyst for protest unseen in the church since the Reformation. Huge numbers of Catholics rebelled. Many, in the jargon of the times, "turned off." But surprisingly few left their church. They stayed, and with their staying the church — for better or for worse, depending on one's reading — became a different place. How different a place? Religious sociologists like Father Andrew Greeley have observed that, although there may have been no noticeable increase in "disidentification" from the church because of *Humanae vitae*, there was nonetheless a noticeable decline in religious devotion and a dramatic departure from many of the traditional orthodoxies in the practice of faith.

In other words, people stayed, but they stayed on their own terms, and thus was born among many that brand of faith some call "cafeteria Catholicism" — a picking and choosing between points of dogma and on mandates relating to religious worship and practice, such as attendance at Sunday Mass.

Others prefer to see this development of independence as an exaltation of the individual conscience (and in Catholic doctrine, conscience still determines the rightness or wrongness of any act), as well as an application of Vatican II's Declaration of Religious Freedom within the church. Either way, our generations are witness to a phenomenon unique in the history of Catholicism.

Will the church survive all the concomitant turmoil and confusion?

Sure. It survived the Crucifixion, didn't it?

# HILAIRE BELLOC, APOLOGIST WITHOUT BLUSH

**THIS WAS THE BIRTH DATE** in 1870 of one of the great Catholic apologists of all times, Hilaire Belloc. Born in France, educated at the Oratory School at Edgebaston (where Newman presided) and at Oxford, Belloc was historian, essayist, travel writer, poet, biographer, sometime sketcher, indomitable controversalist, and of course Catholic militant. He served in the House of Commons from 1906-1910 as the member from South Salford. When he stood for election, he knew he faced a problem of voters' religious bias. He hit it square on. On his very first campaign speech, he appeared, rosary in hand, and announced: "I am a Catholic. As far as possible I go to Mass every day. As far as possible I kneel down and tell these beads every day. If you reject me on account of my religion, I shall thank God that he spared me the indignity of being your representative." The voters loved his candor.

Not everyone else did. Belloc believed that "the Church is Europe: and Europe is the Church." So he wrote in 1920, and underscored the conviction in subsequent books. His critics were many, and not for reasons alone of his Catholic partisanship. Belloc's books were uneven, and his scholarship often suspect. Also attitudes towards Jews left him open to charges of anti-Semitism. But criticism deterred Belloc not one whit. Nor could people ignore him, as a Sheed & Ward blurb once said, any more than they could ignore a tiger on the doorstep.

Books flowed from his pen with such speed that in dedicating *The Cruise of the Nona* to Maurice Baring in 1925, Belloc himself speculated that maybe they ought to be numbered like the streets of America. In which case *Nona* would have been 106 — and Belloc would be writing assiduously until suffering an incapacitating stroke in 1946. He died in 1953, after falling into a fireplace in his home in Sussex, England, near West Grinstead.

# JULY 27

## The Apostles' Creed

1. *I believe in one God, the Father almighty, Creator of heaven and earth;*
2. *and in Jesus Christ, his only son, Our Lord;*
3. *who was conceived by the Holy Spirit, born of the Virgin Mary,*
4. *suffered under Pontius Pilate, was crucified, died, and was buried.*
5. *He descended into hell; the third day he arose again from the dead;*
6. *he ascended into heaven, sitteth at the right hand of God, the Father almighty;*
7. *from whence he shall come to judge the living and the dead.*
8. *I believe in the Holy Spirit;*
9. *the holy Catholic Church, the communion of saints,*
10. *the forgiveness of sins,*
11. *the resurrection of the body,*
12. *and life everlasting. Amen.*

# YESTERDAY'S PRAYERS

**IF FEWER PEOPLE ARE** reciting the rosary (q.v. Oct. 1,2), it follows that fewer are saying the Apostles' Creed. The Apostles' Creed, so called because it came down from apostolic times, is the opening prayer of the rosary. Like the Nicene Creed of the Mass, it is the expression of an act of faith, an assent to a body of truths. More specifically, it is a summary of the principal truths taught by the Apostles — though, it might be noted, neither the wordage nor not all twelve articles of the creed originated with the Apostles and thus in apostolic times. Some words were added later to rebut heresy and to clarify points of doctrine. The phrase "Creator of heaven and earth," for instance, was added to counteract the third-century heresy of Manichaeanism, the sect of synthesis and alleged pure reason that held that the world was created by the principle of evil. Similarly, the word "Catholic" was introduced over time to distinguish the "True Church" from growing numbers of competitors.

The Apostles' Creed doesn't literally belong to yesterday, not being completely forgotten and neglected. But some might need a refresher course in its wording. Hence, here is the Apostles' Creed, numbers inserted, paint-by-the-numbers-style, to identify its separate articles.

# CLARIFYING THE ISSUE OF WHO'S TO BE SAVED

**IN 1949 ROME** was embroiled with a Boston Jesuit, Leonard Feeney, over the meaning of the Latin phrase *extra ecclesiam nulla salus*. Feeney had taken the hard line that the phrase literally meant "outside the church, no salvation," and to bolster his case he invoked Lateran Council IV of 1215, Pope Boniface VIII's 1302 bull on papal supremacy, and the profession of faith sworn to in 1869 by the Fathers of Vatican I — "This true Catholic faith, outside of which no one can be saved...." The problem was that Rome had moved to a new age of pluralism, if not quite yet ecumenism, and the phrase had become something of an embarrassment, a haughty piece of dicta belonging to another time, and no longer to be perpetuated. On this day in 1949 the Sacred Congregation of the Holy Office sought to set the issue straight, declaring:

"Now among those things which the church has always preached and will never cease to preach is contained also that infallible statement by which we are taught that there is no salvation outside the church. However, this dogma must be understood in the sense in which the church herself understands it.... In his infinite mercy God has willed that the effects, necessary for one to be saved, of those helps to salvation which are directed toward man's final end, not by intrinsic necessity, but only by divine institution, can also be obtained in certain circumstances when those helps are used only in desire and longing.... Therefore, that one may obtain eternal salvation, it is not always required that he be incorporated into the church actually as a member, but it is necessary that at least he be united to her by desire and longing...[which] need not always be explicit... God accepts also an implicit desire."

Clear? Not sufficiently so for Vatican II, which said plain out in the constitution *Lumen gentium* that the divine "plan of salvation" included others besides Catholics; in fact, it included the unbaptized as well as the baptized.

## THE POWER OF A CATECHETICAL HOLINESS

**TODAY IN 1859** the man revered in France as a living saint neared his end. He had fallen down several times in his room. Now he fell on the stairs making his way to church. He was placed in his bed. The weather was excruciatingly hot. He was ice cold. Flies buzzed about his face. A Sister of St. Joseph brushed them away with her handkerchief. "Leave me my poor flies," the dying man said. "Nothing worries me but sin." The man was St. John Vianney, curè of Ars, who one day would be declared patron of parish priests.

Ars was the village near Lyons that Pere Vianney transformed by his holiness and simple wisdom into a center of piety and devotion. People flocked there on pilgrimage to hear his daily catechism lesson and to kneel before him in confession. In 1855 alone more than 20,000 pilgrims flocked to Ars, and Vianney was spending between sixteen and eighteen hours a day in the confessional. So much in demand was he as a confessor that he was not even allowed the privilege of being sick. When he was ill, people would kneel at his bedside in confession. When he was dying, they were sending objects to his room for him to bless.

John Vianney died August 4, 1859, and would be canonized in 1925 by Pope Pius XI. But the ceremony of canonization was mere formality to Vianney's legions of admirers; to them he was a saint from the start. His example was that of prayer and of fasting; his method, basically catechetical.

The wonder was the unlikeliness of it all. As a youth John Vianney was a draft dodger. He was of no more than average intelligence, and had trouble as a seminarian for what was called lack of mental suppleness in dealing with theory as distinct from practice. He managed ordination, but was scorned for his lack of learning. Superiors passed him over for promotion. The assignment to Ars was no plum. Ars, in fact, was reputed to be a godless place. Yet he transformed it into a spiritual oasis by the very ordinariness of his holiness.

The Sea of Galilee

# SOME GUESSES ABOUT GALILEE

**IT EASY ENOUGH** to figure out why the fishermen among the Apostles worked the Sea of Galilee instead of the much larger Dead Sea, which was only about 70 miles away. The Dead Sea, 46 miles long and 9.5 miles wide, had no fish; it's five times saltier that the ocean. The Sea of Galilee, on the other hand, 13 miles long and 8 miles at its widest, teemed with fish — which was eaten locally or salted and dried and shipped to places as far off as Spain.

The Sea of Galilee, in Pliny's words, "was surrounded by pleasant towns," and it was to one of them — Capernaum — that Christ moved from Nazareth. Why Capernaum? One guess is because carpenters were in demand in a shipbuilding place like Capernaum, and wasn't Christ a carpenter? He picked up his first Apostles there (Peter, Andrew, James, John and Matthew). He also picked up a lot of lore about boats, navigation and fishing, on which he constantly drew in his preaching. He also worked many miracles there, including the raising of Jairus' daughter from the dead and the curing of the centurion's servant.

Christ left Capernaum, cursing it as he did so (Matthew 11:23), but he stayed about the Sea of Galilee itself, which, coincidentally or not, attracted large crowds of visitors for its tropical climate and reportedly curative waters. Herod himself had built his palace near the warm sulphur springs of Tiberias. In any instance, the area's reputation as a health spa is thought to account for the large number of the sick Christ encountered thereabouts. Mark records the phenomenon: "And when they had passed over, they came into the land of Gennesaret, and drew to the shore. And when they were come out of the ship, straightway they knew him, and ran through that whole region round about, and began to carry about in beds those that were sick, where they heard he was. And whithersoever he entered, into villages, or cities, or country, they laid the sick in the streets, and besought him that they might touch if it were but the border of his garment; and as many as touched him were made whole" (6:53ff).

# JULY 31

The signuature of St. Ignatius

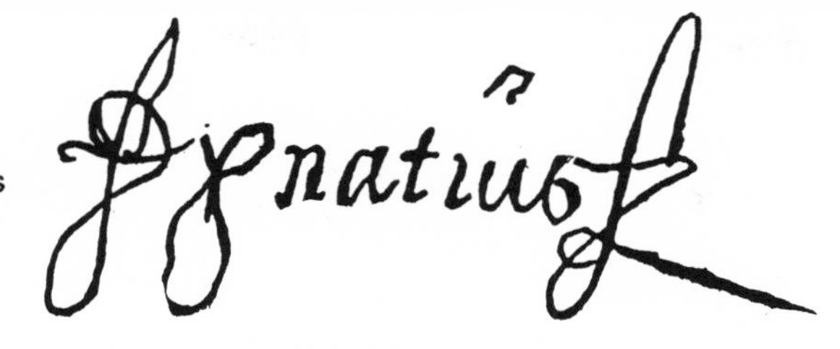

## THE MAN WHO MOBILIZED THE JESUITS

**NO RELIGIOUS ORDER** of men or women has claimed more attention, some welcome, much otherwise, than the Society of Jesus, the Jesuits. Since its beginnings in Paris in 1528, the order has been at the center of most of the church's great controversies and many of its triumphs. It has known more than its share of enemies — and friendly patrons. It has weathered all storms....and today the church honors its founder, St. Ignatius Loyola.

Ignatius wasn't Loyola's birth name; it was Inigo Lopez de Recalde. The Ignatius was adopted out of devotion to St. Ignatius of Antioch. The Loyola? It was linked to the castle to which the young Loyola, then a soldier, was taken in 1521 after suffering a serious leg wound while fighting with the Spanish against the French in the seige of Pampeluna. That would reshape Ignatius Loyola's life, for to kill time during his long convalescence, he took to reading lives of the saints. Struck especially by the lives of St. Francis and St. Dominic, Ignatius Loyola resolved to challenge their legacy and become a saint of comparable renown. Indeed he did through the Jesuit order.

It meant, however, reordering his life, spiritually and intellectually. Trained as a soldier, Ignatius lacked rudimentary learning, so in his thirties, back to school he went, sitting on benches alongside little children to acquire the skills that would enable him to enter the universities at Alcala and Salamanca. In 1528 he left for the Sorbonne, and there he met the five who with him would comprise the core of Jesuit origins: Faber, Lainez, Bobadilla, Rodriguez and of course the famous Francis Xavier (q.v. March 4). They would swear vows in an underground chapel in Montmartre in 1534, but it would be six years before formal recognition was extended the order by the bull *Regimini militantis ecclesiae* of 1540 by Pope Paul III. The bull's title clues to the order's direction. It would be an order of perfect discipline, a militant regiment in the service of the church. Thus, besides the customary vows of poverty, chastity and obedience, members took a fourth vow of special obedience to the pope, the church's leader.

Originally, Ignatius Loyola envisioned a mission in the Middle East for the order, but the disturbed state of affairs in the Levant prompted him to go instead to Rome, where the order was placed at the disposal of the Holy See. The rest is history.

One small footnote: The bull of erection limited the Jesuits to sixty members. So immediate was the success of the order that within three years the quota had been filled. A second bull, accordingly, had to be issued to enable the order to keep growing. The Jesuits' growth, in the view of people of the time, was nothing short of miraculous — but then hadn't Paul III himself said on reading the order's constitution, "The finger of God is here" ?

Ignatius Loyola died on this day in 1556 at age sixty-five, worn down it is said by labors and privations. His order had been formally constituted only sixteen years, but on Ignatius Loyola's death it already numbered twelve provinces, 101 houses and nearly 1,000 members, and was fully launched to fame and controversy (q.v. Jan. 30 and Aug. 7). Its founder would be canonized in 1622 and assigned a feast day of July 31.

# AUGUST 1

Oliver Cromwell

## LIVING AND BELIEVING "BEYOND THE PALE"

**IT WAS THIS MONTH** in 1649 that Oliver Cromwell, Lord Protector of England, quelled the so-called rebellion in Ireland. Read some histories and Cromwell was a tolerant man; read some others and he established an "unexampled prosperity" in Ireland; talk to the Irish, especially Irish Catholics, and one hears quite different. Oliver Cromwell was tyrant and murderer, and whatever else he did for (or to) Ireland, he left it with one of the infamous catch-phrases of history: "To hell or Connaught." The Irish resent him for that.

"To hell or Connaught" is a phrase that pricks the Irish to this day. In historical context, it translates that native Irish, particularly Irish Catholics, were dispossessed of their land and given two choices: death or life in Connaught. Then as now, Connaught, the northwest province of Ireland, just happened to be the stoniest and most impoverished corner of the land.

A second catchphrase of history was expanded — quite literally — by Lord Cromwell's "quelling" of the Irish, the phrase "beyond the pale." The word "pale" derives of the Latin *palus*, meaning a stake or boundary marker driven into the ground to indicate the fencing off of a certain territory. Over time, the "pale" came to signify the area of Ireland around Dublin dominated by the English. For many years before Cromwell, that "pale" had been shrinking in on itself. Cromwell corrected this with his "hell or Connaught" policy. Catholics were shown no mercy, and priests were ordered out of the country. Resisters were shipped "beyond the pale" to the Arran Islands or the Barbados. Those who stayed were hunted down, and as caught, they and their protectors were executed. A thousand priests were driven into exile. The pale, meanwhile, grew to include Ireland's pleasantest, most livable counties.

Today "beyond the pale" is used to indicate any place where social outcasts are consigned. Kipling's poem "Beyond the Pale" accounts for the application.

# THE STORY ON ADAM AND EVE

**EVER WONDER WHAT BECAME** of Adam and Eve? Catholic tradition is extraordinarily vague about them; there are no feasts even to either one in the liturgical calendar. Jewish tradition, on the other hand, is full of detail.

Yes, Adam and Eve were redeemed. They repented and did penance — Adam standing up to his neck in the Jordan for forty days; Eve in the Tigris for eighteen days. Subsequently, God granted Adam's seed the privilege of serving him, and the human race was begun. That's how the story ends; here's how it begins....

According to Jewish lore, the bliss of paradise was short lived, for Adam ate the fruit of the forbidden tree only three hours after his creation. Some masters of Jewish oral law speculate that the fruit was from a fig tree; others, from a vine. Not much opinion favoring an apple, in other words. Whatever, with the Sabbath approaching, God allowed Adam and Eve to remain in the Garden of Eden until the next day, whereupon they were expelled. It was then that the two encountered darkness for the first time, Eden having been a place during the primeval Sabbath of perpetual daylight. Fearful that the end was approaching, Adam repented, and God then revealed to him the gift of fire.

As a further act of repentance, Adam separated from Eve for 130 years, a time during which the spirits and demons came into being. Adam was to live 930 years, though the life-span for his descendants would be 70 years. His burial place was Mount Moriah. Or was it the Cave of Machpelah, where the patriarchs were later buried? Take your choice. As for Eve, she survived Adam. Knowing, however, that her life too would soon end, she related her story in great detail, and said it should be preserved on stone tablets — long lost, alas.

A final note: In the *Midrash*, Adam is reproved by the saints at the gates of paradise for having sinned, thus bringing mortality into their lives; Adam responds: "I sinned but once; and who among you has not committed many more sins than I? You have none to blame for your punishment but yourselves."

# THE RIVAL OF LORETTO AND COMPOSTELLA

**THE YEAR WAS 1538,** and this the last day that one of Christendom's then most famous Marian shrines would be in existence. The previous month the shrine had been despoiled of its wealth; four centuries ago tomorrow its priory would be dissolved and its twenty-two members scattered to their fates.

The shrine was that of Our Lady of Walsingham in north Norfolk, England, not far from the sea. Walsingham was once the rival of the shrines of Our Lady of Loretto and St. James of Compostella. It dated from 1061, and popular belief held that Mary had made it her real home after the desecrations by Mohammedans in the Middle East. Pilgrims by the thousands flocked to the place, following a series of crosses that pointed the way, much as the Milky Way was supposed to point to Mary's home. The trail was called Walsingham Way.

A feature of Walsingham was a wishing well — two wells really. One was directed to kneel between the two wells with the right knee bare, dip the left hand in the water, drink from the palm and wish. The wish would be granted in a year's time, provided one did not mention the wish to anyone or utter it aloud to oneself.

Among those who visited in pilgrimage was the very one who would be the shrine's despoiler — King Henry VIII. Walsingham was Henry's favorite place of devotion, and he went there often, once walking barefoot, to pay homage to the Virgin. But once the break was made from Rome, Walsingham would not spared, not even its revered carved statue of Our Lady. The statue was dismantled and sent to London, where it was burned. Walsingham slipped quietly into ruins. It is said that of all Henry's desecrations, the one that troubled conscience most was that of Walsingham. He thought about it even on his death bed, and consigned his soul to none other than Our Lady of Walsingham.

The shrine was excavated in 1855 and 1955, and pilgrimages have revived to the place. But the days of greatest glory were ended by Henry VIII.

# AUGUST 4

## DID PIUS XII CONTEMPLATE RETIRING IN 1943?

**THE WORLD DEBATES** yet Pope Pius XII's 'silence' in the face of the Holocaust and the systematic extermination of the Jewish people by the Nazis. Was it cold and heartless? Was it sinister? Or was it misinterpreted, and is Pius therefore the victim of a bum rap? The questions are argued endlessly.

A related question, one hardly ever broached anymore, is what if the Nazis had taken Pius XII captive and spirited him away to Germany? What would he have done? Were there contingency plans at the Vatican for such a possibility?

The questions are hypothetical given the playing out of history. But once upon a time the Vatican did ponder them seriously. Indeed, on this day in 1943, the Vatican Secretary of State, Cardinal Luigi Maglione, told Rome's cardinals that the Italian government expected the Nazis to be tough with the pope. Pius would be seized and taken to Munich, along with members of the Secretariat of State.

As it turned out, Maglione was having no pipe dream. Nazi propaganda chief Paul Joseph Goebbels' diary for July 26, 1943 recorded that Hitler talked vehemently of occupying the Vatican and seizing the pope. It did not happen, of course. When the Nazis took over Rome, they halted at the Vatican gates.

But suppose they hadn't halted? What would Pope Pius XII have done?

According to an article in the February, 1988, *Trenta Giorni* by retiring prefect Cardinal Pietro Palazzini of the Congregation for the Causes of Saints, Pius XII had written a letter of resignation and entrusted it to a Vatican engineer named Stoppa. "If I am taken away," he reportedly said, "the prisoner will be Eugenio Pacelli, not Pope Pius XII." Palazzini backed his story with no hard documentation; he was relying on forty-year-old memories, and Vatican historians reacted with skepticism. Still, there's a curious logic to it all.

# A MARIAN FEAST MELTS LIKE SNOW

**THIS IS THE DATE** the church used to observe as the feast of Our Lady of the Snows. It commemorated an event alleged to have occurred during the pontificate of Liberius in the fourth century. According to legend, the Roman patrician John and his wife were without heirs, and made a vow to donate all their possessions to the Virgin Mary if blessed with one. Their petition heard, they then prayed to Mary for a sign as to how their possessions should be disposed. Suddenly, on the night of August 5, in a city where snow seldom fell, never mind in the summertime, snow blanketed a spot on Rome's Esquiline Hill. In obedience to a vision they had that same night, John and his wife sponsored the erection there of a grand basilica in Mary's honor. Initially the basilica was known as Basilica Liberii or Liberiana, after the reigning pope. What is it now? It's the magnificent Basilica of St. Mary Major.

St. Mary Major is the so-called fourth church of Rome. It is the largest dedicated to Mary, and the only Roman church retaining its original form and character, though of course richly embellished over the centuries. The basilica was dedicated by Sixtus III (432-440), and honored Mary under her formal definition as Mother of God. The first gold brought from the New World was used to gild the ceiling of the central nave.

As for the snow business, it is largely discounted. Sixtus III's dedicatory inscription made no allusion to any phenomenon, and historians came to treat the alleged miracle as pious legend. Nonetheless, a feast of Our Lady of the Snows took its place on the calendar. At first the feast was observed only at St. Mary Major, but in the fourteenth century it was extended to all the churches of Rome. Two centuries later Pius V declared it a universal feast, and Clement VIII at the turn of the seventeenth century raised the feast from what was once called "a double rite" to "a double major." All that's gone. Today August 5 appears on the calendar as the feast of the Dedication of St. Mary Major.

# AUGUST 6

## ECCLESIASTICAL HIERARCHS AND RETIREMENT

**FOR SOME OLDER PRELATES,** this was the day the first shoe dropped. Pope Paul VI on August 6, 1966, issued the apostolic letter *Ecclesiae sanctae* directing bishops to submit their resignation from office "not later than at the completion of their 75th year." The second shoe dropped November 21, 1970, with the motu proprio *Ingravescentem aetatem* dealing with mandatory retirement for cardinals. Among much else, *Ingravescentem aetatem* said that no cardinal after his eightieth birthday may enter the conclave and participate in a papal election — which prompted Cardinal Alfredo Ottaviani, eighty, to ask sarcastically why in that event an octogenarian should still be considered capable of filling the chair of Peter. He put his finger on what was a sore point for more than a few: the new legislation covered everyone but the pope, as if the pope and the office were not subject to or threatened by the debilities of age. *Touche.*

Nothing of consequence has changed since. The papacy is still exempt from age limitations, both in terms of eligibility (though it is unlikely anyone eighty or over would be voted to the office) and in terms of retirement.

But, yes, popes can retire, and in the last years of Paul VI's reign there was considerable speculation about the probability and even desirability of his resigning. He didn't, of course, but if he had, he at least would have had canon law on his side. Canon law conceded the right; still does.

The right is worth remarking because when Celestine V resigned in 1294 (q.v. Dec. 5), the church was thrown into turmoil. Could a pope resign? As he had no superior on earth, who was there to accept a resignation? The answer was provided by none other than Celestine's successor, Boniface VIII, who, wouldn't you guess, had encouraged the resignation in the first place. Celestine "deliberated with his brethren," the cardinals, and concurred with them: "the Roman Pontiff may freely resign."

# THE JESUITS RETURN FROM SUPPRESSION

**ON THIS DAY IN 1814,** the Jesuit order, Society of Jesus, was officially rehabilitated, Pope Pius VII signing the bull *Sollicitudo omnium ecclesiarum* ending a forty-one-year suppression. The suppression, which was supposed to be "for all eternity," had been ordered by Pope Clement XIV effective August 16, 1773. All papers of the society were handed over to a special commission, together with titles, deeds and moneys; individual Jesuits were given the option of becoming secular priests; the society with 233 years of history was theoretically no more. Except, of course, the Jesuit society hung on — in Russia and Prussia, where they received a tolerance; and in Italy, France and Austria, where they managed a shadow existence under names such as the Society of the Faith of Jesus and Society of the Sacred Heart of Jesus, thus in the words of historian Manfred Barthel being able "successfully to defy the papal ban without actually disobeying it" — a jesuitical tactic, some might say.

The rap against the Jesuits was more political than theological, certainly in the beginning. Governments resented their power, their wealth, their eloquence, their "meddling," and when Portugal took the bold step of expelling them in 1759, the rush to judgment was on. France followed in 1764, then Spain, Naples and Parma. Pressure soon reached to the papacy to ban the order altogether. Clement XIII refused, but his successor, Clement XIV, was more pliable. In 1773 the Society of Jesus ceased to be — for, as said, forty-one years.

At the time of suppression, the Jesuits had forty-one provinces and 22,589 members, 11,295 of whom were priests. Barthel's book, *The Jesuits*, shows 26,622 members, 19,574 priests, 3,277 scholastics and 3,771 brothers in 1984. The numbers, he observed, are holding firm. The order's influence, however, would seem to be of a considerably different kind from that which caused it many of its problems in the 1700s. Most would agree that's a good thing.

# AUGUST 8

## HOLY HALOS, HOLY HELPERS!

**IN THE SO-CALLED AGES** of faith (credulousness?), cults grew up around a number of saints, not for their holiness or learning, but for alleged ability to do things, like cure headaches and stomach cramps. Thus was born the feast permitted once upon a time for this day — that of the Fourteen Holy Helpers. The feast was remarkably popular in France and Germany (a colorful Bavarian tablet credits the Holy Helpers with saving a mother and her daughters from a shipboard fire July 6, 1845, as they were emigrating to America). But elsewhere it was different. The Fourteen Holy Helpers never made it big in England, nor in the New World. A 1958 source says a church is named for them in Baltimore, but none shows now in the Kenedy's *Official Directory.* So who were the Fourteen Holy Helpers once so regionally famous, and what where their specialties? The lineup was subject to local variations, but here were the regulars, and the why and by whom of their invoking:

1. **Achatius,** against headaches.
2. **Barbara,** against lightning, fire, explosion and sudden death.
3. **Blaise,** against ailments of the throat.
4. **Catherine,** by philosophers, students and lawyers.
5. **Christopher,** by travelers.
6. **Cyriacus,** against eye ailments.
7. **Denis,** against headaches and rabies.
8. **Erasmus,** against cramps and intestinal diseases.
9. **Eustace,** by hunters and against fires.
10. **George,** by soldiers and against skin diseases.
11. **Giles,** against epilepsy, insanity, sterility and demonic possession.
12. **Margaret,** by pregnant women and during childbirth.
13. **Pantaleon,** against tuberculosis and other wasting diseases.
14. **Vitus,** against epilepsy, the "dance" bearing his name.

# HOLY MOSES, HOLY SLEEPERS!

**FROM HOLY HELPERS** to Holy Sleepers....The latter are but half in number, but once upon a time the Seven Holy Sleepers were revered as much as any Fourteen Holy Helpers. In the Roman calendar they were accorded a feast day (July 27) and in the Byzantine calendar two (August 4 and 22), and a great church was erected over their supposed place of repose.

So who were the Seven Holy Sleepers? They were seven "noble young men" of Ephesus — Maximian, Malchus, Marcian, Denis, John, Serapion and Constantine — who, rather than worship an idol, took to the hills and hid up in a cave during the persecution of the Emperor Decius (249-251). All they took with them was a few coins. An infuriated Decius ordered all caves of the area sealed tight, thus entombing the dissidents in their hiding place — he thought.

Two centuries pass, and one day a man digging a foundation for a stable breaks into the cave. The seven sleepers awake, quite rested but very hungry, not having eaten (they presume) since the day before. Maximian dispatches Malchus to the city to buy bread. On entering Ephesus, Malchus marvels at the changes that have occurred "overnight," and proceeds blithely in search of a bakery. A bakery he finds, but there is great commotion when he pays for the bread. The antiquity of the coins! They excite wonder and suspicion. Malchus is hauled before authorities, but under questioning it is soon apparent that a miracle has occurred. Emperor, bishop and a large throng hurry to the cave, where the sleepers, wide awake and relishing their fame, recount their story. Their mission completed, the seven holy sleepers go to sleep again — for good.

In the sixteenth century the historian Cesare Baronius questioned the truth of the story, and the hagiographer Alban Butler in the eighteenth century wrote that maybe it was the relics of the seven that were discovered in 479, not their living, breathing selves. What matter? It's a great story. The church of St. Victor in Marseilles claims the relics of these Christian Rip van Winkles.

# THE DEACON WHO WAS MARTYRED

**OF THE ROMAN MARTYRS** of the early church, few have achieved the popularity of the third-century's St. Laurence. In the fourth century his feast rated a vigil; none besides the Apostles had that honor. In the sixth century the Leonine sacramentary provided him no less than fourteen Masses. In the Middle Ages at least thirty-four Roman churches were dedicated to him. He was even named Rome's third patron saint. Who was this great saint with claim on so many honors and whose feast is marked today? We know only in the vaguest of ways.

According to tradition, St. Laurence was born in Spain, and went with his family to Rome, where he became one of the seven deacons of the city under Pope Sixtus II. During the persecution of Valerian, Sixtus was tried and beheaded. A few days before dying, however, Sixtus prophesied to Laurence that an even more painful death would be his, and, with evil times a-coming, he should begin distributing the church's wealth to the poor. This Laurence did, so that when Valerian's men dropped around to collect the wealth, Laurence produced the poor as the sum of the church's treasury. Infuriated, Valerian ordered Laurence roasted alive on a grid. As the fire grew hot, Laurence reportedly turned to Decius, now in charge, and chided him with the words: "One side has been roasted, turn me over and eat it." Roast live martyr.

The trouble with the story, historians point out, is that it confuses the persecutions of Valerian and Decius, and contradicts an accepted fact of the Sixtus story: namely, that he was not tried but upon his arrest beheaded on the spot. On the other hand, there must be valid reason for honoring Laurence, else how account for the extensive cultus that grew up so immediately around him and his memory? Seven Roman senators were said to have been so impressed by Laurence's witness that they converted on the spot, their conversions marking the beginning of the conversion of Rome itself. This was around 258.

Alexander VI (A detail from a fresco by Pinturicchio)

# THAT MOST HUMAN OF POPES

**THIS WAS NOT ONE** of the most felicitous days in the church's history. It was the day in 1492 that Rodrigo Borgia was elected pope, taking the name Alexander VI. Rodrigo Borgia was said to have fathered six children, four by Vanossa dei Catanei. He is said also to have maintained a mistress after being elected pope, and that her influence resulted in her brother being named a cardinal. He was Alexander Farnese, later Pope Paul III. But it was the four children by Vanossa who were a problem: Juan, Caesar, Lucrezia and Jofre, born respectively in 1474, 1476, 1480 and 1482. It seems probable that Caesar and Lucrezia dabbled in poisons. At any rate, they gave the family name to one of the famous sayings of history: to dine, or to have a glass of wine with the Borgias — a great, but a risky honor. The family, including their father, likewise gave meaning to the word nepotism — Latin for *nepos*, meaning a nephew or descendant. Alexander VI filled many vital church offices from family; son Ceasar, for instance, was named an archbishop at sixteen, though he never bothered to take the post (Valencia) or be ordained.

It was written subsequently that Alexander VI was one pope who never found an apologist. Funny thing, however. He wasn't the disaster he might have been. He was a skillful administrator, and he had the prescience to surround himself with learned men — the best and the brightest, as it were. He fostered the arts (the ceiling of St. Mary Major was of his commissioning) and employed the first gold brought from the Americas by Columbus; he was tolerant towards the Jews (a remarkable Christian quality at the time); he rebuilt the Roman university; he even sought to reform the church, and a commission of his naming actually drafted decrees that foreshadowed Trent. Nothing came of them in his lifetime. The most he proved was that the church, a divine institution, could survive its most human of popes. Alexander reigned from 1492 to 1503.

# AUGUST 12

## THE DAY THE SCHOLARS WERE CHILLED

**THIS IS NO RED-LETTER** day of Catholic history. At least it wasn't in 1950, when Pope Pius XII marked it by issuing *Humani generis*, the encyclical which was to blow the whistle on a generation of church scholars, at least for the time being. Suddenly under a cloud were theologians of the stature of Henri de Lubac, Jean Danielou, Yves Congar, M.D. Chenu and Teilhard de Chardin.

The encyclical concerned itself with so-called false opinions and attempts to destroy Catholic truths by undermining foundations of Catholic doctrine. It didn't name names, but its aim was squarely on France's scholars, many of whom who were advocating a return to the theology of the early church as they probed possibilities of reform and expanded ideas on a thology of the laity. At the same time, the encyclical was emphatic in its insistence on papal prerogatives: "Theology, even when positive, cannot be equated with a purely historical science, since God has given his church, together with those sacred sources [scripture and tradition], a living teacher to illustrate and develop these truths that are contained only obscurely and as it were by implication in the store-house of the faith." Some theorize that with that statement Pius XII was preparing the public for his invocation of the infallibility doctrine proclaimed at Vatican I but never yet directly used — a matter he would change in less than three months, when on November 1, 1950, he would define the doctrine of the Assumption.

That theory seems a mite contorted, but one thing is certain: *Humani generis* put a huge damper on things. Professors lost teaching posts; superiors were removed from office; bishops were charged to keep a strict eye on what was being taught and published within their jurisdictions. Controls would one day relax, and eventually those brought under suspicion would be rehabilitated. But for the time being it was a dark, anti-intellectual period in Catholicism.

# EUCHARISTIC CONGRESSES

**THIS DAY IN 1985,** the 43rd international Eucharistic Congress was in full swing in Nairobi, Kenya, and Pope John Paul II, on the 27th foreign trip of his pontificate (there have been almost two dozen since) to Togo, Ivory Coast, Cameroon, Central African Republic, Zaire, Kenya and Morocco, was making his way there to preside over the concluding ceremonies. If Nairobi in the heart of Africa seemed an out-of-the-way setting for an event one would be inclined to associate more with metropolitan Catholicism, it wasn't — at least not particularly so. Since the staging of the 1964 Eucharistic Congress in Bombay, no site henceforth could be thought unlikely for the event.

Eucharistic Congresses are interesting, if usually triumphal, events. They are arranged, as John Paul II reminded at Nairobi, as "an expression of a particular veneration and love of the universal church for the Blessed Sacrament." In a way, Eucharistic Congresses are the Olympic Games of Catholicism. They're held on a periodic basis, with a central, permanent committee determining the site, choosing between competing cities, then overseeing a program of liturgical services, public addresses, exhibitions, religious spectacles and civic ceremonies built about a unifying theme.

The first Eucharistic Congress was held in Lille, France, in 1881. Since then they have been held at Avignon, Liege, Freiburg, Toulouse, Paris, Antwerp, Jerusalem, Rheims, Paray-le-Monial, Brussels, Lourdes (1899, 1914 and 1981), Angers, Namur, Angouleme, Rome (1905 and 1922), Tournai, Metz, London, Cologne, Montreal, Madrid, Vienna, Malta, Amsterdam, Chicago, Sydney, Carthage, Dublin, Buenos Aires, Manilla, Budapest, Barcelona, Rio de Janeiro, Munich, Bombay, Bogota, Melbourne, Philadelphia Nairobi and Seoul.

For sheer spectacle and drama, however, there was nothing to match the Eucharistic Congress held in Chicago in l926. Read on.»»»

# THE DAY THE CARDINALS' SILKS WERE RUINED

**THE 1926 EUCHARISTIC CONGRESS** in Chicago was two years in the planning, and the excitement generated caught up much of the country. When the *S.S. Aquitania* docked in New York carrying Pius XI's legate to the congress, Cardinal John Bonzano, and an assemblage of cardinals large enough for Rome itself, the city was ecstatic. Some 300,000 persons lined Fifth Avenue as the group proceeded from the docks to St. Patrick's. The train that carried the official party to Chicago was dubbed "the red train"; it was painted cardinal red for the trip. At every stop, huge throngs gathered to shout greetings.

In Chicago, the crowds were unprecedented. Many of the events were held in Soldier Field, where at the start of services, a voice would come over the loudspeaker instructing the men, "You are now in church. Please extinguish your cigars." For the concluding event, however, the scene shifted to St. Mary of the Lake, the seminary of sylvan beauty some distance from downtown, and coincidentally, from many of the facilities needed to handle a large crowd.

Special trains and autos disgorged some 270,000 on the seminary's broad acres, but as the procession of prelates wound its way along a three-mile course an early-summer thunderstorm rolled in from Lake Michigan — it was June 24 — bowing trees, dumping torrents of water, and turning the seminary's paths and lawns into swamps. The marchers, we are told, did not break ranks; there was no where for them to go. They were trapped. Spectators at the edge of the crowd fled to the shelter of the train depot, but panic resulted as more and more people jammed into its limited space. About one hundred persons were injured, ten seriously enough to require hospitalization. The procession, meanwhile, moved on, but by the time the cardinals arrived at the seminary chapel, their long trains of silk (this was before the simplifying of ceremonial robes) were mud-caked and so water-soaked they had to be rolled up and carried, in total ruin. It was all dreadfully bad luck....but also dreadfully bad planning.

# AUGUST 15

## The Memorare

*Remember, O most gracious Virgin Mary, that never was it known that anyone who fled to thy protection, implored thy help, and sought thy intercession, was left unaided. Inspired with this confidence, I fly unto thee, O Virgin of virgins, my Mother! To thee I come, before thee I stand, sinful and sorrowful. O Mother of the Word Incarnate, despise not my petitions, but in thy mercy hear and answer me. Amen."*

## The Salve Regina

*Hail, Holy Queen, Mother of Mercy, our life, our sweetness, and our hope. To thee do we cry, poor banished children of Eve; to thee do we send up our sighs, mourning and weeping in this valley of tears. Turn, then, most gracious advocate, thine eyes of mercy toward us; and after this our exile, show unto us the blessed fruit of thy womb, Jesus. O clement, O loving, O sweet Virgin Mary.*

*Pray for us, O Holy Mother of God*

*That we may be worthy of the promises of Christ.*

## MARY'S SPECIAL SUMMER DAY

**THIS IS MARY'S DAY** and has been since time immemorial, although the event which its commemorates — her assumption, body and soul, into heaven after her death — was not formally declared a dogma of the church until 1950. There are numerous feasts honoring Mary throughout the year, but none has stronger appeal to the populace than the feast of the Assumption. It's a holy day of obligation, of course, and in the reading of the Mass we catch fragments of the phrases threaded together as the Hail Mary, the *Ave Maria*.

Some of the most beautiful prayers in the church's treasury are directed to Mary, but in the revamping of the liturgy, many have been allowed to slip from mind and tongue. This may be the day to recall perhaps the two most popular of Marian prayers. You'll remember them.

# AUGUST 16

## A THEOLOGIAN DEAD BEFORE HIS TIME

**THIS DAY IN 1966** was Jesuit Father John Courtney Murray's last day as mere mortal. He was returning by taxicab to Manhattan after visiting his sister in Queens, when he was stricken with a heart attack. The cabbie rushed him to Whitestone General Hospital, but he was too late. John Courtney Murray was dead at sixty-three, much too young for one with so much yet to contribute to life.

John Courtney Murray's great religious and social achievement was the development of the proposition that church and state could not only be separate, but that in separateness resided greater freedom and fuller theological possibilities for the church itself. This was a radical idea in Catholicism in the 1940s-1950s, and in 1954 Murray was banned by his superiors from writing or lecturing further on the subject. He obeyed.

Murray's day came, however, with Vatican II, though initially he was a pariah — "disinvited" as a *peritus* (consulting expert) from 1962's opening session by the Apostolic Delegate to the United States, then Archbishop Egidio Vagnozzi. New York's Cardinal Spellman corrected that in time for 1963's session, and Murray went on of course to become the principal architect of the council's landmark declaration on religious liberty, *Dignitatis humanae*.

Germany's Bishop Walter Kampe declared that document the "American contribution to the Council." But Murray saw its limitations. He knew that beyond questions of church and state, the document opened a second front on the theological meaning of Christian freedom in the church itself. Specifically he noted that "the children of God, who receive this freedom as a gift from their Father through Christ in the Holy Spirit, assert it *within the church* as well as within the world...." The emphasis is added, but it clues that Murray saw what was ahead for the church in terms of internal dissent and the observance of doctrinal mandates. Alas, he was not alive to help resolve the issues.

## THE BURNING OF THE URSULINE CONVENT

**IN 1834, THIS WAS** an especially tense day in Boston and for American Catholicism. The previous Monday, August 11, a mob had burned down the Ursuline Convent in Charlestown, displacing ten sisters and closing their school with forty-four students. The burning was an act of bigotry — and of panic. To the inflamed Protestant imagination of the time, convents were places of suspicion, places where all sorts of immorality and corruption were said to be seated. Maria-Monk allegations were rife, and non-Catholics worried seriously of "popery" and notions of a Roman Catholic conquest of America. When a seemingly "pious girl," Sister Mary John, "Miss Harrington," slipped out of the convent, sought refuge with friends, then returned to the convent, the wildest suspicions were fueled. She had "escaped" iniquity, had been "spirited back," was being held a "prisoner" against her wishes. The local press poured oil on the story, until on August 11, 1834, a mob ransacked and burned the convent.

The superior, Sister Mary Edmond St. George, led her charges over a rear fence to safety in a nearby farmhouse, where, settled on a sofa, she expressed a wish for a clean handkerchief and a pinch of snuff. But Sister Mary Edmond St. George had left a threat behind. She had promised that some 20,000 Irishmen would avenge any ill fate to the convent. Indeed, Catholics' feelings were inflamed. Crowds of Irish laborers collected in Lowell, Worcester and Providence, and started for Boston to right the wrong against the nuns. It was this rage that Boston's Bishop Benedict Fenwick had to stem. On Sunday, the 17th, he preached at Holy Cross Cathedral, "Father, forgive them, for they know not what they do," and thanks to this and other actions of his the incident passed without one act of Catholic retaliation. A grateful city took notice, for forbearance had triumphed over hysteria. Nonetheless, as we shall see in tomorrow's entry, justice was never completely served in the aftermath.

# POSTSCRIPT TO THE CHARLESTOWN BURNING

**MANY OF BOSTON'S** most distinguished Protestants, Edward Everett and Harrison Gray Otis among them, condemned the Charlestown burning, and an investigation exonerated the Ursulines. Still they remained victims. The state refused to grant indemnity, and the court rendered the legal proceedings a farce. From the mob that participated in the burning, only nine were brought to trial and eight were acquitted, "whether because of the partiality of the jury or through the force of excited and misguided public opinion." The one conviction was in the case of a seventeen-year-old boy who had apparently taken the incident as a lark. Boston's Bishop Benedict Fenwick and the Ursulines promptly organized a successful petition for his pardon. As for the Ursulines, they moved to Roxbury and sought to open a new school there. But threats of violence followed them, and finally they gave up and retired to Canada.

For years afterwards few nuns could be found in the state. In 1849 the Sisters of Notre Dame de Namur arrived to teach in parochial schools, and though their numbers grew steadily, it was not until 1870 that they dared to appear in public wearing religious habits. Their caution was not misplaced. An Irish-Catholic section of Boston was attacked in 1837 with such fury, a state history says, that it "would probably have been wiped out but for the prompt action of Mayor Samuel A. Eliot in bringing out the militia." Bishop Fenwick is recorded as being so despairing of police protection for Catholic churches that he authorized parishes to prepare to defend themselves, and at least one parish had to — St. Patrick's on Northampton Street.

Hysteria was a long time dissipating. In 1853, as an example, George W. Burnap devoted the Dudleian Lecture at Harvard to the topic "The Errors and Superstitions of the Church of Rome," and in it specified as a particularly ominous sign that "a convent had arisen in the sight of Harvard Yard."

# THE SWINGING OF THE PENDULUM FOR SISTERS

**IT IS A SMALL IRONY** that nuns, who in one century would be viewed by elements of society as threatening to the commonweal, would be regarded in the next century, again by elements, as irrelevant and cloistered from the real world. The fact is that even while the pendulum of public opinion was moving between extremes of judgment, religious women were in the vanguard of reform and development as educators, social workers and health-care specialists. It figures. Sisterhoods provided unique opportunities for feminist expression, and sisters became true professionals in the Catholic community. As school principals, hospital administrators and heads of institutions, sisters were in leadership roles before this was common with counterparts in secular society.

Was the sisters' professionalism recognized, was it even appreciated in yesterday's church? Mary J. Oates, a Sister of St. Joseph, offers some interesting perspectives in an essay in the 1985 book *Catholic Boston: Studies in Religion and Community 1870-1970* (Robert E. Sullivan & James M. O'Toole, eds.). Oates notes that in Cardinal William O'Connell's time "sisters were permitted...to *write* papers on school issues, but at conventions and even local teachers' meetings they had to be read by men." On bread and butter levels, she notes many orders were forced to finance themselves through entertainments and solicitations of gifts because sisters' stipends were so small, reaching only $300 per annum by 1937 — housing included, to be sure, but not always board. If the sisters were too successful in supplementing their stipends, they risked the funds' being expropriated by the Chancery. Then too, as teachers in parochial schools, many sisters were technically employees of the parish and at the mercy of the pastor. He could dismiss at will — and sometimes did. Reading Oates, it is not a surprise sisters should act to revolutionize their status in the church, as they have. The wonder is they waited so long.

St. Bernard

# SAINTED MONK OF MONASTIC THEOLOGY

**TODAY THE CHURCH** salutes St. Bernard of Clairvaux, its *doctor mellifluus*, as Pius XII called him in 1953 on the eighth centenary of his death. Bernard of Clairvaux was born near Dijon in 1090, and as Benedictine monk, abbot and monastic theologian he left an enduring mark on monastic life and the spirituality of the church. He embodied in his writings and the example of his life that theology which aims at an orderly and warm exposition of truth, not so much to discover or develop new thought, but to dispose the soul to prayer and contemplation. As such St. Bernard, monk and mystic, is honored as a representative of the Christian ideal, free from egoism and personalism, that is characterized by self-sacrifice and service to community.

Interestingly enough, Bernard's life was not lived behind walls of his French monastery. He traveled (seeding sixty-eight foundations out of the one he founded at Clairvaux); he preached the Second Crusade (which ended unhappily); he mediated disputes (as between pope and antipope, Innocent II and Anacletus II, in 1130); he engaged in a huge correspondence, only part of which survives, but it is one of the chief historical sources for the period. It could hardly be otherwise. Bernard was at the center of the great events of the day — the disputes too, as over Peter Abelard, whom Bernard opposed fiercely.

He tangled with heretics, preferring the element of persuasion, but, we are told, not being neglectful of the secular arm "in cases of pertinacity." Fortunately for himself, the dogma of the Immaculate Conception had not then been declared, else the heresy hunters might have come a-calling on him. The Assumption Bernard seemed willing enough to admit, but the truth of the Immaculate Conception he held doubtful. But then the doctrine was still evolving — in fact, it was not officially defined until 1854 (q.v. Dec. 8).

Bernard of Clairvaux died on this day in 1153, "consumed by sickness and austerity." He was sainted in 1174 and named a doctor of the church in 1830.

# AUGUST 21

## "A JUG OF WINE...AND THOU"

**THIS IS THE TIME** of the new wine, and to whom might we be thankful? Would you believe Noah, he of the ark? He's the Bible's first vintner. As will be recalled from Genesis, the first thing Noah did on leaving the ark was to plant a vineyard. The fruit in, he got totally drunk from its juice and he passed out, leaving his loins exposed. A strain developed between him and son Ham, when Ham spread the tale about. By contrast, Noah's other sons, Shem and Japheth, decently took a garment and covered the father's nakedness, being careful to avert their eyes. For this they were blessed.

There's no suggestion in the Bible that Noah was an alcoholic, that he had gotten drunk before, or again afterwards. So why did it happen on the occasion of Genesis 9:18-27; how come Noah got so terribly drunk as to pass out?

*The Interpreter's Bible* is full of theories. *Escape*: "Noah wanted to escape from what he remembered." *Avoidance*: "He wanted to escape from what he realized he had to do"; after all, he was to be a second father of the human race. *Readjustment*: Lost was the "concentrated simplicity" of the womb of the ark; Noah had to face the real world. *Power....idle optimism*, etc. Forget it. The simplest, most logical explanation for Noah's big drunk is that Noah was "Mickey Finn-ed" — by himself. Being unacquainted with the effects of fermented grape juice, he drank too much, and wham!

Footnote: When Noah was born, his father Lamech exclaimed, "This same shall comfort us concerning our work and toil of our hands, because of the ground which the Lord hath cursed." Was Lamech prophesying that this son of his would be instrumental in removing the curse pronounced against Adam (Genesis 3:17ff)? Or, as some mirthfully suggest, was he prophesying the discovery that would be Noah's of that beverage "that maketh glad the heart of man" (Psalm 104:15), and likely has some medicinal value as well? Whatever, wine certainly did not stunt Noah's longevity. He lived to the grand old age of 950!

# QUEENSHIP VERSUS "PRIESTHOOD" OF MARY

**TODAY'S FEAST ON** the church's calendar is the Queenship of Mary. It's a relatively new feast, universal observance being ordered only in 1954 by Pius XII. It's also a curious feast. It's point was to commemorate the high dignity of Mary, but it did so in the context of a dignity whose day is largely passed — that of monarchy. There's a monarchy in England, but not many places else these days. Therefore there aren't many queens with us anymore. Even England's Queen Elizabeth II will be succeeded by a king, not a queen.

Could Pope St. Pius X have been more on the mark? In 1906 he promulgated an indulgence of three hundred days for devout recitation of a prayer of his composing addressed to *Maria MaterwMisericordiae.* The prayer dwelled not so much on the *queenship* of Mary as the *priesthood* of Mary! For instance, the prayer hailed Mary, "Mother of the High Priest Christ, Priest likewise and Altar." Later the prayer declared: "Although you did not accept the sacrament of ordination, nevertheless whatever dignity or grace is conferred therein you received in full measure," before concluding, "Mary Virgin Priest, pray for us."

The London *Tablet* recently recalled Pius X's prayer, noting it was not long before Vatican officials grew uneasy about the direction this devotion inspired by Pius X was leading. "There was no movement for the ordination of women at the time, but at least in the matter of taste, if not of doctrine, it was beginning to run off the rails." Exacerbating matters was the circulation of popular images of Mary vested as a priest. Never mind that medieval art frequently depicted Mary in the role of priest, and that even today a painting in the church of St. Praxedis in Rome shows the Eucharist being celebrated by women of the second century. By 1913 the Vatican had had enough. Authorities ruled that "the image of the Blessed Virgin Mary dressed in priestly vestments is to be condemned," and Pius X's prayer was quietly consigned to oblivion.

# JOHN PAUL II ON MARY'S "PRIESTHOOD"

**CONTINUING WITH** yesterday's item....Where does Pope John Paul II stand on the issue of the priesthood of Mary? He made his position known at a gathering of bishops in Rome on February 11, 1988. Mary is an outstanding model "for us pastors," John Paul II declared, a model of perfection, and her contribution is indispensable and complementary. But priest? No, she is not.

By coincidence, John Paul II's comments followed hard on speculation in The *Tablet* about a painting in the Louvre entitled *Le Sacerdoce de la Vierge*, "The Priesthood of the Virgin." In the painting, Mary is "splendidly apparelled" in priestly vestments — alb, stole, cincture, chasuble — and half turned from an altar. At her feet is the Christ child, surely, their left hands joined, his right hand clutching the hem of the chasuble. The altar is bare except for a candle and candlestick, but ten acolytes, in the form of little angels, are shown carrying processional cross, chalice, missal and censer — all of which, remarked The *Tablet*, suggests a Mass. A scroll in one corner of the painting reads, *Digne vesture au prestre souverain*, "vestments worthy of a high priest."

The *Tablet* noted that the painting was reproduced in the 1948 book *Art in Mediaeval France* by Joan Evans, and that originally the picture was given to the cathedral of Notre Dame d'Amiens by Jean de Bos, master of a confraternity in honor of the Virgin Mary in 1437. The *Tablet* further remarked on depictions of Mary as a priest in early illuminated manuscripts and on a 1916 image banned by Rome of Mary garbed as a priest. The *Tablet*'s point was more one of curiosity than anything else. In fact, apropos to the Amiens painting, it observed that Jean de Bos, the donor, was a mercer, a dealer in textiles, and that "the painting may not be so much a daring theological statement as a piece of pious trade promotion." Interesting too, however, is the question: Had John Paul II read The *Tablet* item and decided to head off further discussion?

# TRUSTEEISM AND THE AMERICAN CHURCH

**ONE OF THE NETTLING PROBLEMS** of the early American church, one that would persist in one form or another until the middle of the nineteenth century, was that of lay trusteeism, or more correctly its abuse. The problem was born of the dearth of clergy available to administer the church's multiplying parishes. As one historian has remarked, "priests were as scarce as saints." One solution was to place control of parish property in the hands of laity. The idea was new in Roman Catholicism, but it had an intoxicating appeal in the U.S., where religious freedom and the example of Protestant congregations commended its trial in the American church. The idea even had the early approval of Archbishop John Carroll, the first American bishop.

The idea never worked, however. Controversies sprang up, and relationships deteriotated between clergy and their parishioners, priests and their bishops. Nationality also became a factor, as rivalries quickened between Irish and German laity. In Norfolk, Virginia, one vestry went so far as to try to bring its grievances before Thomas Jefferson. He wisely walked wide of the matter.

There were some pretty stormy trustee fights — as at St. Peter's parish in New York in the 1780s, and then another in 1820 at St. Mary's Cathedral parish, Philadelphia. The latter reached all the way to Rome, when an excommunicated priest was accepted by the trustees as pastor, then, backed by the trustees, sought civil protection after church authorities tried to oust him.

Finally on August 24, 1822, Pope Pius VII admonished the American church, declaring the polity then arising there "totally unheard of" and a subversion of laws "not only ecclesiastical but divine." Gregory XVI added his opinion in 1841, saying: "We wish all to know that the office of trustee is entirely dependent upon the authority of the bishop, and that consequently the trustees can undertake nothing except with the approval of the ordinary." Case closed.

# A CHURCH OF NUMEROUS RITES

**ASK ALMOST ANY CATHOLIC** how many rites there are in the church and the answer will be two: the Eastern Rite and the Latin Rite. That's wrong. The church has seventeen major canonical rites of Eastern derivation, and in pockets of the Latin or Western Rite, the dominant and most populous rite of the church, there are another half-dozen small rites.

But first, just what is a rite? It's an ecclesiastical grouping comprising people organically united in the Holy Spirit, the seven sacraments and the one universal government, but differing in liturgy, ecclesiastical discipline and spiritual heritage. All approved rites are accorded equal dignity within the church, and of course all come under the spiritual care of the pope.

Here they are, as listed by the *New Catholic Encyclopedia*, taking first the Eastern Rites:

From the Patriarchate of Alexandria, two canonical rites: the Coptic and Ethiopian.

From the Patriarchate of Antioch, three canonical rites: the Sprian, Maronite and Malankar.

From the original Byzantine Church, nine canonical rites: the Bulgarian, Greek, Georgian, Italo-Albanian, Melchite, Rumanian, Russian, Serbian and Ukranian.

From the East Syrian Church, an offshoot of the Patriarchate of Antioch, two canonical rites: the Chaldean and Malabar.

The Armenian Rite.

There is dispute over several smaller groups. Some Hungarians of the Byzantine Rite claim theirs as an independent canonical rite, as do some Uniates of Volinia and Bieloruthenia. But, by and large, the seventeen listed are the commonly accepted rites of the East. As for the Western church, read on.»»»

# AUGUST 26

## THE RITES OF THE WEST

**THERE WERE AT ONE TIME** as many or more variant rites in the Western church as in the Eastern. It was Pope Pius V (q.v. April 30) who curtailed them, or most thereof, with the bull *Quo primum* of July 14, 1570.

It was this bull that imposed the Roman Missal on the Western church. The missal, which was to survive virtually intact into the twentieth century, aimed to bring uniformity of worship to the West. The church had traditonally cherished its various rites, and had protected them against fundamental changes or mixing. But, a kind of liturgical chaos was spreading in the West, so great in fact that the issue came before the Council of Trent, which formed a commission to deal with the issue. The Roman Missal resulted, seven years after the council's close. It was published by Pius V, and inevitably it brought about a thinning out of the medieval variant rites that then abounded in the West. But, again, not all of them.

*Quo primum* allowed variant (non-Latin) rites to continue to exist, but a historical continuance of at least two centuries had to be proven. This provision enabled religious orders with so-called Monastic Rites — notably the Dominicans, Carthusians and Carmelites — at least modified usage of their old ways. It also enabled rites peculiar to specific dioceses to continue serving the faithful of their respective areas. Thus to this day in the Latin or Western Rite one finds local rites existing as liturgical islands of a sort in a huge Latin sea. Four to be exact, as follows:

— Ambrosian Rite, peculiar to the Archdiocese of Milan, Italy.

— Mozarabic Rite, in use in the Archdiocese of Toledo, Spain.

— Lyonese Rite, centered in Lyons, France.

— Braga Rite, established in the Archdiocese of Braga, northern Portugal.

So is the Catholic Church a monolith? Not liturgically.

# AUGUST 27

Mother Teresa

## THE NOBEL PEACE PRIZE GOES TO A NUN

**ONE OF THE GREAT CATHOLIC HEROES** of the 20th century was born on this day in 1910 in Skopje, Albania, now a part of Yugoslavia. She was Agnes Gonxha Bojaxhiu, but you know her better as Mother Teresa, the modern-day apostle to the poor and the sick.

Young Agnes Bojaxhiu went to India at age 17 as a missionary in the order of the Sisters of Loretto, and after twenty years in Calcutta as a teacher in a private school, she asked permission to live outside the convent and minister to the poor. Moved by the plight of Calcutta's street people, she founded her own religious order, the Missionaries of Charity in 1948. Two years later, the order received canonical approval from Rome, and began a phenomenal worldwide growth. Currently the order has some two hundred branches in fifty Indian communities and nearly twenty-five countries, operating schools, hospitals, orphanages, youth centers and shelters for the poor.

Apostles of the poor frequently go unrecognized, but that has not been Mother Teresa's fate. In 1979, she was awarded the Nobel Peace Prize, the first time the peace prize had been given, in the words of the Nobel Committee, "for work undertaken in the struggle to overcome poverty and distress in the world, which also constitute a threat to peace." Interestingly enough, Mother Teresa was no surprise winner. By 1979 she was the long-established candidate to receive the award. She was the sixth woman to win it.

Her apostolate is an innovative one. Her order inevitably came to Harlem, and in 1982 it opened a house in Jenkins, Kentucky, its first in rural United States. In 1987 Mother Teresa sought to set up a house near Chernobyl for evacuees of the nuclear accident. Permission never came, but with eyes on Russia, it is hard to believe Mother Teresa will not one day be there.

# AUGUST 28

### The Act of Contrition

*O my God. I am heartily sorry for having offended thee. I detest all my sins, because I dread the loss of heaven and the pain of hell, but most of all because they offend thee, O Lord, who art all good and deserving of all my love. I firmly resolve by the help of thy grace to confess my sins, to do penance, and to amend my life. Amen.*

## YESTERDAY'S PRAYERS

**THE "ACT OF CONTRITION"** isn't exactly yesterday's prayer, but one wonders how often people recite the prayer that most Catholics learned as youngsters alongside the Our Father and the Hail Mary? To most the words of the Act of Contrition are familiar indeed, but do the new generations know the intonations as well as Catholic seniors do?

There are variations to this prayer, of course, but usually only small ones. The prayer was recommended as a part of one's night prayers and before receiving communion. And, of course, it was an integral part of confession, what is known now as the Rite of Reconciliation. One said the Act of Contrition as the priest extended his Latin absolution.

So why might the Act of Contrition be slipping into the category of yesterday's prayers? One reason is because confession of sins to a priest has become so much a part of the past for many Catholics. Sixty percent of American Catholics no longer avail themselves of the sacrament, according to a survey of the American bishops cited by *Newsweek* March 13, 1989.

Another reason why the prayer might be slipping into the cobwebs of use is because the New Rite of Penance, which mandates an expression of contrition, does not specify recitation of the Act of Contrition as such. Penitents may use that formula, if they wish. But they also may substitute a completely different formula of their own wording, thus for some obviating the necessity of ever learning it in the first place. More tomorrow.

# THE NEW RITE OF RECONCILIATION

**THE LITURGICAL EVOLUTION** of the old Sacrament of Confession into the new Rite of Reconciliation was completed in 1973, with the approval by Pope Paul VI of the revised ritual for the confessing and forgiving of sins. The United States bishops mandated its use as of February 27, 1977, though, as mentioned, the old form could still be used by those preferring so. The new ritual differed from the old in setting (reconciliation "rooms" replaced confessional "boxes" or "cubicles"), in emphasis (the social, or communal and ecclesial aspects of sin and conversion were to be stressed), and in method (the new rite offered three ways for celebrating the sacrament: individually; with groups in the course of a community celebration which included individual confession; and in special circumstances with groups in the course of a community observance with general confession and general absolution following.

The more common of those three options seems to be the first. Proponents of the new form see it enriched by such additional elements as scriptural exhortations and readings, responsory prayers and a dismissal in peace. The Latin absolution of the old form, *Ego te absolvo a peccatis tuis, in nomine patris* etc., has been replaced. The formula according to the New Rite of Penance is: "God, the Father of mercies, through the death and resurrection of his Son has reconciled the world to himself and sent the Holy Spirit among us for the forgiveness of sins; through the ministry of the church may God give you pardon and peace, and I absolve you from your sins in the name of the Father and of the Son, and of the Holy Spirit."

The penitent, who has previously asked to express sorrow for his or her sins, "using a formula you know or your own words," responds Amen. The priest then gives thanks of God, prays his mercy will endure forever, then speaks the dismissal or prayerful farewell of his own devising. A final word tomorrow.

## JOHN PAUL II ON "CONFESSION"

**THE RADICAL DECLINE** in the numbers of Catholics availing themselves of the sacrament of reconciliation elicited from Pope John Paul II the apostolic exhortation of December 2, 1984, *Reconciliatio et Paenitentia*, "Reconciliation and Penance in the Mission of the Church." The document was in a sense a post-synodal reflection on the proceedings of the 1983 Synod of Bishops, which pondered the diminished sense of sin in the world and the need for redemption, and in that context the decline in the administration and reception of the sacrament of penance. John Paul emphasized the need for reconciliation and penance with words such as these:

"...Sin is a product of man's freedom.... As a rupture with God, sin is an act of disobedience by a creature who rejects, at least implicitly, the very one from whom he comes and who sustains him in life. Sin, in the proper sense, is always a personal act since it is an act of freedom.... To acknowledge one's sin...is the essential first step in returning to God. To become reconciled to God presupposes and includes detaching oneself consciously and with determination from the sin into which one has fallen. It presupposes and includes, therefore, doing penance in the fullest sense of the term: repenting, showing this repentance, adopting a real attitude of repentance — which is the attitude of the person who starts out on a road of return to the Father.... [P]enance is closely connected with reconciliation, for reconciliation with God, with oneself and with others implies overcoming that radical break which is sin. And this is achieved only through the interior transformation or conversion which bears fruit in a person's life through acts of penance. Reconciliation, in order to be complete, necessarily requires liberation from sin, which is to be rejected in its deepest roots."

The pope's point: Get back to confession — I mean, reconciliation.

## KEEPING HEAVEN EVER IN VIEW

**BRITONS PAUSED** on this day in 1988 to mark the three hundredth anniversary of the death of John Bunyan, Catholics among them. Bunyan wasn't a Catholic. In fact, he suffered persecution for the Baptist cause during the Restoration, being imprisoned for refusing to give up preaching. Still, he is honored today by Catholics and Protestants alike for the depth of his spirituality and for his constant reminders, in Canterbury's Archbishop Robert Runcie's words, of "the destination of our Christian journey, nothing less than heaven itself."

John Bunyan lived from 1628-1688, and his master work, of course, was *The Pilgrim's Progress*, the narrative with the famous line, "So he passed over, and the trumpets sounded for him on the other side." *The Pilgrim's Progress* allegorized the life of a man named Christian from conversion to death. Once called Graceless, of the race of Japhet, Christian grows disenchanted with life in the City of Destruction, and goes in search of salvation. Christian's doubts are giants, his sins a bundle, his bible a chart, his minister an Evangelist, his conversion a flight from Destruction, his cohorts people with names like Worldly Wiseman, Faithful, Hopeful, and Giant Despair, owner of Doubtful Castle.

Bunyan wasn't gentle. Pope and Pagan, for instance, were giants whose caves Christian can only pass after reciting verses from the Psalms to protect himself from devils issuing from one of the gates of Hell. Pope sits at his cave's mouth "crazy and stiff with age...grinning at pilgrims as they go by and biting his nails because he cannot come at them."

Gordon Wakefield calls *The Pilgrim's Progress* "the all-time best seller of English Protestant spirituality." But Catholics share John Bunyan's legacy. Henri Talon wrote a stellar life of Bunyan forty years ago, and when England's Cardinal George Basil Hume issued *To Be a Pilgrim* in 1984, he prefaced it with Mr. Valiant-for-Truth's words, "Who would true valour see,/Let him come hither."

# THE DONATION OF IRELAND

**THE ONLY ENGLISH POPE** of history died on this day in 1159. It is likely that few tears were shed for him in Ireland. Certainly he is not endeared now in Irish memories. The English pope was Adrian IV.

Adrian was born Nicholas Breakspear, and came to prominence as a papal legate in Scandinavia, where he was saluted as the Apostle of the North. He worked primarily in Norway, establishing a hierarchy (previously there had only been "court" bishops) and reforming customs and instituting reforms, decreeing for instance that no person might roam armed about the towns except the twelve who formed the king's bodyguard. He arrived back in Rome something of a legend, and instant favorite for the papacy when Anastasius IV suddenly up and died. And to be sure, he was elected pope, unanimously, on December 4, 1154.

Adrian's five-year reign is remembered, by the Irish especially, for the bull *Laudabiliter*, which handed over Ireland to Henry II of England — the Donation of Ireland, as the act is known to history. English eyes had long been fixed on Ireland, and so were Rome's eyes, though for different reasons. Rome disliked the independent ways of the Irish church and was anxious to bring it and its fifth-century ecclesiastical customs into line with the rest of Christendom. So, acting under the "Donation of Constantine," the forged document which gave the pope authority over all islands of the Roman empire, Adrian IV "donated" Ireland to the Henry and the English "to hold by hereditary right." As one historical source (British) remarks, "It was conveniently forgotten that Ireland had never been in the Roman empire, and so had not even been Constantine's to give away." Thus neither Adrian's either.

The suggestion exists that because he was born in England, Adrian made Ireland over to the Angevin monarch. The allegation probably does not merit serious attention, but don't try to persuade some Catholic Irish it doesn't.

# SEPTEMBER 2

## THE POPE OF WORLD WAR I

**LIKE FORGOTTEN WARS** there are forgotten popes, and the two coincided in World War I and Benedict XV. Benedict's predecessor was canonized, and the cause of two or three of his successors is being promoted. But ask the person in the pew about Benedict XV, and you're almost guaranteed to draw blanks. His fate is anonymity, the lot too of his papacy.

Benedict was elected pope on this day in 1914, and though his reign was given over to World War I and its problems, it was also overwhelmed by them. During the war years, 1914-1918, Benedict was able to persuade the combatants to observe a truce on Christmas Day, but when the war was over he was excluded from the peace deliberations. The exclusion was quite deliberate. A clause in the secret Treaty of London, made between the Allies and Italy in 1915 prior to Italy's entry into the war, specified the pope's omission.

Why would the pope's "input" not be welcome? Undoubtedly because his neutrality rankled, and his sympathies were preceived, not unreasonably, as being more on the side of the Central Powers than the Allies. A partnership of anti-clerical France, Protestant England and Orthodox Russia did not inspire this pope's commitment to the Allies' cause. Benedict permitted no diplomats from the warring nations to live in the Vatican. However, in alluding to the war, he refused to call belligerent states by name, and expressions of outrage over what he called this "useless war" thus often rang hollow; e.g., Benedict's 1916 condemnation of Germany's occupation of Belgium: "We see minority nations, even those invested with high dignity, shamefully outraged and a number of peaceful citizens taken from their homes and deported to distant regions."

Among critics, the Italian Pope Benedetto XV became Maldetto XV; he was the accursed, not the blessed. Benedict was able to effect the exchange of many prisoners of war and bring about an improvement in care of the wounded. But when he offered his own peace plan in 1917, both sides rejected it.

# THE FLAG AS RELIGIOUS ICON

**ON THIS DAY** in 1777 the congressional resolution went into effect adopting the stars and stripes, "representing the new constellation," as the flag of the United States, and designating June 14 as Flag Day, the day for its honoring. That Betsy Ross designed the flag is now regarded as a piece of patriotic fiction, but that's about all the revisionism that is allowed so far as the flag is concerned. National flags are the banner of patriotism everywhere, but nowhere is this truer than in the United States.

Of course, patriotism, as Samuel Johnson remarked, is the last refuge of a scoundrel, but the American flag — well, as President George Bush proved with his emphasis on the Pledge of Allegiance and his visit to a flag factory during his 1988 campaign for the White House, it's impossible to wrap yourself too tightly in its red, white and blue imagery.

Catholics of a certain age knew all that. They grew up reciting the pledge each morning in parochial school, and later had the image of flag constantly reinforced by Cardinal Spellman, who made it a point on his travels as military vicar to descend from planes waving a small American flag. Dr. Tom Dooley, the 1950s paragon of all patriotic and religious virtue, out-Spellmaned Spellman. He flew the American flag from his jeep while doctoring in Southeast Asia after his discharge from the Navy, and distributed miniature American flags to his patients — almost as if flags were medicine for the spirit, as pills were for the body.

Charles Sumner, Massachusetts' nineteenth-century abolitionist senator, said the person "must be cold, indeed," who can look upon the flag "without pride of country." There's no arguing the point. But what of those who look on the flag and apply it idolatrously? They're the ones to guard against.

# SEPTEMBER 4

## The Angelus

*The Angel (angelus) of the Lord declared unto Mary.*

*And she conceived of the Holy Ghost.*

*Hail Mary, full of grace, the Lord is with thee. Blessed art thou amongst women and blessed is the fruit of thy womb, Jesus. Holy Mary, Mother of God, pray for us sinners, now and at the hour of our death. Amen.*

*Behold the handmaid of the Lord.*

*Be it done unto me according to thy Word. Hail Mary....*

*And the Word was made flesh.*

*And dwelt among us. Hail Mary....*

*Pour forth, we beseech thee, O Lord, thy grace into our hearts; that we, to whom the incarnation of Christ, thy son, was made known by the message of an angel, may by his passion and cross be brought to the glory of his resurrection. Through the same Christ, our Lord. Amen.*

## YESTERDAY'S PRAYERS

**SCHOOLS ARE REOPENING** from summer vacation, and for those who attended parochial school in the old days, here's an old memory to recall. Remember when September meant returning not only to the books, but also to prayers — prayers that perhaps haven't been said since. Like the Angelus, the prayer that honored Mary and the Incarnation. For eight years we said it before being dismissed for lunch. How many could say it now without prompt cards?

Once upon a time, church bells chimed three times a day for the Angelus — 6 a.m., noon and 6 p.m. — and the devout paused in prayer. Yesterday, indeed.

# SYNODS OF BISHOPS AND COLLEGIALITY

**A PRINCIPAL PREOCCUPATION** with the Fathers of Vatican II was the establishment of a vehicle that would continue to foster collegiality among the church's leaders. Several times the subject was broached, and this month in 1965 Paul VI responded with the document *Apostolica sollicitudo*, chartering a central church institute known as the Synod of Bishops, the synod to convene at intervals to deal with matters of moment in the church and "to encourage close union and valued assistance between the Sovereign Pontiff and the bishops of the entire world." Since 1967, synods have been held on a regular basis.

Actually there are three kinds of synods:

**Ordinary synods,** which since 1971 have been meeting every three years to discuss such topics as "Evangelization in the World" and "The Role of the Christian Family in the Modern World." Each episcopal conference is allowed a specific number of delegates according to national members (the U.S. has four, England two), and the pope may nominate 15 of the total membership.

**Special synods,** which are devoted to the affairs of a church of a particular region and usually involve the pope and bishops of the region. Examples would be the synods concerned with the Netherlands in 1980 and the Ukrainian Church in 1980 and 1985. (The 1989 synod between the pope and U.S. cardinals and archbishops was more in the nature of a special meeting.)

**Extraordinary synods,** which are supersummits of a sort. Membership is limited to the presidents of episcopal conferences or their equivalents, heads of the Roman *dicasteries*, and of course the pope, who sets the agenda, names the officials, decides the duration, and writes the summary document. In 1969 Paul VI called an extraordinary synod to discuss the reception of *Humanae vitae* (q.v. July 25), and in 1985 John Paul II scheduled an extraordinary synod for purposes of assessing the work of Vatican II (q.v. Oct. 24-27, et al.)

Though a new creation, the synod seems collegiality's permanent partner.

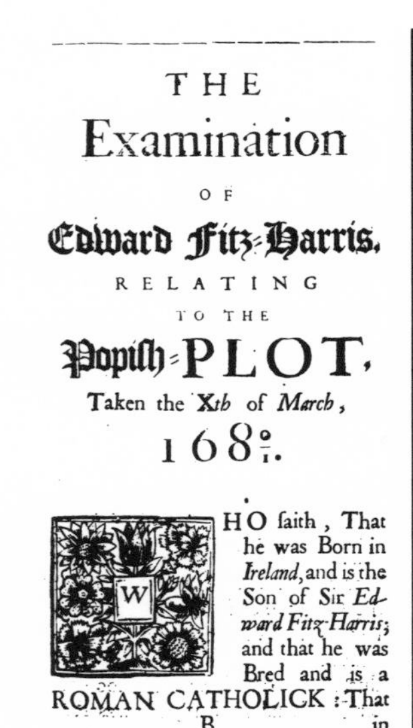

THE

Examination

OF

Edward Fitz-Harris.

RELATING

TO THE

Popish-PLOT.

Taken the Xth of March,

168⁰⁄₁.

WHO saith, That he was Born in Ireland, and is the Son of Sir Edward Fitz-Harris; and that he was Bred and is a ROMAN CATHOLICK: That

B in

Published by Order of the House of Commons. 7

formed and Discharged of His said Command; whereupon He went to Paris, and having but little Money, He lived there difficultly about a year.

IN One thousand six hundred seventy-two, going to take his leave of Father Gough an ENGLISH PRIEST at Paris, He said to this purpose.

YOU are going for ENGLAND, within these two years you will see the CATHOLICK RELIGION Established there as it is in France.

THE Examinant asking him how that could be, since the KING was a PROTESTANT; He answered, if the KING would not Comply, there was Order taken and things so laid, That he should be TAKEN OFF or KILLED.

THAT the DUKE of YORK was a CATHOLICK, and in his Reign there would be no Difficulty of doing it: This Examinant then ask-

ing

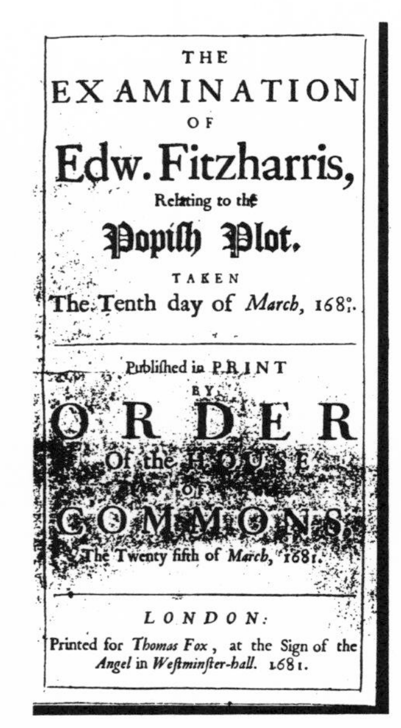

THE

EXAMINATION

OF

Edw. Fitzharris,

Relating to the

Popish Plot.

TAKEN

The Tenth day of March, 168⁰⁄₁.

Published in PRINT

BY

ORDER

Of the HOUSE

OF

COMMONS.

The Twenty fifth of March, 1681.

LONDON:

Printed for Thomas Fox, at the Sign of the Angel in Westminster-hall. 1681.

Published by Order of the H. of Commons. 17

IRELAND, and the Father promised this Examinant a Regiment of the Men so to be Raised, and Armed in IRELAND, and the Design was to restore that Kingdom to its former Owners, subject to the FRENCH.

HE also desired him to send him all the LIBELS that came out in LONDON; and said, That LIBELLING the KING and the GOVERNMENT, was a thing necessary to be done, in order to Distaste the KING, and make him Afraid and Jealous of his People.

THAT he knew Mr. Everard at PARIS, in One thousand six hundred sixty five, and hath since continued and encreased his Acquaintance with him; that the Opinion of Father Patrick, was an Encouragement to him to

E to

Pages from a 1681 document relating to the Popish Plot

# TITUS OATES, MISCHIEF MAKER

**TITUS OATES IS KNOWN** by history as the infamous fabricator of the Popish Plot, a scheme which played on seventeenth-century Protestant suspicions of Catholics in England by alleging a vast Catholic conspiracy to murder Charles II, burn London, massacre non-Catholics, place James on the throne, and bring about in sum a suppression of Protestantism in the country.

On this day in 1678 Oates, a pretending Catholic, made an 81-article deposition outlining the alleged plot before Middlesex magistrate Sir Edmund Berry Godfrey. When Godfrey was found murdered shortly afterwards, excitement rose to fever pitch, and Parliament rushed into session to pass a new test act excluding all Catholics from power. Arrests and witch trials followed, and before ending some three years later a score or more prominent persons were executed for treason, including five Catholic peers of Parliament, the secretary of the duchess of York, several Jesuits, and the archbishop of Armagh, Oliver Plunket, now sainted.

As for Titus Oates, he achieved great wealth by his spurious revelations, and a handsome pension. But as his story of a Popish Plot came more and more to be doubted, he fell into disrepute, and was pilloried, whipped and imprisoned for three and a half years. Eventually he received a royal pardon, and his pension was restored, though at a much smaller figure. He joined the Baptist Church and became preacher at Wapping. He was the source of more trouble there, before being formally expelled as a Baptist as the result of a financial scandal. Titus Oates died in 1705. He wasn't greatly missed.

# SEPTEMBER 7

## HOISTING ONESELF ON ONE'S SYLLABUSES

**THIS WAS THE EVE** of the day Pope Pius X's encyclical *Pascendi dominici gregis* burst upon the church in 1907. Concerned with the doctrines of "Modernists," the encyclical formalized the decree *Lamentabili sane exitu* of two months before and gave the church an updated syllabus of errors to complement Pius IX's 1864 syllabus, *Quanta cura*. In a set of sixty-five propositions, the new syllabus condemned the chief propositions of Modernism, the name given to a so-called synthesis of all heresies. Among much else, it specified penalties for those refusing obedience to ecclesiastical authority, those who show a love of novelty in history, archaeology or biblical exegesis, and those who neglect the sacred sciences or appear to prefer the secular sciences to them. *Pascendi* spawned the "Oath against Modernism," which was taken by clergy and professors of philosophy and theology at Catholic seminaries from 1910 to 1967, when it was replaced by a much more abbreviated profession of faith.

Pius X's syllabus was essentially doctrinal in its focus, but it came atop a whole series of nineteenth-century papal condemnations of indiscriminate kind which had the effect of turning the church away from a host of critical human issues and political developments. For instance, the church's head was turned when great issues of democracy arose, so that decades after most everyone else had faced up to freedom of conscience and political and social equality, the church was having to state itself on the subjects, a matter to which much of Vatican II was given. In the years since, the church has deeply involved itself in the struggles of the modern world, but it was too long absent from the scene.

The syllabuses are dead documents in today's church. But they took their time dying. They also left many unfairly impugned in their wake — including one man who eventually became pope. To his amazement, Angelo Roncalli, the future John XXIII, once found himself reported to Rome as a possible Modernist.

# A SAMPLING FROM A SYLLABUS OF ERRORS

**WHAT DOES A SYLLABUS** sound like? Here are sample propositions from the sixty-five condemnations itemized in Pius X's decree *Lamentabili sane exitu*. All errors, they "are being daily spread among the faithful," said *Lamentabili*. "Lest they captivate the faithful's minds and corrupt the purity to faith," they are condemned herewith (the numbers correspond to those of *Lamentabili*):

2. The church's interpretation of the Sacred Books is by no means to be rejected; nevertheless, it is subject to the more accurate judgment and correction of the exegetes.

5. Since the deposit of faith contains only revealed truths, the church has no right to pass judgment on the assertions of the human sciences.

9. They display excessive simplicity or ignorance who believe that God is really the author of the Sacred Scriptures.

17. The fourth Gospel exaggerated miracles not only in order that the extraordinary might stand out but also in order that it might become more suitable for showing forth the work and glory of the Word Incarnate.

44. There is nothing to prove that the rite of the Sacrament of Confirmation was employed by the Apostles. The formal distinction of the two Sacraments of Baptism and Confirmation does not pertain to the history of primitive Christianity.

52. It was far from the mind of Christ to found a church as a society which would continue on earth for a long course of centuries....

53. The organic constitution of the church is not immutable. Like human society, Christian society is subject to perpetual evolution.

64. Scientific progress demands that the concepts of Christian doctrine concerning God, creation, revelation, the Person of the Word Incarnate, and Redemption be readjusted.

# SEPTEMBER 9

## BLACK BISHOPS AND AMERICAN CATHOLICISM

**IN 1984 THERE WERE** ten black bishops in the United States, and on this day of that year they spoke as a group for the first time in American Catholic history, when they issued the pastoral letter "What We Have Seen and Heard." The letter hailed the maturity of black Catholic Christianity in the United States, and celebrated the "richness of our Black experience," which it described in terms of four major characteristics; black spirituality, in the letter's words, is contemplative, holistic, joyful and communitarian.

The letter was totally innovative; it was also accusatory. It charged that "racism, at once subtle and masked, still festers within our church as within our society," and it cited this racism as the major hindrance to the full development of black spirituality and participation within the church.

A year later, the black bishops gathered at St. Charles Borromeo Church in Harlem to mark the letter's first anniversary. They saw no reason to change one word of their 1984 assessment. "Racism is a sin and must always be on the agenda of the church," said Auxiliary Bishop Emerson J. Moore of New York.

Had the pastoral changed anything? New York's Cardinal John O'Connor conceded at the anniversary observance that "very little" had in fact been done in the year since the pastoral's issuance to bring about the changes sought by black Catholics, but it was clear that, thanks to the pastoral, church leaders were more sensitive to the problem and likely would respond to the challenges.

In the years since, hymnals with gospel favorites of blacks have been introduced; a new standing committee for black Catholics has been established at the Washington headquarters of the United States Catholic Conference; a black prelate has been named to head the archdiocese of Atlanta.... The Catholic world changes slowly in the context of its black members, but it does change.

# SEPTEMBER 10

St. Jerome

## FATHERS OF THE CHURCH

**SO OFTEN THE TERMS** are used "fathers of the church," "doctors of the church." Precisely whom do these categories include? In order:

**Fathers of the church.** Quite simply, they were the first teachers of spiritual things, the molders of the Christian church, by whom men and women were reborn into the likeness of Christ. They were the teachers and writers, noted for their holiness and orthodoxy (though they were not all in every word free from error), who passed on the words of Christ and the Apostles, in the process forming them into the record that comprises the deposit of faith and apostolic tradition.

What age did they span? Ah, that's the difficult question. Some would narrowly define the age as extending from the days of the Apostles to the Council of Chalcedon in 451. But that time frame would eliminate such notable writers and teachers as Gregory the Great, who died in 604, and St. John Damascene, who died about 754. The common practice, thus, is to extend the age of the Fathers well into the Middle Ages. The nineteenth-century French writer Jacques-Paul Migne extends the period all the way to the Council of Florence, 1438-1439, in his *Patriologia Latina Cursus Completus*, but it is generally agreed that this is too wide a sweep. The cutoff date is usually 1153, the year marking the death of St. Bernard of Clairvaux (q.v. Aug. 20).

The consensus is that the greatest of the fathers were Sts. Ambrose, Augustine, Jerome and Gregory the Great in the West; Sts. John Chrysostom, Basil the Great, Gregory of Nazianzen and Athanasius in the East.

One final word apropos Migne. In one sense he was not at all sweeping in defining the age of the Fathers. Bishops sitting in ecumenical councils are called Fathers, in much the same manner as the title is applied to Fathers like Augustine and Jerome. The Fathers of Vatican II, accordingly, can be said to have been Fathers of the church — at least for a time. Read on.»»»

# DOCTORS OF THE CHURCH

**FATHERS OF THE CHURCH** may also be doctors of the church, and in fact several are. But mostly this is an honorary title conveyed on luminaries of learning and sanctity, much as a university might convey an honorary doctorate on an eminent scholar or benefactor. There have only been thirty-two in the whole history of the church. We'll get to the list in a minute, but first the three requisite qualifications for consideration: *eminens doctrina, insignis vitae sanctitas, ecclesiae declaratio* — namely, eminent learning, high degree of sanctity, and proclamation by the church. Benedict XIV (1740-1758) said apropos the third condition that the declaration of doctor of the church may be made either by the pope or a general council. In point of fact, no council has ever conferred the title; the exercising has traditionally been the pope's.

The doctors of the church, all saints of course, are: Albert the Great (c1200-1280), Alphonsus Ligouri (1696-1787), Ambrose (c340-397), Anselm (1033-1109), Anthony of Padua (1195-1231), Athanasius (c297-373), Augustine (354-430), Basil the Great (c329-379), Bede the Venerable (c673-735), Bernard of Clairvaux (1090-1153), Bonaventure (1217-1274), Cyril of Alexandria (c376-444), Cyril of Jerusalem (c315-387), Ephraem (c306-373), Francis de Sales (1567-1622), Gregory Nazianzen (c330-c390), Gregory the Great (c540-604), Hilary of Poitiers (c315-368), Isidore of Seville (c560-636), Jerome (c343-420), John Chrysostom (c347-407), John Damascene (c675-749), John of the Cross (1542-1591), Lawrence of Brindisi (1569-1619), Leo the Great (c400-461), Peter Canisius (1521-1597), Peter Chrysologus (c400-450), Peter Damien (1007-1072), Robert Bellarmine (1542-1621), Thomas Aquinas (1225-1274).

But that's only thirty, you say? Right. There are two more, both recently named, both women — in fact, the *only* women doctors of the church: Teresa of Avila (1515-1582) and Catherine of Siena (c1347-1380). They were named a month apart in 1970 by Pope Paul VI.

# SEPTEMBER 12

## JOHN F. KENNEDY ON CHURCH AND STATE

**WHEN JOHN F. KENNEDY** ran for president in 1960, the big question for some Americans was loyalty. Could a Catholic with loyalties or obediences to a particular religion and presum ably a particular person, the pope, serve as president with unqualified commitments to the Constitution and the oath of office? Then-Senator Kennedy met that question head-on September 12, 1960, in a speech before the Houston Ministerial Association. The speech has been characterized as "the best" of the campaign, to be surpassed in power and eloquence only by the Inaugural Address itself. Certainly it was the most important address of Kennedy's life so far as his personal political survival was concerned. Following is a key passage from that Houston talk:

"I believe in an America where the separation of church and state is absolute — where no Catholic prelate would tell the president (should he be Catholic) how to act, and no Protestant minister would tell his parishioners for whom to vote — where no church or church school is granted any public funds or political preference — and where no man is denied public office merely because his religion differs from the president who might appoint him or the people who might elect him.

"I believe in an America that is officially neither Catholic, Protestant nor Jewish — where no public official either requests or accepts instructions on public policy from the pope, the National Council of Churches or any other ecclesiastical source — where no religious body seeks to impose its will directly or indirectly upon the general populace or the public acts of its officials — and where religious liberty is so indivisible that an act against one church is treated as an act against all...

"That is the kind of America in which I believe, and it represents the kind of presidency in which I believe."

John Henry Newman

# CARDINAL NEWMAN ON CHURCH AND STATE

**JOHN F. KENNEDY** probably won't be the last Catholic to have to answer the charge of a divided loyalty. Certainly he wasn't the first. Al Smith had to cope with the charge in the 1928 election. Nor is the charge endemic to America. Cardinal John Henry Newman came to grips with it in nineteenth-century England, when William Ewart Gladstone was prime minister. He sketched a scenario in which the prince of Wales became a Catholic and the pope bade English Catholics to stand firm in one phalanx for the Catholic Succession. Newman exclaimed that under the circumstances he "could not do as [the pope] bade me." On the other hand, there were cases in which Newman said he could conceivably obey the pope before the state. He explained the seeming paradox in *Certain Difficulties Felt by Anglicans in Catholic Teaching Considered* (Newman was never felicitous in his choices of titles for his books):

"...When, then, Mr. Gladstone asks Catholics how they can obey the Queen and yet obey the Pope, since it may happen that the commands of the two authorities may clash, I answer, that it is my rule both to obey the one and to obey the other, but that there is no rule in this world without exceptions, and if either the Pope or the Queen demanded of me an 'Absolute Obedience,' he or she would be transgressing the laws of human society. I give an absolute obedience to neither. Further, if ever this double allegiance pulled me in contrary ways, which in this age of this world I think it never will, then I should decide according to the particular case, which is beyond all rule, and must be decided on its own merits. I should look to see what theologians could do for me, what the Bishops and clergy around me, what my confessor; what my friends whom I revered; and if, after all, I could not take their view of the matter, then I must rule myself by my own judgment and my own conscience. But all this is hypothetical and unreal."

# SEPTEMBER 14

## HOLY ORDERS, REVISED AND UNREVISED

**FOR MANY CATHOLICS,** clerics most especially, I suppose, this is the date that divides the pre-Vatican II priesthood — or elements thereof — from the new one, for it marks the date in 1972 that Pope Paul VI completed the revision of the steps to holy orders.

Everyone remembers the old system. A candidate for the priesthood advanced through four minor orders (porter, lector, exorcist, acolyte) and three major orders (subdeacon, deacon, ordination) to the Roman collar. The Holy See began a revision of these orders in 1971. Before it was over, those of porter, exorcist and subdeacon were abolished; acolyte and lector survived, open now to lay persons, but with individuals installed rather than ordained to those ministries; the deaconate continued, as since 1967, as a two-tiered clerical order (1) for those going on to ordination, and (2) for those who would be remaining permanent deacons. Untouched was the final order, that of the priesthood.

Will it ever be touched? There has been great agitation in recent years for change. Some would like to see the priesthood opened to women. Some would like to see celibacy laws changed so that priests could marry or remain celibate, according to a free preference. One advantage of the latter change, it is argued, would be the immediate availability of many men who in recent years left the priesthood for marriage, and who would like to minister again as priests. In a time of a critical clergy shortage, it is for some a tempting argument.

The church has resisted change to date, and John Paul II adamantly so — thus his reiterated opposition to changes in the celibacy laws; thus his 1988 apostolic letter *Mulieris dignitatem* ("On the Dignity of Women") reaffirming opposition to female ordination. Change is most unlikely while he is pope. But considering the revisions of 1971-1972, can it be ruled out forever?

# SEPTEMBER 15

## HARVEST-TIME MUSINGS

**DID YOU EVER WONDER** what people of biblical times ate? No need to. It's all laid out in no place other than the Bible itself.

First of all, folks of biblical times ate limited amounts of meat — in fact, before the great flood of Genesis, which only Noah, his family and his animals survived, thanks to his fabled ark, no one ate any meat. It was only after the flood that people were permitted to indulge in meat: "Every thing that liveth shall be meat for you" (Genesis 9:3). There was one restriction: no consumption of animal blood (Genesis 9:4), which meant no sausage of the kind so popular now in Germany and Ireland, and known as blood pudding.

Therefore, what meats were popular? Lamb and veal, for two. We know that from Amos 6:4, where the wealthy are denounced "that lie upon beds of ivory, and stretch themselves upon their couches, and eat the lambs out of the flock, and the calves out of the midst of the stall." In 1 Kings 4:23, oxen, harts, gazelles, roebucks and fatted fowl are added to the meat entrees. The meat was either boiled or roasted, but the Passover lamb was always roasted.

As said, meat was taken in limited amounts, and then only on special occasions. It was not for religious scruples that this was so, but rather because of the scarcity then of domestic cattle and the extravagance of slaughtering animals which were needed for such dietary necessities as milk, cheese and curds. Similarly, fowl of several species were spared for their eggs.

As for fish, it was not a common staple of Old Testament diets, one reason being that Hebrew people had limited access to the Mediterranean Sea. Fish became, however, common fare for people of the New Testament. At least four of the Apostles — Peter, Andrew, James and John — were fishermen, and of course it was fish that figured in the miracle of the feeding of the multitude in Mark 6:38 and Matthew 15:34. Read on for fruit and vegetables.»»»

# SEPTEMBER 16

## YOUR BIBLICAL GREENGROCER

**SO WHAT VEGETABLES AND FRUITS** were biblical folks harvesting around this time? Well, cucumbers, leeks, onions and garlic, among other items. As will be remembered from the March 1 entry, the Israelites developed a taste for these vegetables during their time in Egypt (Numbers 11:5). Those vegetables were probably tastier and more abundant in Egypt than similar products grown in Palestine, for the climate and the soil of Egypt had distinct advantages then over other areas of the Middle East, particularly an unirrigated Palestine. Also, they would be storing up a wide variety of greens and herbs, as known from Genesis 9:3, along with beans and lentils. In fact, beans and lentils were staples. They could be eaten raw, boiled into a pottage or very thick soup, or mixed with flour to increase the flavor and the texture of bread. Millet, a cereal grass, and spelt, a kind of wheat giving a very fine flour, were being harvested, as were barley and emmer, the latter a primitive form of wheat.

Fruits? Melons, to be sure. Olives and grapes, most assuredly — not so much to be eaten as to be made into oils and wines. Apples, of course. A couple of towns and a person in the Old Testament bear the Hebrew name for apple, *tappuah*, and doesn't the loved one in the Song of Solomon (2:5) ask to be plied with apples?: "Stay me with flagons, comfort me with apples, for I am sick of love." The pomegranate fruit was obviously common, being mentioned several times. The date is not mentioned, but there must have been dates, as there are mentions of the palm. Quinces and citrons were being picked. Finally, there was that special delicacy, the fig — which was eaten ripe, dried individually or molded into cakes as food for long journeys. Interestingly enough, the fig was also used medicinally, as in 2 Kings 20:7, where it is recorded as being applied successfully to a boil. Read on.»»»

# SEPTEMBER 17

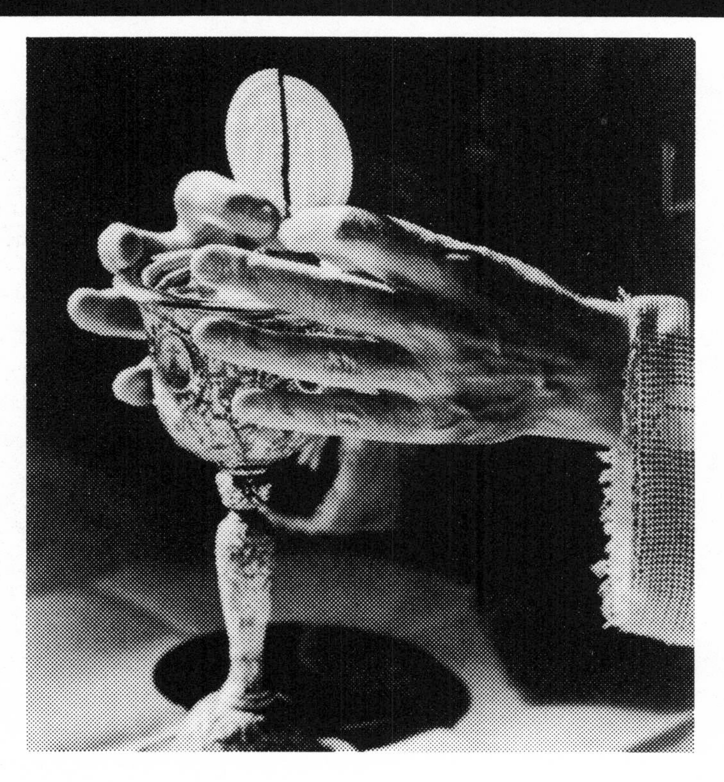

## DEVALUING FOOD FOR THE STOMACH

**THE PEOPLE** of the Old Testament had their sacred meals, and still do, as at Passover. The people of the New Testament adopted a different kind of sacred meal — the Eucharist at the liturgy of the Mass. The action was consistent with biblical philosophy, for as early as Deuteronomy 8:3 the word was preached that "man does not live by bread alone" but rather "by everything that proceeds from the mouth of the Lord." Of course, it was hard to convince everyone of this in days before the sophistication of agricultural processes and storage facilities, when the acquisition of food was the end purpose of one's day and the possession of food the mark of affluence. Food was accounted among the greatest of God's blessings. On interpersonal levels, it was the bond of friendship, the test of fellowship, the most gracious and thoughtful of gifts. Food, like rain and water, was of enormous, indeed vital significance in daily lives, and as families and clans multiplied, food acquired large social and economic contexts to go along with the religious.

Then along came Jesus Christ, and echoing Deuteronomy, he devalued food, as in the Sermon on the Mount: "...Take no thought for your life, what you shall eat, or what you shall drink; nor yet for your body, what you shall put on. Is not the life more than the meat, and the body more than raiment?" (Matthew 6:25). Similarly in Luke 12:22, Christ is quoted, "Take no thought for your body, what you shall eat; neither for the body, what you shall put on."

Christ offered a different kind of food: his own body, his own blood; the food of Christ becomes the bread of life. Previously, the miraculous food of God was manna, the bread from on high with which God nourished the Israelites for forty years in the desert, until they ate of the corn of the Promised Land (Joshua 5:12). In Wisdom 16:20, manna is "the food of angels...with sweetness in every taste." But now there was something better. Proceed.»»»

# SEPTEMBER 18

## THE NEW MANNA OF THE EUCHARIST

**THE NEW MANNA** promised by Christ we know as the Eucharist. It is held infinitely more nourishing than the manna that fell in the desert. It gives life everlasting. John records Christ's guarantee, Chapter 6:35ff:

"'I am the bread of life; he that cometh to me shall never hunger; and he that believeth in me shall never thirst.... No man can come to me, except the Father which has sent me draw him: and I will raise him up on the last day. It is written in the prophets. And they shall be all taught of God. Every man therefore that hath heard, and hath learned of the Father, cometh unto me. Not that any man hath seen the Father, save he which is of God, he hath seen the Father. Amen, amen, I say unto you, he that believeth in me hath everlasting life.

" 'I am that bread of life. Your fathers did eat manna in the wilderness, and are dead. This is the bread which cometh from heaven, that a man may eat thereof, and not die. I am the living bread which came down from heaven: if any man eat of this bread, he shall live forever: and the bread that I give is my flesh, which I will give for the life of the world.'

"The Jews on that account argued with one another, saying, 'How can this man give us his flesh to eat?'

"Then Jesus said unto them, 'Amen, amen, I say unto you, unless you eat the flesh of the Son of man, and drink his blood, you shall have no life in you. Whosoever eateth my flesh and drinketh my blood, hath eternal life: and I will raise him up on the last day. For my flesh is food indeed, and my blood is drink indeed. He that eateth my flesh, and drinketh my blood, dwelleth in me and I in him. As the living Father hath sent me, and I live by the Father: so he that eateth me, even he shall live by me. This is that bread which came down from heaven: not as your fathers did eat manna, and are dead: he that eateth of this bread shall live forever.'"

# JANUARIUS AND THE LIQUIFYING OF BLOOD

**JANUARIUS IS A SAINT** we know little about, but hear of much. This is his feast day, incidentally. Januarius lived in the fourth century, and died for his witness to the faith. Apparently he was cast to wild beasts in the amphitheater at Pozzuoli, but the beasts refused to attack. Timid lions. The axe proved swifter and surer. Januarius died by beheading.

Januarius' remains were interred at Benevento, then moved to Montevergine, and finally, for safekeeping, to the cathedral at Naples. Therein lies St. Januarius' fame, for several times a year a flask said to contain Januarius' blood is produced for veneration, and to the wonder and excitement of the congregation the blood liquifies when exposed before another relic believed to be the martyr's head! It's been doing this going on five hundred years. Is the liquification a miracle? Is it trickery? Is it natural phenomenon? No one knows for sure, as no careful scientific study has been done on this as has been done on other phenomena of a religious kind, such as the Shroud of Turin.

Certain details have been noted, though, regarding the liquefactions. One, the volume of blood appears to vary from one event to the next, and the weight of the reliquary in which the flask is kept had been found to vary in weight by as many as twenty-seven grams. What that proves or disproves no one is quite sure. Heat, likewise, is an ambiguous factor. At a temperature of 86 degrees, it has taken up to two hours for liquefaction of the blood to occur, whereas at 66 degrees liquefaction has taken place within fifteen minutes. On the other hand, failure to liquefy is more frequent in December than in summer.

The liquefaction of the blood of St. Januarius could be a miracle. If so, could there also be "copycat" miracles? One asks, because since the fifteenth century the number of liquefactions has been on the rise in Naples, including one alleged to be the blood of John the Baptist. Maybe it's the geography.

# THE PRISONER OF THE VATICAN

**FOR CENTURIES** popes cherished the temporal power of office as a divine right. Pius IX himself said to Sir Odo Russell in 1862: "My son, the Temporal Domination was given by God to His Vicar on Earth. God alone can take it from Him. The Lord's will be done." Well, by 1870 somebody else's will had been done. Guiseppe Garibaldi completed his invasion of the Papal States and the Italian peninsula was united as a kingdom under Victor Emmanuel. Pius IX in protest shut himself up in the Vatican, and thus began the period that lasted until 1929 when popes held themselves to be "prisoners of the Vatican." The fateful beginning was this day in 1870, when Royalist troops occupied the papal city of Rome, leaving the pope, Pius IX, with only the Vatican buldings.

The Vatican based its claim to Rome and the Papal States, some 18,000 square miles of the central peninsula, on the *Patrimonium Petri,* Patrimony of Peter, a gift of France's King Pepin in 754. In compensation for loss of the territory, the Italian state in 1871 offered Guarantee Laws providing the pope residence in the Vatican, limited rights of a sovereign, an annual remuneration of 3.5 million lire (about $650,000), and several extraterritorial palaces. Pius IX refused and shut himself and successor popes off for fifty-nine years.

Pius IX played hardball. He forbade Catholics to stand as candidates for public office and Catholics who voted in elections did so under penalty of excommunication. The state in reply confiscated church property, secularized monasteries, and conscripted clerics as well as laity. In fact, so unpopular was the church's stand and Pius IX himself that his remains were abused while being transported from St. Peter's to the Basilica of San Lorenzo after his death February 7, 1878. A mob shouting obscenities and singing blasphemous songs pelted the papal coffin with mud and tried to tip it into the Tiber. Police did not arrive on the scene until the incident was over. (cf. Feb. 7)

# SEPTEMBER 21

## A TAX COLLECTOR WHO CAME AND FOLLOWED

**OF THE ORIGINAL TWELVE** who dropped all to follow Jesus, the one who took the greatest occupational risk was perhaps Matthew. Peter and Andrew, for instance, could always return to their boats and fish the sea of Galilee; it was extremely unlikely that Matthew would ever get his job back as a collector of taxes and customs duties in Capernaum.

Matthew, of course, was evangelist as well as apostle, writing the Gospel that is sequentially first (Matthew, Mark, Luke and John) but chronologically second, being written sometime between 70 and 77 A.D.; Mark's is dated between 61 and 67 A.D. (Luke's followed betwen 79 and 85 A.D. and John's between 88 and 98 A.D.)

Matthew wrote in Aramaic, and his gospel account is ledger-like in its orderliness and organization, and mathematic as well. Exactly what one might expect from one whose training was in ledgers and numbers. In fact, Matthew displays a fixation with numbers and combinations in his gospel. There are the seven parables of the kingdom; the seven woes of the Pharisees; the seven invocations of the Lord's Prayer. There are the five disputes of the Pharisees, the five loaves, the five talents. He even divides his gospel into five books. Maybe that's all coincidence, but not the knowledge he displays in his gospel about money and taxes, even down to such fine distinctions as the difference between the indirect tax and the poll tax.

Matthew records in his Gospel (9:9) the circumstance of how he came to follow Jesus, but the facts of his life are meager. The details supplied by tradition are unreliable, partly because of confusion between Matthew and Matthias, the apostle elected to replace Judas. He preached in Judea, Ethiopia, Persia and Parthia, where he was martyred. The Cathedral of Salerno, Italy, claims to house his remains, but who knows for sure they're Matthew's. What we can be sure of is that September 21 is his feast day.

# SEPTEMBER 22

## THE MOST CANDID OF THE EVANGELISTS

**LEST WE OVERLOOK** one of the Four Evangelists, let's follow Matthew with Mark, whose feast back on April 25 was co-opted by another subject. Mark wrote the shortest of the Gospels, and in many respects the bluntest — for it is Mark who records with remarkable honesty many of the faults and foibles of the heroes of Christianity's beginnings.

Mark, for instance, exposes the presence of vanity among the Apostles: "At this they fell silent, for on the way they had been arguing about who was the most important" (9:34). He suggests that they were slow of understanding and wit: "On the contrary, their minds were completely closed to the meaning of events" (6:52). Not even Peter was excepted from the charge: "He hardly knew what to say" (9:6). Mark dares even to lay a bit of observational error about nature on Jesus himself: "Observing a fig tree some distance off, covered with foliage, he went over to see if he could find anything on it. When he reached it, he found nothing but leaves; it was not yet the time for figs" (11:13).

Some exegetes, in turn, have turned Mark unflatteringly upon himself. Mark probably witnessed Christ's betrayal and arrest, and these interpreters have suggested that the anonymous young man who dropped his linen cloth "and ran off naked" as Jesus was seized (Mark 14:50-52) was none other than Mark himself.

It is presumed that Mark was a Levite and from an affluent background, for Peter used Mark's mother's house as a refuge after his escape from prison. That same house was large enough to accommodate sizable gatherings of Christians. In his apostolic mission, Mark traveled with Paul, but not everywhere. In fact, he seems to have annoyed Paul by refusing to go with him to Tarsus. Paul responded in kind by declining Barnabas' proposal that he take Mark with him on his second missionary journey. But Mark made his witness. He was martyred in Alexandria. In the ninth century his remains were brought to Venice, where they are venerated today in the great cathedral of San Marco.

# THE STIGMATA AND PADRE PIO

**SINCE THE THIRTEENTH CENTURY,** the marks of the stigmata — wounds or scars corresponding to that of the crucified — have been claimed or attributed to more than three hundred persons, and the phenomenon had such a grip on the Catholic imagination that September 17 was listed on the calendar as the feast of the Stigmata of Francis — he of Assisi, of course. Of the three-hundred alleged cases of the stigmata, ninety-five percent involved women, most belonging to religious orders, and five percent men, mostly friars or tertiaries of a mendicant order. One of the most famous of the latter died on this day in 1968, barely twenty-five years ago — Francesco Forgione, the Capuchin-Franciscan priest better known as Padre Pio.

Padre Pio was ordained to the priesthood in 1910, and first experienced the stigmata in September, 1918, at the friary in San Giovanni Rotondo, Italy. The happening was greeted skeptically by doctors and clergy, and there was considerable controversy whether Padro Pio's wounds and their bleeding were natural or supernatural in origin. The Vatican, somewhat discomforted, this being the twentieth century and all, forebade Padre Pio to say public Mass and began an investigation of its own. Rumors flew that Padre Pio was to be transferred from San Giovanni Rotondo, and this led to riots by townspeople that left fourteen persons dead and eighty injured. In 1920 the Vatican decided to leave Padre Pio where he was, but it imposed tight restrictions on his public activities that were to last thirteen years. Pius XI lifted them in 1933, saying to Padre Pio's archbishop, "I have not been badly disposed toward Parde Pio, but I have been badly informed about Padre Pio." Padre Pio was never to leave San Giovanni Rotondo, but the world came to him in the form of the devout — to attend his Masses, hear him preach, kneel before in confession. Gift offerings built what was to be his monument, the hospital Casa Sollievo della Sufferenza. Nothing could have been more appropriate given Padre Pio's own lifetime of suffering.

# SEPTEMBER 24

## JUST HOW LARGE WAS THE HOLY FAMILY?

**DID JESUS HAVE BROTHERS?**....That's not exactly a tendentious question. Matthew 13:55 and Mark 6:3 both speak of the "carpenter" or "carpenter's son" who was the "brother" of James, Joses, Simon and Juda. In fact, there's even reference to "sisters." Here is the passage from Mark: "Is this not the carpenter, the son of Mary, the brother of James, and Joses, and of Juda, and Simon? And are not his sisters here with us?"

The gospel passages raise fascinating questions. Might these "brothers" of Jesus be Joseph's sons by a former marriage, in which case they would be step-brothers of Jesus? Or, might they be full brothers, sons born to Mary and Joseph, presumably after the birth of Jesus? Much depends on the answers — especially to the latter question, including the validity of Catholic dogma on the virgin birth and Catholic teaching on the perpetual virginity of Mary.

These questions, incidentally, are not the latter-day interjections of mischief-makers. They were grappled with in the early church. In the fourth century, for instance, a strong school of thought known as the *Epiphanian* held strongly that James, Joses, Simon and Juda were step-brothers of Jesus. Advocates of this theory were known as *Epiphanians*, after the theory's most zealous proponent.

Modern exegesis concedes that the word used in the original Greek texts means "brother." The Catholic contention, however, is that the Greek word is merely a carry-over from the Aramaic used by the first Christians, in which language the word is used to designate a closely defined group of people, such as cousins. Since Aramaic, like Hebrew, had no word for "cousin," it would be logical in the Catholic understanding of things to use the word "brethren" or "brothers" to identify cousins. A modern-day parallel would be use of the word "brothers" by Afro-Americans to designate members of their ethnic group. In any instance, Catholics reject the notion that Jesus had brothers or sisters, and hold instead that he was the one child of a virgin mother.

# SEPTEMBER 25

## THE BEATIFYING OF FATHER JUNIPERO SERRA

**THIS DAY IN 1988** belonged at last to Father Junipero Serra, the Franciscan missionary who lead a group of friars in establishing a chain of twenty-five California missions in the eighteenth century. This was the day he was beatified in Rome by Pope John Paul II. Some had hoped that the ceremony would take place in California itself during the pope's 1987 visit to the country. It didn't, for reasons in dispute. One explanation was that the beatification process could not be completed in time for a formal ceremony of elevation. Another held the reason to be political. Charges had been made that Junipero Serra had mistreated Indians, and, though refuted by a 1986 investigation conducted by the diocese of Monterey, to have beatified Serra in the den of controversy would under this logic have been unseemly.

There was controversy nonetheless. A spokesperson for the American Indian Historical Society criticized the announcement May 4 that the beatification would take place in September, saying: "It's not surprising. The Pope doesn't care about what's been done to us. We thought we could expect something better — that he would hold up the beatification until we could make our case."

As for the pope, there was no doubt in his mind that Serra belonged among the blessed. In the beatification homily he called him "a shining example of Christian virtue and the missionary spirit," adding that Serra's mission to the California Indians stemmed from a desire to "further their authentic human development." "He sowed the seeds of Christian faith amid the momentous changes wrought by the arrival of European settlers to the New World," said the pope. Then, turning the charges of Serra's detractors against them, John Paul remarked that mission work meant Blessed Junipero Serra also had to "admonish the powerful" so that they would not "abuse and exploit the poor and the weak."

Junipero Serra, 1713-1784, is buried at the Carmel Mission in Monterey.

# MORAL TALE WITHOUT A MORAL

**THIS IS** one of those days in the liturgical calendar that was once embarrassingly mixed up with myth. It was assigned to Sts. Cyprian and Justina. Fine, except neither ever existed. Theirs is a "moral tale," composed, perhaps, to impress listeners or readers, but assimilating enough credence over time to delude St. Gregory of Nazianzen and the poet Prudentius.

According to the tale, Cyprian was a pre-fourth-century man of Antioch, a magician specializing in idolatry, astrology and black magic, who blasphemed Christ, disemboweled children to study their insides for portents of things to come, and who murdered in order to secure blood offerings. Pretty nasty guy.

Seemingly, Cyprian's services were procured by one Algaides to help him win the heart of Justina, a Christian beauty of virginal state. Cyprian sicked demons on Justina, but she repulsed these unwelcome beings by blowing in their faces and making the sign of the cross. Frustrated, and recognizing that there was such a thing as a superior power, Cyprian threatened to quit the devil's service. The devil then turned against Cyprian, but Cyprian, having learned from Justina, repulsed him by making the sign of the cross himself.

Everything seemed to be going swimmingly. Cyprian burned his books of magic, embraced the faith and went on to become priest and bishop. Algaides likewise converted to Christianity. Justina, deeply moved by these wondrous happenings, cut off her hair as a sign that she was dedicating her virginity to God, gave her possessions to the poor, and retired to Damascus.

Alas, neither Justina nor Cyprian lived happily ever after; Algaides has been lost at this point. The persecution of Diocletian is unleashed on the land, and Cyprian and Justina by coincidence end up before the same judge. They are tortured, then hurled into a cauldron of boiling pitch. Miraculously spared, they are dragged to the banks of the Gallus, where, no miracles this time, they are unceremoniously beheaded. End of edifying story.

# SEPTEMBER 27

Vincent de Paul

## THE MODEL OF CHRISTIAN CONCERN

**THIS IS THE FEAST** of the saint who motivated Frederic Ozanam (q.v. Nov. 20) and to this day inspires worldwide the work of the St. Vincent de Paul Society (q.v. Nov. 19), none other than Vincent de Paul himself.

Vincent de Paul lived from 1580-1660. The son of French peasants, he spent much of his youth tending his father's sheep on the plains of Landes, a quiet, contemplative occupation that is said to have helped fuse his spirituality. Subsequently, Vincent studied at Dax, Saragossa and Toulouse, was ordained, and became chaplain to Queen Margaret of Valois in Paris. His sermons and work with the poor attracted wide attention, and led to the founding in 1625 of the Congregation of the Missions (known as the Vincentians or Lazarists) to do missionary work among peasants. Later, with Louise de Marillac, also to be sainted, he founded the Sisters of Charity, an order growing out of the "charity confraternities" he organized throughout France and whose apostolic work today as ever is in their name — charity.

Vincent de Paul established hospitals and orphanages, ransomed Christian slaves in North Africa, and made decided contributions to clerical formation through a network of new seminaries. He actually became a figure of large international importance, influencing policies as far away as Poland and Madagascar. Anne of Austria, regent before the accession of Louis XIV, even entrusted him with the appointments to head bishoprics.

A prolific letter writer, Vincent de Paul was also a compelling preacher. His retreats for ordinandi and monthly days of recollection for clergy in Paris were so effective as to gain him a place with the regenerators of the church in sixteenth-century France. He gave new meaning and purpose to the parish, defining it not only as an oasis of spiritual life, but also as a center of charitable and communal activity. Vincent de Paul lived a long life: eighty years. More than two centuries later he continues to cast a long shadow.

# SEPTEMBER 28

## THE POPE WE HARDLY KNEW

**NAME THIS POPE,** who lived in the lifetime of most of us.

He was elected on a fourth ballot after only eight and a half hours of the conclave's deliberations. He was not a favorite for the office, and he had no public aura or reputation as a social reformer. Yet he was hailed on his election as the first "working class" pope, the reason being his father was a laborer and a socialist. This pope was Italian, and though patriarch of Venice before his election, he was something of a Vatican outsider. He had never been a member of the Curia, nor of the diplomatic corps, traditional seeding grounds for new popes. His background was primarily that of a professional theologian and catechist, unglamorous activities that usually do not involve charisma. As pope this man immediately won hearts with his warmth and informality. At his coronation he disdained the traditional papal throne borne by footmen and the bejeweled papal tiara. His first audiences were delightfully casual, and promised a papacy symbolized by a spirit of pastoral simplicity and joy. The first test-tube baby, Louise Joy Browne, was born in England just before his election, and he offered the child "cordial wishes." Though he had certain reservations about such scientific procedures, he declared that he had no right to criticize her parents who "might even have deep merit before God for what they encouraged their doctors to carry out." It was a statement other popes would be unlikely to make. Still this pope was no "barn-burner." He gave no hint of breaking ranks on birth control, married priests or the ordination of women. Nor did he. Who was this pope?

He was born Albino Luciani in 1912 at Forno di Canali, near Belluna, in the Dolomite Mountains southwest of Venice. He was elected to the papacy on August 26, 1978, but served only thirty-three days. On the night of September 28 he suffered a heart attack while in bed. John Paul I, the "September Pope," was dead.

# SEPTEMBER 29

St. Michael fighting the dragon (Woodcut by Albrecht Dürer)

## THE ONCE-HALLOWED DAY OF MICHAELMAS

**THIS IS MICHAELMAS** — "Michael's mass." The first term of the academic year, Michaelmas, begins on or about this day in English and Irish universities. Michaelmas is also the regular quarter-day for settling rents and other accounts. But the origins of the word are distinctly religious. Michaelmas was a festival celebrated on September 29 in the Western church in honor of the Archangel Michael and the other faithful archangels and angels. The festival appears to have grown out of a local celebration connected to the dedication of a church of St. Michael either in Rome or at Mount Garganus in Apulia in southeast Italy. In any instance, at the beginning of the ninth century it was a great day in the church calendar, and especially in Britain, where once upon a time the prize stubble-goose was dressed on Michaelmas Day.

These days the church marks September 29 as the feast of Sts. Michael, Gabriel and Raphael, archangels. Though the dedication is a shared one, it is Michael's name that dominates in the popular Catholic psyche, perhaps because so many Catholics remember when all low Masses concluded with prayers at the foot of the altar, the third of which was to Michael: "St. Michael, the archangel, defend us in battle, be our protection against the malice and snares of the devil. We humbly beseech God to command him, and do thou, O prince of the heavenly host, by the divine power thrust into hell Satan and the other evil spirits who roam through the world seeking the ruin of souls. Amen."

Michael is no New Testament invention. He is twice mentioned in the Book of Daniel as the special protector of Israel. The principal New Testament reference is in the Apocalypse (Revelation) 12:7-9, where St. John writes of the great battle in heaven in which Michael and his angels drove out Satan and his minions, and hurled them down to earth. In the ages of piety, the church honored him by charging him with the care of souls of the faithfully departed.

# AUTHENTICATING THE BIBLE'S WORDS

**THE NEW AMERICAN BIBLE,** a twenty-six-year project and finally the first Roman Catholic-sponsored translation of the Bible in English from original sources, appeared on this day in 1970. That seems hard to believe, but such is the case. The first Catholic Bible in English, the Douay-Rheims Version (1582-1609/10), and its successor, the Bishop Richard Challoner revision (1750), were based on the Latin Vulgate. The original languages of the Bible, on the other hand, were Hebrew, Aramaic or Greek. In other words, for many centuries Catholics who read the Bible in English were reading a work from secondary sources. It is doubtful that anyone's faith was undermined because of that, but it sure makes a hypocrisy of the old Catholic warnings against the King James Bible and condemnations of other so-called unauthentic translations.

In fairness, it is easy to understand the insistence on accuracy. The Bible is the fundamental source of dogma and is central to religious thought and teaching — for Catholics as of course for Protestants, Eastern Orthodox and Jews. Divided into two testaments of seventy-two books — forty-five in the Old; twenty-seven in the New — the Bible is regarded as the inspired Word of God, whether literally true in scientific detail or not. The Bible was written in separate sections and over several centuries before being drawn together into one book in the Christian era. That in itself was no small feat. It was not until the fifth century, for instance, that the canon of the New Testament was stabilized, and not until the Council of Trent in the sixteenth century that this canon received its dogmatic definition.

As for those Catholic warnings and condemnations of yesterday, the irony is that today there is no exclusively Catholic Bible. We now have common or interconfessional Bibles produced in accordance with guidelines agreed on by the United Bible Societies and the Vatican. Ecumenism marches on.

# OCTOBER 1

## THE ROSARY AND THE MONTH OF OCTOBER

**THE MOST POPULAR CATHOLIC DEVOTION** of recent centuries, hands down, is that of the rosary, and this is the month specifically dedicated to its recitation by Pope Leo XIII in the encyclical *Supremi apostolatus officio*. The encyclical was issued in 1883, and fitted a papal pattern of the time. During the Middle Ages, the public functions of the church and the popular devotions of the faithful began intimately to connect. Then, in the nineteenth century, popes began to give over whole months to the popularizing of particular devotions. Thus January was designated to the Holy Name of Jesus; May, Marian devotions; June, the Sacred Heart; July, the Precious Blood, etc.

The rosary's turn came with October, and Catholics of senior generations can recall when scores would turn out on October evenings for recitation of the rosary at the closing of the parish church for the day.

Although this particular evening devotion is rare today, still the rosary retains a popularity. There are ambiguities, though. For instance, deceased Catholics are traditionally laid out with the rosary entwined around fingers. This made particular sense when the rosary was the chief devotion of the Catholic wake. It isn't anymore. Father arrives to lead a Bible vigil or other service of prayer, not to lead a recitation of the beads.

The origin of the rosary is attributed to St. Dominic in the thirteenth century, and followed on the mid-twelfth century development of the "Hail Mary" as a formula of devotional prayer. The practice of meditating on definite sets of "mysteries" (joyful, sorrowful, glorious) while saying the beads came much later. As said, the rosary isn't as popular as it used to be, but there are still those who regard it as the most powerful Catholic prayer of intercession.

# THE ROSARY, ITS MYSTERIES AND FRUITS

**AS REMARKED,** the rosary was pegged to "mysteries," which were intended to translate, upon meditation, into "fruits" in the spiritual lives of those praying the beads. Thus in the old days of devotional Catholicism one had the following linkage between "mysteries" and "fruits" of the rosary:

## **Joyful Mysteries**—Spirit of Holy Joy

1. Annunciation . . . . . . . . . . . . . . . . . . . Humility
2. Visitation . . . . . . . . . . . . . . . Fraternal charity
3. Nativity . . . . . . . . . . . . . . . . .Spirit of Poverty
4. Presentation . . . . . . . . . . . Obedience, purity
5. Finding ofJesus in the Temple . . . . . . . Love of Jesus; devotedness to duties of our state of life

## **Sorrowful Mysteries**—Spirit of Compassion, Contrition and Reparation

1. Agony in the Garden . . . . . . Fervor in prayer
2. Scouring at the Pillar . . . . . . . . . . . Penance, and especially mortification of the senses
3. Crowning with Thorns . . . . . . Moral courage
4. Carrying of the Cross . . . . . . . . . . . . Patience
5. Crucifixion . . . . . . . . . . . . . . . . .Self-sacrifice for God and for neighbor; forgiveness of hurts

## **Glorious Mysteries**—Spirit of Adoration and Faith

1. Resurrection . . . . . . . . . . . . . . . . . . . . . . Faith
2. Ascension . . . . . . . . . . . . . . . . . . . . . . . . .Hope
3. Descent of the Holy Ghost . . . . . . . . . . . Love and zeal for souls
4. Assumption . . . . . . . . Filial devotion to Mary
5. Crowning of Mary as Queen of Heaven. . . . . Perseverance

# OCTOBER 3

## THERESA AND HER SHOWER OF ROSES

**IN THE NEW CALENDAR** of feast days, St. Theresa of Lisieux is accorded October 1; in the old it was today, October 3. Small matter, however, which day is hers; she belongs to modern times. She lived in the nineteenth century, 1873-1897, but she's a twentieth-century saint. She was canonized in 1925 — only twenty-eight years after dying, be it noted — and once was invoked as few other saints.

Still, Theresa of Lisieux was not your typical nineteenth-century nun; she seemed to belong more to the seventeenth. She was more mystical than socially engaged. She did not nurse the plague-stricken, the poor, the aged; she did not perform large, heroic deeds like Joan of Arc or Catherine of Siena. She simply entered religious life at age fifteen — at the Carmelite convent at Lisieux in northwest France — and did nothing but pray, suffer and obey before dying a quiet death at twenty-four. She lived on "a new kind of food." "I found it within me," she wrote, "without knowing how it got there. I simply believe that it was Jesus himself, hidden at the bottom of my poor little heart, acting on me in some mysterious way and inspiring me to do whatever he wished to be done at any given moment."

But what an impact she had. Theresa exerted extraordinary moral influence throughout the Christian world by the example of a life suddenly revealed to the world in an autobiography, *The Story of a Soul*. Everywhere, it seemed, people were adopting Theresa's "Little Way" as an avenue to holiness. Theresa became exemplar for the heroic way she dealt with physical suffering, and doing so when for years she had no sensible perception of God's presence.

On her deathbed Theresa promised to "spend my heaven doing good upon earth," and added she would "let fall a shower of roses." Even as a child she believed she would be a saint, and indeed immediately upon her death cures and conversions of wondrous kinds began to be attributed to her. To believers they were nothing less than that promised "shower of roses."

## GOD'S FOOL, GOD'S MINSTRELS

**FRANCIS OF ASSISI** has to be accounted one of the church's most fascinating saints. He lived at the end of the twelfth, beginning of the thirteenth centuries, and though pious legend says he was born in a stable (it was a latter-day effort to parallel his life to Christ's), the reality is that he belonged to a noble family. After a few brief years of uncertainty, he felt the call to poverty and prayer, and he embraced it with such enthusiasm that people thought him mad, God's fool. His father locked him up in a closet, presumably for his own good. When he was freed, Francis stripped himself of his clothes and said to his father: "Hitherto I have called you my father on earth; henceforth I desire to say only 'Our Father who are in heaven.' "

The rest of course is Catholic folklore of a most inspirational kind: the fabled gestures of love and charity, like the embracing of the leper and the exchanging of clothes with those of the beggar; the gentleness and angelic simplicity of character; the celebrated absent-mindedness which caused him to respond to the question if he intended to marry, "Yes, I am about to take a wife of unsurpassing fairness"...romanticized by Dante and Giotto as Lady Poverty.

Francis drew followers, who wandered about singing for joy, calling themselves the Lord's minstrels. And he founded the religious order Friars Minor — so named, some say, to accent identity with the poorest classes, but maybe too in the context of Matthew 25:40-45 as a reminder of one's humility.

Francis' success was singular, and so was his fame. He traveled widely, but his favorite ground was his native Italy. When he approached villages, church bells rang out, processions of clergy and laity met him with song and prayer, the sick were brought out for healing, and people kissed the ground on which he walked. Francis bore the stigmata, and was only in his mid-forties when he died in 1226. Within two years he was canonized. This is his feast day.

# FRANCIS OF ASSISI'S PRAYER FOR PEACE

**FRANCIS OF ASSISI,** to continue, is the saint associated with peacemakers, and indeed he was an extraordinarily gentle man. He conversed with birds and animals of the field, and when he died larks reportedly collected around the roof of his hut, raising a song to heaven. The marvel of the incident is that the lark is a bird of the morning sun, whereas Francis died in the evening, as sun was setting.

The small paradox is that Francis the peacemaker aspired originally to a knight's career, and in fact was once a soldier, joining in an attack on Perugia, where he was taken prisoner and held captive for a year. This was before the famous dream of 1205 that called him to Christ's service as he was about to join a military campaign under the flag of the Neapolitan States. Francis of Assisi went about preaching forgiveness and repentance, but it was the commitment to peace that formed the dominant facet of his image. Francis' prayer for peace is a favorite with peacemakers to this day:

Make me, O Lord, an instrument of your peace,

Where there is hatred, let me sow love;

Where there is injury, pardon;

Where there is doubt, faith;

Where there is despair, hope;

Where there is darkness, light;

Where there is sadness, joy.

O Divine Master, grant that I may not so much seek to be consoled as to console; to be understood as to understand; to be loved as to love;For it is in giving that we receive; it is in pardoning that we are pardoned, and it is in dying that we are born to eternal life. Amen.

# OCTOBER 6

## JOHN XXIII AND LORETO'S HOLY HOUSE

**IT IS 1962.** The stage was set. In a few days Vatican Council II would open (q.v. Oct. 11). These preliminary days were spent by John XXIII in prayer....and pilgrimage. To be specific, Pope John was just back on Oct. 6 from a pilgrimage to Assisi and Loreto. It was the first time a pope had left Rome officially since 1870, when Pius IX declared himself a prisoner of the Vatican, after the loss of the Papal States. To everyone, the visit to Assisi was readily understandable. Loreto? That was a dubious objective.

Loreto, of course, is the site of the so-called "holy house" in the province of Ancona, where Mary is said to have been born and reared. Except, of course, Mary never lived anywhere near this rocky spot overlooking the Adriatic; she lived in Asia Minor. No problem. The house — a plain stone building, 28 feet by 12.5, and 13.5 in height — in 1294 was carried by angels across the Adriatic to a woods near Recanati, then in 1295 to Loreto. A papal bull by Sixtus VI accepted the authenticity of the house, but Julius II in 1507 was more cautious, favoring the transport of the house but with the qualifier *ut pie creditur et fama est*....Let the believer beware, in other words. Church officials have grown increasingly tentative towards Loreto. Yet John, the pope of enlightment, went there on pilgrimage just before the council. Why?

Who knows? John was a confirmed Marianist. He had been to Loreto before as a pilgrimage — in 1900. He was also dying, and, as Peter Hebblethwaite has remarked, who's to deny a sick, old man the gift of returning to a place near to his heart and his creedal instincts? It is interesting, though. Some feared that John would encourage the theological speculations they were anxious to dampen. John XXIII, interestingly enough, never alluded to the alleged miracle that makes Loreto famous. He dwelled instead on three points: the Incarnation, themes of family life, and the dignity of daily work — with every emphasis directed towards the council that was about to open.

# PIUS XII AND THE AMERICAN LEGION

**AFTER WORLD WAR II** millions of people, Catholic and non-Catholic, beat a path to the Vatican for an audience with Pope Pius XII, still legendary, for as yet spared the criticism of revisionists that would follow with the stagings of Rolf Hochhuth's 1963 play *Der Stellvertreter* ("The Representative" or "The Deputy" in English). Pius XII was ever available to visitors, and none did he greet with greater warmth than Allied soldiers and sailors — and veterans. On October 7 in 1947, a group of American Legionnaires, veterans of World War I and II both, came to call. Pius XII saluted them thus:

"Your spirit does not seem belligerent, but your name is. In ancient Rome the legionnaires were regarded as the best and most trustworthy soldiers, most truly Roman. But they were legioned for one vast level plain of Mars; you are veterans of such fields of battle, never to return to them, we hope, and now are organized as a force for peace.

"Your devotion to your country has been written on the imperishable pages of history of two terrible wars. Remember, the pages that tell the history of peace are no less honorable, and the Legion, we are sure, will write its devotion to country on those pages with no less glory. The Bill of Rights for which men died may be lost later in bloodless battle. In union there is strength, it is true, and strength is a great asset, provided it be expended for a good and worthy purpose. It can be maneuvered and diverted into a channel that leads to no good, neither its own good nor the good of the country that has created it. Such is the weakness of all human organizations.

"Our best wishes, then follow the American Legion. God grant that its members, as they were her glory in war, may be their country's bulwark and honor in peace. We pray God's blessing on you and on all who are near and dear to you."

# OCTOBER 8

## YESTERDAY'S PRAYERS

**NO SET OF PRAYERS** belongs more to yesterday than the Leonine Prayers that once wrapped up low Mass. A whole generation of Catholics has grown up unaware that at the end of every low Mass the priest-celebrant switched from Latin to the vernacular for the so-called "prayers at the foot of the altar": three Hail Marys, Hail Holy Queen (*Salve Regina*) with *Oremus*, prayer to St. Michael the Archangel, and an ejaculation to the Sacred Heart said three times, alternatively with the priest-celebrant.

These were latter-day additions to the Mass, all but the ejaculation being in use in the Papal States from 1859, where they were said for the providence of the States. After the loss of the Papal States in Garabaldi's Italian unification movement, recitation was extended by Leo XIII to the universal church. That was in 1884. Pius X added the Sacred Heart ejaculation in 1904.

With the Lateran Treaty of 1928, however, these prayers were rendered superfluous; there was peace between the papacy and the Italian government. Still, the prayers were not dropped. Pius XI retained them, while shifting their intention to the conversion of Russia. The prayers lasted until being dropped completely in the liturgical revisions mandated by Vatican II.

The *Salve Regina* and *Oremus* are still used in liturgical contexts, though in settings quite different from yesterday.

# OCTOBER 9

John Henry Newman (Drawing by George Richmond)

## JOHN HENRY NEWMAN ENTERS THE CHURCH

**THESE WERE** exciting ecclesiastical times in 1845 England. The Tractarian Movement, which would move Anglicanism toward so-called High-Church principles, was in high gear when suddenly its guiding light announced that he was resigning the pulpit of St. Mary's Church, Oxford, the university church, and going over to Rome. He was John Henry Newman, the Anglican vicar of St. Mary's. This wet, blustery evening of 1845 he was received into the Catholic Church by Father Dominic, an Italian Passionist Father, passing through Oxford.

It is hard to appreciate today the impact Newman's conversion had on the English establishment. He was by all odds the great Christian thinker of the time, and a fateful time it was for religion in an epoch of agnosticism and Darwinism. To many of his colleagues he was the Guy Fawkes of Oxford; for Rome he was a great "catch" of the century, whose conversion stirred dreams of a reversal of the tides that had swept England away from Roman Catholicism. Newman was ordained a priest in 1846 in Rome, and returned to England to establish the Oratory of St. Philip Neri and take up missionary work in Birmingham. In 1879 he was elevated to the rank of cardinal by Leo XIII. It was the ultimate reward, but many disappointments had come in between, including the effort in the 1850s to found a Catholic university of Ireland. The effort set the foundations for University College, now with branches in Dublin, Cork and Galway. But in Newman's time there was only Dublin, and "only a few native or English students attended the house in St. Stephen's Green."

Newman died in 1890 at the grand age of eighty-nine, leaving behind a body of work distinguished in the words of one critic for "pure Christian radiance." His writings were collected into thirty-six volumes in 1895, then supplemented. His most famous work was the treatise *Apologia pro Vita Sua* defending his conversion. An example from the work follows.

# OCTOBER 10

Cardinal Newman (Painting by Emmeline Deane)

## NEWMAN AND THE MATTER OF ORIGINAL SIN

**NEWMAN'S** *Apologia Pro Vita Sua* appeared in composite in 1864, but the religious autobiography had previewed in bi-monthly parts, stirring extraordinary interest and debate. Critics poured over it word by word. Charles Kingsley, for one, accused Newman of holding that truth for its own sake "need not be, and on the whole ought not be, a virtue of the Roman clergy." Notwithstanding, the logic and intimate tone of the *Apologia* routed much of the prejudice and confirmed the sincerity of Newman's convictions.

Herewith is a sample from Chapter 5 of the *Apologia*. It follows on Newman's observations on a world of woe, spotted by the disappointments of life, the defeat of the good, the success of evil, racking mental anguish, the prevalence and intensity of sin, idolatries, corruptions, dreary hopeless irreligion, and the like. Newman continues with the posing of a question:

"What can we say to this heart-piercing, reason-bewildering fact? I can only answer, that either there is no Creator, or this living society of men is in a true sense discarded from His presence. Did I see a boy of good make and mind, with the tokens on him of a refined nature, cast upon the world without provision, unable to say whence he came, his birthplace or his family connexions, I should conclude that there was some mystery connected with his history, and that he was one, of whom, for one cause or another, his parents were ashamed. Thus only should I be able to account for the contrast between the promise and the condition of his being. And so I argue about the world: — *if* there be a God, *since* there is a God, the human race is implicated in some terrible aboriginal calamity. It is out of joint with the purpose of its Creator. This is a fact, a fact as true as the fact of its existence; and thus the doctrine of what is theologically called original sin becomes to me almost as certain as that the world exists, and as the existence of God."

# OCTOBER 11

POSTE VATICANE

IOANNES XXIII
MAGNO CUM PATRUM CONCURSU
CONCILIUM OECUMENICUM
VATICANUM II CELEBRAT

Die Emissionis

## THE DAY THE COUNCIL OPENED

**THIS DAY WAS A THURSDAY** in 1962. Pope John XXIII — smiling gently, quietly weeping, seated in the *sedia gestatoria* — was borne on the shoulders of burly Vatican guards down the central aisle of St. Peter's Basilica. In tiers of seats on either side, resplendent in white damask robes and miters, the world's bishops had taken their places. They cheered. The pope swept his arms in greetings and blessings. After almost three years of preparation, Vatican Council II was being formally opened.

The traditional hymn *Veni Creator Spiritus*, "Come Holy Ghost," was sung, followed by solemn Mass, with the epistle and gospel being chanted both in Greek and Latin to emphasize the universality of the church and the unity between the Eastern and Western churches. It was Pope John's great moment of triumph, the realization of his dream of *aggiornamento* — the word he used to sum up the rationale of a council. *Aggiornamento* means to update, to renew, to revitalize, and the word speedily passed from his lips into the Catholic lexicon as descriptive of the process of reform and renewal in the church.

Not everyone agreed, to be sure, that an *aggiornamento* was called for. Pope John swept them away in his sermon at the Mass as "prophets of doom, who are always forecasting disaster, as though the end of the world were at hand." These people were looking back, or at best sitting too smug. Pope John said it was imperative to face forward, as "Divine Providence is leading us to a new order of human relations." While the church must "never depart from the sacred patrimony of truth received from the Fathers," he stated it must "ever look to the present, to new conditions and new forms of life introduced into the modern world, which have opened new avenues to the Catholic apostolate."

If the modern church has its equivalent of a Magna Carta, that sermon is it. It set the tone of the council, and of the reforms that were to follow.

# OCTOBER 12

## THE DISCOVERER OF THE DISCOVERED

**THE WORD DISCOVERER** is applied these days with cautious qualifiers to those who opened the New World, beginning with Christopher Columbus. On this day in 1492 Columbus "discovered" the Americas, but of course the literal "discoverers" were those who evolved in the Americas or, as is more likely, who crossed to it from Asia via the Bering Strait in prehistoric times. But give Columbus credit. He demonstrated that the world wasn't flat, and he proved to skeptics that there was a world out there beyond Europe and Africa. To be sure, when he touched shore at Watling's Island in the Bahamas group of the West Indies, he thought he was at the approaches to India and China — more likely India, which is why he called the natives he encountered Indians, a misnomer that became permanent. But reaching the Americas was accomplishment enough. Columbus, a native Italian sailing under the colors of Spain, was a bona fide hero of the times.

He returned to Spain with a number of prizes, including several natives, samples of exotically different fruits and vegetables, gold and other precious metals. The gold especially boggled eyes. Spain was poor, having been stripped of its precious metals centuries before by the Romans. Some new source was needed. Columbus, in pious naivete, thought gold from the New World might be used to fund a crusade to "free" Jerusalem from so-called infidels. Spain's Queen Isabella, Columbus' patroness, thought it a good idea too. The idea, however, was never implemented. Spain had more immediate problems. Besides, the lodes were never so rich nor real as imagined. Yet the possibility they might be launched waves of immigration from old Hispania to new Hispania.

The New World thus came first under Spanish influence. But it could have been otherwise. Portugal, France and England said no, before Isabella persuaded her husband, King Ferdinand, to gamble on the man from Genoa.

# OCTOBER 13

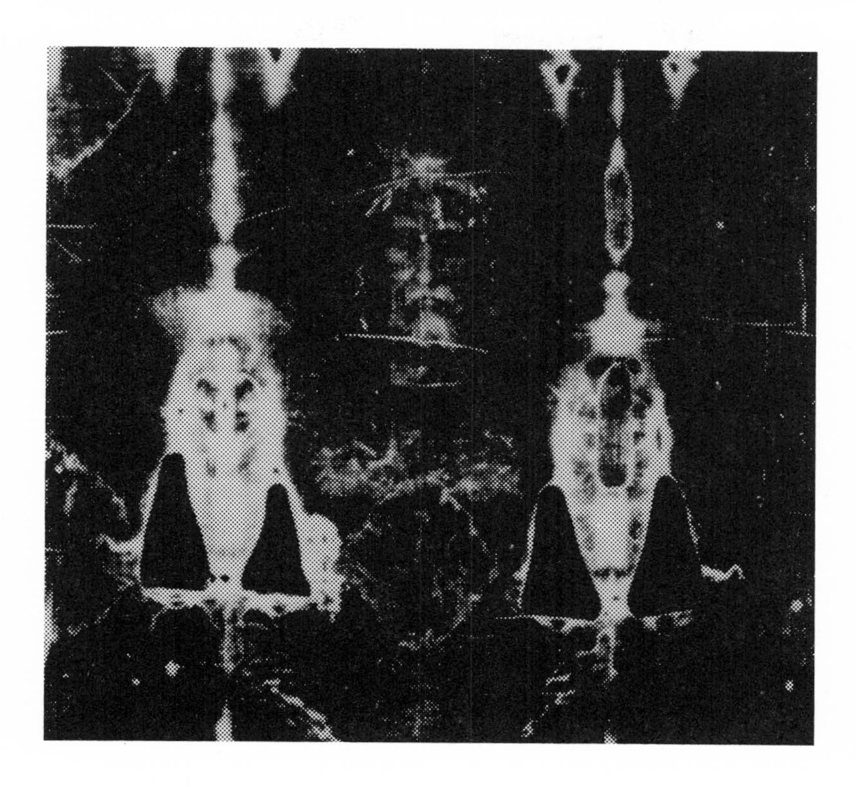

## AN UNSHROUDED SHROUD OF TURIN

**FOR HUNDREDS OF YEARS** millions of Catholics believed the Shroud of Turin to be the actual burial cloth of Christ. Bloodstained and bearing a faint brownish image of a man, front and back, who had been crowned with thorns, whipped, speared and nailed to a cross, the shroud was believed to be some 2,000 years old. On this day in 1988, church authorities conceded on the basis of carbon-14 tests conducted by independent sources that the shroud dated only from between 1260 and 1390, and therefore was at most 728 years old.

To many Catholics the revelation was a deep disappointment, but on the basis of church history others were not surprised. The church never formally accepted the shroud's authenticity, being skeptical because of its incomplete documentation. The shroud could be traced back only as far as 1354, when it came to light in Lirey in the Diocese of Troyes, France. Also, there was no evidence of a shroud in the first centuries of the Christian era — though after references to a shroud were made in the fifth or sixth century "shroud fever" set in, so that by the Middle Ages several places were laying claim to having the true shroud. However, all were discarded as fakes long ago, except for the shroud in the Chapel of Santissimo Sudario of the cathedral at Turin.

So now the Shroud of Turin likewise is not authentic. Is it fair therefore to dismiss it as a mere forgery? Church officials say no, and have encouraged Catholics to continue venerating the shroud as a pictorial image of Christ capable of quickening devotion, as any holy picture might, and capable also of producing miracles. "The church believes in the image and not in the history," commented Turin's Anastasio Cardinal Ballestrero, "because this image of Jesus Christ [on the shroud] in fact is very interesting and the people deeply believe in Jesus." Ballestrero feels, in sum, as do others, that the date of the shroud is not important, but rather its power to lead people to Christ.

# OCTOBER 14

## ELEVEN DAYS THAT NEVER CAME

**WE GO BACK** to 1582. This day that year was the last for the Julian Calendar, the calendar named for Julius Ceasar by which the world had lived since 46 B.C. That calendar was so imprecise that by the sixteenth century the calendar year was running some eleven days behind the sun, throwing everything out of kilter in the ecclesiastical as well as the secular spheres. Several councils of the church, including Trent in its last session in 1563, urged action to correct matters, but the problem seemed to defy solution — that is, until ten years after Trent when three astronomers commissioned by Gregory XIII — Lilius, Clavius and Chacon (Chaconius) — devised a solution. The calendar would be jumped ahead by eleven days from October 4, 1582, to October 15, 1582, and leap years would be introduced into future calendars. The key was the leap-year innovation, for except for thirty-five seconds it offset the difference between the calendar year (365 days) and the astronomical year (365.25 days). Those thirty-five seconds don't count for much; scientists note that it will take about thirty-five centuries for the difference to amount to one day.

The new calendar took Gregory's name, of course, and it's known to this day as the Gregorian Calendar. However, countries divided along denominational lines in accepting the new calendar, Catholic countries adopting it instantly and countries of the Reformation rejecting it. Inevitably, enormous confusion resulted, especially in Germany, divided as it was between Roman Catholicism and Lutheranism. Nor would it be soon before the calendar was universally accepted. England and the American colonies did not accept the loss of their eleven days until 1752. And Orthodox churches still follow the Julian calendar.

The last of the national holdouts was Russia, which waited until this century was a couple decades old before changing over. Thus for Russia the historical paradox: Their "October" Revolution actually took place in November.

# OCTOBER 15

St. Teresa of Avila

## THE ISSUE OF WOMEN AS PRIESTS

**AS ROMAN PONTIFFS GO,** Paul VI was a good friend of feminists. In 1970, he named St. Catherine of Siena and St. Teresa of Avila doctors of the church, the first women even so honored. In 1971 he named the first woman in history to head a Vatican department: Sister Thaddea Kelly; the department dealt with women's religious orders. In 1973 he named a special commission to examine the role of women in the church and in society, an obvious signal that he believed an improvement in status was in order. He even received in audience the American ultra-feminist Betty Freidan. But then on this day in 1976 he in effect said to Catholic women: 'You can go so far, no further.'

For on October 15, 1976, the final 'i' was dotted and 't' crossed on *Inter insigniores*, the document known as the "Declaration on the Question of the Admission of Women to the Ministerial Priesthood." The declaration was not published by the Congregation of the Doctrine of the Faith until the following January 27, but the delay cushioned nothing. The conclusion might generally have been presumed, but for many the reasoning came as a shock. Women were excluded from the priesthood on three grounds.

First was Scripture. Though Jesus was a feminist and acted often against cultural prejudices and in favor of women, he did not personally entrust or include women in the apostolic mission. The implication, the declaration argues, is that it is of divine order: women are not to be ordained priests.

Second was tradition. From apostolic times, the church has only ordained men. The practice thus is normative and expressive of God's will.

Third was theological reasoning. Since a priest acts in the person of Christ and as his image, a priest must necessarily be male. This is the so-called argument of fittingness; symbolism in sacrament requires natural resemblance (maleness) in the person acting *in persona Christi* when the words of the consecration are pronounced. The logic boggled minds. Read on.»»»

# WILL WOMEN BE ORDAINED PRIESTS?

**AS MENTIONED,** *Inter insigniores* stunned by its reasoning even those who had long presumed that any explicit ruling by Rome on women priests would be negative. The Catholic Theological Society of America probed Rome's arguments from Scripture, tradition and anthropology, and in 1978 concluded that it "does not...find that the arguments adduced on the question present any serious grounds to justify the exclusion of women from ordination to pastoral office in the Catholic Church." Feminists applauded, notably those of the Women's Ordination Conference, a "grassroots movement" which organized in 1975 to press the issue of ordination for women. Rome stood its ground, however.

The issue refusing to go away, Pope John Paul II in 1988 issued the apostolic letter, *Mulieris dignitatem*, "On the Dignity of Women." Modestly styled as a "meditation" by the pope himself, the letter forcefully defended women's dignity, but narrowly defined their role in the church and society. The pope essentially characterized women in terms of the "vocations" of motherhood and virginity. Married women and those who "realize their womanhood in a way different from marriage" were told to find themselves in their love for others, and not seek to appropriate to themselves "male characteristics contrary to their own feminine originality." As for women in the church, John Paul II discounted demands for a greater role for women, and of course once again reaffirmed the church's official opposition to female ordination.

Traditonalists welcomed *Mulieris dignitatem*, as would be expected. Feminists, as also might be expected, accused the pope of constructing, in the words of two women, a "static eternalized feminine archtype." So the big question: Has John Paul II's letter settled the matter? No more than did the declaration issued in Paul VI's time. One can look for the issue of women's ordination to persist, if not in terms of equality, then in the context of new forms of ordained ministry to cope with the shortage of male priests.

# PULLING THE PLUG ON "GOD'S MICROPHONE"

**THE PAGES OF CATHOLIC HISTORY** are strewn with forgotten names and movements. Take that of Jesuit Father Riccardo Lombardi and his Better World Movement, a phrase from a speech by Pius XII. Lombardi was known as "God's microphone," and in the 1950s he filled the air of Italy with ringing anti-communist rhetoric. He enjoyed the confidence of Pius, and liked to cite Pius' prediction that "the next pope would call a Council," an idea he endorsed. Indeed the next pope would call a council, but Lombardi's sun was by then set.

The clue to Lombardi's non-future came on this night in 1955. After addressing the clergy of Venice, he dined with the future John XXIII, then the patriarch of Venice, Cardinal Angelo Roncalli. According to new reports, Lombardi is said to have held forth on the importance of his Better World Movement in the context of what he saw as "the new Counter-Reformation," and in his zeal charged that not one bishop of Italy was living according to the precepts of Trent. Roncalli is portrayed as responding mildly, "Dear father, I have studied the Italian situation before and after Trent, and I can assure you that things are much better today." An exasperated Lombardi leaped to his feet and banged the table with such vehemence that the crystal fell to the floor and smashed. "Souls are going to hell and the Patriarch tells me that everything is going well!" "I'm never going to talk here again," he exclaimed.

Roncalli is recorded as being solicitous of Lombardi, following him to his room, where he calmed him by giving him a signed copy of his Lenten pastoral of that year, "Towards Spiritual Renewal." But Lombardi wasn't done yet. With a council in sight, he offered an overview in a book titled *The Council for a Reform in Charity*. Advance publicity claimed the book "was almost certainly approved by the Pope." It was the kiss of death. The book was withdrawn and new translations were prohibited. Father Lombardi belonged to the past.

# OCTOBER 18

St. Luke

## DID LUKE WRITE OUT OF MARY'S MOUTH?

**FUNNY THING** about St. Luke. He is accounted an apostle and an evangelist, but he never actually met Jesus. Nor was he bishop or priest, though he played an important role in the early church as a member of Paul's mission through Asia Minor about the year 50. He was layman to the end.

Luke, a Greek-speaking Gentile, was one of the first converts to Christianity. He was a doctor by profession (Paul refers to him as the "beloved physician" in his letter to the Colossians, 4:14), and was therefore well educated. Certainly his Gospel is the most literate of the four, and the most Marian-centered — perhaps because Mary herself might logically have been the source of much of his information. In any instance, it is in Luke's Gospel, and Luke's alone, that one finds the narrative of the Annunciation to Mary that she had been chosen to become the mother of Jesus; the account of the Visitation of Mary to her cousin Elizabeth; the Presentation of Jesus in the Temple; and the finding of Jesus in the Temple, after he had become lost. Similarly, though all four evangelists relate the story of the Nativity, Luke provides additional details that could easily have been supplied by Mary.

Of course, in recording those events in Mary's life, Luke gives to history not only the joyful mysteries of the rosary (q.v. Oct. 2), but also some of the church's most beautiful prayers, including the Angelus (q.v. Sept. 4), the Magnificat (q.v. May 31), and the first phrases of the Hail Mary (q.v. May 2).

Luke makes other contributions to the New Testament that are unique, most notably the parables of the good Samaritan (10:33-37), the prodigal son (15:11-32), and the barren fig tree (13:6-9).

Luke was in Rome with Paul during the time of Nero's persecutions, but he escaped martyrdom. According to one second-century writer, he went to Greece, where, "serving the Lord faithfully, unmarried and childless [he] died at the age of 84...full of the Holy Spirit." Today is Luke's feast day.

# NORTH AMERICA'S JESUIT MARTYRS

**WITH THE COMING** of the automobile, Auriesville in Montgomery County in upstate New York became an especially popular destination — a pleasant drive, and a spiritually rewarding one. It still is an objective for the devout, for at Auriesville is the shrine of the North American Martyrs — Sts. Isaac Jogues, John de Brebeuf and companions, whose feast the church observes on this day. They were a Jesuit group serving in what was then known as the missions of New France, and they were martyred in the seventeenth century by Mohawk Indians, mainly because the Indians held them to be sorcerers and thus responsible for natural problems that had come into their lives. For instance, Isaac Jogues, the most famous of the martyrs, died because he was deemed responsible for a tribal sickness and a blight that had hit Mohawk crops in 1646. Isaac Jogues' martyrdom was an especially cruel one. He was met in September of that year by an Indian party near Lake George (a water called Horicon by the Indians and for a time known as the Lake of the Blessed Sacrament, thanks to Jogues). The Indians stripped Jogues naked, beat and slashed him with their knives, then led him captive to Ossernenon, the village that is now Auriesville. The following October 18 they finally dispatched him. Jogues was tomahawked and decapitated. His head was fixed to a palisades spike and his body hurled into the Mohawk River.

Jogues' companions, in addition to de Brebeuf, were Anthony Daniel, Gabriel Lalemant, Charles Garnier and Noel Chabanel, all Jesuit priests, and two lay missionaries, Rene Goupil and John Lelande. Their martyrdoms were stretched out between September 22, 1642, and December 9, 1649, one as cruel as the next. Pope Pius XI canonized the group June 29, 1930. Meanwhile, the site of the Mohawk village where the martyrdoms occurred was purchased in 1884, and the shrine was developed that attracts pilgrims to this day.

# ORESTES BROWNSON, OUTSPOKEN LAYMAN

**ONE OF THE GREAT CONTROVERSIALISTS** of nineteenth-century America was Orestes Augustus Brownson. Political theoretician, philosopher, publisher, author, Brownson flitted about the intellectual landscape with astonishing effect and influence. He moved in and out of several Protestant churches; he was ordained a Universalist minister; he joined with Robert Dale Owen and Fanny Wright in their "war on marriage"; he flirted with Transcendentalism — then in 1840 he penned so strong a condemnation of democratic principles (advocating abolition of penal codes, private ownership and all forms of Christianity) that President Martin Van Buren ascribed his defeat for re-election to Brownson's unwelcome support. But Brownson was yet to drop his biggest bombshell. To the astonishment of all who knew him, he became a Catholic on this day in 1844, being received into the church in Boston by Bishop John B. Fitzpatrick.

For Brownson, being Catholic meant merely that the setting had changed. He continued as flamboyant controversialist, though now specializing in Catholic themes. There was a famous falling out with Bishop John Hughes of New York, and the orthodoxy of some of his theological views was frequently called into question; Newman, for instance, invited him to join the faculty of his Catholic university in Dublin, then scratched his name. Still, he was an uncompromising champion of church interests, and unrelenting in his attacks on the "opposition."

Brownson advanced his reviews in his own journal, *Brownson's Quarterly Review* — where, incidentally, he did not hesitate to criticize individual Catholics. Jesuits, the hierarchy and leaders of Catholic immigrants were favorite targets. He even questioned the pope's claim to temporal power by divine right, a daring position with the papacy striving mightily to preserve the Papal States. Brownson not only survived, but was commended by Pius IX for his activities in behalf of the church in the U.S. He died in 1876.

# OCTOBER 21

## ANIMAL LOVERS OF THE BIBLE

**THE CHRISTMAS CRECHE** (q.v. Dec. 15) is familiar even to the smallest of children, complete to the animals hovering about, gazing in wonder and warming the Christ Child with their breaths. It's a pleasant scene, except highly imaginative. Luke, the one evangelist to go into detail about the Nativity, speaks of a manger, but makes no mention of animals being present. But it was a stable; maybe Joseph shooed them off for sanitation's sake.

Whatever, animals figure prominently in the Bible, there literally being hundreds of references to them. But of course. Animals figured intimately in everyone life — for food, labor, transportation and sacrifice.

We know that Christ rode about on an ass, as when he entered Jerusalem in triumph on Palm Sunday (John 12:14). But what other animals are mentioned in the Bible? Well, there's the ape, badger, bat, bear, boar, camel, deer, sheep, fox, goat, horse, hyena, leopard, lion, mole, mouse, whale, wolf, ram — one could go on and on. Deuteronomy 33:17 and Job 39:10, for instance, mention the unicorn; was the unicorn an imaginative concoction, or was there such a species and it became extinct? And what of the "behemoth" mentioned in Job 40:15; is that a reference to what we now call the hippotamus? Fascinating!

Incidentally, the most spectacular animal passages in the Bible are in Job, as of the wild goat, ass, ostrich and horse. The horse passages (39:20-25) are especially graphic: "...the glory of his nostrils is terrible. He paweth in the valley, and rejoicest in his strength: he goeth on to meet the armed men. He mocketh at fear, and is not affrighted; neither turneth he back from the sword. The quiver rattleth against him, the glittering spear and the shield. He swalloweth the ground with fierceness and rage: neither believeth he that it is the sound of the trumpet. He saith among the trumpets, Ha, ha; and he smelleth the battle far off, the thunder of the captains, and the shouting."

Job is a treasure trove for zoologists and for animal lovers generally.

# THE PAPACY AND ITS FORMER MONOPOLY

**ROME HAD NOT SEEN** such excitement in years to compare to this day in 1978. The church was formally installing its youngest pope (fifty-eight) since the election of Pius IX at fifty-four in 1846, and its first non-Italian pope since the Dutch pope, Adrian VI, more than 450 years before. The new pope was the cardinal from Krakow, Karol Wojtyla, a surprise choice whose announcement the throng of Conclave watchers gathered in St. Peter's Square had greeted with the exclamation, *Ecco. E il Polacco*; imagine, the Polish cardinal! That was October 16; six days later excitement had ebbed not one bit. Wojtyla, now John Paul II, accepted the symbols of office in the elaborate ceremony of installation, then plunged into the crowd to shake hands. The crowd went wild with joy.

A dozen years into the reign of Pope John Paul II, it is hard to appreciate the novelty of his choice, so thoroughly has the office absorbed the nationhood of the man. It might have been otherwise, as Avignon papacies demonstrated. John Paul II, however, has been so impartial a pope nationally that, should the rest of his reign be as the past, there should be neither problem nor worry about electing as pope one from wherever, so long as he is best qualified.

How unusual was the choice of the Wojtyla? Well, over the past millennium, only twenty-two of the church's 125 popes have been non-Italian. Of the twenty-two, twelve were French, four German, two Spanish, one English, one Portuguese, one Dutch and finally one Polish. That might seem a fair distribution to some, but remember from 1523 until 1978 every pope had been Italian. Over four centuries the papacy had come to be associated exclusively with Italians, and the generally transnational character that Italians brought to the office argued for continuance of the practice. But a Polish pope has demonstrated that this transnational quality is not unique to a particular hierarchy, that others than Italians alone can preserve and dramatize the church's universality and the breadth of faith. There will be more non-Italian popes.

# OCTOBER 23

## THE PASSING OF EMBER AND ROGATION DAYS

**SO MUCH** has gone by the boards in the so-called new church. Does anyone remember Rogation Days? Or Ember Days? They passed back in 1970.

Rogation Days were days of special prayer with a history dating to the fifth century. There was no fast or abstinence connected with them. Mainly they were days on which one petitioned for a bountiful harvest or protection against calamity, and on which one did penance for sin. A major Rogation Day was observed in April, and three minor days of rogation were marked immediately preceeding the feast of the Ascension.

Ember Days had an even earlier history, going back to the third century and probably originating as Christian replacements for the seasonal fetes of agrarian cults. Gregory VII in the eleventh century prescribed their observance by the whole church in the four seasons of the year, specifically the Wednesdays, Fridays and Saturdays following: (1) Dec. 13, the feast of St. Lucy; (2) the first Sunday in Lent; (3) Whitsunday, the seventh Sunday after Easter; and (4) Sept. 14, the Exaltation of the Cross. Primarily penitential in character, Ember Days were days of fast and abstinence that made the first full week of Lent tougher, and which brought a touch of Lent to the universal church three more times of the year. Ember Days were also occasions of special prayer for clergy nearing ordination.

Rogation Days and Ember Days were replaced by the 1970 "Instruction on Particular Calendars" of the Vatican's Congregation for the Sacraments and Divine Worship directing dioceses, at times designated by the local ordinary, to observe "days or periods of prayer for the fruits of the earth, prayer for human rights and equality, prayer for world justice and peace, and penitential observance outside of Lent."

And such is the case until now.

# OCTOBER 24

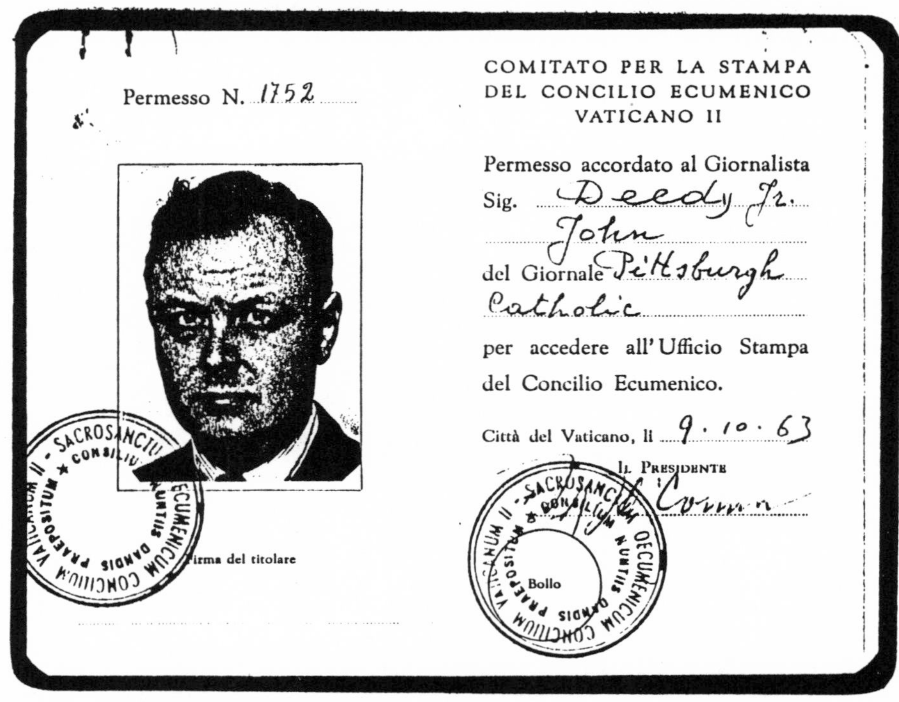
Permesso N. 1752

COMITATO PER LA STAMPA
DEL CONCILIO ECUMENICO
VATICANO II

Permesso accordato al Giornalista
Sig. Deedy Jr.
John
del Giornale Pittsburgh
Catholic
per accedere all'Ufficio Stampa
del Concilio Ecumenico.

Città del Vaticano, li 9 . 10 . 63

Il Presidente

Firma del titolare

Bollo

Author's press credentials for Vatican II

## REFLECTING ON VATICAN COUNCIL II

**THIS TIME IN 1965** Vatican Council II was rushing to a close. Between now and December 8, the day of the council's close, eleven of the council's sixteen documents would be promulgated. Three were issued in 1964 and two in 1963, including *Sacrosanctum concilium*, the Constitution on the Sacred Liturgy, which was to change so radically the ways of Catholic worship. But then, Vatican II radically changed everything in the church, when theoretically it was only supposed to let in a few draughts of fresh air. But hasn't it always been such?

The last thing in Martin Luther's mind when he hammered his theses to the door of the castle church in Wittenberg was a church separate and distinct from Roman Catholicism. And the last thing in Pope John XIII's mind in calling his "pastoral" council was a Catholicism substantively different from the one the church had nurtured and developed over centuries, if not millennia.

But history has a way of playing tricks with seemingly lesser events, and just as the gesture at Wittenberg was the catalyst for a Protestant church, so did Pope John's "pastoral" council set forces in motion the full extent of which, it is safe to say, are not completely known, though already they have produced a "new" Catholicism.

Pope John's hopes for his council were radical only in terms of the church's ancient and institutionalized conservatism. A church reformed and renewed? Yes, John wanted that. A church snatched from the hands of the "prophets of doom"? — his words, remember! He especially wanted that. A church of expansive human compassion, a church more attuned ecumenically, a church more open to the world? Yes, he wanted all that too. On the other hand, he wanted a church "that did not depart from the sacred patrimony of truth received from the Fathers," where doctrine was orderly and safeguarded, and where consciences were formed in "faithful and perfect conformity" to authentic teaching. His legacy was one without the other. Why? Read on.»»»

# OCTOBER 25

## REFLECTING FURTHER ON VATICAN II

**POPE JOHN'S COUNCIL** gave the church a deeper understanding of its nature; it gave it a purer liturgy, episcopal collegiality (imperfect to be sure), and a keener appreciation of the role of the laity (males more than females, however); it put the church at last in line on religious freedom (or at least abreast of Roger Williams); it repudiated old libels against the Jews, some of which had been codified in the church's official liturgy; it conceded the operativeness of the divine in churches other than solely the Catholic Church. Considerable advances all of these.

But the church of "most splendid light" that John saw evolving from a council which could produce all this developed instead into a shadowy and fractious church of no little crisis, one in which there was diminishing conformity and an astonishing degree of doctrinal free-lancing, not only on the part of a supposed ill-formed laity, but also among the church's professionals, its priests and theologians. And why should *that* have happened?

Scapegoats are easy to find. The bishops who voted so bravely in Rome to reform the church, then acted so timidly when it came time to reform their own dioceses, can be faulted for letting momentum slag and conciliar impetuses slip away. Inevitably reform then would devolve into a tug-of-war between liberals and conservatives, until many in the middle ground would throw up their hands in boredom and/or disgust. Rome's tailoring of the meaningfulness of certain conciliar decisions and its efforts to put brakes on how far reform might logically go did not help much either. The people in the pews began to shuffle their feet. The postconciliar Synods of Bishops would presumably re-energize the thrusts of the council, but they were managed into irrelevance when not opened up to certain topics (celibacy) and concerned parties (laity). Then there was *Humanae vitae*, which shut a door Vatican II had gently nudged open. That "most splendid light" of John's vision dimmed perceptibly. Read on.»»»

## CONTINUING TO REFLECT ON VATICAN II

**THE DIMMING** of John's "most splendid light" was accompanied by considerable turmoil. There's no denying a cause and effect relationship between the two, but there's no easy categorizing as to what produced what. The question is, is it all bad?

A surface reading of the script might say so. However, to look at today's church and see only disappointment, revolt and reaction may be to miss the complete picture. Something very positive may be at work, not including the possibility that an age of enlightenment has come to the Catholic Church, liberating the thinking of theologians and the consciences of the laity.

If that is what is happening, it should come as no surprise. Something had to give. Too many double standards existed. The imperatives of the non-Catholic conscience, for instance, could not be affirmed, as they were at Vatican II, while the imperatives of the Catholic conscience were held subservient to the exercise of Catholic authority, as was attempted. The conciliar principle of "the Holy People of God shar[ing] in Christ's prophetic office," with all that encompasses by legitimacy of the collective conscience, could not be articulated as policy and then suspended when a particular thrust ran counter to papal preference. Nor could the emphases on "personhood" any longer be subdivided so as to mean one thing for non-Catholics and something else for Catholics — and within Catholicism itself, one thing for lay persons and something else for men and women religious.

In a word, the real story of what has happened in Catholicism since the council may be that as Rome sought to draw boundaries on the carry-over from Vatican II, much as a rancher might merely move his fences when enlarging the ranch, there were those free spirits who were not content with merely more room to range in. They saw new horizons and strained towards them. Read on.»»»

# CONCLUDING THE REFLECTING ON VATICAN II

**ONE CAN APPRECIATE** Rome's dilemma over much of what has happened since Vatican II. It had to react, sometimes sternly, if only to control the sweep of change. To have stood by and done nothing would have amounted to a virtual blessing of a new dogmatic and moral theology for Catholicism, with a new concept of church, a new concept of religion inevitably emerging. More especially, to have stood by would have been to bless — four centuries late — a great deal of what the Reformation was all about, notably with respect to conscience, freedom and authority. Granted, Vatican II dealt with all three of those topics, but in the controlled contexts of the times, when perimeters could be set and their outward limits respected. Hence the reaction, which stiffens markedly with John Paul II. Rome doesn't want a new Reformation.

Which raises another question, not so much whether Vatican II was per se good or bad, but whether the church would have been better off without a council. To say yes, it would have been better off, is to lay on the council the blame for the turmoil the church has experienced the past two decades; that can't be done, not logically. To say yes is also to presume that had the lid stayed on everything the church today would be the same as it was, say, in the 1950s. Impossible! The problems of skepticism and doubt, of repudiation, rejection and drainage were coming, every one of them, and for a thousand and one reasons — perhaps the most obvious being that a more sophisticated Catholic had taken his/her place in what had become a creaking, archaic institution. Besides, the church does not exist in a vacuum. What was happening in the wider society — the questioning of old ways, the dysfunction societies experienced, none more so than the United States — inevitably affected the church too — indeed, made it easier for some to understand what was happening in the church. So is the church better off because of the council? Let's answer this way: Things would be a whole lot worse had there been none.

# OCTOBER 28

## FDR'S MISSTATEMENT ON A NAZI CHURCH

**MANY EPISODES OF HISTORY** which loom large, then lose their significance and fade quickly into oblivion. One such occurred on this date in 1941, when President Franklin D. Roosevelt took to the airwaves to announce the existence of a Nazi directive of thirty points for "the abolition of religion as we know it." The directive envisioned establishment, after German victory, of a "German National Church," one which would replace all traditional churches and be based on an "entirely new religious concept related to National Socialism."

Roosevelt's talk attracted attention worldwide, including at the Vatican, which harbored fears of precisely such a development. Hitler, however, mocked the "revelation" in a speech in Munich, and for once spoke the truth. Yes, the directive was German in origin, but it was the 1930 handiwork of a man named Bildt of Stettin, who had been arrested that year for disturbing a religious convention with his fulminations. Roosevelt had been misprogrammed. The Allies ignored the speech. Rome filed it away with the note, "Not to be published."

But as Anthony Rhodes notes in his 1973 book *The Vatican in the Age of the Dictators (1922-1945)*, Roosevelt's information, while inaccurate, was likely connected with events which were then taking place — namely, a fourteen-point plan being drawn up by the Nazi Reichstathaler of Wartegau in occupied Poland for regulating the religious situation there. One point would eliminate the juridical "personality" of the church and reduce it to a simple association known as the National German Roman Catholic Church, with no canonical laws of its own and no relations with Rome. The plan never came to full fruition. Nonetheless, the very idea struck terror into the hearts of Polish Catholics, many of whom felt that they were being abandoned to their fate by Rome. It was not until 1943, when Pius XII spoke out gloriously on behalf of Poland in a speech June 2 before the College of Cardinals, that Polish fears were ended.

# OCTOBER 29

## THE VISION OF MACAULAY'S TRAVELER

**THOMAS BABINGTON MACAULAY,** the English statesman, poet, essayist and biographer, is perhaps best remembered for his *History of England*, which enjoyed enormous popularity when the first two of its five volumes appeared in 1849, and which is read yet as one of the most colorful tracts of the times.

Two especially vivid images were left by Macaulay in his writings. First is "Macaulay's schoolboy," an imaginary person invoked so often to rout political opponents that the "boy" became proverbial. Macaulay, for instance, would take exception to a statement and precede his response with the phrase, "As any schoolboy of fourteen would know," or, "As every schoolboy knows...." He did it so often that the phrase "Macaulay's schoolboy" has passed into the language as a classic put-down.

The second of the great images bequeathed by Macaulay is that of the New Zealand traveler. It is one frequently invoked by Catholic speakers in making the point that, however bad the circumstances of the moment might seem, history is on the church's side.

Now Macaulay was not, in that felicitous nineteenth-century phrase, of the Roman Catholic persuasion. But there was much in Roman Catholicism that he respected and admired, and it showed lustrously in the review-essay that appeared in October, 1840, of von Ranke's *History of the Popes*, in the immortal lines:

"She [the Roman Catholic Church] may still exist in undiminished vigor when some traveller from New Zealand shall, in the midst of a vast solitude, take his stand on a broken arch of London Bridge to sketch the ruins of St. Paul's."

Macaulay employed the same image at other times to make the point that the Roman Catholic Church is likely to be still making its witness when the world around it is reduced to rubble heaps. Obviously, no one is anxious to see the latter come to pass, but the optimism of the former should bolster the spirits of anyone inclined to doubt the durability of the church.

# "HOCUS-POCUS" AND SEASONAL TRICKS

**IT'S THE SEASON** of trick or treat, of hocus-pocus and all that stuff. *Hocus-pocus*? Everyone knows what the words are meant to signify; they clue to a trick played on someone, a hoax, usually innocent. But where do the words *hocus-pocus* come from? The seventeenth-century archbishop of Canterbury, John Tillotson, speculated that the term was a corruption of the Latin *Hoc est corpus*, a telescoping of the words of the Eucharist in the Latin church, (the actual Latin is *Hoc est enim corpus meum*), and that the words were used "in ridiculous imitation of the priests of the Church of Rome in their trick of Transubstantiation." Tillotson's is the common theory, but there are others.

Like *hocus-pocus* being the first words of a longer pig-Latin formula used by a late Middle Ages juggler or conjurer while working his tricks, then picked up by others. Thomas Ady records the possibility in *A Candle in the Dark* (1655): "I will speak of one man...that went about in King James his time...who called himself, The Kings Majesties most excellent Hocus Pocus, and so was called, because that at the playing of every Trick, he used to say, Hocus pocus, *tontus talontus, vade celeriter jubeo*, a dark composure of words, to blinde the eyes of the beholders, to make his Trick pass the more currantly without discovery."

A further theory links *hocus-pocus* to Ochus Bochus, a wizard and supposed demon of Scandinavian mythology, though several sources discount any connection from him to the Latin Mass. Maybe there isn't. On the other hand, Swedish and Norwegian children are said to use the phrase *hocus-pokus fileokus*, just as American Catholics of senior years can remember merrily chanting *hocus-pocus dominocus* in childhood years. Both phrases ring of leitmotifs from the Latin Mass — the *Filioque* of the Creed, and the *Dominus*, used throughout the Mass.

Where does all this leave us? Back with Tillotson, most likely.

# OCTOBER 31

## TRICK OR TREAT, IT'S HALLOWEEN

**HALLOWEEN.** Most everyone knows where the word came from. It derives from All Hallows Eve, the name given to the vigil of Hallowmas, which we now know as All Saints' Day. Historically, though, Halloween is a combination of pagan holiday and Christian holy-day vigil.

The Romans celebrated the day as the festival of Pomona, goddess of gardens, and they dipped into stores being laid away for winter for one last feast. Nuts were roasted, and apples were plunked into tubs of water for the sport of apple-ducking. Ducking for apples was long wildly popular, and in places far removed from Rome. In medieval England everyone bobbed for apples on Halloween, and the custom crossed the waters to the New World.

The ancient Celts, on the other hand, called this day "Samhain" or "end of summer," and they observed it as the end of the growing season. That sounds innocent enough, except it is from those same Celts that many of the scary and spooky customs of Halloween derive. For the Celts harbored the Druidic belief that on October 31 Saman, lord of death, brought together all the wicked who had died within the past twelve months and been condemned to inhabit the bodies of animals. Thus the Celtic night echoed with the terrible sounds of keeners and screechers, and for protection people lit fires atop hills to keep the ghosts away. The practice of dressing up as a ghost is a carry-over from those times. So is the practice of treating those who knock on one's door. Better a treat than a trick, was the prevailing wisdom.

In Scotland and Wales, Halloween bonfires were lit well into this century. The custom was to place in the fire's dying embers as many small stones as there were people present, A check was made in the morning, and if any of the stones had been displaced, it was believed the person represented by the stone would be dead within the year. Chilly stuff, but the stuff of All Hallows Eve.

# NOVEMBER 1

## A DAY FOR HONORING THE UNSAINTED SAINTS

**SAY WHAT YOU WANT** about this holy day: It's one of the most popular on the church's calendar. The feast commemorates all those in heaven without any specified feast day of their own. It can be said thus to be a family feast, the day on which one prays for all those not formally canonized — like one's mother and father, one's grandparents or beloved relative, one's children...in a word, all whom we know in our hearts to be in heaven.

November 1 is a marvelously inclusive feast, which is why, along with Christmas, Easter and the Ascension, it ranks from one end of the earth to the other as the most commonly observed of the so-called optional holy days. Nothing surprising about this. The feast has tradition going for it. It dates from the fourth century, and has been a fixture on the church's liturgical calendar since 835 and the pontificate of Gregory IV, when at Gregory's insistence Louis the Pious fixed the date for the feast's observance as November 1 and Gregory himself imposed the obligatory Mass-observance rule. Back when trappings counted for much, the feast was marked with a vigil and an octave. It was, in a word, a feast of the first rank. Still is for most Catholics.

Early scholarship connected the feast of All Saints to the consecration of the Parthenon in Rome to Holy Mary and the Martyrs, which would have situated its observance on May 13. More likely the feast originates in the establishment by Gregory III in the eighth century of an oratory in St. Peter's for the relics "of the holy Apostles and all Saints, martyrs and confessors, of all the just made perfect who are at rest throughout the world."

All Saints is a uniquely Catholic feast. At the time of the Reformation, the Lutheran and Anglican churches at first retained it. But they let it lapse, and despite efforts at revival it is still lapsed among Protestants.

# NOVEMBER 2

## REMEMBERING THE FAITHFULLY DEPARTED

**ONE WOULD EXPECT** the feast of All Souls to have existed at least as long as All Saints. It hasn't. All Souls is more a medieval than an early-church feast. Its origins are found in Peter Damiani's *Life of St. Odilo*, namely in terms of a pilgrim returning from the Holy Land who found himself cast up on a desolate island and in the company of the resident hermit. The hermit told of a chasm between great rocks from which arose constantly the cries of the tormented. They came from that place called Purgatory, and along with the cries came what? Deprecations from the keepers of the tormented against the faithful — especially the monks at Cluny — for the efficacy of their prayers. Seems these prayers were rescuing souls from a fate the tormentors would have otherwise inflicted. They were going to heaven. On his return to France, the pilgrim informed the abbot of Cluny of the experience, and, impressed, the abbot set apart November 2 as a day of prayerful remembrance for the faithfully departed that they might the sooner achieve the Beatific Vision. From Cluny the observance spread to other Cluniac communities, thence among Carthusians, thence the dioceses of France. All this occurred around the year 1000.

French remembrance soon became a feast of the church, though not a holy day of obligation. Indeed, the feast achieved such popularity that around 1888 Pope Leo XIII was asked if priests might be allowed *trination* privileges on that day — that is, permission to celebrate three Masses. He said no, but was reversed in 1915, when Benedict XV, out of love for the soldier dead of World War I, said yes.

All Souls isn't observed so popularly as it used to be, nor so quaintly. Once upon a time Catholics believed that the dead returned to their homes on All Souls Day, and they left a collation — milk, biscuits, cakes — as a welcome. Today many Catholics doubt the very existence of a Purgatory.

# NOVEMBER 3

## THE "END" OF FATHER COUGHLIN, CHARLES E.

**THIS WAS THE DAY** in 1936 that incumbent president Franklin D. Roosevelt won re-election by defeating Republican Alfred M. Landon of Kansas and a third-party candidate named William Lemke of North Dakota. Lemke's name is not the least bit important in American history, except in the context of Father Charles E. Coughlin, the radio-priest out of Royal Oak, Michigan, who then commanded the ears of millions of listeners. Coughlin's National Union for Social Justice supported Lemke — not only supported him, but Father Coughlin vowed to quit his controversial radio program if his candidate did not receive 9-million votes. Lemke received a mere 891,858. Coughlin did indeed go off the air, but he returned a few months later, saying he did so at the dying request of his bishop, Michael J. Gallagher of Detroit. Gallagher's successor, Bishop (later Cardinal) Edward Mooney, was of a different stripe. He quickly brought the pressures of canon law to bear on Coughlin. What finally silenced him, though, was not canon law but a national radio code which forbade controversial broadcasters air time unless they were part of a panel. Coughlin was forced to cancel his 1940-1941 radio series, and his power base was gone.

One can only grasp the force of a man like Father Coughlin by realizing the power of radio in pre-television days. Radio reigned, and for many there was no program of political and social commentary to rival Father Coughlin's Sunday afternoon broadcast. He held audiences spellbound, while careening them over an ideological roller coaster. Early in his career he popularized the slogan "Roosevelt *or* Ruin." Later it became "Roosevelt *and* Ruin." He harrangued against what he called a British-Jewish-Roosevelt conspiracy. He was anti-Semitic, pro-Nazi, anti-Communist. After his silencing, Father Coughlin faded into a pastoral quiet overseeing his Shrine of the Little Flower. He lived to 1979, but he was effectively dead as a national figure on this day in 1936.

# NOVEMBER 4

Miguel Molinos

## PUTTING THE QUIETUS ON QUIETISM

**IT WAS TWO DAYS** after the event, but Rome buzzed still with the news in 1687: Pope Innocent XI had issued the bull *Coelestis pastor* condemning sixty-eight propositions of the Spanish priest Miguel de Molinos, founder of Quietism, and with that bold stroke Quietism was consigned to the church's heresies.

The church has known exotic heresies over the centuries, but there has been none before or since to top Quietism, a complicated movement that swept France, Italy and Spain, partially as an outgrowth of the sixteenth-century mysticism of St. Teresa of Avila and St. John of the Cross. Quietism in sum was a mood or proposition of disinterested love or holy indifference in which the soul lost all wish for action and reached a summit of perfection by surrendering a sense of proprietorship in itself. It was to remain passive while God acted within, even in matters of love. Passivity, in fact, was the one test of holiness.

The reverse of the coin was stamped with sex. The soul was to resign itself to the devil's intrusions, and put away all scruples and doubts, especially in matters carnal. Most particularly, carnal happenings, whether committed alone or with others, were not to be mentioned in confession, because by not confessing them the soul overcame the demon or devil and in the process acquired a "treasure of peace" that produced a closer union with God.

Inevitably the movement won ardent disciples, like Jeanne Marie Guyon (1648-1717), a widow who brought her holy zeal to the French court with what is said to have been notable success. Her most illustrious convert was the theologian and writer Fenelon, then tutor to the Duke of Burgundy. It is recorded that "they met, they pleased each other, and their sublime amalgamated."

As for Molinos, he was arrested by the Inquisition and sentenced to life imprisonment, where he was to be perpetually clothed in penetential garb, and ordered to recite the Creed and the rosary and to confess four times a year.

# NOVEMBER 5

## "...REMEMBER THE FIFTH OF NOVEMBER..."

**THIS IS THE DAY** when Englishmen (and women) carry "guys" through the streets, light bonfires, and set off fireworks. It's Guy Fawkes Day. No particular Catholic celebration this. To the contrary. It's the day that marks the saving of Parliament (the building) and James I (the king) in 1605 from Catholic conspirators who hoped to do both in and thereby stir an uprising in the Midlands that would restore Catholic prerogatives in newly Protestantized England. Guy Fawkes, one of a band of five whose number eventually grew to thirteen, was caught red-handed in a cellar beneath the House of Lords, along with some twenty barrels of gunpowder, just hours before the appointed time for their explosion. History knows the episode as the Gunpowder Plot.

Like all stories, there are two sides to this one. A Catholic plot of some kind was undoubtedly initiated, and it indeed did involve gunpowder. But how broad a plot was it, and was entrapment involved? There's a school of thought that holds the government knew well beforehand of the plot, and its limitations, but allowed it to proceed for purposes of its own.

One objective seems to have been an inflating of guilt of those responsible for the plot from a small band of zealots, acting independently and on their own authority, to the larger body of Catholics, and the Jesuits in particular. A wide conspiracy was never proven, but the mere allegations served official ends. The plot intensified Protestant suspicions of Catholics, and was used as an excuse for more rigorous enforcement of the recusancy law, which among other things levied fines on those who refused to attend Anglican worship.

As for the "disgruntled papists," they died. Under torture, Guy Fawkes divulged the names of his co-conspirators, and they were hunted down, dragged through the streets, and executed. As a message to others, their heads were publicly displayed on pikes. Not pretty.

# NOVEMBER 6

Bishop John Carroll

## THE AMERICAN CHURCH'S COMING OF AGE

**THIS WAS THE DAY** in 1789 that Pope Pius VI issued his brief *Ex hac apostolicae* erecting the diocese of Baltimore and appointing Father John Carroll as first bishop. It was a choice not lightly made. Catholics were then held in considerable suspicion, and there was question whether the time was right for so momentous an exercise of authority. But Episcopalians had elevated a bishop of their own in 1784 with no negative repercussions, and this lent encouragement. Rome went ahead, braving even to choose as bishop a priest who had been ordained a Jesuit, an especially adventurous choice given the suspension of the order in 1773 by Clement XIV. Some worried that Jesuit property interests would be adversely affected, but they weren't.

As for the choice of Baltimore as the see city, it seems to have been based on Baltimore's central location more than anything else. The United States was then an eastern seaboard country and Baltimore was as good a hub as any other. Many state capitals were chosen on the same basis of geography.

As for John Carroll, he chose to go to England for the ceremonies of elevation to the episcopacy. A number of reasons were involved. He hoped to raise money for the projected college of Georgetown; he hoped to entice his English friend Charles Plowden to become its first president; finally, he hoped to recruit priests for the United States from among the English clergy. Carroll did in fact receive some substantial gifts, but Plowden turned him down and the English clergy were in demand for parishes in their own country.

John Carroll's ordination as bishop took place August 15, 1790, in the private chapel of Lulworth Castle. The presiding prelate was the aged Benedictine, Bishop Charles Walmesley, Senior Vicar Apostolic of England. Bishop Carroll arrived back in Baltimore in triumph on December 7. In 1808 he was promoted to archbishop, and died in 1829, a true hero of American Catholic history.

## De Profundis

*Out of the depths have I cried unto thee, O Lord.*

*Lord, hear my voice: let thine ears be attentive to the voice of my supplications.*

*If thou, Lord, shouldest mark iniquities, O Lord, who shall stand?*

*But there is forgiveness with thee, that thou mayest be feared.*

*I wait for the Lord, my soul doth wait, and in his word do I hope.*

*My soul waiteth for the Lord more than they that watch for the morning: I say, more than they that watch for the morning.*

## YESTERDAY'S PRAYER....AND TODAY'S TOO

**ONE OF THE MOST MOVING PRAYERS** in the entire liturgy is the *De Profundis*, the Old Testament psalm which Catholics chant in remembrance of the dead. Indeed, it is the prayer for the dead used more than any other. The psalm is number 129 or 130, depending upon one's version of the Bible; printed here is the King James Version, #130. The *De Profundis*, the prayer for pardon and mercy and the sixth of the Penitential Psalms, seems especially appropriate to recall in the month during which the church remembers the faithfully departed:

# NOVEMBER 8

St. Martin of Tours

## A GOOSE FOR ST. MARTIN'S DAY

**ST. MARTIN OF TOURS' FEAST** is observed on November 11, but it was on this day that he died in 397. St. Martin is revered as one of France's great saints, and why not? He was a bishop; he fought the good fight against heresies (Arianism and Priscillianism); he pioneered Western monasticism, promoting the practice even before St. Benedict; he also worked all kinds of miracles. For example, he three times raised a person to life who was apparently dead; he cured a woman with an issue of blood (as did Christ), a leper with a kiss, and a paralytic by pouring oil (sic) in his mouth. He traveled the country roads, St. Martin did, destroying pagan sanctuaries as he went. A pagan's sword raised against him is said to have fallen impotent. Against popular opinion, he ordered a sacred tree felled, and to prove the rightness of his order, he placed himself in the path of the tree's fall. The tree miraculously swerved aside. You've got to admire a man (saint) like that.

Why is his feast observed three days after his death, rather than on the memorial date itself? Probably because it was intended to substitute for the Roman feast of Bacchus. Inevitably, St. Martin's feast (Martinmas — Martin's Mass) retained some of the features of the feast of Bacchus (the Bacchanalia), which may be why St. Martin is regarded as the patron saint of bartenders and drunks. Incidentally, the phrase "Martin drunk," meaning terribly drunk, comes from the association of St. Martin's feast with revelries celebrating Bacchus.

Another phrase connected with St. Martin is "Martin's goose," a term for a bothersome animal. How come? Because, while calling as a peacemaker in his diocesan village of Candes, St. Martin is supposed to have ordered a goose killed for his dinner, and fell mortally ill while eating it. Again, that was today in 397. Thereafter a "Martin's bird" was traditionally sacrificed on "Martinmas" — except you could go hungry, if you chose.

# NOVEMBER 9

## CHRISTENDOM'S MOTHER CHURCH

**BLINK AGAIN!** This is a feast honoring the dedication of a basilica, that of St. John Lateran in Rome.

What's a feast honoring a building doing on the church's revised, pruned-down calendar? The answer is that St. John Lateran is no run-of-the-aisle church building. St. John Lateran is the mother church of all the churches of Rome, and of the world for that matter.

The basilica was founded by Constantine back in the fourth century, and was known as the Basilica of the Savior during the time of Sylvester I (314-335). In a word, the basilica predates its neighbor, St. Peter's. St. John Lateran was destroyed and rebuilt several times before the present basilica was raised in the seventeenth century.

The eminence of St. Peter's once belonged to St. John Lateran. Popes lived here — most all of them, in fact, before the papacy was carted off to Avignon in 1305 — and, of course, the basilica was the site of five general ecumenical councils: Lateran I (1123), Lateran II (1139), Lateran III (1179), Lateran IV (1215), and Lateran V (1512-1517). A lot of church history was defined here, including the eucharistic term "transubstantiation."

St. John Lateran follows the lines of the classical basilica, with nave and four aisles. Its facade was built in 1775 by Alexander Galilei, and among the building's mumerous showpieces are bronze doors requisitioned from the Curia at the Forum by Pope Alexander VII (1655-1667). Here too are the remains of Sylvester II (999-1003), the French pope, who was the first to proclaim the "necessity" of the Crusades for the "rescue" of the Holy Land — foolhardy adventures that were to extend over a two hundred-year period, roughly.

St. Peter's may have superseded St. John Lateran as a tourist attraction, but St. John Lateran will forever enjoy a unique place in church history.

# NOVEMBER 10

## THE FIRST OF THE POPE LEOS

**THERE HAVE BEEN** thirteen Pope Leos, and today belongs to the first, the pope who alone of pontiffs shares with Gregory I the surname The Great. Leo the Great reigned from 440 to 461, and came to grips with three of the great heresies of the early church: Manichaeanism (which argued the inherent evil of matter), Pricillianism (which viewed marriage as diabolical and saw a Kingdom of Light coexisting with a Kingdom of Darkness), and Nestorianism (which denied the unity of the human and divine natures in Christ). To deal with the last proved the knottiest of the three problems. Tensions came to a head in 449 when Leo sent a letter to the Nestorian-dominated Synod of Ephesus setting forth in precise detail the doctrine of the dual natures, human and divine, existing in the one person of Christ. The letter was submitted but never read at the synod. The papal legates were in fact lucky to escape with their lives from violent theologians who, it is recorded, "shouted for the dividing of those who divided Christ." Leo forthwith declared the acts of the council null and void, thus consigning Ephesus to the "robber synods" — that is, unlawfully-called church assemblies. Two years later, the Council of Chalcedon was assembled, and Leo's letter was resubmitted and adopted by acclamation. This time the theologians shouted, "Peter has spoken by Leo!" Leo's letter set forth the creed on the nature of Christ that to the letter has been the church's ever since.

Leo's letter anchored his place in church history, but the legend doesn't stop there. It was Leo who confronted Attila the Hun at the confluence of the Mincio and the Po in 451, as Attila was advancing on Rome, and by the sheer power of his rhetoric persuaded him to turn back. Leo was less successful a few years later when the Vandal chief Genseric arrived at the gates of Rome, but so great was his standing that the Vandals tempered their vandalizing.

# ANOTHER DAY FOR REMEMBERING

**WE OBSERVE THIS DAY** in the United States as Veterans Day. Those a little older remember it as Armistice Day, the holiday marking the war to end all wars, World War I, which ended in 1918. But, then, we have had several wars since, haven't we, so of course we need an umbrella designation for the honoring of the nation's fallen heroes. This is that day.

November 11, however, was not forever a day of military commemoration. Go back a while, way back, and November 11 was the first day of winter. We're talking about when the Julian calendar was in effect. Then as now in the northern hemisphere November was a foreboding month, the time when the weather changed for the worst. This precise day was when the calendar season officially moved from gentle autumn to bold, cold winter.

The old Anglo-Saxon words for November were *Windmonath*, "wind month," and *Blodmonath*, "blood month." Live in England — or Chicago, Canada or the New England shore, for that matter — and one can understand why. April may be the cruelest month, as T.S. Eliot said, but November can give it a run for that designation. A "cheerless" month, Thomas Hood once said of November, "no shade, no shine, no butterflies, no bees,/no fruits, no flowers, no leaves, no birds." William Ernest Henley would agree. "November glooms are barren beside the dusk of June," he wrote in *Invictus.* But we all know that.

Actually, not everyone has been completely jaundiced about the month. Governor Willam Bradford of Plymouth Colony, for one, chose November as the month for "thanksgiving unto the Lord," hence the holiday to dome later in the month.

Even the Romans weren't so despairing of November. In fact, in Roman times, this very day, November 11, set the stage for *epulum Jovis*, the sacred banquet two days hence honoring Jupiter, the supreme deity of the ancient Romans. The Romans actually regarded November as an auspicious month, at one time, it is said, thinking of renaming it in honor of their emperor from 42 B.C. to A.D. 14, Tiberius Claudius Nero Caesar, whose birthday fell on the 16th. The proposal was beaten back when one of the senators posed the question: "What will you do, Conscript Fathers, if you have *thirteen* Caesars?"

# BRIDGE BETWEEN EAST AND WEST

**TODAY THE CHURCH** marks the feast of the person whose martyrdom in 1623 helped assure the survival of the Catholic Slavonic church — St. Josephat. Josephat was born John Kuncevic in 1580 in the Lithuanian town of Volodymyr. Ecclesiastically, it was a time of great Uniate-Orthodox tension between Ruthenian and Ukrainian Christians. Josephat entered the Basilian monastery at Vilna at age twenty-four, proceeded to priesthood and, reluctantly, the episcopacy. He served as bishop of Vitebsk and later archbishop of Polotsk.

In an age when the clergy was largely unlettered, seldom preached and rarely bothered about catechetical instruction, Josephat was a paradox. He was committed to learning and instruction — as well as to the culture of the East. His liturgical and spiritual orientations were distinctly Byzantine. Still, he maintained a strict loyalty to Rome, and this was to cost him his life. There was an intransigence in Josephat toward schismatics, and even opposition to concessions extended them by the central Polish government, which then controlled the area. So it was that on a visit to Vitebsk he was cut down with an axe by nationalists, then shot. Immediately, miracles began to be attributed to him. Within five years his cause was introduced, and twenty years after his death he was beatified. Canonization followed in 1867.

When Pope John Paul II in 1983 created the fourth diocese in the United States for the care of the Ukrainian Catholics whose spiritual roots go back to Josephat, it was named the Ukrainian Catholic Diocese of St. Josephat, in honor of Josephat Kuncevic. The diocese — headquartered in Parma, Ohio — embraces Ohio, Mississippi, West Virginia, Kentucky, Tennessee, Alabama, Georgia, North and South Carolina, Florida and western Pennsylvania — a vast area of 494,000 square miles. The diocese numbers around 12,000 members, according to recent count, but tradition counts more than numbers. The diocese memorializes a bridge between East and West.

# THE BISHOPS ADDRESS ECONOMIC ISSUES

**SIX YEARS OF WORK** by a committee of bishops headed by Archbishop Rembert G. Weakland of Milwaukee culminated on this day in 1986, when the body of the American bishops approved by 225 to 9 votes the pastoral letter "Economic Justice for All: Catholic Social Teaching and the U.S. Economy." This was the famous letter in which the bishops declared that the "litmus test" of the justice or injustice of any society was how it treated its poor and powerless, and in that context they endorsed the policy of a "preferential option for the poor," calling it one of social justice, not charity.

There was much more in the 115-page document. The bishops condemned job discrimination against women and racial and ethnic minorities. They scored the U.S. tendency of recent years to make "national security the central policy issue" of government. They branded militarization and politicization of foreign developmental aid as a grave distortion of the way aid should be handled. As for poverty in the U.S., the bishops termed it "a social and moral scandal," and proceeded to ask for more economic planning, less military spending, expansion of welfare programs, and a regular review of policies.

Not everyone agreed with the bishops' conclusions and recommendations. Indeed, not everyone agreed that the topic was within the proper purview, much less the competence, of the bishops. But then, back in the 1950s, not everyone agreed that the bishops should be involving themselves in civil rights issues.

One interesting spin-off of the national economic pastoral has been the energizing of some state conferences of bishops in related regional problems. Maryland's bishops, for instance, issued a laundry list of recommendations in 1988, which asked in sum that the state spend $60 million more on programs for the poor. What did Governor William D. Schaefer say? "Everything they're interested in, I subscribe to." Obviously, it doesn't hurt to speak up.

# NOVEMBER 14

## THE U.S. BISHOPS FACE RACIAL SEGREGATION

**APROPOS RACE RELATIONS,** the American bishops were never known particularly as leaders, although individual bishops did have proud moments. St. Louis' Archbishop Joseph E. Ritter integrated his parochial schools seven years in advance of the 1954 Supreme Court ruling ending segregation in public schools, and Washington's Archbishop Patrick O'Boyle beat the Supreme Court by six years. Similarly, Raleigh's Bishop Vincent S. Waters in 1954 integrated all institutions of his see, churches included. Still, segregation continued as a major social problem. On this day in 1958 the American bishops as a body faced the issue in a pastoral letter, "Discrimination and the Christian Conscience." They posed the question, "Can enforced segregation be reconciled with the Christian view of our fellow man?" and answered no for two reasons:

"1) Legal segregation, or any form of compulsory segregation, in itself and by its very nature imposes a stigma of inferiority upon the segregated people. Even if the now obsolete Court doctrine of 'separate but equal' had been carried out to the fullest extent, so that all public and semipublic facilities were in fact equal, there is nonetheless the judgment that an entire race, by the sole fact of race and regardless of individual qualities is not fit to associate on equal terms with members of another race....

"2) It is a matter of historical fact that segregation in our country has led to oppressive conditions and the denial of basic human rights for the Negro. This is evident in the fundamental fields of education, job opportunity and housing. Flowing from these areas of neglect and discrimination are problems of health and the sordid train of evils so often associated with slum conditions.... May God give this nation the grace to meet the challenge it faces. For the sake of generations of future Americans, for indeed of all humanity, we cannot fail."

# THE MAN WHO "MENTOR-ED" AQUINAS

**IN A DAY** when the thought of Thomas Aquinas (q.v. Jan. 28) is often equated with entrenched conservatism, it is difficult to imagine there could ever have been a time when the opposite was the case — when his thought would have been regarded as dangerously new and revolutionary. But so it was.

This day honors the man who was Aquinas' mentor and also his defender — Albertus Magnus, better known perhaps as Albert the Great. Albert was a luminary of the thirteenth century — "the wonder and miracle of his age" in the words of his contemporary, Ulrich Engelbert, a scholar rivaled only by Roger Bacon in the universality of his knowledge. Albert the seasoned professor came in contact with the much younger Aquinas at the University of Paris, and the bonds of friendship and intelligence were instantly forged. Albert and Aquinas were fellow Dominicans, of course; they were also confirmed Aristotelians, though not slavishly so. Albert was to become a bishop, but resigned to pursue the intellectual life as professor at the University of Cologne. He and Aquinas stayed in close touch, and looked forward to being together at the Council of Lyons called in 1274 by Gregory X. When Aquinas died en route, Albert was crushed, and lamented that "the light of the church" had been extinguished. The mentor thus outlived his hearer, but the mentor/disciple relationship was to continue on. One of Albert's last acts was to return to Paris to defend Aquinas' memory against charges of unorthodoxy and his writings of being too favorable to pagan philosophers — charges Albert was to hear of himself.

Detractors discounted Albert as the "ape of Aristotle," but Dante placed him with Aquinas among the great lovers of wisdom in his Heaven of the Sun. (Dante used Albert's doctrine of free will as basis for his ethical system.) In 1622, Gregory XV beatified Albert, but it was not until 1931 that he was finally canonized and named a doctor of the church. This is Albert's feast day.

# NOVEMBER 16

## ST. GERTRUDE, GREAT AND MYSTICAL

**THE CHURCH** honors St. Gertrude on this day....St. Gertrude the Great, actually. Gertrude was never officially canonized. She's a saint by acclamation, and the only female one to whom the title "great" has been given.

Gertrude was born in the mid-thirteenth century. Nothing is known of her parentage, not even her family name. What's known is that before age five (sic) she was made an oblate of the Benedictine house of Helfta in Germany. The monastery was a prosperous one, and Gertrude as she matured became its proudest boast. It is written that she was a person of exceptional charms, who had the gift of winning hearts and minds. Then in her twenty-sixth year she began to experience visions, and these would be constant until her death in 1301 or 1302. With the visions came a keen interest in theology and the Scriptures. She wrote in what has been described as the glowing richness of a Teutonic genius. The Lord himself is said to have been so pleased with her writing that he told Gertrude: "I have placed this book thus upon My Heart, that every word contained therein may be penetrated with Divine sweetness, even as honey penetrates bread. Therefore, whoever reads this book devoutly will receive great profit for his salvation. I consecrate by My benediction all that is written in the book, that it may promote the salvation of those who read it with humble devotion."

There's also the story that once, when Gertrude was ill and unable to attend Mass, Our Lord came down and himself celebrated Mass for her in her room. Now that's service for you.

Gertrude is credited with possessing the gift of miracles and of prophecy, but her humility was such, it is recorded, that "she wondered how the earth could support so sinful a creature as herself." Her special piety was devotion to the heart of Jesus, and hagiographers thus credit her with being a precursor of the devotion to the Sacred Heart that blossomed in the seventeenth century.

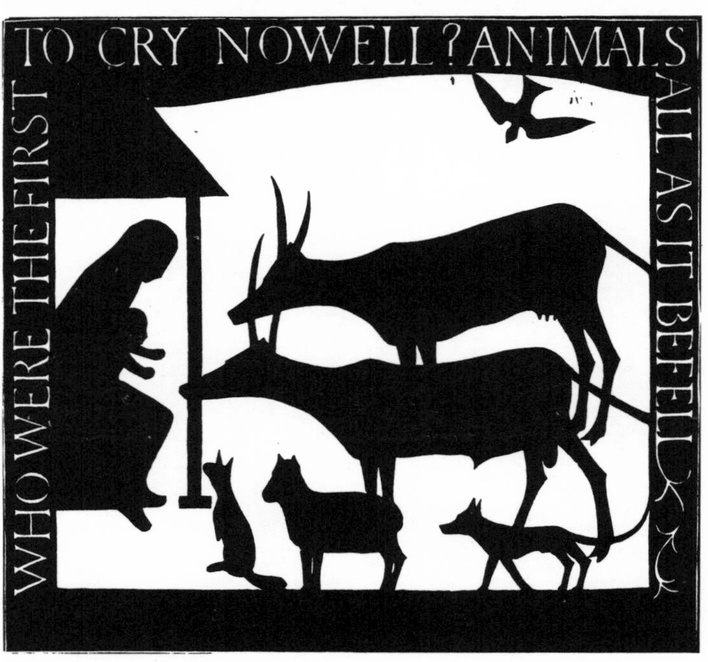


Woodcut by Eric Gill

## MAN OF THE ARTS, FLESH AND SPIRIT

**THE NIGHT** of November 16, 1940, was another violent one for England. The Luftwaffe was raining bombs on the London area when a call went out from Harefield House Hospital in Middlesex to the chaplain to hurry with the holy oils, a patient was dying. In the chaplain's words, "guns were banging and bombs were bursting all around." But he got there. A doctor tried to deny the priest entrance to the patient's room lest administration of the last rites, as they were called then, would unnerve the patient and hasten death. The priest entered anyway, and the patient said, "Thank God, Father, you've come." The rites were administered, and a few minutes before five o'clock in the morning the patient was dead.

He was Eric Gill, famed British sculptor and artist, designer of type faces (e.g., Perpetua and Gill sans-serif), printmaker, author, theoretician — a man of the spirit, and also of the flesh. Gill did not scruple at the erotic, and viewed the naked body as something of an icon. He thought no end to life worse than the fate of growing old like Rodin, "carving ladies' bottoms with great technique and no inspiration." He was certainly spared that.

Eric Gill lived from 1882-1940, and it is as a man of the spirit that he left his most pronounced marks. The heroic-sized stations of the cross in Westminster Cathedral — five-foot square carvings of Hoptonwood stone on massive piers — are his. So also are delicate woodcuts of Madonna and Child, initial letters of biblical motif, and inspired interpretations of the Bible, from Solomon's Song of Songs to the birth of the Christ child at Bethlehem.

A convert, Eric Gill was no doctrinaire religionist, no flaunter of the faith, as some converts tend to be. Basically, he held that to be religious meant to believe in order, and order implied a God's ordering. He liked Catholicism's grasp of the point. Much is made, not unreasonably, about Gill's robust sexual habits, but after everything is said, he remains the integrated Christian artist.

# NOVEMBER 18

## CATHOLICS AND THE READING OF THE BIBLE

**THE CATHOLIC CHURCH** was once so concerned about the absolute dogmatic precision of the Word that it practically surrendered the Bible to others. The Bible was in every home...where it collected dust. As a book to be read, the Bible was not. Leo XIII began to change that on this day in 1893, maybe, with the encyclical *Providentissimus Deus*, a response to rationalists who were attacking the accuracy of the Bible. Leo also wanted to rehabilitate the Bible among those who should be reading it, his flock. His was the first of a series of papal exhortations respecting the Bible. In quick succession came:

— November 15, 1898, a letter from Leo to the Minister General of the Friars Minor containing directives on the use of the Bible in preaching;

— December 13, 1898, a decree from Leo granting an indulgence of three hundred days for reading the Bible at least fifteen minutes a day;

— September 8, 1899, an encyclical from Leo, *Depuis le jour*, applying the directives of *Providentissimus Deus* to the education of the clergy;

— March 27, 1906, an apostolic letter from Pius X detailing instructions for Scripture studies in seminaries;

— September 8, 1907, an encyclical from Pius X, *Pascendi dominici gregis*, condemning Modernists' attitudes towards sacred Scripture;

— May 7, 1909, an apostolic letter from Pius X establishing the Pontifical Biblical Institute in Rome, for the promotion of biblical studies;

— September 15, 1920, an encyclical letter from Benedict XV, *Spiritus Paraclitus*, citing St. Jerome's love for and understanding of the Bible;

— April 30, 1921, an encyclical from Benedict XV, *In praeclara summorum*, commending Dante's appreciation of sacred Scripture.

One could go on. But the question must be asked of Catholics: Have papal documents such as these changed much? Do Catholics actually read the Bible?

# THE FACES AND HANDS OF CHARITY

**ONE OF THE ENDURING MARKS** of the Christian, we are told to believe, is his or her ability to love others, whatever the circumstances. On this day in 1845, one of the most important agencies of Christian love, the Society of St. Vincent de Paul, was introduced into the United States, with the inauguration of the first American conference in St. Louis.

The Society of St. Vincent de Paul was founded in Paris in 1833 by Frederic Ozanam (q.v. Nov. 20), a professor of literature at the Sorbonne. A lay initiative, the society had an immediate impact and rapid growth throughout the Catholic world, and still does today what it pledged on its founding in 1833: help those in need of help; no questions asked, no means tests applied.

The interesting thing about this society is how few people are consciously aware of its existence — which is understandable; a hallmark of the society is anonymity. A central conviction of the society is that, while the works of the organization may be publicized, the members must not. What do the society's works translate to? To nothing less than a formal embrace of the corporal works of mercy — feeding the hungry, sheltering the homeless, comforting the afflicted, clothing the naked, visiting the sick, burying the dead. In a recent year, society members in the United States volunteered 2 million hours of time to the poor and the institutionalized, while some $47.5 million was expended in direct grants by the more than 4,000 parish conferences.

Once upon a time, the Vincent de Paul Society was a solidly male bastion; it was founded by Ozanam as an association of men. But of late women have been moving into the society, beginning in Europe. In the United States, female membership lags, but even here the composition of the group is changing.

How does one in need or one wishing to participate in its good works get in touch with the society? It's as simple as dialing the nearest rectory.

# FREDERIC OZANAM, MR. VINCENT de PAUL

**FREDERIC OZANAM** was only twenty when, with seven colleagues, he founded the Vincent de Paul Society, in his words, to "insure my faith by works of charity." The society was named after the much admired seventeenth-century French saint, who was himself known for an all-embracing charity. Frederic Ozanam lived only to age forty— he died of consumption — but to the end he was an active member and zealous propagator of the society, traveling extensively in its behalf. By his death, the society was widely celebrated, numbered upwards of two thousand members, and had already crossed the ocean to the United States.

Interesting enough, in his lifetime Frederic Ozanam was known more as a Catholic intellectual than a Catholic organizer. He gained attention at eighteen for a pamphlet against Saint-Simonianism, the vaguely socialist doctrine that would put the direction of the modern industrialist state in the hands of scientists and strip religion of dogmas into what would be called a New Christianity. Numerous other important writings and contributions of an intellectual sort would be credited to Ozanam — so many, indeed, that one scholar wrote that Ozanam had "no doubt administered a healthful antidote to the prevalent notion, particularly among English-speaking peoples, that the Catholic Church had done far more to enslave than to elevate the human mind." He was trained in law, but his knowledge of Dante and medieval literature generally made him a man of broad cultural grasp. He was one of the most esteemed scholars of his day.

Frederic Ozanam moved in imposing circles. He associated with the Ampere family, including Andre Marie Ampere, the scientist who gave his name to the unit of electrical current we know as the ampere. Ozanam chummed too with luminaries of the neo-Catholic movement, among them Chateaubriand, Lacordaire, Montalembert and Ballanche. But perhaps closest to his heart were his colleagues in charity, the anonymous associates of his Vincent de Paul Society.

# NOVEMBER 21

Detail of "Presentation of the Virgin at the Temple" by Titian

## A MARIAN FEAST OF MYSTERY

**IT WOULD BE HARD TO FIND** on the church calendar a feast more obscure than today's, the Presentation of Mary. For one thing, the feast tends to be confused with the February 2 feast of the Presentation of Jesus; for another, there's no mention of a Presentation of Mary in the Gospels. One finds it only in apocrypha, such as the Protoevangel of James, the Gospel of Pseudo-Matthew and the Gospel of the Nativity of Mary. According to those sources, at age three Mary was presented in the Temple by her parents, Sts. Anne and Joachim, in fulfillment of a vow to be brought up and educated in the shadow of sanctuary.

Observance of the feast began in the East — probably Syria, said to be the "home of the apocyphra." The feast is not found in the eighth century Menology of Constantinople, but liturgical documents of the eleventh century amply record its observance. The 1166 constitution of Manuel Comnenos, for instance, lists the feast as one of the first rank, a day on which the law courts did not sit.

The feast was introduced into the West by the French in the fourteenth century, when Gregory XI (1370-1378) was presiding over the papal court at Avignon. Still, doubts about the feast obviously persisted. Sixtus IV (1471-1484) incorporated the feast into the Roman breviary, but Pius V (1566-1572) in turn struck it from the calendar. Sixtus V (1585-1590) brought it back, shortly after his election. The feast is still on the church's calendar, though it is doubtful many Catholics could explain offhand the significance of the feast.

Notwithstanding, the feast has had an unusually strong appeal. Artists have immortalized the event, and religious groups have adopted it as the name of their order, notably the Congregation of the Presentation of Mary, founded in France in 1796 for the education of young children, and subsequently strongly present in the parochial schools of Canada and the United States.

# NOVEMBER 22

## THOSE DAYS OF ORGANIZED BIGOTRY

**CATHOLICS WERE** relatively late-comers to the United States. In fact, it was not until 1820 that they began to arrive in appreciable numbers. By 1840, there were still only 663,000 Catholics in the U.S., mostly of German and Irish origin. They totaled to a relatively small percentage of the national population, but it was large enough to excite fears among American Protestants, who worried for their jobs and their religious ascendancy. So it was that on this day in 1842 Philadelphia Protestants organized the American Protestant Association, ninety-four ministers proclaiming "Popery...subversive of civil and religious liberty." The association was one of several that would spring up, warning of the "errors of Popery" and "dangers" born of Rome.

Associations such as these helped spawn in 1853 the American or Know-Nothing Party (so named because the typical answer of members to questions about the party's activity was "I don't know"). The party enjoyed prominence for several years in a campaign to deny political office to all but the native born. The party broke up with the Civil War, but found a successor in the American Protective Association (APA), another secret organization that played on nativist fears of growing Catholic influence in schools and public institutions. The APA came into being in 1893 in Clinton, Iowa, and made significant gains in the 1894 elections. But by 1900 the APA was dying, its ranks split over the issue of "Bryanism" and free silver. The association lingered on until 1911, still managing to cause mischief — though nothing to equal in enormity the bogus encyclical, published in the *Patriotic American* of Detroit, in which Leo XIII was alleged to instruct Catholics to rise up on the feast of St. Ignatius — July 31, 1893 — and massacre all heretics.

Bigotry against Catholics lingered in the country until being finally buried in the 1960 election. The APA was its last organized gasp.

# ROME, CANTERBURY AND RAPPROCHEMENT

**IN 1987,** ecumenists were assessing repercussions from an event twenty-four hours earlier in Rome. Pope John Paul II had beatified eighty-five Anglo-Welsh Roman Catholics who had been executed for religious reasons in England between 1584 and 1679. The *beati* — sixty-three priests and twenty-two laymen — had long been venerated as martyrs of Britain's penal laws, but their formal elevation by Rome was unusual because it took place at a moment in history when the Church of Rome and the Church of Canterbury had drawn closer together in ecumenical dialogue and were beginning to clear away centuries-old problems of theological kinds. Reaction to the event was muted, however, thanks largely to Canterbury's Archbishop Robert Runcie, who commented that whereas once Rome's honoring of the eighty-five would have fueled distrust, "today we can celebrate their heroic Christian witness and together deplore the intolerance...which flawed Christian convictions."

The real strain in Anglican-Roman Catholic ecumenical relations was to come fifteen months later, when on February 11, 1989, the first female bishop in the worldwide Anglican communion was consecrated in Boston by the Episcopal diocese of Massachusetts, Rev. Barbara Clementine Harris. Several branches of Anglicanism had been consecrating female priests for some years, to Rome's great displeasure. But the elevation of a woman to the episcopacy was a far more dramatic action and created large new ecumenical obstacles for Rome.

The development in Massachusetts was not endorsed by Archbishop Runcie, whose Church of England has sought to hold the line even on women priests. Pope John Paul II, however, has not been as understanding of Runcie on the women-clergy issues as Runcie was on that of the beatifications. In his "state of the church" address early in 1989, for instance, John Paul, reflecting back, characterized Runcie as a "shadow" on his previous year, saying he caused him "deep hurt" — apparently for only weakly resisting the ordination of women as priests and as bishop.

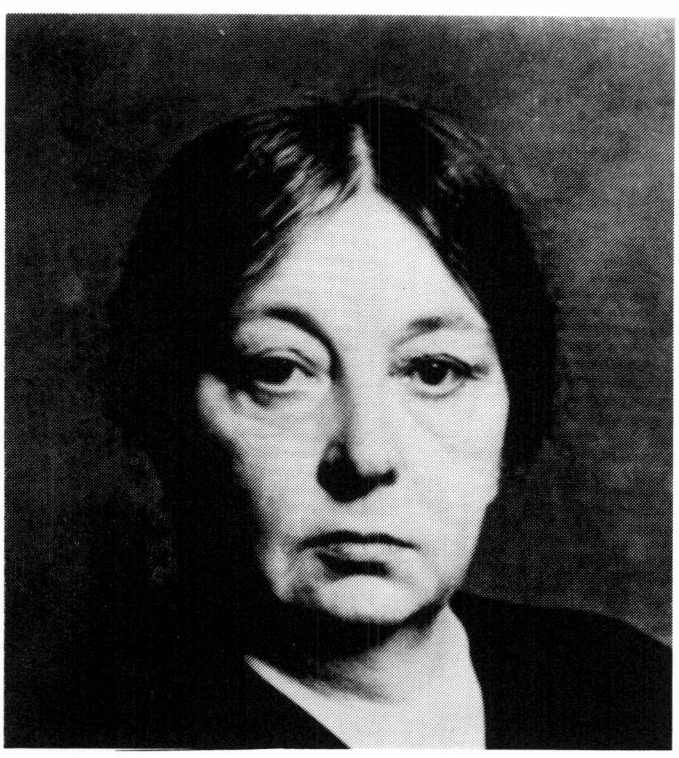

Sigrid Undset

# A CONVERT AND NOBEL LAUREATE

**SHE WAS** one of Scandinavia's most distinguished writers, and she was received into the Catholic Church on this day in 1924. She was born in Denmark in 1882 of a Danish mother and Norwegian father, and she was raised in Oslo, when that city was known as Christiana. She grew up in a home steeped in the legend, folklore and history of Norway, and indeed in later years she would garb herself as a Norse matron of the Middle Ages as she presided over a restored 1000-year-old house filled with medieval antiques. When the Nazis invaded Norway in 1940, she fled to the United States, where she lectured and wrote in behalf of Norway's government-in-exile. She had extra reason to oppose the Nazis: her son Anders was killed by them. She returned to Norway at war's end, and she died there in 1945. Who was she?

Maybe you'll recognize her from her books. She was a master of the historical novel, though she also wrote essays, mainly on saints, and a biography on St. Olav. In the early 1920s she wrote the trilogy *Kristin Lavransdatter*, dealing with Norwegian life in the thirteenth and fourteenth centuries, and followed this with the tetralogy *The Master of Hestviken*. Her fame sealed, she was awarded the Nobel Prize for literature in 1928. Correct! Sigrid Undset.

Sigrid Undset worked and reworked the themes of love and marriage, guilt and loyalty, but very much as a traditionalist. She was no feminist, and in fact had little time for the great women's issues of her day, including the suffragette movement and feminine emancipation. As a Catholic, she was also the thorough traditionalist, and she seemed to solve all conflicts by strictest Catholic precepts. For instance, in conjunction with her conversion to Catholicism, she dissolved her marriage to the painter Anders C. Svarstad, presumably because theirs was an invalid marriage, he having been wed before and his first wife still living. Would even the church insist on that today?

# NOVEMBER 25

Illuminated leaf of a Benedictine Book of Hours; France. 1435

## THE CANONICAL HOURS

**AMONG THE JEWISH CUSTOMS** perpetuated by the Fathers of the early church was that of praying at given hours of the day. The Jews prayed three times a day (at the third, sixth and ninth hours), but the practice was expanded in the Christian tradition. Thus early on, to the Jewish hours of prayer were added midnight (commemorating when Paul and Silas sang in prison), dawn and evening, bringing the number of prayer hours to six. In the sixth century, Benedict, the patriarch of Western monasticism, added a seventh to commend the example of the psalmist who exclaimed, "Seven times a day do I praise thee because of thy righteous judgments" (Psalm 119:164). Before all was finished, the day was divided into eight parts, each with its prescribed prayers. In monasteries, in canonical life and among the devout, these became known as the canonical hours. Where observed, the canonical hours are:

*Matins*, theoretically the canonical hour for midnight, but in time usually observed before dawn, or, as in France, on the preceding evening in accordance with the old proposition that "evening and morning were the one day."

*Lauds*, proper to sunrise, but mostly grouped with *Matins* as morning prayer.

*Prime* (first hour, 6 a.m.), *Terce* (third hour, 9 a.m.), *Sext* (sixth hour, noon) and *None* (ninth hour, 3 p.m.). *Prime*, *Terce* and *Sext* are the so-called "little day hours" and eventually came to be combined into the one observance.

*Vespers*, also known as *Evensong*, and commonly marked at sunset.

*Compline*, meaning "completion," the end of the day, bedtime. Technically the hour of observance was 9 p.m., and was intended as a time of prayer for protection during the darkness. *Compline* came to be combined with *Vespers*.

Prayers for the canonical hours (the *Magnificat*, *Nunc dimittis*, etc.) were collected into books, often handsomely illuminated and gorgeously bound. These were known, naturally, as Books of Hours.

# NOVEMBER 26

Teilhard de Chardin

## TEILHARD DE CHARDIN'S LAST CHAPTER

**ON THIS DAY** in 1951 the famous Jesuit paleontologist and theologian of evolutionary Christology, Teilhard de Chardin, arrived in New York on his "exile" from France. Pius XII had issued *Humani generis*, the encyclical warning against attempts to distort Catholic truths, the year before, and among others he clearly seemed to have Teilhard in mind. Teilhard concluded that he had become "an embarrassment" to the church's leadership, and his superiors concurred, suggesting that "a shelter out of France" would be best for all concerned. Teilhard headed for the United States.

What had made Teilhard de Chardin so controversial? It was his theory that evolution, then a dirty word in Catholicism, was a continuing Christological process with "man" (humankind) the very "arrow" of evolution. Evolution, in turn, was an irreversible process planned by God and converging ultimately on God, as the universe perfected itself through the evolving intelligence of man. Teilhard posited a starting point (Alpha) and a goal (Omega), each in effect being God, so that what began in God returned in time to God.

Teilhard circulated his writings through papers he called *clandestins*. Viewed nervously by his superiors, he was forbidden to publish publicly. He was also denied teaching positions — a huge humiliation for a man whose research had extended from central Asia across the East Indies to Africa's sub-Sahara, who had a part in the discovery of Peking Man, and who had contributed enormously to scientific knowledge on the origin of life.

In New York, Teilhard considered himself "a bird of passage," never feeling "completely at home." He suffered severe bouts of depression before dying of a heart attack on Easter Sunday, 1955. It was a sad ending for one so notable. Only a handful showed for Teilhard's funeral Mass, and only two accompanied the remains to their final resting place in the Jesuit cemetery above Poughkeepsie.

# BRINGING LAW AND ORDER TO THE CHURCH

**NO INSTITUTION,** ecclesiastical or otherwise, runs itself without a body of rules and regulations, and in the Catholic Church they are embodied in what is known as the Code of Canon Law. On this day in 1983, the latest, updated code went into effect, though promulgation by Pope John Paul II was the previous January 25. It is a code of 1,752 canons (some 700 fewer than the one it replaced), and is grouped by subject matter into seven books. The code governs everything from holy day observances to the church's laws on marriage.

One would expect that the devising of a code of canon law would have been one of the few steps taken by the Fathers of the church. Interestingly enough, it wasn't, for the simple reason that it didn't seem particularly urgent. Early Christians lived with the popular belief that the Second Coming was imminent, or just a short time away, so why trouble with something so complex as a body of laws? Besides, there was Roman law, and this was an eminently fair code in its day. The early church was not without some regulations, but when ecclesiastical law was silent, the church actually followed Roman law.

Naturally an arrangement of shared civil and ecclesiastical canons would be satisfactory for only so long. As the church developed and expanded, it would need a body of law all its own. The wonder is that it got not just one; it got scores of them. The period between the end of the ninth and middle of the twelfth century, for instance, saw no less than forty systematic collections of canon law arrive on the books. There was, in fact, such a plethora of collections that many feared a loosening of ties to a central authority in Rome. In the Western church various attempts were made to digest these collections into a single canon, but this wasn't accomplished until 1918, our twentieth century. It was thought that that code would last indefinitely, maybe forever. But time does not stand still, not even for Rome. The 1918 code lasted only until 1983.

# NOVEMBER 28

## THE TRADITION OF CANONIZING SAINTS

**NOVEMBER, AS MENTIONED,** is a month for remembering the faithfully departed. But, as the first day makes plain it's also a month for honoring the heroes of the faith — the anonymous saints, to be sure; but also the officially credited, the formally canonized.

Protestants don't run about canonizing their saintly figures, and the Catholic propensity to do so has sometimes been likened to pagan apotheosis. There's a distinct difference between the two, but the church was a long time drawing it. In fact, the defense of the process was not laid out in hard, specific terms until Benedict XIV's *De servorum Dei beatificatione et beatorum canonizatione*, and Benedict reigned from 1740-1758. It was a long time coming.

Canonization is today a complicated procedure, involving a number of preliminary steps, including being declared venerable, then blessed, before being pronounced a saint. But the sainting of those of heroic virtue was once a fairly simple process, rooted mainly in cumulative public acclaim rather than the results of bureaucratic investigations. For example, the sainthood of Flavianus was a happening of the eleventh session of the Council of Chalcedon in 451, the Council Fathers exclaiming in unison: "Flavianus lives after death! May the martyr pray for us!" But then martyrs always were special cases.

The interesting thing is that before the strong centralization of the church in Rome, bishops could make determinations of sainthood, presumably on the basis of proximity and familiarity, in the instance of local figures of holiness and sanctity. Inevitably the tradition would be vulnerable to enthusiasms and partialities, if not worse, and some dubious "saints" would creep into the calendar. It wasn't until the close of the eleventh century that popes — notably Urban II and Calistus II — began to gather to Rome exclusive authority to determine who qualified to be honored as a saint. Read on.»»»

# NOVEMBER 29

An. et vol. LXXV    9 Aprilis 1983    Pars I, N. 4

ACTA APOSTOLICAE SEDIS

COMMENTARIUM OFFICIALE

*Directio:* Palazzo Apostolico - Città del Vaticano — *Administratio:* Libreria Editrice Vaticana

ACTA IOANNIS PAULI PP. II

CONSTITUTIO APOSTOLICA

Modus procedendi in Causarum canonizationis instructione recognoscitur et Sacrae Congregationis pro Causis Sanctorum nova datur ordinatio.

IOANNES PAULUS EPISCOPUS
SERVUS SERVORUM DEI
AD PERPETUAM REI MEMORIAM

DIVINUS PERFECTIONIS MAGISTER et exemplar, Christus Iesus, qui una cum Patre et Spiritu Sancto « unus sanctus » celebratur, Ecclesiam tam-

## WHAT IS EQUIVALENT TO CANONIZATION?

**OLD PREROGATIVES** die as hard in Catholicism as anywhere else, and so it was that local bishops continued to canonize their saints. It was not until 1634 that Urban VIII brought the practice to an abrupt end with a bull reserving exclusively to Rome the right to canonize.

Looking back, the wonder is how well the system worked when popes were not central to the canonization process and guidelines varied according to time and place. Some of the church's greatest saints were raised up when the system was at its loosest — among them St. Thomas of Canterbury, St. Francis of Assisi and St. Anthony of Padua, all of whom were formally sainted within three years of their death. That could not happen today because of such elements as time intervals, interrogations, examinations, hearings, confirmation of required number of miracles, etc., being built into the process.

The regulations are detailed and officials involved are irrevocably bound by the process, except for one person — the pope. How come? Because canonization has traditionally been regarded as an infallible exercise of the church's authority, and the pope is infallible, right? He can dispense from the usual formalities of canonization (beatification too). He can even canonize out of the blue, so to speak, by invoking the procedure known as "equivalent canonization." Equivalent canonization is a pope's definitive declaration on behalf of a person for whom a canonization has not been introduced, but with whom a public *cultus* has been connected, usually for more than one hundred years. Many saints have come onto the liturgical calendar through this process, among them Sts. Norbert, Bruno, Peter Nolasco and King Stephen of Hungary. John XXIII exercised the prerogative in 1960 in behalf of St. Gregory Barbarigo, a seventeenth-century Venetian who was three times a frontrunner for the papacy and never made it. Tomorrow we'll see that the practice continues.

# THE BEATIFICATION OF "IL BEATO"

**IN 1983,** Pope John Paul II bypassed usual canonical procedures and issued on his own initiative a decree beatifying the fabled Florentine painter and Dominican friar, Giovanni da Fiesole, better known to history as Fra Angelico. Within thirty years after his death in 1455, Fra Angelico was popularly referred to as *Il Beato,* the beatified, but there was no quibbling over John Paul's decision to formalize what had once been proclaimed.

Fra Angelico was a person of exquisite talent, and also of remarkable sanctity. Exceedingly devout, self-denying and humble, it is said he never took up a brush without praying at the same time, and further that he never revised a work out of the conviction that what God had allowed to happen should remain as is. Fra Angelico specialized in religious themes — the Last Supper, the coronation of Mary, scenes from the lives of Sts. Stephen and Laurence, Cosmas and Damien, etc. To Fra Angelico painting was a form of prayer. He felt that those who painted Christ should be with Christ, and as if to give meaning to the words he is known to have wept on painting a Crucifixion.

Fra Angelico was born in Tuscany in 1387 (the "Fiesole" was merely the name of the town in which he took his vows as a Dominican), and was much favored at the Vatican. According to the sixteenth-century art historian Giorgio Vasari, Fra Angelico was offered the archbishopric of Florence, but shunned the advancement out of feelings of inexperience and unworthiness for so exalted and responsible a station. As artist, Fra Angelico painted assiduously, and though some do not rank him with Fra Lippo Lippi or Giotto, artists of the same genre, his work is characterized by undeniable genius. Its special character is a rapt and devotional fervency. The expressions of Fra Angelico's subjects display a near-beatitude, which some find smug, but which others see reflecting conviction in a heavenly life behind a veil that only an artist's eye can penetrate.

# DECEMBER 1

## THE ENERGIZING OF THE WORKS OF MERCY

**IT IS AN INTERESTING PARADOX.** December is the month when consumerism is king, and when religious leaders seem so distraught by rampant commercialism that they are impelled to be constantly reminding believers that 'tis the season to be other than just merry. And, truly, December is a pretty crass and tinsel-ly time. Strangely enough, it is also the month when the corporal and spiritual works of mercy are more real in people's lives than at any other time of the year — certainly, the corporal works. The often-maligned media can claim as much credit for this as the churches, thanks to Christmastime campaigns on behalf of the homeless and poor — some run in conjunction with churches, to be sure, but others, like the *New York Times'* fund for the needy, wholly independent of ecclesiastical auspices. Those who participate often do not realize the deep religious context of their gesture. By the same token, those running the appeals do not stress, probably don't even sense, the holy thing they are about, believing likely as not that theirs is a non-theological activity arising out of some human instinct or guiding rule of humanism, like the Golden Rule. Fine, except the Golden Rule is thoroughly grounded in the Scriptures, appearing in Luke immediately after the Beatitudes, "Do unto others as you would have them do unto you" (Luke 6:31).

So what are these corporal and spiritual works of mercy that take on flesh, as it were, at Christmastime? Parochial-school graduates remember them thus:

The corporal works of mercy: To feed the hungry; to give drink to the thirsty; to clothe the naked; to visit the imprisoned; to shelter the homeless; to visit the sick; to bury the dead.

The spiritual works of mercy: To admonish the sinner; to instruct the ignorant; to counsel the doubtful; to comfort the sorrowful; to bear wrongs patiently; to forgive all injuries; to pray for the living and the dead.

# DECEMBER 2

## "FISH ON FRIDAY" CATHOLICISM

**FOR MANY CATHOLICS** this was the day in 1966 that demonstrated beyond any doubt that the church could change, *really* change. It was the day when henceforth abstinence from meat on Fridays year-round would no longer be required of American Catholics. The regulation implemented the letter of Pope Paul VI apostolic constitution of February 17, 1966, *Poenitemini*, which totally reorganized ecclesiastical disciplines relating to fast and abstinence.

In reality, Paul VI did not give Catholics absolute *carte blanche* on Fridays. They were expected to substitute other forms of penance or, by choice, perform works of charity or piety in place of abstinence from meat.

But, of course, it was the change in the "fish on Friday" rule that produced the impact. Except for Spain and Portugal, which enjoyed papal exemptions, Catholics worldwide were brought up on the principle that eating meat on Friday was not just a sin, but a mortal sin. As the Gilmary Society's 1913 *Catholic Encyclopedia* stated: "...the law of abstinence embodies a serious obligation whose transgression, objectively considered, ordinarily involves a mortal sin. The unanimous verdict of theologians, the constant practice of the faithful, and the mind of the church place this point beyond cavil."

Naturally wagsters had a field day. One cartoonist sketched two perplexed devils in the hot and crowded bowels of hell, one asking the other: "What are we going to do with all those people who are here for eating meat on Friday?"

In the United States, Catholics are expected to observe Ash Wednesday and Good Friday as days of fast and abstinence, and Fridays of Lent as days of abstinence. The other Fridays involve alternative works of penance. But, as distinct from the past, emphasis is on voluntary compliance. The church is no longer in the business of consigning people to perdition for dietary reasons.

# DECEMBER 3

Al Smith

## BREAKING THE PRESIDENTIAL ICE

**THE BIRTH OF THEIR SON** on this day in 1873 did not seem an auspicious event, except maybe to the parents — the father, a truck-wagon driver; the mother, a piece worker in an umbrella factory. They lived on New York's Lower East Side, and were desperately poor. Yet their son grew up to be a four-term governor of the state of New York, and a White House aspirant. Indeed he won the Democratic Party's presidential nomination in 1928, becoming the first Catholic ever nominated for the presidency by a major American political party. The person was Alfred E. Smith, of course. Al Smith lost the election to Herbert Hoover in a campaign which was so rife with religious bigotry that many doubted a Catholic could ever hope to be elected President. To be sure, one would be, John F. Kennedy, though that would be more than thirty years later.

There has been no Catholic president since Kennedy, but today Catholics run routinely for the office; there is no so-called religious test for them now. But there certainly was in Al Smith's day. Bigots equated a vote for Smith to a vote for the pope, and this routed him. To be sure, there was the issue of "Demon rum" (these were prohibition times, remember), and Smith's Tammany Hall and big-city backgrounds didn't exactly help beyond the Hudson. But religion was the big factor; Protestant-nativist hysteria dominated the ballot box.

Whether Al Smith would have been a good president is anyone's guess. But he certainly was a great governor. He streamlined state government, reduced taxes, improved parks and recreational facilities, promoted low-cost housing, advanced welfare benefits, expanded educational systems, launched the first broadly conceived mental-health service in the country, and upgraded health and hospital programs. He was a man whose knowledge and vision far surpassed his eighth grade education. Al Smith lived until 1944, serving in his last years as chief executive officer of the then-new Empire State Building.

# THE DAY LATIN DIED FOR GOOD

**ASK THE AVERAGE PERSON** in the pew the change since Vatican II that personally has had the greatest impact, and chances are she or he will say the adoption of the vernacular for the Mass. This was the day in 1963 that was pivotal for American Catholics in that regard; it was the day that the American bishops, assembled in Rome for the council, voted "to make full use [in the American church] of the vernacular concessions" provided in the council's Constitution on the Sacred Liturgy. It was a step of historical significance, but the immediate impact was lost in events of state. The country was still transfixed in grief over the slaying two weeks before of President Kennedy.

As for the vernacular, it did not come overnight. Change was dribbled out in steps, as if anything too sudden would shake the foundations of faith. The hesitancy produced an unsettling note of a different kind; for several years Catholics were subjected to a Mass completely out of synchronization not only with its past, but also where it was headed. The timidness in going to the vernacular was never easy to understand. To be sure, time was needed to prepare translations and have them approved. Even so, in other countries the church moved more quickly to a fully vernacularized Mass than in the U.S.

Looking back, no Vatican II change made more sense than going to the vernacular. There was enormous attachment to the old Latin, but Latin itself was a third-century innovation to the Mass. Hebrew, Aramaic and Greek preceded Latin as the language of the Mass. Latin was adopted because it was the language of Rome, and as such that of commerce, law, literature, the army, and the administration of Western Europe. The logic that brought Latin to the Mass applies in its replacement. Simply put, to be understood, one must communicate with people in words they understand.

Celestine V

# THE POPE WHO PITCHED IT IN

**THIS DAY IN 1294** Celestine V, the former Pietro del Morrone, was pope five months to the day; a week and a day hence he would be gone — not dead, just gone. He would reign less than six months. How come so short? Because Celestine resigned — December 13, 1294 — the last, maybe the only pope ever to do so. (The facts are obscure in nine earlier possibilities.) Celestine's a saint now, being canonized in 1313. But qualities of sainthood do not guarantee a successful papacy. Celestine's reign was a disaster.

Pietro del Morrone, a simple monk of Benedictine roots, was in his eightieth year, living in the mountains as an anchorite, when a divided conclave tapped him. The church had been without a pope for two years and three months, the papal conclave being hopelessly deadlocked between the Orsini and Colonna factions of Rome, when Pietro del Morrone wrote a conclave cardinal that unless the conclave settled soon on a new pope, God would visit a severe chastisement upon the church. Pietro del Morrone's message was as from God himself, and the cardinals seized on it as a cryptic sign from on high for solving their impasse. They elected Pietro del Morrone pope, then a delegation trooped off into the mountains of Abruzzi to ask him to accept. He did, taking the name Celestine V.

Many churchmen regarded Celestine's election as an elaborate farce, and in many ways it was. Certainly he was an incompetent pope. He granted the same benefices to three or four parties; lavished favors carte blanche; followed no protocol. More seriously, under the influence of King Charles of Naples, he named twelve cardinals, seven French and the rest, save one, Neapolitans — thus setting the stage for the Avignon papacy and the Great Western Schism of 1378-1417, when Christendom was divided between two and three papal obediences.

The situation was headed from bad to worse. Perhaps sensing as much, Celestine resigned. His successor "en-celled" him, and he died in 1296.

# DECEMBER 6

## "AND A YOUNG CHILD SHALL LEAD THEM...."

**THE PSYCHE** of Middle Ages Catholics was wondrous in its naivete and innocence. Catholics then could burlesque particulars of faith, often to the great dismay of church leaders, yet intend no contempt in the irreverence, at least not consciously. Take an event that occurred annually on this day in England. Catholics of cathedral parishes elected a boy-bishop, dressed him in episcopal robes complete to miter and crozier, attended him with other young boys dressed as priests, and invested him with actual authority. At Salisbury, the boy-bishop exercised a patronage and could make appointments. He traveled the town dispensing blessings, and performed other liturgical rites, though he didn't say Mass or hear confessions. It was such great fun that ordinary parishes got into the act, raising up boy-bishops of their own.

It was all part of the Feast of Fools, a quasi-religious festival which was intended as a counterpart of secular festivities known and presided over by the "Lord of Misrule." The religious burlesque could be as short as one day, or it could run to December 28, Holy Innocents Day — a story in itself.

The "boy-bishoping" was no mere English custom, and several councils sought to limit it before the Council of Basel (1431) issued an outright prohibition. English Catholics did not conform immediately. Henry VIII outlawed the boy-bishop business in 1542, but it was revived by Queen Mary in 1552, before finally being abolished by Elizabeth I. Nor did Catholics fall readily in line elsewhere — as in Germany, where the custom was introduced in 828 (in honor of St. Gregory, patron of schools) and where it hung on as late as 1799. There the practice was to elect the boy-bishop, vest him, attend him with two boy-deacons, then process him to the parish church, where he preached a sermon. No doubt the sermon evoked belly laughs. But then so do many of today's sermons.

# DECEMBER 7

Gerard Manley Hopkins (Watercolor by Anne Eleanor Hopkins,1859)

## GERARD MANLEY HOPKINS AND *THE WRECK*

**WHEN GERARD MANLEY HOPKINS,** the British poet, entered the Jesuits in 1868, two years after his conversion to Catholicism, he burned his manuscripts and resolved to write no more. But a tragedy occurred which ended that resolve. Five German Franciscan nuns, exiles of the Falck Laws, drowned when the ship Deutschland, America-bound out of Bremen, went down between midnight and dawn in a wild storm off the English coast. The date was December 7, 1875, and Hopkins, like all readers of *The Times* of London, was emotionally stunned by the paper's account of how five nuns, "hands clasped," drowned together, "the chief sister, a gaunt 6 ft. high, calling out loudly and often, 'O Christ, come quickly!' till the end came."

On a hint from the superior that someone commemorate the event in poetry, Gerard Manley Hopkins returned pen to paper and produced the poem that proved his masterpiece, *The Wreck of the Deutschland.* The poem was written in what he called "sprung rhythm," a set series of accented syllables per line along with a varying number of unaccented ones. It was the poem's content, however, that startled. It told of the "tall nun's" faith and her vision of Christ at the heart of the storm, but the beginning of the poem was a personal testament, in which Hopkins reflected on his own spiritual crisis and conversion. The Jesuit journal *The Month* withdrew it before publication for being too "daring." Today the poem is a mainstay of virtually every anthology of religious verse.

Gerard Manley Hopkins was born in Stratford, England, in 1844, and died in 1889 in Dublin, where he held the chair of Greek at the Catholic University. His influence on modern poetry was considerable. He was one of the first to avoid metrical lines and poetic diction, and take short cuts in grammar, thus sharpening a complex, patterned, but highly individual poetic style.

# DECEMBER 8

## A RECENT FEAST AND A CONFUSED ONE

**TODAY IS A HOLY DAY** of obligation, and I warrant there's no holy day more confused in Catholic minds than this one. Example: An American in Rome, the spiritual and intellectual capital of universal Catholicism, arrived in a tourist bus before the Palace of the Propaganda Fide, just off the Corso, and was told by the guide that the giant column in the piazza with the Marian statue atop commemorated the Immaculate Conception — "Mary's virgin birth of the child Jesus." "Excuse me," said my friend, "the Immaculate Conception has nothing to do with the virgin birth."

Of course, it doesn't. The Immaculate Conception refers to Mary's being born free of Original Sin, and being preserved from sin in a life filled with grace. It's an entirely different doctrine from that of the virgin birth.

The feast of the Immaculate Conception is celebrated in the universal church — including the United States, where it is coincidentally observed as the nation's patronal feast. The United States, to explain, is dedicated to Mary under her title of the Immaculate Conception, and has been since 1846. Curiously enough, this was eight years before the dogma of the Immaculate Conception was itself officially declared. But then Rome has often been prescient. The Immaculate Conception was defined in 1854 by Pope Pius IX.

The paradox is that when the American bishops some years later were coordinating holy days among dioceses of the country, and deciding which would be observed nationally, they did not propose to include the Immaculate Conception. They considered having but four holy days: Christmas, Ascension, Assumption and All Saints. It was only at Rome's urging that the Circumcision (as the January 1 feast was then known) and the Immaculate Conception were included. When was this? 1884.

# A PRAYER TO COMMUNICATE IN DEATH

**FATHER PIERRE TEILHARD DE CHARDIN,** whose life we reflected on last month, left the world more than a complex theory of alphas and omegas and Christological evolution. He left also some remarkable meditations on the process of living and dying, and those elements of reality that people begin to feel with age; namely, that less is often more, and that the small is often more beautiful than that which is grand and complex. This paradoxical insight infuses Teilhard's theory that growth in God requires a concomitant diminishing of self. He applied this thought in a beautiful prayer that should appeal especially to those who have begun to put on great years. Teilhard's prayer:

"When the signs of age begin to mark my body (and still more when they touch my mind); when the ill that is to diminish me or carry me off strikes from without or is born within me; when the painful moment comes in which I suddenly awaken to the fact that I am ill or growing old; and above all at that last moment when I feel I am losing hold of myself and am absolutely passive within the hands of the great unknown forces that have formed me; in all those dark moments, O God, grant that I may understand that it is you (provided only my faith is strong enough) who are painfully parting the fibres of my being in order to penetrate to the very marrow of my substance and bear me away within yourself.

"You are the irrestible and vivifying force, O Lord; and because yours is the energy, because of the two of us, you are infinitely the stronger, it is on you that falls the part of consuming me in the union that should weld us together. Vouchsafe, therefore, something more precious still than the grace for which all the faithful pray. It is not enough that I should die while communicating. Teach me to communicate while dying."

Detail from painting of Mother Cabrini titled "Saint Among the Skyscrapers" by Robert J. Smith

# SECURING THE FAITH OF ITALIAN-AMERICANS

**WHEN MOTHER CABRINI,** the young Italian orphanage director, decided she wanted to become a missionary, she thought first of going to the Far East. Her mind was changed by Pope Leo XIII, who told her, "Not to the East, but to the West....You will find a vast field for labor in the United States." Mother Cabrini landed in March, 1899, and launched on an apostolate from New York to Seattle that would see her canonized in 1946 as St. Frances Xavier Cabrini — the first American citizen to be so honored; twenty-nine years before the first native-born American would be sainted, Elizabeth Bayley Seton.

Pope Leo's advice to Mother Cabrini was hardly unexpected. Italian immigrants to the United States weighed heavily on his mind, and on this day in 1888 he addressed a plea to American bishops asking their cooperation in easing the lot of these immigrants. The letter opened:

"How toilsome and disastrous is the condition of those who for some years have been migrating out of Italy to the regions of America in search of a livelihood that is so well known to you that nothing is to be gained by dwelling on it. Indeed, you see these evils at first hand and several of you have sorrowfully called our attention to them in repeated letters. It is to be deplored that so many unfortunate Italians, forced by poverty to change their residence, should rush into evils which are often worse than the ones they have desired to flee from....."

Leo was especially concerned for the health of the souls of the immigrants, and he noted that he had founded in Piacenza a college to train priests as ministers to immigrants. He asked they be received with "fatherly love," and be extended "necessary faculties for exercising the sacred ministry among their countrymen." The request fostered the growth of Italian nationality parishes.

# AN INTERNAL ECCLESIASTICAL OBLIGATION

**TODAY WAS A SUNDAY** in 1988, but no ordinary Sunday. It was the Sunday approved by the United States bishops for the first-ever nationwide collection for the retirement needs of members of religious orders, especially of women. The bishops authorized the collection at their 1987 November general meeting, scheduling it for ten years, unless the needs are met before then.

Those needs have been widely publicized. Long underpaid (and exploited), religious order people suddenly found themselves in the 1980s with fewer hands and funds with which to cope. Traditionally the sisterhoods — who in terms of numbers are by far the most involved —took care of their own, and with great and justifiable pride. When a sister retired or became infirm, she went to the motherhouse or a home specially maintained by her community, where she was supported psychologically, physically and spiritually by members of her own order. Alas, the world changed. The ratio of working sisters to retired sisters declined; the ranks of new recruits thinned; veteran sisters had to be recalled to do work once done by novices; there was no big, soft financial cushion to slump back on. By and large, it was not much different for religious orders of males. Still the sisterhoods were hit the hardest.

A 1988 analysis put the minimum unfunded liability in meeting the health-care and retirement requirements of these groups at close to $3 billion. Why isn't the money there? The reason is not mismanagement. As one sister said, the problem is born of "an imbalance between the numbers of working and retired members, escalating costs of health, *and* longevity." The old especially are not being replaced. The median age of women religious is 64; of men, 56.

The December collection is the bishops' way of saying they're not going to abandon the nuns, or the brothers and fathers, to their fate. No one should.

# DECEMBER 12

Our Lady of Guadalupe

## AN OLD FEAST WITH NEW RELEVANCE

**THIS IS** a relatively new feast on the U.S. liturgical calendar, but one that promises to become more popular as Hispanics grow in numbers and influence in the American church. It is the feast of Our Lady of Guadalupe, commemorating the apparitions of the Blessed Virgin Mary to Juan Diego, an Indian in his fifties, at a hilly place called Tepeyac, northwest of Mexico City, between December 9 and 12, 1531. In the first apparition, the Virgin instructed Juan Diego to visit Bishop Zumarraga and instruct him to build a church on the site where she appeared. To quicken credibility with the bishop, the Virgin told Juan Diego to go among the rocks of the hill, pick flowers and bring them along on his audience. Juan did as he was told, picking scrawny mountain flowers and placing them in an apron-like mantle. When he unfolded his mantle for the bishop, magnificent out-of-season roses fell to the floor, and beneath them a life-size image of the Virgin, miraculously painted on the mantle. This image is that of Our Lady of Guadalupe that Catholics worldwide know so well today, and revere — particularly those of Hispanic background.

The Virgin's church got built, of course. The first sanctuary was erected in 1533, to be succeeded in time by a grander monument, since designated as a basilica. It is today one of Mexico's proud religious monuments.

Meanwhile, a succession of popes — twelve at the very least — expressed their love and veneration of the holy image of Our Lady of Guadalupe. Benedict XIV in 1754 declared Our Lady of Guadalupe patroness of "New Spain." Leo XIII sent couplets of his composition to the basilica, and they are to be found today at the foot of the image, carefully preserved. Pius X declared Our Lady of Guadalupe patroness of Latin America. Pius XII in 1945 named her "Queen of Mexico and Empress of the Americas."

# LUX, LIGHT, LUCY

**IN THE HOUSE-CLEANING** that followed Vatican II many parish churches pitched out their *kitsch* — those brightly colored plaster statues of saints that had cluttered the premises for decades, elevating and insulting piety and devotion at the one time. In Boston's North End there's a church that resisted all such temptation (St. Leonard's), and among its "treasures" is one of a blinded woman, demurely dressed, holding her eyes before her *on a plate*.

That statue is of St. Lucy, whose feast the church marks today. She's invoked against eye problems, but in truth not much is known of Lucy. Legend has it that she was the daughter of an affluent Sicilian who suffered martyrdom during the persecution of Diocletian. But she didn't go easily to her reward. Denounced as a Christian by a suitor, she was first condemned to suffer the shame of prostitution, but when it came time to ship her off to a bordello, she proved impossible to move. So they tied her to a stake and heaped faggots around her. Once again no luck; she wouldn't burn. Thereupon, the sword was drawn, and she was tortured, blinded and dispatched. The Church of San Giovanni Maggiore in Naples claims to possess those precious relics, her eyes.

Now all that may be true, or not. No mind. She was honored in the canon of the old Latin Mass; check the *Nobis quoque peccatoribus*. And though the names of others have been expurgated, Lucy's still appears on the liturgical calendar with a feast day of her own. But then the church always has been partial to its virgin-martyrs. The word Lucy, incidentally, derives from the Latin *lux* for "light." Lucy was associated with festivals of lights, and this was reflected in the prayer of her Mass: "Harken unto us, O God, our salvation, that as because of the festival of blessed Lucy we rejoice, so by reason of our feeling of loving devotion may we become better grounded in doctrine."

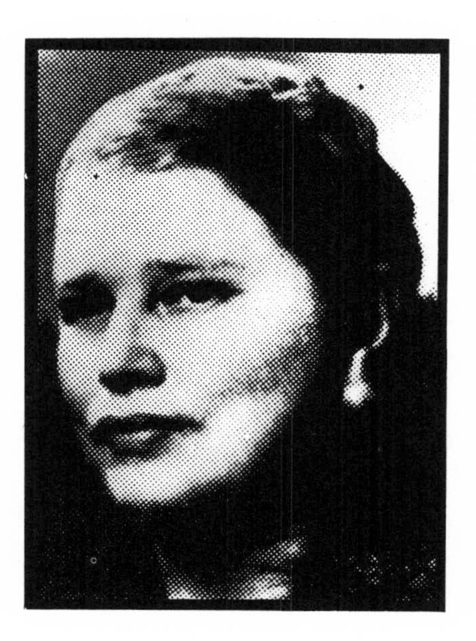

## A CATHOLIC CONSCIENCE OUT OF RUSSIA

**IN A LOG CABIN** in the remote Ontario of Combermere, one of the century's most remarkable laywoman died on this day in 1985. She was Catherine de Hueck Doherty, Russian-born but a large player in the golden age of Catholic social action on this continent. Her influence was especially strong in the 1930s, 1940s, 1950s, as she went from platform to platform across the United States thundering in Catholic settings against racism, and berating Catholics for their segregated parishes, schools, religious orders and lay societies. "Don't you know that the Catholic Church is just a front for capitalism, and that all their talk about the poor is hypocrisy," she would exclaim.

Her crusade spawned Friendship House, an inter-racial movement based on social justice through nonviolence and simple living, with houses in Harlem and impoverished quarters of Toronto, Chicago and Washington, among other cities. Her disciples lived among the poor and sought to bring the witness of Christ to people who felt they were ignored by the church.

To escape "growing internal tensions" in her movement, she moved in 1947 to Canada with her husband, the famed Chicago journalist Eddie Doherty. There she founded Madonna House, a training center for the lay apostolate, and organized a new lay community that today claims twenty-one mission houses. Her husband preceded her in death by ten years, but before dying became a priest of the Melkite Rite. The two had pledged themselves to a celibate relationship in 1955.

Catherine de Hueck Doherty's life divided into two radically different apostolic experiences — first, one of social activism; then one of withdrawal in the spirit. It was a curious evolution, but it gave her an impact in two worlds. Her name was often breathed with that of Dorothy Day, but she also had enormous impact on Thomas Merton, acknowledged in *The Seven Storey Mountain.*

# THE CHRISTMAS CRIB

**IT IS ABOUT THIS TIME** that families are bringing out of storage the *creche* or Christmas-crib set, and setting it up in a place of honor as a prayerful reminder of Christ's birth in Bethlehem. It is a holy custom, one which is generally credited to St. Francis of Assisi, although the practice was in fact known prior to his time.

St. Francis gets the credit, because in 1223 he laid before Honorius III plans for a scenic representation of the principals and place of the Nativity, an idea to which the pope is said to have responded enthusiastically. Come Christmas, Francis was at Greccio, where with the help of his friend Giovanni Velita, he proceeded to build a crib, and he arranged about it figures of Mary and Joseph, the shepherds and animals commonly associated with the event.

But that's not the end of the story. Legend has it that Francis acted as deacon at Christmas midnight Mass at Greccio, and as the choir chanted and the *et incarnatus est* was intoned, Francis genuflected in meditation on the marvel of the Incarnation, when, lo and behold, what appeared in his arms but a babe surrounded by a brilliant light. It was the Christ Child. Giotto commemorated the legend in a painting to be found in the Basilica of St. Francis at Assisi.

The devotion inspired by St. Francis spread, and today churches throughout Christendom set up Christmas cribs during the Nativity season. The Fransciscan church of Ara Coeli in Rome has one of the largest and most beautiful. It must be hard, though, to compete with the claims of the Basilica of St. Mary Major across town, which is said to house five of the six pieces of wood that formed the actual Nativity crib. Taken from a sycamore tree, the relics are reputed to have been brought from the Holy Land in the 640s during the pontificate of Theodore I, who feared they might fall into the hands of pagan marauders.

# FRANCIS THOMPSON'S LABYRINTHINE WAYS

**WHEN DOROTHY DAY** was in her Bohemian phase, she used to hang around the back room of Jimmy Wallace's saloon, a mecca of sorts for young intellectuals at Fourth Street and Sixth Avenue in Greenwich Village. It was there on a bitterly cold winter night that Eugene O'Neill, mouth grim, eyes sad and breath heavy, arrested attention by reciting from memory *The Hound of Heaven*, the haunting, beautiful poem that allegorizes the pursuit of reluctant humankind by the grace and redemption of a persistent God. That poem was the masterpiece of Francis Thompson, who was born on this day in 1859.

A sad, pathetic man, Francis Thompson. Failed seminarian, failed medical student, a failure at every job he ever held, Francis Thompson read de Quincey's *Confessions of an English Opium Eater*, then himself headed down the road of drugs. But he wrote, and wrote well, and in 1887 he used his last half-penny to post some poetry and an essay to Wilfrid Meynell at *Merry England* magazine. It was a year before Meynell and his wife Alice got around to reading the submissions, and they were deeply impressed. Unable to contact Thompson, they went ahead with their publication, trusting the author would see it. He did, and called at the office of *Merry England*. Thus began a beautiful friendship and literary patronage.

The Meynells took Francis Thompson into their home, and Thompson began to move in the fascinating circle of the Meynells' friends — the young Belloc, Ruskin and Browning, Coventry Patmore, George Meredith and others. His health had been undermined by the years on the streets and a bad case of tuberculosis. Francis Thompson died at forty-seven in 1907. He was buried in St. Mary's Cemetery, Kensal Green. In the poem "To My Godchild" he set down his own epitaph:

"Look for me in the nurseries of Heaven."

# DECEMBER 17

DANIEL IN THE LION'S DEN
Daniel 6, 16-23

## THE "WUNDERKIND" OF THE OLD TESTAMENT

**THERE'S NO CORRESPONDING FEAST** in the Western church, but in the East this is the day on which Daniel is remembered. Daniel, of course, is the protagonist of the Old Testament book which bears his name and which he reputedly wrote — "reputedly," because the book (moral fiction in content, not strict history) seems to have alternated in languages, and thus likely evolved as a series of separate parts over a considerable period of time.

Whatever, Daniel is the Bible's *wunderkind*, a kind of Jack Armstrong and Tom Swift wrapped in one, experiencing exotic challenges and, naturally, always triumphing — he, that is, and his three companions. Their Hebrew names were Hananiah, Mishael and Azariah, but most of us know them by the names given them in their Babylonian captivity: Shadrack, Meshach and Abednego. Daniel, whose name in Hebrew means "my judge is God," was assigned the name Belteshazzar.

The Book of Daniel relates the adventures of the four of them — and at least two of the stories are as familiar as any in all literature. One is that of Shadrack, Meshach and Abednego in the fiery furnace (from which the three emerged unsinged, though the fire, stoked with brimstone, pitch, tow and faggots, rose forty-nine cubits into the air). Daniel isn't mentioned at all here, but he dominates the other famous story — you guessed it — the story of Daniel in the lion's den (where an angel of the Lord shut the lions' mouths, rendering them as kittens in Daniel's presence).

There are other fascinating tales — the food test, King Nebuchadnezzar's dream, the handwriting on the wall, Nebuchadnezzar's vision of a great tree — followed in the book's second part by Daniel's visions of the four kingdoms inimical to God before the establishment of God's own kingdom for his chosen people. Overall purpose of the Book of Daniel: to underscore God's commitment to his people and to encourage faithfulness to the ancestral religion.

# DECEMBER 18

## THE PROPHET DANIEL AS HERCULE POIROT

**DID I SAY** in yesterday's entry that Daniel was a kind of Jack Armstrong and Tom Swift? Make him a Hercule Poirot too, for one of the stories in the Book of Daniel casts him in the role of detective. This is the story of chaste Susanna, which appears as Chapter 13 or an appendix — although not consistently in all versions of the Bible. Catholic versions have always accepted the story as canonical Scripture, but other canons have omitted it (including the King James Bible), apparently regarding it as less than totally edifying for reflecting on young womanhood and the probity of judges.

The story is a familiar one: Susanna took noontime walks in her husband's garden, where she came to be spied upon and lusted after by two elders. One warm day Susanna decided to bathe, and dismissed her maids so that she could do so chastely. Privacy she did not have, however. The elders sprang from their cover and demanded her favors. Susanna shrieked and help came, but the elders turned accusers. They claimed to have caught Susanna *in flagrante delictio* with another man, who, they said, managed to flee. Susanna protested her innocence, and Daniel proved it by cross-examining the witnesses, who had been separated one from the other, and tripping them up with a simple question: "Tell me under what tree you surprised them?" A mastic tree, responded one; an oak, replied the other. The former is a small evergreen; the latter, a tall, majestic tree. Ah ha, said Daniel, their "fine lie" would cost them their heads. Which it did, they being put to death in accordance with the biblical law laid down in Deuteronomy 19:18-21: "...And the judges shall make diligent inquisition: and behold, if the witness be a false witness, and hath testified falsely against his brother; then shall ye do unto him as he had thought to have done unto his brother; so shalt thou put the evil away from among you."

Chaste Susanna's story has been dubbed literature's first detective story.

# DECEMBER 19

## THE "O" ANTIPHONS OF ADVENT

**THE ANTIPHON** is one of the most ancient prayers of the church. The origin of the word is Greek, and in the literal sense means "sounding in answer." The first usage in the church thus related to one part of a choir responding in answer to another, as in the singing of alternate verses of the psalms. By the sixth century, however, the meaning had broadened in the Western church, the antiphon becoming the refrain that accompanied the alternation. The usual usage today is to describe a short verse or text, usually from Scripture, recited in the Liturgy of the Hours (q.v. Nov. 25) before and after psalms and canticles. Whatever, some of the most beautiful antiphons are those of Advent, and specifically of the seven days preceding the vigil of Christmas.

These Advent antiphons are known as the "O" antiphons, because each of the seven begins in the Latin with the interjection "O" — (1) *O Sapientientia*, (2) *O Adonai*, (3) *O Radix Jesse*, (4) *O Clavis David*, (5) *O Oriens*, (6) *O Rex Gentium*, (7) *O Emmanuel*. Addressed to Christ the Lord under one or another of his scriptural titles, the antiphons salute Christ's majesty, then conclude with a petition on the coming of the Lord. Each is quite brief, as we shall see in tomorrow's entry, but each has a poetic and scriptural exquisiteness, and constitute in sum one of the most beautiful features of the Advent liturgy as the church prepares for the observance of Christmas. The antiphons are in a sense the great antiphons, the liturgical heralds of Christmas.

The "O" antiphons have been around for centuries (eleventh-century manuscripts reflect their usage), and are sung with special solemnity at vespers. The antiphons are assigned to that hour because it was believed that Christ was born as man in the evening. For similar reason they were attached to the Magnificat, thus honoring her through whom Christ came into the world.

# DECEMBER 20

## THE ANTIPHONAL HERALDS OF CHRISTMAS

**IN THE VERNACULAR,** these are the "O" antiphons of Advent:

*December 17*: "O Wisdom, You came forth from the mouth of the Most High, and reaching from beginning to end, You ordered all things mightily and sweetly. *Come*, and teach us the way of prudence!"

*December 18*: "O Adonai (God of the covenant) and Ruler of the house of Israel, You appeared to Moses in the fire of the burning bush, and on Mount Sinai gave him Your Law: *Come*, and with an outstretched arm redeem us!"

*December 19*: "O Root of Jesse, You stand for an ensign of mankind; before You all kings shall keep silent, and to You all nations shall have recourse. *Come*, save us, and do not delay."

*December 20*: "O King of David and Sceptre of the house of Israel; You open and no man closes; You close and no man opens. *Come*, and deliver him from the chains of prison who sits in darkness and in the shadow of death."

*December 21*: "O Rising Dawn, Radiance of the Light eternal and Sun of Justice; *Come*, and enlighten those who sit in darkness and in the shadow of death."

*December 22*: "O King of the Gentiles and the Desired of all, You are the cornerstone that binds two (the Jews and Gentiles) into one; *Come*, and save poor man whom You fashioned out of clay."

*December 23*: O Emmanuel (God with us), our King and Lawgiver, the Expected of nations and their Savior: *Come*, and save us, O Lord our God!"

# THE APOSTLE OF FAITHLESS DOUBTERS

**IN THE OLD LITURGICAL CALENDAR,** this was the feast of St. Thomas. It seemed fittingly placed, coming at it did then within a few days of the Incarnation, God's assuming of human flesh in the Second Person of the Trinity. For Thomas was the doubter, of course, and it was only when he touched the flesh of the risen Christ that he finally believed.

The story is as familiar as any in the New Testament. It appears in St. John's Gospel, 20:24-29.

Christ's loyalists were gathered in the upper room, doors locked out of fear and seeking to build confidence with the sharing of what one commentator called "women's tales" of a resurrection, when Christ appeared among them. But Thomas was not present, and when he was told the story he was skeptical, saying, "Except I shall see in his hands the print of the nails, and put my finger into the print of the nails, and thrust my hand into his side, I will not believe." Eight days later, when Christ appeared again, Thomas was invited to do exactly that, and we know Thomas' cry; it is for many their prayer at the elevation of the host during the consecration of the Mass: "My Lord and my God."

Thomas was the pessimist from the beginning, believing, for instance, the mission to raise Lazarus a foolhardy one — "Let us also go that we may die with him" (John 11:16) — and at the Last Supper questioning Christ and where he was headed (John 14:5-6), only to receive the sublime answer, "I am the way, the truth, and the light; no man cometh unto the Father, but by me."

Thomas was an energetic Apostle, preaching in Persia, Medea and India, before being martyred near Madras. But his name has never shaken its past. It is still synonymous with that of the faithless doubter. The Roman Rite now observes St. Thomas' feast on July 3; the Eastern Rite on October 6.

# TO CATHOLICISM VIA TRANSCENDENTALISM

**ONE OF THE MOST INTRIGUING FIGURES** of nineteenth-century American Catholicism is Father Isaac Hecker, founder of the Paulists. He came to Catholicism via Transcendentalism, the New England religious movement that engaged the intellectual elite of the day — Emerson, Thoreau, Alcott, Channing, Margaret Fuller of *The Dial*, and Sophia Peabody, who became Hawthorne's wife in 1842. To be sure, Hecker was at best on the fringes of the movement, and he did not stick around long, believing that Transcendentalism overexalted human nature. He made his commitment instead to Catholicism, converting in 1844 and subsequently becoming a Redemptorist. He was assigned as a missionary to immigrants, and he achieved such fame as a lecturer and defender of the faith as to be in demand in New York, Boston, Detroit, St. Louis, Chicago, and points in between. But life as a Redemptorist had its complications, and conflict erupted between the American community and superiors in Rome over evangelical methods. Hecker went to Rome to clarify matters, and quickly found himself expelled from the order. Pope Pius IX, however, was supportive, and urged Hecker to consider formation of a new order to continue his work. The result was the institute known as the Missionary Society of St. Paul the Apostle — more popularly, the Paulists. The group is headquartered today in Scarsdale, N.Y., and has a strong presence in publishing while pursuing missionary, ecumenical and pastoral assignments.

As for Isaac Hecker, his name surfaced in death in connection with "Americanism," the so-called heresy of the end of the century (q.v. Jan. 23). Actually, it was all a misunderstanding. The heresy was a pipe dream, and so was Hecker's connection to it in life or death. No one could have been more loyal to the church and Catholic doctrine. Hecker died on this day in 1888.

# DECEMBER 23

## A VENERABLE WOMAN NOW BLESSED

**THIS IS THE FEAST** of one of Canada's most remarkable women, Marie Marguerite d'Youville. Beatified since 1959, Mother d'Youville was the first North American native to found a religious order — Sisters of Charity, but better known as the Grey Nuns of Montreal. Blessed Marguerite is saluted as Canada's apostle to the poor, but her influence has spread far and wide. Her order is well known in the United States, notably the northeast.

Marie Marguerite d'Youville lived from 1701-1771, and her lot wasn't an easy one. She was married to a lout, and found herself widowed with three children and a heavy debt after eight unpleasant years. Her burdens actually inspired her. Out of her own poverty, she helped others who were poor, and she steered two sons to the priesthood. Community oriented, her vision and skills rescued a local general hospital from debt and ruin, and those she mobilized in the effort became the core of the Grey Nuns' order. The hospital was entrusted to her care in 1747, and from the start it accepted the most difficult of cases — epileptics, lepers, the insane, the incurable — cases other hospitals preferred to shun. The hospital was destroyed by fire in 1766, but Mother d'Youville's order grew and spread across Canada, opening other hospitals and adding foundling homes and orphanages to its apostolates of mission and care.

Times change but the old traditions continue. The Grey Nuns of Montreal still welcome the most trying of cases, and nothing attests clearer to this than the order's 305-bed hospital in Cambridge, Massachusetts, for the rehabilitation and care of the chronically sick. Incidentally, that hospital was once known as the Holy Ghost Hospital for Incurables; it is now called simply Youville Hospital.

No change of name could be more appropriate.

## "AND THE WORD WAS MADE FLESH..."

**THE VIGIL OF THE INCARNATION:** the assumption of human nature by the Second Person of the Trinity, God the Son. The Incarnation is the central doctrine of Christianity. It is a supernatural mystery coincident to Christ's earthly life and continuing in the eternal in Christ's concern with the Father for the salvation of humankind. God the Son is human and divine. As God he is invisible, incomprehensible, timeless; as man he is visible, comprehensible, bound by time. The mystery of it all is conveyed in the magnificent, albeit somewhat sexually chauvinist, prologue to St. John's Gospel:

"In the beginning was the Word, and the Word was with God, and the Word was God. The same was in the beginning with God. All things were made by him, and without him was made nothing that was made. In him was life, and the life was the light of men. And the light shineth in the darkness, and the darkness did not comprehend it. There was a man sent from God, whose name was John. This man came for a witness, to give testimony of the light, that all men might believe through him. He was not the light, but was sent to give testimony of the light. That was the true light, which enlighteneth every man that cometh into this world. He was in the world, and the world was made by him, and the world knew him not. He came into his own, and his own received him not. But as many as received him, to them he gave power to become the sons of God, even to them that believe in his name. Who are born not of blood, nor of the will of the flesh, nor of the will of man, but of God. And the Word was made flesh and dwelt among us, and we saw his glory, the glory of the only-begotten of the Father, full of grace and truth."

When that gospel prayer was said at the end of every low Mass, knees genuflected at the words *And the Word was made flesh.* Christ was born among us.

# DECEMBER 25

## IS CHRISTMAS REALLY CHRIST'S BIRTHDAY?

**FUNNY THING** about Christmas. No feast is the church surer of than the birth of Christ, but it really has no idea on what day Christ's birth occurred. Before December 25 was decided upon, a number of days were in the running, especially January 6 and March 25. There was even sentiment for a May date, because some early chronologists calculated the birth to have occurred in the twenty-eighth year of the reign of Augustus on the twenty-fifth day of the Egyptian month Pachon; May 20 to be precise.

December 25 was the date favored in Rome, however — partly to coopt the Roman civil holiday commemorating the birthday of Mithra, the Unconquered Sun. This brought charges of sun-worship and idolatry on the Roman church from some Christian communities, but Rome held firm. By the fourth century, December 25 was the fixed date for the observance of Christmas in the Western church. The East gradually fell into line, but the fact remains that until the fifth century there was no general consensus on when Christmas should come on the calendar.

The irony is that some early Christians did not even want an observance of Christ's birthday. Origen, for instance, in his eighth homily on Leviticus, repudiated the keeping of Christ's birthday "as if he were a king Pharoah." That was around 245.

The larger irony, though, is the feast's Mithraic angle. Because Mithra is associated with the winter solstice, the observance of Christ's birth on December 25 may be thus said to be governed more by the distance of the sun from the celestial equator than by any message from heralds singing from on high — more by the sun's entering the sign of Capricorn than by a star's fixing itself above a stable in Bethlehem. Still what difference does that make? The important thing is that God was born of woman to redeem humankind.

# STEPHEN, THE CHURCH'S PROTOMARTYR

**SAINT AUGUSTINE SAID,** "If Stephen had not prayed, the church would not have gained Paul." He was referring to Stephen's martyrdom, and his prayer as stones were pelted upon him, "Lord, do not count this sin against them." Paul was present, but hadn't joined in the stoning, being repulsed by the crime. However, he did hold the coats of those who did. Nice guy. Eventually Paul became a Christian, of course, and, as Augustine remarked, Stephen's prayer helped the process. But poor Stephen, he died. He was the church's first martyr. This is his feast day.

What was Stephen's crime? The story is told in the Acts of the Apostles, Chapters 6 and 7. Accused as a heretic, he dared to confront the high priest and members of the Sanhedrin before whom he was brought to trial with a precis of the Old Testament that we are told reduced its members to rage. The Sanhedrin and loyalist onlookers tried to block their ears and shout Stephen down, but Stephen, filled with the Holy Spirit, would not be shut off. Rage mounted, until finally he was rushed out of the city and put to death.

Stephen's "crime," his discourse, is reported at length in Acts. It's a tough, uncompromising, accusatory speech, which ticks off the rejections and persecutions of God's prophets through Old Testament history, and which sees old impulses culminating in the betrayal of the "Just One." The "Most High does not dwell in buildings made by human hands," Stephen exclaimed. The heaven is his throne. "Look," he continued, "I see the heavens opened, and the Son of man standing on the right hand of God."

In the old church calendar Stephen enjoyed a second feast, August 3, the finding of his body. Today's feast commemorates the martyrdom. But how many know it? The feast is largely lost in the wake of Christmas.

# DECEMBER 27

St. John the Apostle

## THE EVANGELIST DEPICTED AS AN EAGLE

**THIS IS THE FEAST** that honors the closest of Christ's companions — St. John, Apostle and Evangelist. His feast has been observed on this date since before the fifth century, a detail which testifies to the respect in which he was held from earliest times. But then, why not? John may even have been a cousin of Jesus; that is, if one accepts intrinsic biblical deduction that John's mother and Mary were sisters. For sure, he and James the Greater were brothers — sons of Zebedee, in fact. (Wouldn't you guess. Church history would preserve the father's name and not the mother's. Ah yesterday!)

Ecclesiastical art frequently depicts John as something of a wimp, with his head on the master's breast at the Last Supper and all. Fact is, he and James were known for their fiery dispositions — "sons of thunder" Christ called them (Mark 3:17). And he had rank. His name, along with those of James, Peter and Andrew, appears first in all lists of the Apostles. He was present at the raising of Jairus' daughter (Mark 5:37), the Transfiguration (Mark 9:2) and the Agony in the Garden (Mark 14:33), but when he and his brother approached Jesus for special favor when he came into his glory, Jesus countered with a demand for willingness to suffer martyrdom (Mark 10:35-41). We read that the other ten Apostles, on hearing of the request, were indignant with John and James for their special pleading.

Interesting enough, John was the only one of the Apostles not to suffer martyrdom — though tradition had it that he was once pitched into a cauldron of boiling oil before Rome's Latin Gate but was miraculously preserved. There was once a feast marking the incident on the church's calendar, May 6, but it was excised as ahistorical. It is probable that John lived to be near one hundred and died in Asia Minor. His symbol in art is that of an eagle. Know why? Because of the soaring theological height of the prologue of his Gospel (q.v. Dec. 24).

The Slaughter of the Innocents (Detail from a woodcut by Albrecht Dürer)

## HOLY INNOCENTS AND UNHOLY FUN

**THIS IS THE DAY** the church honors its first martyrs — the children ordered slain by the troubled Herod in his manic attempt to kill the child born King of the Jews. It is the church's feast of the Holy Innocents. The church ordinarily does not accord the honors of the altar to infants, as it is impossible because of age for infants to perform the necessary deliberate acts denoting heroic virtue to warrant the distinction. It makes an exception for the Holy Innocents because of their unique role in salvation history.

Over the centuries, this day has been marked by Catholics in radically different ways. Today peace activists and anti-abortionists use the day to accent the sanctity of life by bringing attention to evils that threaten or attack life directly. In the Middle Ages, on the other hand, the day was one of great levity, an occasion for the indulging of children and for extravagant expressions of nonsense. As an example, the Society of Lincoln's Inn, an inn of court in London, elected a "King of the Cockneys" for the day.

There's been a dark side to the day as well, however. Holy Innocents was long considered an unlucky day on which to begin anything, the notion being that what began on December 28 would never be finished. Young couples thus did not marry on this day. On levels of state, France's Louis XI forbade official business on this day, and when England's Edward IV realized that his coronation was set for December 28, he had the ceremony put off to the next day.

Again, all that was back in the Middle Ages. People are more sophisticated nowadays, and maybe a mite more civilized. For instance, in England not since the seventeenth century have children been reminded of the somber origins of Holy Innocents Day by being whipped in their beds on awakening. Things do improve. But one can see why the Irish called December 28 "the cross day of the year."

# DECEMBER 29

The Knights of Henry V strike down Thomas at Canterbury

## FOUL MURDER IN CANTERBURY CATHEDRAL

**BEFORE THOMAS MORE** — four centuries before, in fact — there was another Thomas who braved the king's wrath on issues of faith and principle, and paid for it with his life. This was Thomas a Becket, chancellor to Henry II and later archbishop of Canterbury in twelfth-century England.

It was as archbishop that Thomas came into conflict with the king. Henry wished to reassert the rights exercised earlier by William the Conquerer, such as the trial of clerics and the excommunication of offenders; Thomas asserted papal prerogatives. When Henry demanded assent to the Constitutions of Clarendon embodying the customs of the past, Thomas bolted. For six years he was an exile in France. An easy truce enabled him to return in triumph to England, but the truce was short-lived. Henry, annoyed with Thomas' refusal to withdraw certain censures, marked him for assassination with casual words meant to be taken as command or permission to kill Thomas as traitor to the crown.

The foul deed was carried out December 29, 1170, by four knights who rushed upon Thomas in the north aisle of the unlocked cathedral, and sought to drag him outside. Thomas a Becket resisted and was slain on the spot, his last words being, "I accept death for the name of Jesus and for the church."

T.S. Eliot renders those final words more poetically in *Murder in the Cathedral*, his exquisite drama dealing with this dark episode of history:

> Now to Almighty God, to the Blessed Mary ever Virgin,
>
> to the blessed John the Baptist, the holy apostles Peter and Paul,
>
> to the blessed martyr Denys, and to all the Saints, I commend my cause and that of the Church.

The murder shocked the papacy and the conscience of Europe. Within three years Thomas a Becket was canonized as a martyr, and Canterbury was a place of pilgrimage second only at the time to Rome and Compostella in Spain.

# DECEMBER 30

## THE WAY THE CHURCH USED TO SOUND

**CATHOLICS TALK** of the ways their church has changed, but one of the biggest changes goes unnoticed or unappreciated: its tone of voice. The church speaks authoritatively, but it does not speak so imperiously, nor for that matter with such sexual chauvinism, as once upon a time. How did the church used to sound? This was Pope Pius XI speaking in the encyclical on Christian education, *Rappresentanti in terra*, as 1929 drew to a close:

"...Since education consists essentially in preparing man for what he must be and for what he must do here below, in order to attain the sublime end for which he was created, it is clear that there can be no true education which is not wholly directed to man's last end, and that in the present order of Providence, since God has revealed himself to us in the person of his only begotten son, who alone is 'the way, the truth and the life,' there can be no ideally perfect education which is not Christian education.... [A]ll education belongs preeminently to the church... Again it is the inalienable right as well as the indispensable duty of the church to watch over the entire education of her children, in all institutions, public or private, not merely in regard to the religious instruction there given, but in regard to every other branch of learning and every regulation insofar as religion and morality are concerned."

Did anyone else have any competence in the matter of education? "The state may...reserve to itself the establishment and direction of schools intended to prepare for certain civic duties and especially for military service," said Pius XI, "provided it is careful not to injure the rights of the church or of the family in what pertains to them."

Christian education remains an issue close to the church's heart, as indeed it should. The church speaks on the subject, but it doesn't bully the issue, nor others, as it once did. For that, "Amen."

# THE VISION OF PARADISE

**WHAT MORE FITTING CONCLUSION** for a Catholic Book of Days than St. John's vision of paradise in the concluding book of the Bible, the Book of Revelation, or Apocalypse? The Apocalypse is replete with symbolism, but any Christian can thrill to John's look to the holy city, and hope in terms of herself or himself. The translation is that of the King James Version, beginning with Chapter 21:

> And I saw a new heaven and a new earth: for the first heaven and the first earth were passed away; and there was no more sea.
>
> And I John saw the holy city, new Jerusalem, coming down from God out of heaven, prepared as a bride adorned for her husband.
>
> And I heard a great voice out of heaven saying, Behold, the tabernacle of God is with men, and he will dwell with them, and they shall be his people, and God himself shall be with them, and be their God.
>
> And God shall wipe away all tears from their eyes; and there shall be no more death, neither sorrow, nor crying, neither shall there be any more pain: for the former things are passed away.
>
> And he that sat upon the throne said, Behold, I make all things new.... It is done. I am Alpha and Omega, the beginning and the end. I will give unto him that is athirst of the fountain of the water of life freely.
>
> He that overcometh shall inherit all things; and I will be his God, and he shall inherit my son...
>
> And there came unto me one of the seven angels which had the seven vials full of the seven last plagues, and talked with me, saying, Come hither, I will show thee the bride, the Lamb's wife.
>
> And he carried me away in the spirit to a great and high mountain, and shewed me that great city, the holy Jerusalem, descending out of heaven from God,
>
> Having the glory of God: and her light was like unto a stone most precious, even like a jasper stone, clear as crystal;
>
> And had a wall great and high, and had twelve gates, and at the gates twelve angels, and names written thereon, which are the names of the twelve tribes of the children of Israel...
>
> And I saw no temple therein: for the Lord God Almighty and the Lamb are the temple of it.
>
> And the city had no need of the sun, neither of the moon, to shine in it: for the glory of God did lighten it, and the Lamb is the light thereof.
>
> And the nations of them which are saved shall walk in the light of it: and the kings of the earth do bring their glory and honour unto it.
>
> And the gates of it shall not be shut at all by day: for there shall be no night there.
>
> And they shall bring the glory and honour of the nations unto it.
>
> And there shall in no wise enter into it anything that defileth, neither whatsoever worketh abomination, or maketh a lie: but they which are written in the Lamb's book of life...
>
> And they shall see his face: and his name shall be in their foreheads."

## BIBLIOGRAPHY


Abbott, Walter M., S.J., general ed. *The Documents of Vatican II.* New York: Guild Press, America Press and Association Press, 1966.

Allen, Leslie. *Liberty: The Statue and the American Dream.* New York; Statue of Liberty Ellis Island Foundation, 1985.

Benet, William Rose. *The Reader's Encyclopedia.* New York: Crowell, 1955.

*Book of Kells, The*, Reproductions from the Manuscript in Trinity College, Dublin, with a Study of the Manuscript by Francoise Henry. New York: Knopf, 1974.

Bush-Brown, James and Louise. *America's Garden Book.* New York: Scribner's, 1980.

Brantl, George, ed. *Catholicism.* New York: Braziller, 1962.

Carruth, Gordon. *The Encyclopedia of American Facts & Dates*, eighth edition. New York: Harper & Row, 1987.

*Catholic Encyclopedia.* New York: The Gilmary Society, 1913.

"A Catholic Home Encyclopedia," supplement to *The Holy Bible.* Chicago: The Catholic Press, Inc., 1950.

Chambers, R., ed. *The Book of Days.* Philadelphia: Lippincott, 1863.

Cheetham, Nicolas. *Keepers of the Keys.* New York: Scribner's. 1983.

Cogley, John. *Catholic America.* New York: Dial Press, 1973.

Coulson, John, ed. *The Saints: A Concise Biographical Dictionary.* New York: Hawthorne, 1958.

Daniel-Rops, Henri. *The Protestant Reformation*, vols. 1 and 2. Garden City, New York: Image Books, 1963.

Daws, Gavan. *Holy Man: Father Damien of Molokai.* New York: Harper & Row, 1973.

Delaney, John J. *Dictionary of American Catholic Biography.* Garden City, New York: Doubleday, 1984.

Delaney, John J. and James Edward Tobin, *Dictionary of Catholic Biography.* Garden City, New York: Doubleday, 1961.

Deedy, John. *American Catholicism: And Now Where?* New York: Plenum, 1987.

________ *The Catholic Fact Book.* Chicago: Thomas More, 1986.

________ *Seven American Catholics.* Chicago: Thomas More, 1978.

________ *Literary Places, A Guided Pilgrimage: New York and New England.* Kansas City: Sheed, Andrews and McMeel, 1978.

________ "Roman Catholic Church" entries, *Collier's Encyclopedia Year Book.* New York: Macmillan, 1971-1988.

Deretz, J., and A. Nocent, O.S.B. *Dictionary of the Council.* Washington and Cleveland: Corpus, 1968.

Duggan, Alfred. *The Story of the Crusades.* New York: Image Books, 1966.

Ellis, John Tracy. *Documents of American Catholic History.* Milwaukee: Bruce, 1962.

________ *Catholics in Colonial America.* Benedictine Studies. Baltimore: Helican, 1965.

________ *American Catholicism*, second edition, revised. Chicago: University of Chicago Press, 1969.

________ *American Catholics and the Intellectual Life.* Chicago: Heritage Foundation, 1956.

Encyclopedia Britannica, eleventh edition. New York: Encyclopedia Britannica Co., 1911.

Encyclopedia Britannica, fifteenth edition. 1987.

Fairman, Milton. "The Twenty-Eighth International Eucharistic Congress," *Chicago History*, Chicago Historical Society, Chicago, Illinois, vol. 4, no. 4, Winter 1976-1977.

Farrow, John. *Damien the Leper.* New York: Image Books, 1965.

Foy, Felician A., O.F.M., ed. *Catholic Almanac.* Huntington, Indiana: Our Sunday Visitor Press, 1985.

Fesquet, Henri. *The Drama of Vatican II.* New York: Random House, 1967.

Fogarty, Gerald P. *The Vatican and the American Hierarchy from 1870 to 1965.* Wilmington, Delaware: Michael Glazier, 1985.

Fremantle, Anne, ed. *The Papal Encyclicals in Their Historical Context.* New York: Putnam, 1956.

Greeley, Andrew M., et al. *Catholic Schools in a Declining Church.* Kansas City: Sheed & Ward, 1976.

Granfield, Patrick. *The Papacy in Transition.* Garden City, New York: Doubleday, 1980.

Gheon, Henri. *Secrets of the Saints.* Garden City, New York: Doubleday/Image Books, 1963.

Hardon, John A. *Christianity in the Twentieth Century.* Garden City, New York: Doubleday, 1971.

Harmon, Nolan B., ed., et al. *The Interpreter's Bible.* New York: Abington, 1956.

Harvey, Sir Paul. *The Oxford Companion to English Literature.* Oxford, England: Clarendon Press, 1953 edition.

Hatch, Jane M., ed. *The American Book of Days.* New York: H.W. Wilson, 1978.

Hebblethwaite, Peter. *Pope John XXIII.* Garden City, New York: Doubleday, 1985.

________ *Synod Extraordinary.* Garden City, New York: Doubleday, 1986.

Hendrickson, Robert. *Encyclopedia of Word and Phrase Origins.* New York: Facts on File, 1987.

Hennesey, James, S.J. *American Catholics: A History of the Roman Catholic Community in the United States.* New York: Oxford University Press, 1981.

Hirsch, E.D., Jr., et al. *The Dictionary of Cultural Literacy.* Boston: Houghton Mifflin, 1988.

Hoehn, Matthew, O.S.B. *Catholic Authors: Contemporary Biographical Sketches, 1930-1947.* Newark: St. Mary's Abbey, 1948.

Hudson, Winthrop S. *Religion in America.* New York: Scribners, 1965.

Hughes, Philip. *A Popular History of the Catholic Church.* New York: Macmillan, 1962.

________ *The Church in Crisis: A History of the General Councils, 325-1870.* Garden City, New York: Image Books, 1964.

Jedin, Hubert. *Ecumenical Councils of the Catholic Church.* New York: Deus Books, Paulist Press, 1961.

John, Eric, ed. *The Popes: A Concise Biographical Dictionary.* New York: Hawthorne, 1964.

Johnson, Paul. *Pope John Paul II and the Catholic Restoration.* New York: St. Martin's, 1981.

Landman, Isaac, ed. *The Universal Jewish Encyclopedia.* New York: Universal Jewish Encyclopedia Co, 1948.

Kenny, Herbert A. *Israel and the Arts.* Boston: Quinlan Press, 1988.

Lasance, F.X., et al. *The New Roman Missal.* New York: Benziger Brothers, 1937.

Leckie, Robert. *American and Catholic.* Garden City, New York: Doubleday, 1970.

Longford, Lord. *Pope John Paul II.* New York: Morrow, 1982.

May, Herbert G. *Oxford Bible Atlas.* London: Oxford University Press, 1962.

Miller, Madeleine S., and J. Lane Miller. *Harper's Bible Dictionary.* New York: Harper's, 1952.

McGurn, Barrett. *A Reporter Looks at American Catholicism.* New York: Hawthorne, 1967.

Martos, Joseph. *Doors to the Sacred.* Garden City, New York: Doubleday, 1981.

Maynard, Theodore. *The Story of American Catholicism.* New York: Macmillan, 1941.

________ *Great Catholics in American History.* Garden City, New York: Hanover House, 1957.

Morrow, Louis LaRavoire. *My Catholic Faith,* silver jubilee edition. Kenosha, Wisconsin: My Mission House, 1961.

Murphy, Francis X., C.SS.R. *The Papacy Today.* New York: Macmillan, 1981.

*New Catholic Encyclopedia.* New York: McGraw-Hill, 1967, with supplements of 1974, 1979 and 1988.

O'Dea, Thomas F. *American Catholic Dilemma: An Inquiry into the Intellectual Life.* New York: Sheed & Ward, 1958.

Parsch, Pius. *The Church's Year of Grace.* Translated by Rev. William G. Heidt, O.S.B. Collegeville, Minnesota: The Liturgical Press, 1962.

*Reader's Digest Book of Facts.* Pleasantville, New York, 1987.

*Reader's Digest Illustrated Story of World War II.* Pleasantville, New York, 1969.

Seldes, George. *The Vatican: Yesterday, Today, Tomorrow.* New York: Harper & Brothers, 1934.

Smith, George D. *The Teaching of the Catholic Church,* vols. 1 and 2. New York: Macmillan, 1948.

Sullivan, Robert E., and James M. O'Toole, eds. *Catholic Boston: Studies in Religion and Community.* Boston: Roman Catholic Archbishop of Boston, 1985.

Thurston, Herbert, S.J., and Donald Attwater, eds. *Butler's Lives of the Saints*; revised and supplemented. New York: Kenedy, 1956.

Ward, Kaari, ed. *Jesus and His Times.* Pleasantville, New York: Reader's Digest Association, 1987.

Ward, Maisie. *Return to Chesterton.* New York: Sheed & Ward, 1952.

In citing the Bible, no one particular translation has been used in this book. Some biblical quotes come from memory and therefore trace back to one's religious roots, one's schooling. This inevitably means a certain use of the Douay/Rheims Version, which is the biblical text most Catholics of my age grew up on. There has also been a reliance on the King James Version of the Bible, which we Catholics did not grow up on. The King James Version is frequently credited, but where not, is always recognizable — for the majesty of its language.